THE MYSTERY OF JESUS FROM GENESIS TO REVELATION

YESTERDAY, TODAY, AND TOMORROW

THE MYSTERY OF JESUS

FROM GENESIS TO REVELATION

YESTERDAY, TODAY, AND TOMORROW

VOLUME TWO

THE NEW TESTAMENT

Dr. Thomas R. Horn, Donna Howell, Allie Anderson

DEFENDER

CRANE

The Mystery of Jesus from Genesis to Revelation: Yesterday, Today, and Tomorrow
Volume 2: The New Testament
By Dr. Thomas R. Horn, Donna Howell, Allie Anderson

ISBN: 978-1-948014-62-5

Cover design by Jeffrey Mardis

CONTENTS

VOLUME TWO

THE NEW TESTAMENT
Matthew–Jude

When reading Scripture in modern times, it is easy to read Malachi 4 (the last chapter in the Old Testament), turn the page, and begin reading Matthew 1 (the first in the New Testament), expecting it to pick up with what happened next. Readers often assume that a mere page-turn represents an equally fleeting increment of passing time. The continuity fosters this assumed cohesion between the two divisions of the Bible as well: While the Old Testament centers on mankind's interaction with God the Father and foretells of a coming Messiah, the New Testament completes the story by announcing the Messiah's arrival upon the earth, covering the events of His salvation work, describing the dawn of the Holy Spirit amidst mankind on the Day of Pentecost, and showing Christians what is expected of them.

Yet, the amount of time that passed between these two printed pages was vast—nearly four hundred years. Moreover, it was a time in which many cultural elements were cemented into place, which impacted the way the world received the Messiah when He did come. The truth is, God was silent for nearly four centuries (to His people,

Israel, as a whole, though perhaps not to the sincerely seeking individual during that time). The prophets had stopped speaking. The promised Messiah had not arrived. Those who saw their desolate position as the rendering of judgment waited for God's mercy to fall upon them.

Any realistic attempt to deeply comprehend the New Testament requires a close look at a few main concepts of what God's people were facing at the time Christ entered the picture. This period began when the voice of God to His prophets ceased, and ended with the birth of Jesus. For four hundred years, many events happened on earth, but Scripture does not cover any of them. Therefore, we will, but briefly. (We will also explain a few more paramount factors related to what was going on in this area of the world as we draw closer to the narrative of Jesus' death.)

INTERTESTAMENTAL PERIOD

L et's rewind to the oft-overlooked Intertestamental Period—the powder keg upon which the events of Christ's life combusted. Some of these details were mentioned in volume 1 of this series where they were relevant. But here, we'll crunch together a short review, as it assists us in showing the formation of different sects of Judaism.

The Formation of Jewish Sects

During the exiles, Babylon rose to power and overtook the Southern Kingdom. It invaded Jerusalem, sacked the Temple, looted its treasures, and returned its land with the plundered goods and many captive/ enslaved Jews, who were then exiled in Babylon for the next seventy years. Within the century following Babylon's rise, Persia had invaded and overtaken the region, displacing Babylon's rule. The Persian king then allowed the exiled Jews to return to Jerusalem. Most of these Jews embraced the Law and adhered to it steadfastly all of their days. Their release from Babylon flooded Jerusalem with a new type of Jew: the extremely legalistic follower of God.

Greece rose to dominance within this political realm between, approximately, 800 BC and 150 BC, with its apex around 330 BC. The multiregional conquests of Alexander the Great around this time had hundreds of years to culminate into a culture heavily dominated by Grecian influence by the time of Jesus' birth, from the eastern Mediterranean borders and Egypt, further east through territories known in the modern world as western India. The basics of human expression and exploration—art, science, religion, philosophy, language, etc.—then formed a near one-world government and civilization that directed the ancient world.

Judaism—though still very much in existence, thanks to the tolerant leadership of Ptolemy and his successors (who ruled over Jerusalem and Palestine before the Seleucid dynasty)—was not the most popular belief system. The Ptolemic governments protected the Hebrews' right to worship the God of the Jews and operate within their own Jewish institutions, but there still remained a sense of societal superiority of the Greek ways of life over that of Yahwism.

Then, in 168 BC, Hellenist Antiochus Epiphanes (or Antiochus IV) gained political control over the Seleucid throne, and his oppression of the Jews went to the extreme. God's people were forced by royal decree to worship Greek pagan gods and eat meats that did not align with the food designated as acceptable within the Mosaic Law. Antiochus' struggles with Egypt led to provoking anger, to the point that the Jews became his primary target, and Jerusalem fell under persecution and destruction. Most of the city was plundered and looted by Antiochus' army, and a pig was sacrificed on the altar of the Temple as an act of supreme desecration and rebellion against the Jewish God. The Jews' corporate shock only fed the wicked hunger of this dictator further; soon, the people of God were forced to personally raise pagan temples to Greek deities and sacrifice unclean animals upon them in their scattered villages. Many Jewish men, women, children, and babies lost their lives resisting these various attacks against their religion when the persecution increased, leading to the abolishment of circumcision and the burning of precious scrolls containing Hebrew Scripture. Puritans of the Jewish ways of life had more reasons to loathe their Samaritan neighbors—the partly Jewish offspring of the exiled generations—who cooperated fully with Antiochus' rulings.

Between 146–131 BC, Rome incrementally overtook the Greek Empire, but the remaining Greek influence was so potent that Grecian cultural elements were largely absorbed into the Roman culture (explaining why the term "Greco-Roman" is a common descriptor in New Testament studies). Despite ruling with an iron fist, Rome was able to establish peace between many regions that had previously been held in political friction with one another. This created a setting where, for the first time ever in this region, multi-ethnic and culturally diverse peoples lived alongside one another. This fostered a distinct set of circumstances in which Jesus walked during His time upon the earth—much different than that of the Old Testament. The populace surrounding Jesus would not be an isolated collective of traditional Jews, but rather a mingling of people from all walks of life and backgrounds, and their response to Him would likewise be different than that of an Old Testament Jewish village trained to watch for the Messiah.

All of this shifting and turmoil led to the Maccabean (or "Hasmonean") Revolt, when a prominent Jewish family resisted the armies of Antiochus and won many battles, leading to a major clean-up job in Jerusalem and the Temple. Afterward, there was much feasting and rejoicing, leading to the historic Festival of Lights, which became Hanukkah (or the Feast of Dedication). The leaders of the Maccabean revolt and the Seleucids, after much plotting and plans for revenge on both sides that were eventually abandoned, agreed instead to a peace treaty: The Jews would be allowed to worship as they wished, while the Seleucids retained political control of Palestine.

As time passed, religious safety through intensifying legalism became the preferred way for the Jewish watchmen, who vividly recalled the persecution of exile and vowed to guard against allowing society to fall into the same trap. And since, to them, God was remaining silent (through His cessation of speaking through prophets), these individuals made a lifestyle of chasing heightened piety—protecting the Old Testament Law—and cracking down increasingly on anything that might seem to drift between man and God. Gradually, the more pious men elevated themselves to the station of self-appointed guardians of virtue, identifiers of sin, and public correction committees within their communities. Hellenistic Jews butted heads with conservative Jews, who saw them as compromising with the secular world system, while civil wars broke out throughout Judea and surrounding regions. These conflicts (as well as other numerous political factors) contributed to the eventual rise of the Roman Empire under the exasperated Roman general, Pompey.

However, the history of the clash between Jewish sects led to the fragmentation of a people who were once united in Yahwism. Because Hellenistic Jews had introduced new forms of Jewish worship, there was no longer "one way to God" through a central, Mosaic form of worship as there had once been. Now, Yahwism took on many varying forms. (One way to consider it is to think of the difference between Catholics and Protestants, or "non-Catholic Christians." Though both groups are "Christian denominations," they are as different as black and white in many of their divergent systems of worship, culture, and lifestyle.)

Pharisees, Essenes, and Zealots

The Hasidim movement was led by strictly pious Jewish priests who maintained devout lives under the Mosaic Law and the study of the Torah. Because of their firm adherence to holiness concepts, this group gained the reputation of being painfully legalistic, turning their noses up to any group that didn't adhere completely to their religious ideas. Their views and reverent practices went even beyond the ritual and ethical requirements of the Hebrew Scriptures, bringing new (and unnecessary) customs into their daily habits. But however "holy roller-ish" they appear to historians today, the Hasidim movement sprang from a good motive (even if it was a bit of an overreaction): resisting the secularization of Judaism.

From within the Hasidim movement came the Pharisees…

Probably no teaching on the planet is powerful enough to get this concept through the heads of today's Christians, who largely see the Pharisees as the New Testament's villains, but we will state it anyway in hopes that at least our readers will get it: They were not evil men! At least, *that was true of them in the beginning.* The word "Pharisees" translates to "the separated ones," and that's precisely what they tried to be: separated from the world. In fact, their resistance to worldly culture is a stance we can all learn from, so long as the West continues to treat God's Word as "hate speech" and shove it further and further into obscurity. The mistake the Pharisees made was not one of wicked intent, but one of being human and attempting to please God in ways that humanity naturally limits. Their obsession centered on following every detail and letter of God's Law, and over time, they lost sight of who the Law was supposed to benefit. They became so intense about upholding the rules that their standards of holiness became an outward show instead of an inward work, thereby causing them to abandon the very lost souls God had always intended His people to reach. The Pharisees set out to be separated from the sin in the world. They ended up being separated from anyone they deemed sinful, which was everyone who didn't think the way they did…and this was true despite the fact that their first goal was to seek and make converts. (Kinda like us, in modern times, engaging in interdenominational squabbles within the Body of Christ, believing we have the answers when we don't always, and refusing to be open-minded to others whose theology doesn't align with ours. Though many Christians have risen above this—thank God!—there are still occasions when putting a Pentecostal in the same room as a Baptist can be more threatening to our welfare than pummeling a beehive with a bat at a church potluck. Ahem…back to history.)

Though the Pharisees were primarily made up of middle-class laymen, not priests (which is kind of surprising, considering their influence amid a community that, until this point in history, had championed the priests' authority), the Jewish Midrash (a sort of "study guide" or "commentary" for the books of the Law) was their brainchild. The scribes often originated from this sect as well. Their job description changed over time. Old Testament scribes, like Ezra, were similar to what we would today call a "secretary": someone who keeps excellent records and organizes important documents and legal papers. By the time of the New Testament, this had shifted to involve copying, studying, and interpreting the books of the Law. In addition, societies during the New Testament days considered scribes to be more like lawyers than priests (like Ezra). Due to the endless hours of dedication of these men to interpreting the Hebrew Bible, their word became the law of the Jews who were trained under them. This also partly explains why, while Jesus walked among the people, the "Oral Law of the Jews" (or the "oral tradition" we sometimes hear about in sermons) became so pronounced in Jewish teaching of the day. Because the world was changing rapidly with the spread of Hellenism, some of the then-modern issues of sin were not directly addressed in the Hebrew Bible, so they began to extend the Law into the Oral Law to address these progressive problems using updated language. (Example: Scripture does not address Internet porn addiction, but it does address sexual immorality. A preacher today might "extend" biblical teachings to apply to pornography, and rightfully so.) But quickly, the Pharisaic interpretations of the Law in their contemporary times became so important to them that the knowledge of it became a prerequisite for any rabbi in training. Eventually, the Oral Law or oral tradition came to replace the Law, itself, even if no first-century Pharisee or scribe would ever be willing to view it in those terms. (Note that not every scribe was a Pharisee, but every scribe's word was final on any matter of Law, and the Pharisees prized the Law above all else. This is why the Pharisees and scribes are so often grouped together in Bible studies.)

The Essenes, who also stemmed from the Hasidim movement, didn't believe in reforming culture and society to fit Jewish convictions like the Pharisees did. Instead, the Essenes left society altogether and dispersed into small, monastic communities in unpopulated or wilderness areas. They did believe there would be political and public reform, but they allowed such change as God's responsibility, directly, not men's. Their focus was every bit as much, if not a great deal more, upon holiness standards in living, but the Essenes' reclusive ways of life did not earn them the same reputation as legalists like it did for the Pharisees. John the Baptist is believed to have been an Essene, as his wild, and some would say "crazy," appearances and uncompromising preaching style resembled what we know of the Essenes. Likewise, since the Essenes' fundamental purpose in ejecting themselves from society was to prepare themselves for the Messiah, it stands to reason this would have been John the Baptist's personal resolution. The Dead Sea Scrolls discovered in the '40s and '50s around the caves of Qumran are also likely of Essene origin.

The zealots materialized at the same time as the Pharisees, and their theological and religious roots are comparable. For the most part, they lived in the middle of nowhere, much like the Essenes. What made them different was their willingness to pursue societal revolution by means of bloodshed. Their fanatical nationalism led also to their refusal to pay taxes and resistance to earthly governments (which may have had something to do with why they avoided public life). This faction radically opposed Rome, and their main goal was to see it overthrown. Idolatry was the worst of evils and, like their early ancestor/brother Phinehas (Numbers 25:7–13), they believed God should be defended zealously, even if it meant death. Righteous vengeance was not a problem. (Note that Simon, one of Christ's main disciples, was a zealot [Luke 6:15].)

The Pharisees were the most powerful Jewish sect in the smaller villages around Jerusalem, while the Sadducees were most influential in the heart of Jerusalem.

Sadducees

The Sadducees were wealthy, upper-class, aristocratic Jews trickling down from the leaders of the Maccabean Revolt who were bold enough to resist secular politicians who endangered their Jewish culture. Ironically, this positioned the Sadducees to become supremely authoritative in both political and spiritual matters of Jerusalem when the earlier battles became later negotiations with Rome. In other words, they were the Jewish spokesmen in the Hebrews' spiritual capital; they mediated between the Romans and the Jews. Not everyone in Jewish circles was happy with this arrangement. They didn't always make decisions that flattered everyone's personal needs, and they tended to mix religion and politics in most of their verdicts. Nevertheless, their position gave them tremendous power, which is why the Sadducees were frequently heads of the Jewish court systems (high priests and chief priests) in Jesus' day. The maintenance of Rome was a righteous duty, they believed, so—paradoxically—these "priests" were found lacking in their dedication to Jewish concepts of purity and tradition, nor were they in agreement with the Oral Law of the Pharisees.

Theologically speaking, the Sadducees differed greatly from the Pharisees, disbelieving in such concepts as resurrection or angels. For them, life after death was just a grave named Sheol. They rejected the Wisdom literature and the prophetic records of Israel's history, considering the books of the Law to be the only legitimate scriptural literature worth reading. They were not usually concerned with seeking converts, and with a "chosen ones" approach, almost all who were accepted into their circles had done so by "inheritance" (they were born into their roles).

The Hellenistic Jews

Although the "liberal" Hellenistic Jews drew a gasp from the more pious groups of their day, their ways of life were not always a deliberate statement against the holiness standards of their forefathers. Often, the Hellenistic Jews were a product of hundreds of years of cultural shifting since the conquests of Alexander the Great. Their ancestors were almost always linked to the exiles, so their origins traced to some of the intermarriage that occurred when some Israelites who had established lives of their own chose not to come back when they were freed. In choosing to remain in distant, foreign lands, they eventually dropped certain religious rites (such as circumcision) from their practices, and many of them did not speak Hebrew.

Samaritans

One settlement just outside of Judea is said to have formed as a direct result of this intermarriage practice, though it's not certain whether Samaritan ancestry traces to the time of the Assyrian Exile or the Babylonian Exile. (Most literature states Assyrian. Note that some early Samaritan historical documents deny this, but a deep study of Israelite history in 2 Kings 17:24–41 shows that intermarriage is probably the true origin of the mixed race in the Gospels.) Some scholarly sources go into great detail about the hybridization of the Samaritans' religion, stating that, because their ancestry traced to Assyrian gods, their worship was both Jewish and pagan in nature. Since Yahwism is monotheistic, they could not be considered Orthodox Jews, and since Yahweh abhors the gods of the pagans, they could not be authentically pagan. If these sources are true, they would have been somewhat of a scandalous people to those on either side. Either way, they practiced Yahwism in many ways similar to the Jews' worship practices. One major difference was the Samaritans' belief that Mt. Gerizim was truly the holy mountain upon which to conduct their worship (a subject that came up between Jesus and the Samaritan woman at the well in John 4), but this fact alone is not enough to explain why they were so hated by the Jews, with whom they shared so much in common.

The beginning of the hostility between the Jews and Samaritans has never been nailed down. However, one popular theory is that they held differing political alliances with the dynastic authorities prior to Jesus' birth, pitting the two groups against each other. Other theories include their embrace of Hellenism and their resulting willingness to go along with Antiochus VII. Josephus also wrote:

> Now there arose a quarrel between the Samaritans and the Jews on the occasion following:—It was the custom of the Galileans, when they came to the holy city at the festivals, to take their journeys through the country of the Samaritans; and at this time there lay, in the road they took, a village that was called Ginea, which was situated in the limits of Samaria and the great plain, where certain persons thereto belonging fought with the Galileans, and killed a great many of them.[1]

But whatever the cause, by Christ's birth, the Jew and the Samaritan were natural-born enemies (a detail that becomes important in New Testament reflection).

Sanhedrin

The Sanhedrin was a Jewish civil governing institution, not a "people." When reading most biblical translations today, the words "council" and "court" refer to them. This institution is hard to trace to its root, though it is believed that it could be as old as Moses' "seventy elders" (Numbers 11:16–24).

At the dawn of the New Testament era, a Sanhedrin court could be any group of seven or more that met in synagogues throughout Palestine. The Sanhedrin of Jerusalem, however, was comprised of seventy-one men made up of scribes and elders, and both Pharisees and Sadducees were welcomed (though many were Sadducees, including the high priest).

The Sanhedrin did not have the sole authority to condemn a criminal to death. Rome reserved that right. However, readers of the New Testament quickly learn, Rome didn't care to get involved in most Jewish disputes, allowing a vast level of political and criminal-justice autonomy in their court systems. When it came to the death penalty for an offending Jew (such as Jesus), the Sanhedrin had the power to recommend a sentence of death to the local Roman governor, who would make the final decision (an important detail in the Gospel accounts).

Jewish Expectations

Though the different sects within Judaism around the time of Christ could often coexist in society, they had faced centuries of breakdown and internal weakening that resulted in a people that were no longer united. The constant bickering between Hellenists and the classic Hebraic Jews alone was enough to strangle any hope they may have had in restoring the national identity, pride, and community that their forefathers had maintained. Eventually, the authority of the Sadducees built a fortress of control over Jerusalem, while the villages and towns in rural areas began to stick to their synagogues, and it was, in a sense, two different manifestations of religious lifestyles. Those in rural towns were frequently angered by what religio-political schemes went on in the holy city, while

residents of Jerusalem saw the rural "peasant Jews" as illiterate and ignorant country folk. Intolerance bred on both sides, and tension within the
Jewish believers in Yahwism led to the near death of their dreams that
God would carry out His promises of giving them the glorious Kingdom
the prophets had once spoken over them. Many individuals and sects
abandoned belief in the prophets altogether!

In addition to all of this, Rome wasn't always a friendly dominion
for Jewish residents. Some earlier secular authorities within the Roman
government, as we have discussed, protected the Jews' freedoms (including their exempt status from having to serve in the Roman military),
but the anti-Semitic attitude on a social level grew palpably tense. In 40
BC, Herod the Great was declared "king of the Jews," and much went
downhill from there when he decided to start murdering the baby boys
of the Hebrews in an attempt to cut off the messianic line. (To readers
who know post-biblical history, it would be a little over a century from
this declaration that the Jewish-Roman wars would begin and lead to
the eventual destruction of Jerusalem and the Temple again in AD 70,
in large part as a result of the zealots' provocation.) Nobody appeared
to be good candidates for Israel's neighbors, and they couldn't even
get along amongst themselves! The Galilean Jew was friendlier and
more acquainted with international travelers than the haughty, proud
Judean Jew, so even above and beyond the splintering of sects were
social factions that provided an additional layer of segregating walls.

Where could they place their hope, then?

So, although the exiles were finally over, Jerusalem was reestablished, and the Temple had been rebuilt, the Jews' expectations of
God's promises of grandeur, justice, and lands flowing with milk and
honey had not yet been realized.

Little did the Jews know this same Hellenistic, one-world system
that eventually led to their internal squabbling and eventual political oppression was precisely the vehicle that facilitated the spread of
their God's messianic revelations to nearly all people of surrounding
regions who then conveniently knew how to communicate...

The Hebrew Bible was translated into Koine Greek circa 250 BC in the Jews' intellectual capital, Alexandria. (Note that Jerusalem would always be their *spiritual* capital, so long as the Temple stood.) This was the dawn of a new era for the Jews, who now had the Septuagint translation of God's Word, or, "the Greek Bible." People far and near would now be able to read the same message that the Jews were claiming to be the only religious truth, but in their own common language. Though this era sounds like an advertisement for Judaic revival—and to some degree, it was—the grander design, the redemptive plan of God, actually showed this to be a more important development in the spread of the Gospel...a story that was about to unfold in real time.

Since Genesis, a Messiah who would crush the serpent's head had been promised, and since then, the heroes of Israel's history had not stopped citing that very Messiah would be the fulfillment and completion of all woes. He would be a King unlike any king, ruling and reigning in His Kingdom that would never end upon land that would produce unending life, healing, and sustenance. In every relapse of the Hebrews' sin, those who mourned their wickedness and turned from their ways looked forward to a day within their own lifetime that this King would arrive as the Redeemer to right every wrong. But that's not to say they understood exactly what—or who—they were waiting for...

Whispers of how the Messiah would arrive and how He would act had made their expectations certain: He would be preceded by the prophet Elijah, who would prepare the way for Him amid the waiting throngs. He would rise up like King David, but would be even better than King David, ruling the lands as far as the eye could see and, with a mighty shout, His great army made up of unlimited military numbers and strength like the world had never seen would destroy Rome and free every Jew from oppression. No earthly politician would be able to compare to His wisdom in leading a successful administration, a government with only the purest civil, ethical, constitutional, diplomatic, and doctrinal ideologies that would reach the whole planet with the most impeccable interpretations and binding applications of Yahweh's laws. His throne would be established in Jerusalem, and every knee would bow to Him in acknowledgment that He was the supreme King. Instead of associating Himself with the poor, or with sinners, He would be surrounded by a never-ending lineup of servants draped in only the finest of purple linens hemmed in threads made of gold, while the sinners would fall to their death in His presence and cease to exist, their souls in Sheol for eternity. Judaism would be the only world religion, and the factions and sects within it would unite, surpassing even the glory days of the patriarchs. Sickness and disease would never be heard of again, and the children of Israel would inherit a paradise, paid for in blood by the extinction of its oppressors. This man's strength and leadership in battle would mute even the strength and leadership of the Maccabees.

What a Leader this Man would be!

At least, that's what they *thought* He would be...

According to the *Psalms of Solomon*, an apocryphal manuscript written and added to by mostly Pharisees up to the fifth century AD, the Jews believed the Messiah would "make the land and people holy again, drive away evildoers, establish just rule over Israel and the nations, and bring glory to God and blessing to the righteous (Ps. Sol. 17:26–46)."[2] (It's not clear to scholars why the Pharisees would have named this book after Solomon when the writings were so late in history, but perhaps it was because the author followed his style.) This source's radical language speaks of a Messiah who would, in order of the verses therein (and without repeated statements, of which there are many):

- Cleanse all of Jerusalem from the nations that ever had or ever would again seek its destruction;
- Prevent all sinners from inheriting any blessings of wisdom;
- Humble every sinner's ego and "rub out the arrogance of the sinner like a potter's vessel";
- Obliterate the support of the wicked "with an iron rod";

- Bring to extinction every pagan nation through merely a "word of his mouth";
- Watch as the Gentiles run from the very threat of His appearance;
- Accuse, rebuke, and criticize the actions of all sinners "by the word of their heart";
- Gather all holy people together and lead them in perfectly realized righteousness, becoming history's grandest Judge over all the tribes of Israel who are "sanctified…by God";
- Permanently eliminate any and all injustice or wickedness from ever touching God's elect again;
- Intimately and immediately recognize and know who are, and who are not, the true children of God;
- Return all of Israel's scattered tribes back to their rightful places "upon the earth" (alternatively, this verse could be interpreted to say that He will divide them into *new* tribes);
- Do away with all foreigners and expel emigrants, deportees, refugees, and exiles from among them who are not of God's elect;
- Judge all people and all nations in wisdom and righteousness, maintaining rule over all "under his yoke," glorifying Yahweh "over all the earth";
- Cleanse and sanctify Jerusalem, restoring it to what it was in the beginning;
- Accept visitations and gifts from national leaders who arrive like "utterly weakened sons" from all over the world who travel just to "see his glory," and He will be a King over them, "taught by God";
- Execute flawless judgment "in his days among them" who "all are holy";
- Achieve all military success without having to place His dependency "in horse and rider and bow";
- Accomplish battle victory without relying on gold or silver;
- Avoid having to rally "hopes by many for the day of war" because the only hope necessary is "the hope of God";

- "Show no mercy" to any nation who fears Him;
- "Bring down the earth" with only an eternally effective "word of his mouth";
- Bless all of Yahweh's sons and daughters with "wisdom and joy";
- Have no trace of sin within Him, so that He is the appropriate leader of the physical world;
- Be the strongest Man of God in history, which God has ordained Him to be "by the Holy Spirit";
- Exercise the epitome of wisdom, counsel, understanding, strength, and righteousness, with which the Lord will be with Him always;
- Have strong hope in the Lord;
- Show that no one man or army would ever show strength against Him;
- Display the utmost works as a result of His mighty fear of God;
- Refuse to allow weaknesses of any men;
- Lead with all equality; and
- Eradicate arrogance and all oppression.[3]

It's clear the Jews were correct in only a few areas. The rest of their expectations were most definitely based in human interpretations stemming from rabbinical teaching that had thousands of years to steep. (Our subsequent section, "*HIS* Kingdom?! This Guy Has to Go!" will go deeper into these ideas; this area is to show what the Jews expected before He came, whereas later we will compare these concepts to what He actually said and did.)

Despite the fact that the people of Israel had seen a mighty and miraculous deliverance in the form of Moses, it was always clear to them that Moses was a man of mighty strength whom God used to free His people. There was always clarity amongst God's people regarding the distinction between being *God* and being a *man* through whom God worked. Alongside the many other elements that set Yahweh apart from gods of pagan religions was the fact that, until now, God had never come in the *flesh*.

In non-Jewish religions, there were plenty of "god-men" whose legends were regaled across generations. The most well-known example of this is Hercules, supposedly born of a mortal woman and Zeus, but history is riddled with tales of god-men, demigods, and even Egyptian pharaohs who were also considered gods in their culture. Thus, up to now, the lack of a god in the flesh was one element that set Yahweh apart from other pagan gods. As a result of the claims of Jesus being God, Himself, or the Son of God, many traditional Jews suspected (and accused) Him of blasphemy, while those outside Jewish tradition were much more open-minded about this notion. (This likely contributed to the influx of Gentiles in the early Church, and why it struggled with so much pagan invasion: those who easily adopted the notion of a "god-man" and were familiar with the power that Jesus showed during His lifetime flooded the New Testament church, bringing their idolatrous former religions with them.)

Though we noted earlier that the Pharisees' original motive and intent was based in holiness and purity, by the time of Christ, much of that had changed. (This is, yet again, another lesson we can draw from them. We can and should follow their patterns of abstaining from the ways of the world. Yet, with that goal in mind, we should never become so "arrived" in our theology that we become egotistical.) Although there were certainly sincere Pharisees, Scripture records their conduct around Jesus as arrogant (Luke 18:11), pretentious (Matthew 23:5), incredibly judgmental (John 7:49), money-hungry (Luke 16:14), self-exalting (Matthew 23:6), narrow-minded (Matthew 23:4), and as not concerned with "justice, mercy, and faithfulness" (Matthew 23:23; cf. Luke 11:41–44).

Adding to this, the Pharisees disagreed with Jesus about the Sabbath (Matthew 12:1–2), tradition (Mark 7:1–5), and fellowship with sinners/tax collectors (Luke 5:30). They openly declared Christ was casting out demons by the power of "Beelzebub" (Matthew 12:24), and bore a false witness (John 8:13). They demanded signs from Him (Matthew 16:1) and tried to "trap him in his speech" (Matthew 22:15).

It's therefore not surprising that they couldn't believe the humble Jesus from Galilee was the Messiah.

But who would this Messiah really be? How would He compare to what they had predicted and imagined?

The Gospels answer that question in abundance.

NEW TESTAMENT

At the launch of the Old Testament volume of this series, we briefly covered the word "testament" and concluded that it means the "evidence," "will," and "contract" of God.

When Jesus came on the scene in human form, this "contract" was updated to reflect fresh stipulations and clauses for us, the beneficiaries of this document, which was amended because of the work He performed on the cross. Therefore, just as with the Old Testament, the New Testament could alternatively be called the "Evidence of Christ," the "Will of God and His Anointed," or simply, the "New Contract." (It's important to note that just because it is referred to as "New" does not mean that there can ever be a subsequent "Third Testament" or beyond. The fact that the whole "Old" document speaks of and points to the "New" means that God's self-revelation is completed in Christ and this "New Testament" is the explanation of that completion. Neither Testaments speak of or point to a continuing revelation of God. The end of the second Testament describes the apocalyptic last days upon the earth, so the Bible closes permanently with that book.)

Just as with the First Contract, the new record is God's self-revelation, a legally binding agreement in writing between two parties—God and humanity—and it came pre-signed by the first Party. What we wrote earlier applies again: God is "bound by the pact of what is stated within this text," and we are given the free will to make a choice: either sign it with our hearts and honor it with our actions or ignore it. If we choose to go with the latter plan, God will respect that choice, but when we die, we will not reap the afterlife profits the contract promises.

Before, we said, "What we must *never* do is sign the contract and then be found in breach of its conditions and clauses." That is truer now than ever as we step into the world of the New Testament, as the orders stated within it apply to us in this current state of the nuptial agreement between us and God as metaphorical Husband. More simply, this New Contract is what we believers live by right now, in this modern world, regardless of how the legal terms compare to those who have chosen not to participate in the pact. If we "sign," or accept Christ, and then are found in breach of the terms, we may be held accountable to the "goats clause," which stipulates that we may be among those in that terrifying day who are told, "Depart from me, ye cursed" (Matthew 25:41).

But it's crucial that we remember: The New Testament is not just a "Book of Helpful Tips." Nor is it merely a document that distinguishes benefits from losses depending on how the material "helpful tips" are applied. Such an approach is impersonal, turning God and His Son into a "celestial Santa" who gives us presents when we've been good. The New Testament is a living, breathing thing (Hebrews 4:12a; John 6:63; 2 Timothy 3:16). It speaks life and blessing into its readers and hearers, improving not only our prospects in the afterlife, but in this current life as well. Following the contract of God improves our time on this earth literally, physically, socially, psychologically, emotionally, and spiritually. Considering who Jesus was while He was in human form, what He came to do, and what that means for us *now* is to heap upon ourselves the very best life.

The popular hashtag, "#MostBestLife," is appreciated by the fallen world around us, regardless of religion, and suggests that someone has found a way of living that improves this temporal space. Another one, "#YOLO"—meaning "you only live once"—promises to deliver enjoyment as well, though it often shows up while someone is carrying out an act of, well, stupidity (like jumping off a bridge, or getting drunk and running in front of a bus, just to say it happened).

The Word of God fulfills something these human, secular pursuits cannot. When we start to truly apply the wisdom the Bible offers, we don a new pair of lens, seeing with clarity what really matters. We truly do, as #YOLO states, only live once…so it's crucial that we live our "most best life." That life is not one that pleases *us* and gives us blessings, though that is often the result of choosing to live biblically, but one that pleases God and sacrifices all we want in trade for a higher calling and purpose that will result in better outcomes in the afterlife (like reaching the lost at all costs). This is what it means to fully appreciate the New Contract and the lives that were lost (both Yeshua's and His disciples) to put it into circulation.

One important disclaimer is needed before we proceed: Our original goal for this work was to expand on Christ beyond any other book Defender Publishing has ever released, while also maintaining a certain word and page limit, so as not to produce a product that will be overwhelming to read. With that in mind, a true "expansion work" on the subject of Christ can create, and has many times created, books that bleed into thousands of pages like a multiple-volume set of encyclopedias. As we are choosing to avoid this, there may be parts of Jesus' story or the theology behind what He has done (both in His earthly lifetime and beyond) that we don't cover at length.

One example is the woman at the well (John 4). Few readers are aware that this woman—if the Eastern Orthodox tradition, the Church fathers, Byzantine hagiographers, and ancient Greek sermons from the fourth to the fourteenth century accounts of her are true—went on to: 1) become the first female preacher, evangelist, and revivalist in human history (as evidenced also in her ministry to Sychar in John 4); 2) be baptized by the apostles; 3) be baptized in the Holy Spirit on the Day of Pentecost; 4) receive a new name meaning "light"; 5) travel to Rome and personally challenge Emperor Nero; 6) survive multiple attempts on her life (including poisoning, which she drank and lived beyond; beatings, which she emerged from without so much as a broken fingernail; and a trip to the furnace, which she emerged from like the three friends of Daniel); 7) convert the emperor's daughter and all her handmaidens; 8) convert the jailors and many in her region of Rome following her eventual imprisonment; and 9) finally meet her end (after a very successful ministry converting hundreds more) in an ironic and poetic way—by being thrown into a well.

This account, and a nearly unlimited number of others (as well as theological expansion on some teachings, such as the Beatitudes or the Sermon on the Mount), could be covered in this book, but again, we've instead chosen to focus on who Christ was during the days He walked the earth, what His teachings inflamed among the leaders of His time (religious and secular), His trial, and the writings that materialized after His Ascension. This should answer the question: "Why didn't the authors talk about [fill-in-the-blank-topic]?"

Let's begin.

Matthew, Mark, Luke, and John

IT HAD BEEN FOUR HUNDRED YEARS of silence, and the people of God were, once again, weary in waiting. Rome was a powerhouse that oppressed the Jewish way of life. Roman Imperialism, the stronghold that established the wonderful *Pax Romana* (the "peace of Rome"), both promoted the worship of pagan gods upon the inhabitants of Rome and attempted to inaugurate its emperors and their families as gods, themselves (an element of the Roman state religion called the Imperial Cult).

There was no time like the present for the long-awaited Messiah to come on the scene, and the Gospels detail that arrival.

The Reason There Are Four

Matthew, Mark, and Luke are called the "Synoptic Gospels" because they present one unified narrative, while John is more theological in his approach. "Synoptic" derives from a Greek word meaning "to see with" or "to see together." "Gospel" means "good news." So the term "Synoptic Gospels" refers to these three books that "see the Good News together." Christians who are young in the faith often ask the question: Why are there *four* Gospels? Why not just one longer book that puts all this information together? We will answer this question before we continue, as the answer helps readers more efficiently understand the next four books of the Bible (five, including Acts, which was written by Gospel author Luke).

We know that it's a controversial idea at first, but we need to always remember that, although we do benefit tremendously from these writings today, the books were not written "to us today." All four Gospels were penned by men who were responding to audiences of their day who were confused about the Messiah for various reasons rooted in their vastly different cultures. Therefore, though each of the Gospels may address the same historical events, each is packaged in ways that best answer the questions of diverse people groups.

Matthew's Audience: The Jews

Matthew wrote to the Jews, primarily. He understood more than the other Gospel authors what the Jews expected from their Messiah, and why they couldn't believe in Him after He appeared in a way that was so different than what anyone had anticipated. Matthew's book is included first in the canon for this reason; it serves as a sort of "bridge" between what was written in the Old Testament and the fulfillments of it in the New.

Matthew's intent was not to simply tell the story, but to show, with dramatic illustrations that referred to Old Testament Scripture more than any other Gospel writer, how Jesus was the "Benefits" that the former "Old Contract" outlined for its "beneficiaries." Although we can't say whether Matthew personally spent years of his life ministering to, say, the Romans, his Gospel account was specifically written to answer questions that were Jewish in nature. This is why He didn't go out of his way to explain Jewish customs or religious rituals and practice, because his audience already had great familiarity with these concepts. Likewise, this explains why Jesus, in Matthew, is viewed as the One who came to fulfill the Mosaic Law, not to abolish it (a subject that neither the Romans nor Gentiles would have cared as much about). Further, Matthew boldly calls out religious leaders whose activities were evil and impure in their intent (again, outside of the Jews, nobody would have held any innate anxiety about this). More heavily than the other Gospel writers, Matthew emphasizes Jesus' teaching and compares it with traditional Jewish teachings ripe out of the synagogue. Such examples include the Sermon on the Mount (5–7).

Mark's Audience: The Romans

Mark's writing style is more intense (just read how many times he uses the word "immediately" in his narrative!). History shows that his was actually the first of the Gospels to be completed, and it's the one considered most accurate in its chronology. (That's not to say the book of Mark is the most accurate Gospel, as all are in agreement about what happened. The other Gospel writers sometimes explain events out of order, to be organized in the way that's most effective. Lots of Bible study books today begin with the New Testament and reflect back on the Old so readers can start by learning about who Jesus is and was as a human before looking back on what the Old Testament Scriptures said of His Coming. This is out of chronological order, but to new Christians, it might be the best order so they aren't bogged down by trying to understand prophecies of the Christ they haven't yet learned about. Instead, they get right into reading about who and what He was, and *then* when they dig into the Old Testament studies, they can read and interpret the prophecies in light of what they already know. (This is merely one example of why the Gospel writers, other than Mark, might have felt compelled to tweak the order of their narratives. Matthew tended to group the miracles together to make a strong statement of Christ's divinity, whereas he addressed Jesus' teachings in another lump so his readers could view these two aspects of Jesus—His miracles and His teaching—in a relative and structured way.

The reason Mark is sometimes called "John Mark" is because of the effect Hellenism had on the Jews' naming of their children. "John" was his Jewish name, but his parents, like just about all others of his day, would have also given him a Greek/Roman name, which was "Mark." His Gospel was not for the Jews as Matthew's was, but it was for an audience made up of, most specifically, Romans. We can conclude this for a long list of reasons, but to simplify: Mark didn't start with genealogy or lineage that would link Jesus to the Davidic line; he didn't focus as much on what the Old Testament predicted; the overall writing style doesn't appeal to issues that were important to the Jews, such as religious customs or prophecy; and his "Gospel of action" (with words like "immediately," "as soon as," "at once," and "quickly") reflect the Roman appreciation for a fast-moving story filled with a central Character who embodies power and action.

Luke's Audience: The Gentiles

Luke was a physician who traveled quite a bit. Unbeknownst to some, he was also a Gentile (see Paul's words in Colossians 4:10–14). Whereas a Christian likely doesn't balk at this, the idea that a Gentile's writing would ever be included in the Holy Word of God would have been a scandal to the Jews. His audience, unlike Matthew's, was not for the Jews. However, in contrast to Mark, it was not for only the Romans. Luke was therefore a Gentile who wrote to all Gentiles in general, especially the Greeks.

As the Gentiles were about to be included in the promises of God, and the Greeks were an enormous population of Gentiles, then a Gospel explanation of who Jesus was and what He accomplished was needed not just for the Jews and Romans, but for all those new in the faith coming from the Greek, Gentile world at the time. This explains why Luke's book emphasizes salvation for *all*. As Matthew's Gospel bridged the gap between the two Testaments, Luke's bridged the gap between the rumors of the Jewish Messiah and the first worldwide ecclesiastical assembly (the early Church). As the longest and most history-centered of all the Gospels, Luke (called the "careful historian" by scholars) also covers events that happened before the other Gospel narratives begin (like the full account of John the Baptist and Jesus' teaching in the Temple at age twelve). No doubt this instruction about Jesus' background and personality would appeal to the Gentiles and to the Greeks, whose former theology was well accustomed to the idea of "god-men" (like Hercules).

Today, we're blessed that there is such a three-way overlap between the "Synoptics" (Matthew, Mark, and Luke). This is so for a number of reasons, but we will state two: 1) the more witnesses tell the same story but from different angles, the more solid the argument for the authenticity of the account (our justice system in the United States relies on this truth); 2) though the Gospels do tell the same story, their unique approach sometimes results in a certain detail being addressed in one or two, but not all, Gospels, collectively giving us a wider coverage of what happened historically than we would receive if we had fewer documents.

John's Gospel: A Theological Manual for the Early Church

As for the Gospel of John, it's clear that the unique language connects to a trainload of Jewish theology, making many in the academic world believe John's audience was principally Jewish. However, his language and purpose differ from Matthew's.

Whereas Matthew showed *fulfillment* of long-standing, Jewish beliefs, John explained what those Jewish beliefs and customs *were*.

His frequent clarification of certain Jewish customs and traditions

illustrates that he was writing to people who needed such clarification in the first place, so it's far more logical to believe his audience
was of a Gentile nature—unfamiliar with rabbinical teaching. But
his emphasis on theology also makes his Gospel different from the
Synoptics. The writers of the Synoptics used their narrative of Jesus'
actions, signs, miracles, and prophetic fulfillments along the way as a
means of establishing Jesus' authority and divinity. John flipped this
order, using theology to prove the narrative's legitimacy in history.
His audience was therefore most likely Gentiles who were entirely
unfamiliar with the messianic teaching of the rabbinical world, but
it goes beyond that as well. The early Church did not have the New
Testament that would equip them to witness to the world, but they
were, as people of God, included in the command to fulfill the Great
Commission, and witnessing will always be part of that. How would
one go about spreading "Good News" in an efficient manner if they
didn't know the roots of their belief system?

The well-developed Gospel message as it's preached from the
pulpit today is a product of hard-working men and women over
thousands of years who compiled historic notes and poured into the
Scriptures to rebuke heresy and produce the kinds of study materials
we have available to us now. Today, if a person wishes to witness to
a friend who is on the verge of believing but has a specific issue that
is causing them to hesitate, a quick jaunt to the local bookstore or
library, or an online book-shopping session offers volumes of books
that can provide immediate answers. In John's day, so much closer to
the time of Christ (and before our secularized world started treating
Jesus' story as if it's irrelevant), Jesus' work on the cross was brand
new. Believers were popping up everywhere because of this "man who
gives salvation to all," and they felt inspired to tell everyone as much
as they could. But teaching materials were slim in that day, and fewer
people knew the term "Son of God" was *not* simply another reference
to one of the Greek "god-men."

John's Gospel was, therefore, a sort of training manual for the early Church that explained not only what happened to a historical Man-God named Jesus, but also who He was and is in His eternality—before His birth, and after the cross. The Gospel of John's *true* audience was anyone who believed in Him and wanted to tell others about Him responsibly. Since that also includes modern Christians, it's safe to say that, in God's miraculous providence, John's Gospel was written for all people and all times.

We plan to tackle the beginning of the story of Christ mostly in chronological order, using all four Gospels simultaneously along the way. Then we will shift gears to focus on the miracles, teachings, and actions of Jesus in relative groups.

Most Bible studies separate John from the other three books and tackle his work by itself, citing its complicated, deep nature as the reason. If this study was only on the New Testament, we would likely agree and give it the same treatment. However, *our* readers have been, from the beginning of this book, studying the entire Bible along with us, including the complicated bits about Davidic lines, kinsman redeemers, prophetic pictures, and the unfathomably dense concept of the protevangelium in Genesis. We have no doubt that, although John's Gospel is not as "storybook-like" as the others, our readers will be able to appreciate and fully comprehend his work alongside the others. That said, chronological order does, in fact, take us back to the very, *very* beginning, prior to the creation of the world.

The "Word"

In the very first verse of John's Gospel, we read: "In the beginning was the Word, and the Word was with God, and the Word was God." Later in the same chapter, John states: "And the Word was made flesh, and dwelt among us" (1:14a).

From this, the earliest chronological event in any of the New Testament narratives, we already have our first radically fulfilled prophecy. The Word, which "was God," was "made flesh, and dwelt among us." In short, John is telling his readers that God became a human in the Man of Jesus. Recall what Isaiah said in our discussions of the prophets: "and they will call him Immanuel." As stated earlier, "Immanuel" is Hebrew for "God with us" (also see Matthew 1:23, where Matthew translates the name for Jewish readers).

But what does it mean that Jesus is a "Word"?

In the early stages of Greek Stoic philosophy, as influenced by Aristotle and later Heraclitus, the word *logos* described the existence of rationality and reasoning, or one's ability to accumulate and retain knowledge. Because this is the quality that separates humanity from animals—and that's proven in the fact that humans can speak but animals cannot—the word *logos* quickly became associated with the act of speaking. Since speech requires saying words, the Greek *logos* translates into the English "word."

In the Hellenistic world, debating philosophy was seen as the very purpose of one's existence. Nothing else in the entire universe matters for individuals if they cannot take in information, use their capability of reasoning to rationalize and organize that information into coherent thoughts, process a philosophical conclusion, and then share that finding with others through the vehicle of speech. It was the act of profound thinking that civilization was built upon.

In fact, studies of New Testament culture and background explain that a public social game called "challenge and riposte" was played among those who fancied themselves to be great orators and philosophers. Winning this challenge meant establishing one's self with the highest attainable honor in Christ's day, and this is precisely what the Pharisees were doing when they publicly went against Jesus. One Ashland Theological Seminary professor of New Testament and Greek studies, a theologian named Dr. David deSilva, reiterates:

> The challenge-riposte is essentially an attempt to gain honor at someone else's expense by publicly posing a challenge that can-

not be answered. When a challenge has been posed, the challenged must make some sort of response (and no response is also considered a response [or a "failure" of the challenge]). It falls to the bystanders to decide whether or not the challenged person successfully defended his…own honor. The Gospels are full of these exchanges, mainly posed by Pharisees, Sadducees or other religious officials at Jesus, whom they regarded as an upstart threatening to steal their place in the esteem of the people.[4]

It's crucial to understand that the cohesive process of the human mind, and the ability to respond to that process with words, is what the Greek word *logos* embodied. But as this process is the basis of human intelligence, simply stringing together intelligible vocabulary in a native language wasn't enough to really exemplify the depth of this term. For example, walking into a marketplace and asking someone, "Where's the bread?" most certainly does exercise one's ability to communicate that he wants bread and process the speech that is required to find it. But this simplistic use of language would not satisfy what the Greek philosophers demanded in the exchange of rhetorical persuasion that would be worthy of the word *logos*. A better picture of *logos* as a philosophical term is represented by such a question as, "What is the meaning of life?" or "Why are we here?"

In the natural world, there is order: Grass grows, the sun rises, the wind blows, and rain falls. There is also a natural order instilled within humanity: Lies hurt feelings, treason gets you killed, smiles spread happiness, and so on. All of this is observable, and it all takes reasoning to comprehend. To the Hellenistic philosophers of Christ's time, *logos* came to take on new, cosmic-origins meaning as the "order of the natural world," and this concept was taught in schools and universities of that day: "[*Logos* is] a universal principle of order: *Logos* orders the world; it is the design that directs everything; it is the foundation for human wisdom…. For the Stoics, god, nature, and *logos* were one and the same."[5] The Greek gods, it was believed, would use *logos* to utter something aloud, and that thing would come into being or begin to exist in that moment, a "divine command" process known as *logos spermatikos.*

John's Gentile and/or Hellenistic readers would have instantly known what it meant to call Jesus, *or* the Father, *or* both, the term *logos.* The teaching John gives us here is as true today as it was when he wrote it: For those of us who believe in the Bible and its claims of the Creation event, God didn't just "use" *logos* (reasoning and logic) to create the world; He *was Logos* (Reasoning and Logic) when He created the world. With that in mind, read these verses again: "In the beginning was the Word, and the Word was with God, and the Word was God....And the Word was made flesh, and dwelt among us" (1:1, 14a).

Jesus, our Savior of Salvation, was there in the beginning, *already present* with God, and He *was* God, and *then* He was made flesh and dwelt among us, fulfilling Isaiah's prophecy: "God with us," Immanuel. To bring it down to the simplest of terms: Jesus is the personification of reasoning, and, before the earth even existed, this God named Reason came and dwelt among us. This brings clarity to the following verses 3–4: "All things were made by him; and without him was not any thing made that was made. In him was life; and the life was the light of men." These first four verses again from Brian Simmons' *Passion Translation* are somewhat enlightening after considering all of this:

> In the very beginning God was already there. And before his face Was his Living Expression. And this "Living Expression" Was with God, yet fully God. They were together—face to face, In the very beginning. And through his creative inspiration This "Living Expression" made all things, For nothing has existence Apart from him! Life came into being Because of him, For his life is light for all humanity.[6]

Before assuming that this is just a poetic rephrasing, it's worth noting that Simmons produced this translation by taking the Aramaic into consideration, and this is an etymologically responsible move. We can see this in Isaiah 48:13a, which, in the KJV, says, "Mine hand also hath laid the foundation of the earth," but in Aramaic, it said, "By my word, I have founded the earth."[7] Simmons, in footnote "c" regarding "Living Expression" in John 1:1, states:

> As translated from the Aramaic, which can also mean "Manifestation." The Greek is Logos, or "Word," or "Message," or "Blueprint." Jesus Christ is...the Living Expression of all that God is, contains, and reveals. Just as we express ourselves in words, God has perfectly expressed Himself in Christ.[8]

To John's audience, calling Jesus this term meant that by His very existence, He outperformed the greatest philosophers in all of human history, and all of creation—humans, animals, plants, weather—owes itself to Him and bows to His authority. The rest of John's opening statement relies on understanding the mystery of the Trinity or Godhead. And whereas that topic is supremely complicated (don't worry, we won't go into it at length here), it's a plain teaching of Scripture that Jesus is the Creator alongside the Father. Though this boggles the minds of many Westerners who have been brought up hearing the Father was "the Creator," implying that He was the only member of the Trinity who could create, other verses in the New Testament attest to the fact that Jesus is, *also*, the Creator (Colossians 1:16; Hebrews 1:1–2). Furthermore, if Jesus is not the Creator, then He is a created being, and thus does not share eternality with the Father. Paul wrote in 2 Corinthians 5:17, "Therefore if any man be in Christ, he is a new creature: old things are passed away; behold, all things are become new." How can we put faith in a spiritual recreation—a literal "new creature" theology when we become a follower of Christ like this verse states—if Jesus wasn't the Creator?

Now, is there some theological response that suggests these Creators of the Trinity would have functioned in different areas? Meaning that by some divine prerogative, the Father created the world "through" Jesus, as equal Partner in the formation of the cosmos? That is what Scripture suggests, yes. Hebrews 1:2 says the universe was created *through* Christ, while the following verse says both Trinity Members share the same nature; Deuteronomy 6:4 says that God is "one"; 1 Corinthians 8:6 says, "But to us there is but one God, the Father, of whom are all things, and we in him; and one Lord Jesus Christ, by whom are all things, and we by him." The Holy Spirit was involved in Creation as well (Genesis 1:2). As the Hebrew word for "spirit" means "breath," we read in Psalm 33:6, "By the word of the Lord were the heavens made; and all the host of them by the breath of his mouth." We should understand that God is "One," and God is three Persons, so as a united front, all three Persons were involved in Creation.

If Jesus is the "Word," and the Father "spoke" things into existence and those things "were so" (Genesis 1), then the Father created the world through the Son as an active agent in carrying it out. The proof John was showing Jesus as eclipsing the Greek gods is also shown in his next verse: "In him was life; and the life was the light of men" (John 1:4). The Greeks believed the gods lived in a realm unknown to us, a realm made of light. Our light on this planet only reflects the perfect light of that realm, they thought. Therefore, in Jesus, John said, was the superior light over all gods, and from Him, the life of mankind sprang. He wasn't just "like the other gods" who each represented light and created one or two things that they were thus known for (like Athena/Minerva "the goddess of reason" or Poseidon/Neptune "the god of the sea" and so on). Jesus created *all things* as an active agent alongside the Father, and mankind—the most intelligent and *logos*-capable creation in existence—came from Him who originated both light (Genesis 1:3) and the life of men that held within them a reflection of that holy and pure light.

Another prophecy is fulfilled in this connection: Isaiah said that the One who came to save would be this Light, "a light of the Gentiles" (42:6), and it is to Gentiles everywhere that John the Baptist "came for a witness, to bear witness of the Light, that all men through him might believe" (1:6–9).

Let's continue by considering our famous forerunner (and likely Essene), John the Baptist (unrelated to the writer of John's Gospel), whose story is outlined in Luke 1:5–25, 57–80.

The Forerunner

Luke jumps right in explaining that John the Baptist's parents, Zacharias (alternatively, "Zechariah") and Elizabeth, were too old to have children. This was more than just a disappointment for them, since Jewish culture placed a high value on lineage and producing offspring that would carry on their ways of life and maintain their presence upon the earth in every age. So the couple prayed fervently for a miracle. Zacharias was a priest serving in the Temple at the altar of incense when the archangel Gabriel appeared to tell him he was going to have a son, then proceeded to prophetically describe him:

> Fear not, Zacharias: for thy prayer is heard; and thy wife Elisabeth shall bear thee a son, and thou shalt call his name John....and he shall be filled with the Holy Ghost, even from his mother's womb. And many of the children of Israel shall he turn to the Lord their God. *And he shall go before him in the spirit and power of Elias, to turn the hearts of the fathers to the children,* and the disobedient to the wisdom of the just; *to make ready a people prepared for the Lord.* (Luke 1:13, 15–17; emphasis added)

Remember that, unless otherwise specified, we are using the biblical translation that has been the most commonly read since its production in 1611, the King James Version (KJV), due to many readers' familiarity with its treatment of language. However, that places upon us the responsibility of offering up occasional clarity.

The name "Elias" is Greek. In Hebrew, it's "Elijah."

If necessary, turn back to the Old Testament study and review the very last prophet, Malachi, under "The Prophets" subsection. One of Malachi's statements, spoken through him by the Lord, was the exciting proclamation: "Behold, I will send my messenger, and he shall prepare the way before me!" (Malachi 3:1). Later, God said through Malachi, "I will send you Elijah the prophet before the coming of the great and dreadful day of the Lord: And he shall turn the heart of the fathers to the children…lest I come and smite the earth with a curse" (4:4–6). So here, in Luke, Zacharias is carrying out the Temple duties when suddenly Gabriel the angel appears and tells him, nearly word for word, that his own son, John, will be imbued with the same spirit and power as Elijah, of whom Malachi spoke.

Note this is not a doctrine of reincarnation. This is not literally the "rebirth" of Elijah, as scholars acknowledge: "John was not Elijah revived from the dead, but his ministry was to be characterized by a similar prophetic earnestness, a passion for reformation, and a forthright denunciation of ungodliness. His ministry was to be, in reality, a fulfillment of Malachi's prophecy."[9]

Elijah had, in Old Testament times, been one of the boldest, bravest prophets to ever challenge God's people during their seasons of wicked idolatry (1 Kings 18:21–40). Here, the "spirit" (read: "integrity," "courage," and "passion") of Elijah was being bestowed upon Zacharias' son, John, who would be instilled with the Holy Spirit for this work even before his birth! In fact, the popular verse that tells of John's physical appearance (he wore clothing of camel's hair and a belt; Matthew 3:4) details almost exactly the same clothing as Elijah (a garment of hair and a belt; 2 Kings 1:8).

John the Baptist's role as the forerunner would be for two purposes: 1) to prepare the people spiritually, and 2) to identify the Lord when He arrived (which we will address later). Regarding the first, theologians are not certain if the note about turning "the heart of the fathers to the children" meant John would reestablish a special bond among the Jews, or if it referred to a return to the glory days of Israel—the "children" being those alive on the day Gabriel met with Zacharias and the "fathers" being the unity that existed under the patriarchs. Either is possible, but one naturally leads to the other, so it's likely God intended both interpretations. Readers who may have skipped our reflection on the Intertestamental Period should really consider reading that section before proceeding. It takes understanding the fragmented state of the Jews of that time to really appreciate what is happening here in Luke. *Barnes' Notes* relates this state of the Jews to this verse:

> In the time of John the Jews were divided into a number of different sects.... They were opposed violently to each other, and pursued their opposition with great animosity. It was impossible but that this opposition should find its way into families, and divide parents and children from each other. John came that he might allay these animosities and produce better feeling.... He would restore peace to their families, and reconcile those parents and children who had chosen different sects, and who had suffered their attachment "to sect" to interrupt the harmony of their households.[10]

Most academic material on the Intertestamental Period acknowledges that many Jews just before Christ's appearance were dealing with extreme doubt in the promises of God. If they could speak for themselves, they would surely explain that four hundred years passing since the last anointed prophet of God could likely do that to even the most faithful of His devoted followers when they had been used to the words of the prophets among them for so long. One of John the Baptist's central goals would be to restore unity and "turn the heart of the fathers to the children," thus making the holy nation of God let go of their petty disputes and be spiritually prepared for what was going to happen next. That's a huge undertaking! That is probably why Zacharias—likely one of the devout Jews that had given his life to Yahweh in spite of great doubt—couldn't believe his very own son would be the powerful "preparer," and he was thus stricken dumb (Luke 1:20). Zechariah's son John would be eight days old when the older man would be able to speak again.

Mary

Meanwhile, just months into Elizabeth's pregnancy, the same archangel Gabriel appears to a young virgin betrothed (engaged) to a carpenter named Joseph, saying, "Hail, thou that art highly favoured, the Lord is with thee: blessed art thou among women" (Luke 1:28). After we read about how shocked she was by this announcement, we see Gabriel go on to state the oft-repeated proclamation:

> Fear not, Mary: for thou hast found favour with God. And, behold, thou shalt conceive in thy womb, and bring forth a son, and shalt call his name Jesus [Hebrew, *Yeshua*]. He shall be great, and shall be called the Son of the Highest: and the Lord God shall give unto him the throne of his father David: And he shall reign over the house of Jacob for ever; and of his kingdom there shall be no end. (Luke 1:30–33)

We're sure you caught it, but just in case: Isaiah 7:14 was just fulfilled in this moment: "Therefore the Lord himself shall give you a sign; Behold, a virgin shall conceive, and bear a son..." Matthew not only mentions this event, he interprets it in light of the prophet Isaiah: "Behold, a virgin shall be with child, and shall bring forth a son, and they shall call his name Emmanuel [Greek spelling], which being interpreted is, God with us" (1:23).

> Then said Mary unto the angel, "How shall this be, seeing I know not a man [being that I'm a virgin]?"

And the angel answered and said unto her, "The Holy Ghost shall come upon thee, and the power of the Highest shall overshadow thee: therefore also that holy thing which shall be born of thee shall be called the Son of God. And, behold, thy cousin Elisabeth, she hath also conceived a son in her old age: and this is the sixth month with her, who was called barren. For with God nothing shall be impossible."

The protevangelium, the Gospel promise of Genesis, has finally, after the whole of human history up to this point, begun!

Can you even imagine what must have been going through Mary's mind?

Keep in mind we're not talking about an average-aged virgin fiancée by today's standards. The Bible doesn't mention Mary's age, but extrabiblical, historical documents written in the first and second centuries AD indicate she was between the ages of twelve and fifteen, making her between about thirteen and sixteen at the end of her pregnancy nine months later. As girls in ancient Israel were frequently promised to a man as soon as they reached puberty, this is not an unbelievable age to associate Mary with. (Note that, unlike today, a marriage to a young girl was not immediately consummated, so a girl of twelve could be betrothed for quite some time before she faced more adult situations.) Though some young women today experience pregnancy, the circumstances are obviously different; their pregnancies likely result from either promiscuous choices or tragic and dark scenarios involving coercive actions of a men upon minors. Both possibilities (and any other we can imagine) involve more "educational experience" than a girl at this age should be familiar with. Mary had never "known" a man. At the same age as many of our youth today who are playing with Barbie dolls and braiding hair, Mary was informed through a frighteningly awesome angelic appearance that her childhood was over in an instant. Hers was the "seed" that was about to produce God, Himself, "among us" in the form of a Baby:

Immanuel. Genesis 3:15, as a reminder, reads, "And I [God] will put enmity between thee and the woman, and between thy seed and her seed; it shall bruise thy head, and thou shalt bruise his heel."

In our study of Genesis, we considered how odd the reference to a "female seed" would have sounded to the ancients. The emphasis in Israel's culture was upon the seed of males—and there has never been any such thing as a "seed" in a female's reproductive system. Isaiah prophesied about the Baby Immanuel being born of a virgin, which is the Hebrew *alma*. Some have pointed out the literal translation of this word in Hebrew is "young woman" or "young maiden," and not necessarily "virgin." But the biblical usage and context would render a non-virgin female absurd, as scholars are aware: "There is no instance where it can be proved that *alma* designates a young woman who is not a virgin. The fact of virginity is obvious in Gen 24:43 where *alma* is used of one who was being sought as a bride for Isaac."[11] This utterance from Isaiah about Immanuel coming from the womb of an untouched maiden would likely be the only other time in history up to that point that a reliable voice in the Jewish nation would place such emphasis on the offspring of a *woman*. Though they knew already that no man would even be involved in the Messiah's birth, to the hearers of Isaiah's words as recorded in 7:14, a light must have gone on: *Ohhh… That's why we've been talking about the "seed of a woman."*

We can only imagine the surprise some of the Israelites felt when they initially began to fully comprehend that God, back in the Garden of Eden and in the presence of the only two people in existence, was prophesying out of His own mouth that the Messiah wouldn't even have a biological father. Of course they had heard the prophecy many times before it happened, but the shock of seeing such a phenomenon come to fruition is likely not one that can be prepared for. Jesus was a miracle, an authority over natural law, as early as the beginning of the world and humanity.

As far as the maiden whose "seed" would carry the Child, we find her described in the apocryphal *Protoevangelium of James*, a document important to the early Church until circa AD 500 when it fell out of circulation as a result of Pope Gelasius' rejection of it. The *Anchor Yale Bible Dictionary* openly attests the *Protoevangelium of James* "had a tremendous impact in the early church."[12]

Important disclaimer: That doesn't mean it should be read as a Holy-Spirit-inspired book equal to the canon. What it *does* mean is that, while the Church was in its infancy in the first century and people were still just hearing about who Mary and Jesus were, vindictive rumors about Mary's virginity were popping up and the heresy needed to be corrected—the answer to which was, in part, this early apologetic that strove to reaffirm her innocence. Some believers wince at hagiographical literature (*hagio*, "holy," thus "holy biographies": extrabiblical accounts of the early saints), believing it wrong to consider what they say because they are not inspired Scripture. There's a stigma linked to these documents that often results in a raised eyebrow or two when they're brought up in biblical research. We find it interesting that these same readers will study, and even quote from, biographies on their own historic heroes—Albert Einstein, Abraham Lincoln, Winston Churchill, Charles Dickens, William Shakespeare—and never even think about how similar that practice is to reading a hagiography. They browse the local bookstore, pick up a story on a historical figure, believe it's filled with truth, and even share what they've learned with others, usually without even questioning or confirming the facts outlined in the books. But if it involves information about a Bible character, the general consensus appears to be: "If it's in the Bible, I'll believe it! If it's not in the Bible, it's hogwash! All we ever need to know is in the Book." The value of hagiographies is not in accepting every single word at Holy-Spirit-level value, but in seeing that they do tell another perspective of the story, some of which might be based in truth since we were not there to say otherwise.

That said, *if* some of the details told in the *Protoevangelium of James* happen to be as true as many in the first several centuries believed it to be, then Mary was actually quite popular...and she may have had some warning that God planned to involve her in His Redemption plan in some way. From chapters 6 and 7 of this ancient writing, we read:

> And when she was a year old, Joachim [Mary's father] made a great feast, and invited the priests, and the scribes, and the elders, and all the people of Israel. And Joachim brought the child to the priests; and they blessed her, saying: "O God of our fathers, bless this child, and give her an everlasting name to be named in all generations."
>
> And all the people said: "So be it, so be it, amen."
>
> And he brought her to the chief priests; and they blessed her, saying: "O God most high, look upon this child, and bless her with the utmost blessing, which shall be forever."...

The narrative goes on to say that, from an early age, Mary actually lived in the Temple (which wasn't necessarily uncommon; Anna from Luke 2:36–38 also lived in the Temple), and when she was twelve years of age, the priests were concerned that she would defile the Temple with her presence now that she was old enough to start her menstrual cycle (which was a complicated issue in the cleanliness laws). Not wishing to embarrass her, they quietly sought the Lord over the issue, and were led to host an event for the widowers of Judea to come and claim this beloved young virgin for a wife. The rods of all widowers were gathered together and presented to the High Priest, who prayed over them in the Temple, after which they were returned to their owners. Joseph—whose character calls himself "an old man" in this narrative, wherein he is a widower with children from his first wife—reached for his rod and a dove came out from it, landing on his head: a sign from God that he was the chosen husband for the virgin, Mary. Because of his age and the fact that his new betrothed was very young, Joseph did not consummate the relationship. Instead, as a carpenter, he left to work on a building project, promising young Mary the Lord would protect her as she lived amidst her community without him for a time. (Later, he would return to find her pregnant by the Holy Spirit.)

Again, though we do not claim that the noncanonical *Protoevangelium of James* is as reliable as the Bible, it offers one sweet detail that can inspire a smile for the woman whose "seed" would be the Messiah prophesied in Genesis: During the time Zacharias was stricken dumb from his lack of faith in Gabriel's announcement regarding John's birth, Mary was at her new home spinning the scarlet and "true purple" threads that would be a part of the new Temple veil. The Temple priests decided that she, along with six other virgins (totaling seven, God's number and the number of completion or fullness), would been given this privilege.

What a poetic picture. If this part of Mary's life is true, then the hours she spent laboring at her spinning needle at home, in the earliest days of her pregnancy with the Christ Child, contributed to the completion of the heavy cloth at the doorway to the Holy of Holies. Under the Old Covenant, the veil marked the only consecrated site where mankind was allowed to meet directly with the presence of God (Exodus 30:6). Therefore, with this great honor bestowed upon her by the Temple priests, Mary's craft would relate in adding scarlet (the color of the Lamb's blood that was slain) and "true purple" (biblical colors of true royalty and kingship) to the meeting place of God and men. One day, the son she carried, *the Son*, would die on a cross for all mankind, announcing in the unseen, spiritual realm an eternal victory over the enemy...and that veil would tear from top to bottom (Matthew 27:51; Mark 15:38; Luke 23:45). King Jesus, who is alone worthy of true purple threads, would be the Lamb whose scarlet blood gave *all who believe* in Him access to the Holy of Holies—an all new, invisible, but ever-present meeting place for God and man, accessible anywhere in the world and at any time—through "a new and living way, which he hath consecrated for us, through the veil, that is to say, his flesh" (Hebrews 10:20).

Christ's flesh became the new and living veil.

And whether or not the apocryphal account of Mary is true, God
the Father knew from the beginning the Son's body and blood would
become the doorway to the Holy of Holies for all believers, as He
stated to the world's first two finite, imperfect humans in Genesis.

Another question that arises regarding Mary is how this virginal
birth would have looked to those in her community. The Messiah's
Coming through the womb of a virgin had been prophesied since Isaiah,
so it wasn't a new concept. However, certainly, there would have been
doubters amid Israel when the news spread, making a very uncomfortable situation for Mary, whose integrity would have been under fire. In
the Bible, this issue is not addressed. In the *Protoevangelium of James*,
the midwife confirms our suspicions, marching into Mary's presence
in unbelief, saying, "Show thyself; for no small controversy has arisen
about thee."[14] In other words, "Let's see this big belly everyone's talking
about. You're the talk of the town around these parts!"

(In the interest of closure, the story goes on to say the midwife proceeded to deliver the Christ Child and, because of her lack of faith, a
great, searing, fiery pain spread throughout her hand. She prayed right
there on the spot and was healed, and a voice told her to keep secret the
things she had seen until after the Child had officially made Himself
known to Jerusalem. The identity of the midwife is a fascinating topic.
Her name in verse 10:1 of the *Protoevangelium* is "Salome." Records
unanimously dismiss the idea that she might be connected to the daughter of Herodias who shared her name. However, according to many
historical interpretations, this is the same Salome who married Zebedee,
giving him sons James and John, who grew up to be two of Jesus' twelve
disciples. If this is true, then this midwife is the same Salome who had
ministered to Jesus and remained in His presence from Galilee to the
cross [Mark 15:40–41], and was with Mary Magdalene and Mary the
mother of Jesus when the three went to anoint their Savior's body with
sweet spices and found the tomb empty [Mark 16:1–3].)

Everything we know today about the culture at the time of Mary
suggests that she would have been more than merely controversial,

but she handled herself admirably. An excerpt from Donna Howell's *Handmaidens Conspiracy* slows down the narrative and allows her story to be felt at a deeper level, depicting Mary as the warrior she truly must have been in order to accept this responsibility. Though a portion of this excerpt gets a little ahead of where we are in the account, the conclusion is about the person of Mary, so we will include it in this section so we can connect with her character. After Gabriel's announcement:

> If we let the weight of what just occurred in Mary's life settle within our thoughts, the bravery and boldness of this young woman at this moment in time is extraordinary, if not unfathomable. In an instant, Mary transforms from a scared little girl to a spiritual warrior with a determination that would make Joan of Arc pale in comparison. She responds with tenacious heroism: "Behold the handmaid of the Lord; be it unto me according to thy word" (1:38).
>
> Christians have read and celebrated this narrative for so long in a culture that paints her as a quiet, gentle, and mild-mannered saint that the authority Mary shows in her words here has been traded for the image of a woman bowing her head in docile servitude. Yes, servitude was an enormous part of the big picture regarding Mary, absolutely. By accepting such an inconceivable task as carrying the Son of God into the world in a day and age when a premarital pregnancy would have likely resulted in the death penalty by stoning or, at the very least, banishment from her family and the rest of her people, Mary was no doubt an illustrious servant— first and foremost. Everything stable in her life was now at risk, and she accepted the mission of the Lord despite that. However, it is *because of* such factors, as well as the obedience and humility in her response, that we can catch a glimpse of the warrior within. Her submission to the messenger of God does not relate weakness, but *tenacity!* She had every reason to be afraid of the earthly, societal repercussions of being pregnant before marriage—thousands of

unimaginably awful hardships undoubtedly lay ahead of her—but she didn't waver for an instant. This is not to say that she didn't feel fear, as Luke 1:29 states that she did. But it is to say that she did not allow the fear to rule her. She immediately cast away all concepts of leading a normal life and did the bravest, most warrior-like thing any human in her position could have done: She submitted herself to being the mother of the most important Man this world has ever known, and she did so without any experience whatsoever. She didn't just agree with Gabriel's decree, she *owned* her role bravely despite all human reasoning.

Had she been selfish, she might have said, "But wait! What about my betrothed? What about the people in town? What about my parents? Everyone will think I am tainted by indiscretion! I will be killed, or made to leave my people and wander the world alone. I am chaste. This is not a fair thing to ask of me!" Had she lacked confidence, she might have said, "Surely not I, messenger. I am a girl of humble means. Joseph is only a carpenter. I cannot give the King of kings a full life. I have never raised a child, and I cannot possibly know how to guide this Child, the Son of God." Had she allowed any one normal, human emotion to lead her response, she would have revealed that she was still only a child—perhaps more befitting of the modern ideas we have of the "meek and mild" Mary. Instead, she said, "Behold the handmaid of the Lord; be it unto me according to thy word." It's as if she downloaded ten lifetimes' worth of maturity in a matter of seconds.

What bravery! What valor!...

What *leadership*!

We all know what happened next, but rarely do we pause and reflect upon the enormity of it.

When Joseph discovers she is pregnant, he plans to discreetly divorce her, believing that she has given herself to the temptation of promiscuity, but he is halted by an angel in a dream who tells him that Mary has, in fact, been impregnated by the power of God. The angel instructs Joseph to support her, and the carpenter obeys (Matthew 1:19–25)....

When that precious Savior arrived, it was through the body of a simple, innocent girl who, in seconds, became a dynamic woman of brute-force tenacity in the face of all odds...

And the list grows even longer regarding Mary's womanly strength. Once the Son of God was born to her, Mary left home with her new husband and traveled more than two hundred miles within the first few years—Nazareth to Bethlehem, seventy miles; Bethlehem to Jerusalem round-trip, twelve miles; Bethlehem to Egypt, more than forty miles; and Egypt to Nazareth, one hundred-plus miles—all without the modern conveniences of a vehicle or paved roads. Far from any concept of a homebody female plucking chickens near a stove and squeezing fresh fig juice, Mary was a voyager. A journeywoman! She fearlessly packed up the family's mule and carried their belongings—as well as her infant (and later toddler)—from place to place as the Lord directed, regardless of potentially harsh weather conditions, dangers of the road, marauders by nightfall, or any other concerns that might have made another woman long for baking bread and sweeping the floor. It's likely that Mary knew how to tie sailor's knots, build fires, assemble a tent, and locate nearby food and water sources. What a resourceful woman she must have been.

But the greatest challenge was ahead of her, and it was one she met with equal grit and determination.

When the Christ child grew up and Joseph was gone, Mary willingly went to the foot of the cross and revealed a whole new level of bold heroism as she watched her boy bleed to death slowly and painfully. Her little boy... Her little *Yeshua*. The babe who had moved inside her belly. The babe whose knee boo-boos she had kissed and whose smile she would only ever see in memory until her journey through the Paradise Gate.

The boy whose knowledge of Scripture was so impressive that He held His own amidst the intellects in the Temple. How proud she must have been of Him, the sweet and loving Messiah…and how unwaveringly fearless she was to remain by His side while He suffered.

Mary was as much a servant as any human could possibly be, but she was more than that. Far more. Mary was a dauntless, unflinching *fortress* of strength.

Mary gave birth to and cared for the one and only Son of God. Isaiah's prophecy about the virgin had now been completed, and though the Bible is silent on the subject, we know for certain there were those (Mary, Joseph, Zacharias, Elizabeth, and likely others) who knew who this Messiah was from birth.

Elizabeth, Mary's cousin who was pregnant with John the Baptist, knew instantly.

Right after the conception, Mary went to Elizabeth's house and greeted her. When she did, the baby in Elizabeth's belly "leaped in her womb," and, without Mary having to say a word about the message Gabriel had given her, Elizabeth greeted her as "the mother of my Lord" (Luke 1:41, 43). John the Baptist's birth is not covered at length in the Word. Really, all we know of him is in Luke 1:80, where we read he "grew, and waxed strong in spirit, and was in the deserts till the day of his shewing unto Israel." This describes the life of an Essene, who would have gone into the wilderness and sought only preparations for the Messiah until he was ready to emerge and provide for the world what he had been called to do.

Birth of the Christ Child

The Jews were serious about genealogy. As stated, proving who was related to whom was a big deal when bringing in a new life. Ideally, the new child would make a family proud and account for righteousness in a culture where honor and kinship means everything. Therefore, Matthew, a tax collector and thus a professional of legal documentation in his day, and Luke, the "careful historian," included in their Gospels the lineage of Christ.[16]

Joseph, a man of good character, cared enough for Mary not to publicly humiliate her, so when he arrived and found her pregnant, he sought to secretly divorce her, but the Holy Spirit informed him the pregnancy was legitimately of God (Matthew 1:19–21). As a result, Joseph stood by his young wife (and they did not lie together until after Jesus was born: 1:24–25). A grand census was taken, forcing everyone to return to their home cities (Luke 1:1–3). Joseph was of the lineage of David, so he returned to the City of David, Bethlehem (1:4–5), where the Messiah hailed from His mother's womb.

This fulfilled what had been foretold by the prophet Micah: "Bethlehem...out of thee shall he come forth unto me that is to be ruler in Israel; whose goings forth have been from of old, from everlasting" (5:2).

And it is about right here that all the nativity plays go cross-eyed...

See, many of us have the idea that Mary and Joseph went door to door and nobody had any room because of the barrage of travelers responding to the census, so they just went and birthed in a barn of one innkeeper who impersonally went about his business in the most uncaring fashion. Actually, Luke 2:7 has been misread for two thousand years. In the KJV, this reads: "And she brought forth her firstborn son, and wrapped him in swaddling clothes, and laid him in a manger; because there was no room for them in the inn." This last word translated "inn," in Greek, is *katalyma*, and it is the same Greek word used in Luke 22:11: "And ye shall say unto the goodman of the house, 'The Master saith unto thee, Where is the guestchamber [*katalyma*], where I shall eat the passover with my disciples?'" Depending on their financial situation, the Jews' homes could be small, one-bedroom hovels, but they could also be large enough to house multiple generations so that as sons and daughters grew up and married, they could move to their own chambers. But as was often the case in those times, if a husband moved, the wife went with him. The empty rooms would then be converted into guestrooms to welcome fellow righteous Jews. Because it's explicitly stated in the original language that Jesus was born in a *katalyma* (guest room or guest chamber), the most likely scenario was that He was delivered in someone's personal home, though Bethlehem was a poor area, so it would have been smaller than we imagine those in Jerusalem. The narratives don't indicate who the home belonged to, nor do they say Joseph and his pregnant wife went into a "barn." In fact, that word in Greek is *apotheke,* and it shows up in Luke in several places referring to both "barn" and "grain room" (or "garner"; 3:17; 12:18; 12:24).

Yeah, but it also says Jesus was laid in a "manger"…

That it does. And in those days, the animal-feeding troughs, as well as the animals, were brought into a room of the house in areas where they might otherwise be stolen or killed. Further, the body heat of the animals helped to provide extra heat when the nights got cold.

An incalculable number of scholars recognize this "small house/guestroom" scenario as one of the most probable theories and far more likely than the classic nativity scene in movies and plays. Trent Butler, in his commentary on the book of Luke for Holman's New Testament series, says it's not at all unreasonable to conclude that "Joseph found a small one-room house," and the Baby was laid "in the animal trough attached to the wall that their room shared with the animals' quarters."[17] Leon Morris, in InterVarsity Press' commentary, notes this prospect, saying, "It is also possible that the birth took place in a very poor home where the animals shared the same roof as the family."[18] *New Bible Commentary* says "the traditional picture of a surly innkeeper refusing admission to the needy couple is somewhat dubious."[19] The NET translation notes by Biblical Studies Press likewise acknowledges that "there is no drama in how this is told. There is no search for a variety of places to stay or a heartless innkeeper. (Such items are later, nonbiblical embellishments.)"[20]

Bringing a cow into the living room today may not be how *we* choose to heat our homes, but it was common practice then. In Luke 13:15, where we read that Jesus asked, "doth not each one of you on the sabbath loose his ox or his ass from the manger, and lead him away to watering?" may have been a reference to an inside manger. Otherwise, why would they untie their ox and lead it to the water they kept one foot away from the food in the barn, as this verse otherwise nonsensically suggests? Surely someone in Israel could have found a longer rope...

In Jesus' day, many homes were built up in caves and along the sides of mountains, kind of like a berm house today, for stability and warmth. Early interpretations of this story (including the *Protoevangelium of James*) acknowledge that Mary and Joseph were lodging in a "cave." Therefore, the most likely location of the birth of Christ was a personal home, in what would have been the entryway or the foyer, since there was "no room in the guest room," and the "crib" was an animal's feeding trough.

That's just a fun little tidbit we can smile about this Christmas.

Here's another happy holiday thought: In Luke 2:8–20, we read about the angels' worship of the newborn Savior as they hovered and sang in the skies above the shepherds. Verse 12 states the shepherds are given a sign by which they can recognize the Savior: "Ye shall find the babe wrapped in swaddling clothes, lying in a manger." (The "swaddling clothes" are similar today as they were then, in both fabric and purpose. A new mother would tightly wrap the baby to protect the infant's limbs as well as to imitate the snugness the baby had felt and found comforting in the womb.) Not surprisingly, the shepherds were quick in their willingness to drop everything, run to find this Baby in swaddling clothes, and then tell everyone what they had seen; the people who heard the news were amazed (Luke 2:15–18).

One popular Christmas concept is the shepherd was a lazy, despised man (a rumor having much to do with some baseless claims made by Aristotle who wasn't a Jew and didn't even live near this part of the world). This was never based in reality. The biblical narrative shows Abraham, Moses, and David were all well-esteemed shepherds, and the "shepherd" has always been a reference in the Jewish world for those who "guard" God's "flock" (or people; Psalm 23:1; Isaiah 40:11; Jeremiah 23:1–4; Hebrews 13:20; 1 Peter 2:25; 5:2). That's not to say it wasn't a hard job with some serious down sides; that part was real. Shepherding was difficult, because it disrupted the cleanliness laws (manure, blood from wounds, afterbirth of new animals, slaughtering and dealing with the bodies for food, insects and rats around the livestock, etc.). As such, the shepherds were frequently kept from joining God's people in Jerusalem for feasts and worship. So whereas we would never want to perpetuate the misleading idea that shepherds were men of bad reputation, we need to be real about the fact that they were massively overlooked whenever Israel had a gathering, and that likely whenever someone in the Jewish community had a big announcement, the shepherds generally weren't expected to be involved.

What's more, the shepherds in the Palestinian area had many goals for their sheep, but one in particular stood above the rest. Historians make no small issue about the Jewish pilgrims who would come from all over the territory to Jerusalem for the Passover. The lambs had to be thoroughly checked for perfection, and the accommodations that holy city had to prepare (including the installation of countless extra ovens for the feast) was an enormous task. Any Jew, no matter what trade he was involved in, spent the majority of the year preparing for this one feast alone. Even the roads to Jerusalem had to be repaired annually after all the foot traffic into and out of the city had ceased. The population of Jerusalem was around twenty thousand any other time of the year, but during the Passover feast, it climbed to a staggering one hundred and seventy thousand![21] Selective breeding for the "spotless" lambs was a science that required shepherds to engage all of their time in raising and ritualistically cleansing the animals, preparing special food, and maintaining their health. (This careful breeding could only supply so many lambs, though. Later, we discuss some of the shady practices going on during Passover by religious leaders who angered Jesus when He cleansed the Temple.)

All this, and the men who tended these sheep were regularly excluded while their brothers took the livestock they had raised and used them as Passover sacrifices to cover their own sin. Months of feeding, watering, shearing, cleansing, breeding...yet who would atone for *their* sin? (Few scholars address this question. Those who do suggest they had to participate before or after Passover, when they would have, once again, been segregated from their people.)

Here, we have a beautiful picture of the angels ministering *first* to the shepherds of the field. God, in His divine grace, saw fit to include these men in the accounts of Christ's birth before any others. Perhaps it's because He saw that their lives were dedicated to the practice of atonement, even if their own animal sacrifices were complicated and may have had to be put off until another day when they could have their own, private Passover-like observance, and He wanted to honor that.

Or, perhaps, it's because He knew His Son would one day be *the* Lamb who atoned for all in one work, and the shepherds, for their contribution to the atonement of their people, needed to be recognized...

The shepherds were slaving away in a field of the very lambs this Baby had come to replace, and they were the first to know about it! And now, they were about to meet *the* Lamb! What a considerate thing for God to do! What a thoughtful and compassionate Lord we serve!

We're not through debunking some of the images we see each December on Christmas cards. This next example doesn't have a misinterpreted Greek word or an Aristotle rumor behind it. Frankly, we don't know *where* this idea comes from, but it latched on at some point and an army of oxen can't haul it away from our contemporary culture: Remember how the three kings followed the star of Bethlehem on a long journey over unrelenting hills of desert sand until they arrived at the stable surrounded by donkeys, camels, and hay nestled around the swaddled Christ Child? That was great, wasn't it? Heartwarming!

Except it didn't happen.

The very next thing that occurred in the life of Christ following His birth in a small home was an eight-day wait until His circumcision. Then, after "the days of her [Mary's] purification according to the law of Moses were accomplished"—which Leviticus 12:1–8 clarifies to be forty days from a male baby's birth (thirty-three days after circumcision)—"they brought him to Jerusalem, to present him to the Lord" in the Temple (Luke 2:22–38). The offering for the common Jew at this visit was a lamb and either a dove or pigeon, but if the parents couldn't afford it, they were allowed to choose two birds. Mary and Joseph only sacrificed the birds (2:24), showing that they were financially underprivileged. While they were present at the Temple, they met up with Simeon and Anna. The Holy Spirit had revealed to Simeon that he would see the Messiah before he died; it was the Spirit of God who led Simeon to the Temple for that divine appointment. His words about the Baby were precious, as he began with the statement that he could now die in peace (2:29). He went on to speak to Yahweh, showing his belief: "For mine eyes have seen thy salvation, Which thou hast prepared before the face of all people; A light to lighten the Gentiles, and the glory of thy people Israel" (2:30–31). Even the Gentiles would be reached!

Jeremiah, in his Lamentations, repeatedly sought solace for his anguish. At one point, a supernatural reassurance overtook him, and he proclaimed, "Therefore have I hope...great is thy faithfulness!" (3:21b–23). The confidence that overtook him looked forward to the day of Christ's arrival. In his prophecy to the people, Jeremiah said, as instructed by the Lord, "I will turn their mourning into joy, and will comfort them, and make them rejoice from their sorrow" (Jeremiah 31:13). It was the same faith in this preternatural security that led Isaiah to prophesy, over and over, that all of Israel would find "comfort" in God's plan (Isaiah 40:1; 49:13; 51:3; 52:9; 54:11; 61:2; 66:13).

On Jesus' first trip to the Temple when He was forty days old, a man named Simeon was so comforted that he was ready to die in peace.

Mary and Joseph marveled at his quick recognition of the Baby Messiah, but a tough mixture of joy and heartbreak was delivered to Mary in that moment: "Behold, this child is set for the fall and rising again of many in Israel; and for a sign which shall be spoken against; Yea, a sword shall pierce through thy own soul also, that the thoughts of many hearts may be revealed" (Luke 2:34–35).

Mary likely couldn't have known just yet how true Simeon's prophetic words were. Her soul would be pierced tremendously by her Son's death.

Anna's specific response is not recorded, but the Word says she gave thanks to God for the Messiah and, just like the shepherds, she rushed to tell everyone that "redemption" had come to Jerusalem (2:38). For some, "redemption" was great news. For others, such as the sorcerers involved in the lucrative business of wowing the crowds, it was the end of everything.

Unbelievable Political Implications of the Magi

In the book of Luke, the three wise men or three kings are not mentioned. Mary and Joseph headed straight back to Galilee: "And when they had performed all things according to the law of the Lord, they returned into Galilee, to their own city Nazareth. And the child grew, and waxed strong in spirit, filled with wisdom: and the grace of God was upon him" (2:39–40). So, sometime between their departure from the Temple (Luke 2:39), when Jesus was forty days old, and Jesus speaking with the rabbis at age twelve (Luke 2:42), the "three wise men" visited them in a "house" (Matthew 2:11). We apologize to Hallmark and anyone else whose cheery Christmas greetings are ruined by this, but Jesus was not fresh from the womb during their visit, and He most definitely wasn't in a stable.

The story goes that these men came from the East to worship the "King of the Jews," and Herod, feeling a bit intimidated by other royalty, called his men to report where this new King could be found. After he had his answer—wherein the chief teachers of the Law quoted from Micah 5:2 about Bethlehem—he attempted to trick the travelers, saying he wanted them to go find the Newborn and report back to him precisely where He was so Herod could "worship Him also." The men left at once, following a bright star as a navigation tool. They arrived at Mary and Joseph's residence sometime later, and they gave gifts and offered up praise to the young King. God warned them in a dream not to report back to Herod (Matthew 2:1–13). Herod, enraged, ordered that all male babies in Bethlehem and the surrounding vicinity be murdered (2:16).

(By the way, if the reader is wondering whether these claims about a bright star during Christ's birth are true: Note that, although we don't plan to deal with that topic here, we will say quite a number of astrological phenomena took place at that time. Any of those documented, historical night-sky spectacles could have been what Matthew wrote about. More information on this is found in many books and Bible study tools as well as in online discussions.)

Getting back to the subject at hand: First, we need to address the idea that there were "three" men of any kind. One legend names them Gaspar, Melchior, and Balthasar, which no doubt has added to the idea that there were three. However, those names have not been confirmed in in any historical record and are therefore false. Scholars behind the *Faithlife Study Bible* note that "given the dangers associated with travel in the first-century Near East, the magi probably traveled as part of a larger entourage."[22] The *Lexham Bible Dictionary* also reports that Eastern traditions from early Christianity place *twelve* men in this group.[23] (There are many other sources we could cite, but you get the idea.) Gold, frankincense, and myrrh—the gifts they brought for the

Christ Child—are the most heavily cited reason for there being three people, as it is imagined each carried one.

Second, who exactly *were* those "wise men" or "kings"? Were they just super smart guys? Rich kings from distant kingdoms? Were they magicians, as the alternative "magi" seems to imply? Technically, the word for "wise men" is the Greek *magos*; before that, it was the Hebrew *rb mg*. The etymological tracing of this word continues to link to the concept of the sorcerers in Babylon and later Persia. In fact, the only time it is used in the Bible outside the birth-of-Christ narrative is in in the book of Acts, in reference to "a certain sorcerer, a false prophet, a Jew, whose name was Barjesus" (13:6, 8). This kind of troubled past for the term is probably why "wise men" is preferred. This is understandable, since the narrative describing the magi depicts them as having the purest of intentions at the time of Christ. The "kings" idea may have first come from Tertullian, from whom the Eastern tradition attributes, or it may have been well-meaning Christian interpreters who connected it to Psalm 72:11, which states that all kings will bow to the Child. Yet, the men's access to their three expensive gifts and to the inner court of King Herod does make it possible that they were indeed kings, so we're not ruling that out. After a lengthy weigh-in from many scholars, however, extrabiblical literature's treatment of this word in use at the time of the New Testament make "royal court officials" (a king's councilmen) the most likely possibility.[24] Their proficient skill in reading the stars almost certainly made them astrologers of that day, which was a common job for royal advisors of ancient kings as well. All of these associations put together, especially as linked to the term "magi," makes a divining position in the royal court a real possibility. They may have been heralded in their local area as the kind of "wise men" who practiced sorcery, witchcraft, and divination, predicting coming kings and proving to be accurate (by powers not of Yahweh, much like the reproducers of magical miracles in Pharaoh's court in Moses' time). This would explain why their trip to visit Herod was taken seriously and resulted in the king's witch hunt.

Third, the magi left Herod's presence and found Jesus as a "young child" in a "house" (Matthew 2:11). Herod had ordered the killing of every baby boy under age two, which was an age the king decided would be appropriate based on when the magi had met with him, placing Jesus near that age. Scholars agree that Jesus was a toddler living with Mary and Joseph in a regular Jewish home at this time.

Fourth, a surprising number of people find it comforting to believe these men were Jews, as it would show at least a few more of God's people recognizing Jesus as the Messiah (as the accounts of His life account find that a rare occurrence). This is doubtful. Had they been Jewish, they would have: 1) already known their own Scripture would send them to Bethlehem because of the prophets; 2) sought Scripture to see what it said of the Messiah's birthplace; 3) sought the advice of a learned holy man. The fact that they sought secular King Herod as a means to locate the Jewish Messiah proves they were not Jewish.

By straightening these images out to reflect history more accurately, we don't wish to destroy the picture of the magi. In fact, we're hoping to achieve the opposite: Underneath all of today's cultural misinterpretations and miscalculations about these travelers is a sweet, endearing glimpse of the Father!

If scholars and the Greek historian Herodotus are correct in their estimates of who this "entourage" of more than three people was, then the magi were deeply entrenched in Zoroastrianism (though it wasn't called that at the time).[25] The ancient *Arabic Gospel of the Infancy of the Savior* states outright that the "magi came from the east to Jerusalem, as Zoroaster had predicted" (7:1). The book of Daniel acknowledges the presence of these followers of Zoroastrianism—astronomers, enchanters, dream interpreters, and visionaries—who were everywhere in the king's courts in Babylon (see Daniel 1:20; 2:2; 4:4; 5:7). Daniel, in its later Greek form translated during the Hellenistic period, shows this kind of *magoi* were "flourishing in every corner of the Babylonian kingdom of Nebuchadnezzar."[26] According to the historian Tacitus, this form of kingly advisement from Zoroastrian prophets was alive and thriving in the subsequent Roman Empire as well.[27] Scholars frequently cite that Simon the sorcerer from Acts 8:9–24 was this kind of magi. The list goes on and on showing that the magi, the "wise men" from this narrative of Christ's birth, were pagan priests "engaged in occult arts"[28] and predicting the future for kings who took them seriously because their prophecies frequently played out as predicted. (These "magician-astrologers" are sometimes referred to in scholarly circles as "magiastrologers.")

The ancient, sixth-century BC religion of Zoroastrianism taught that Ahura Mazda, the god of light (according to Zoroaster, the religion's founder) was the *one and only* true god—there could be no other. Ahura Mazda was involved in a ceaseless battle against the evil spirit Angra Mainyu, who was equal in power to this god, though opposite in moral nature and character. The theology of Zoroastrianism at the time of Christ was staunchly monotheistic (though it did have a bizarre, seven-entity "Trinity-type" concept), so there is no way disciples of Ahura Mazda would have followed another god (or God) on their own. Yet here, we may actually be witnessing a whole group of them following the star to Mary and Joseph's house to worship this tiny Boy, offer Him gifts, and then proceed to take heed from the One True God, Yahweh, not to report back to Herod: "And being warned of God in a dream that they should not return to Herod, they departed into their own country another way" (Matthew 2:12).

Do you realize what this means?!

These men were *Gentiles!* (And even if they *were* Jews, they were "Babylonian Jews who dabbled in black magic and star worship,"[29] so they couldn't have been pure.) They may possibly even been soothsaying clairvoyants who received oracles from the gods for their king back home. Yet, they fell to the ground and worshipped the Savior while He was still bouncing His little body on and off the furniture, with more adoration and sincerity than almost all the "holy men" Jesus would ever know. Don't you see it? How adorable! They demonstrated their belief in choosing to carry out the act of worship even when there was no palace, castles, or opulence. A wee Munchkin King became their King in an instant, probably because the same Source that told them to avoid Herod had led them there in the first place, no doubt operating partly through the mouth of whichever king had sent them.

Somewhere in the ancient world, Gentiles in need of saving were seeking redemption that could never come from Ahura Mazda or any other "little-*g* god." Yet it's obvious by the narrative they were honestly seeking and were open-minded to redirection. Yahweh, in His limitless wisdom and love, well before Jesus would accomplish His work on the cross, prompted them not only to seek and find, but to *worship* this little King of the Jews. Yahweh remained in contact with them supernaturally, leading them on a completely different route home so they could not be intercepted and questioned by Herod or his men. God cared for a group who, as far as the evidence shows, didn't have even the foggiest clue who the real Power in the universe was, and He cared well enough to personally intervene on behalf of their very souls. Before the Gentile world knew anything about this Man who died for their sin, a lot more than "three" men were likely immersed in a world of astrology, sorcery, divination, and who knows what else, and God led them to the Savior.

Sorry, but that image is *far* more beautiful than the warm fuzzies holiday greeting cards offer…and it goes well beyond just this group of magi. Nativity plays skim over what was really happening with the visit of these men. Ever wonder why Roman powers (like Herod) would even care about some prophecy about the Jews and a random baby born to them in a small town called Nowheresville-Bethlehem? (Yes, Bethlehem was the "City of David" to the Jews, but its social and economic standing in Christ's day was somewhat pathetic in comparison to, say, Jerusalem or one of the other cities that had Jewish influence on the surrounding, pagan world.) They weren't Jews, they didn't follow God, and they didn't have much reason on an earthly political level to care what Jewish prophecies claimed, so what gives?

The Jews had a long history of Yahweh's miracles they continued to teach as fact (and rightfully so), so when the magi—whom scholars believe to have been collectively the supreme source of prophetic wisdom in the pagan history of Babylon, Media, and Persia—took their warnings seriously, so did the pagan/secular world. This wasn't an ordinary Baby. This wasn't a regular son of Israel whose parents were making claims about deity. Nor was He old enough yet to have personally made claims that would challenge the government like so many false messiahs before Him had done in recent history (Acts 5:38–39). This "following" had not developed by the persuasion of a man who had the faculties of a full-grown manipulator who could draw attention to himself in his own power, his own speech, his own *logos* or challenge-and-riposte showdowns in the marketplaces. The wealthiest kings of the world were sending their men on long journeys from faraway kingdoms with incredibly costly gifts to pay homage to, and worship, this Boy that was prophesied to be the King of all kings!

And that act of faith just may have broken something in the unseen realm...

In case there's still any doubt that the real identity of the magi are far from what's portrayed on Christmas cards, here's one more theory from the archives of history. We find it in a letter from Church father Ignatius to readers in Ephesus almost exactly a hundred years after the magi paid homage to the Christ Child. Ignatius wrote: "How then was [Christ] manifested to the world? A star shone in heaven beyond all the stars... By this all magic was dissolved."

Whoa... What? All magic was what?!

Yep. Watch this:

Ignatius immediately went on to explain that "all things"—that is, practices that used to work in the invisible dominion of magic, sorcery, and the occult—"were disturbed."[30] To put it plainly, the arrival of the star God sent as a sign of Christ's birth of Christ and the faithful response of the magi who followed it "broke" the capability of the dark arts to operate against the laws of the natural world any longer!

Want more evidence? You got it…

Just a few books later, we see in Acts chapter 8 the account of Simon the magician. It begins with the statement: "But there was a certain man, called Simon, which beforetime in the same city used sorcery" (Acts 8:9). "Beforetime" clearly refers to something that had happened in the *past*—that is, before Simon's day. Subsequent verses document that Simon converted to Christianity, but when he saw the power of God producing supernatural wonders and signs, he offered to pay the disciples to show him how they were accomplishing it (8:18–19). If this story is reinterpreted in the light of Ignatius' theory, we can see how Simon's sorcery used to work through the powers of darkness before the star and the magi obliterated this power from the land. Then, Simon converted, the motive behind which is anyone's guess (but it reads like a "may as well" decision, since his skill in the occult was no longer a paying gig and "salvation" would sound sweet to anyone in his suddenly threatened position). But the second he saw the power of God through the disciples, he mistook it for a newer form of sorcery—one he had no knowledge of, and, being a magician at heart, he offered to buy into it. Despite all the other valuable lessons this narrative teaches (not the least of which is that God's power cannot be purchased), we see what might be historical evidence that Simon: 1) *had* magical ability at one time in the past; 2) lost it for some reason unknown to him; 3) and then jumped at the chance to regain his lucrative skill when he saw that "the magic had returned." It hadn't, of course, but we can see why he would think such a thing.

If sorcery and magic were such common elements in the pagan cultures of the Bible, why don't we see that dark influence today? (This is a different question than why we don't see miracles of God as much in today's world—a question we answer in the subsequent "Miracles of Jesus" section.) In contemporary society, we have stage or street magicians and illusionists (David Copperfield, Criss Angel, David Blaine, etc.), but we don't have "real" magic like there appeared to be in various accounts throughout the Word. Why not? Where did that power go? Ignatius' theory, if true, proves the narrative concerning the magi goes far beyond what we could have imagined from any church's theatrical production. The magi very well may have been the men whose faithful act of following God to the Babe dismantled the dark arts so Jesus' birth would carry one more layer of authority over the world!

Whatcha think of those cards now, eh? If you're a playwright, you've *gotta* write this!

Without a doubt, the true back story of the magi glorifies God in potentially unimaginable ways. The star over Bethlehem—and the magi's faithful response to the voice of Yahweh in following it and avoiding Herod on their way back—may have truly "broken" something for all sorcerers. Every earthly king in surrounding territories (and perhaps globally) could have possibly awakened one day to discover that the King prophesied through the mouths of ancient Jewish messengers had indeed arrived. If the Jews were correct in their interpretations of what this King would do, then He was "coming to take the throne from kings" and establish His own glorious Kingdom on earth. This Child who was now only a toddler would someday grow into an adult, establish an army, take down Rome, and exact vengeance upon those in the Roman Empire who contributed to the persecution of the holy race, the Jews believed.

Signs were everywhere!

The magi's arrival fulfilled the prophecy of Isaiah 60:6, which said important men would arrive on camels and "bring gold and incense; and they shall shew forth the praises of the Lord" (60:6). It was happening then, in Herod's time, and if the Jewish chiefs of the Law in his court were as knowledgeable about the messianic prophecies as they appeared to be when they immediately offered the answer about Bethlehem being the birth location of the Child, then Herod was in trouble. Isaiah had also said: "For unto us a child is born…and the government shall be upon his shoulder… Of the increase of his government…there shall be no end, upon the throne of David, and upon his kingdom, to order it, and to establish it with judgment and with justice from henceforth even for ever" (Isaiah 9:6–7).

Herod the Great (the father of Herod Antipas, who reigned at the time of Christ's birth) had been declared "the king of the Jews" (yes, that exact moniker) in 40 BC. Prior to that, the term was used by the priest-kings of the Maccabean revolt who went against the Roman powers and won (if only temporarily; review the section titled "Intertestamental Period"). Thus, the very term "king of the Jews" was an inflammatory, provocative, political nickname being tossed around by nationalistic Jewish rebels for years before Herod Antipas was approached by the magi. Matthew 2:2 says when the magi went to Herod Antipas, they asked, "Where is he that is born King of the Jews?" Though the magi likely had no idea how mutinous their words to Herod were, this question flew like sharp slap to the face of the entire Herodian line. Had someone from Herod's own kingdom said it, the magi probably would have been tried for treason—it was *that* serious. But far from taking it as an insult and demanding why the magi would have been so preposterous as to assign that name to another, Herod attempted to gain their help in locating this threat. When they didn't return, Herod flipped out and had *all* the baby boys killed. Nobody was going to take *his* throne!

Other magiastrologers in Rome's history had likewise seen the bright stars rising in the sky (or other astrological phenomena) as marking the birth of conquering rulers. For instance, in 356 BC, one of the great temples of Artemis/Diana burned down. As the flames touched the heavens, the Persian magi ran around in a panic saying it was a sign in the sky that great peril was coming to Asia.[31] According to the Greek historian, Plutarch, that was the same evening Alexander the Great was born, whose conquests dominated the whole of Western Asia and Northeastern Africa (so their predictions were correct!). The king of Pontus in northern Anatolia between 120 to 63 BC, Mithradates the Great (Mithradates VI Eupator), was one of the most profound enemies of Rome, having waged the Mithridatic

Wars in an attempt to de-Hellenize Asia and drive out Roman forces. Though his efforts were not successful, they had proved such a threat that he would go down in history as the greatest king who ever ruled Pontus. His birth was accompanied by a new star in the night sky, the magi said (and they were correct *again*).[32] Herod Antipas no doubt grew up hearing these stories. His Roman political contemporaries would have certainly had centuries to steep in these facts or legends as well, paving the way for mass superstition about which bright and shining supernova in the sky might be hailing which conqueror to usurp the throne.

The states of the Roman Empire, itself—the most powerful government on the face of the earth—were starting to feel threatened by the very existence of this holy birth, and Herod's panicked reaction to have all the males under two in the area killed proves that.

The last thing anyone needed in secular government then was for the Toddler to mature into a Man who would speak of ruling kingdoms…and then, from their perspective, that's just what He did.

From Birth to Adulthood

Following the visit from the magi to the humble domicile of Mary and Joseph, God sent Joseph a dream warning him of Herod's intentions: "Arise, and take the young child and his mother, and flee into Egypt, and be thou there until I bring thee word: for Herod will seek the young child to destroy him" (Matthew 2:13).

As Matthew explained two verses later, this was a fulfillment of Hosea's prophecy, "When Israel was a child, then I loved him, and called my son out of Egypt" (Hosea 11:1). Matthew 2:15 stated that Joseph "was there until the death of Herod [with Mary and Jesus]: that it might be fulfilled which was spoken of the Lord by the prophet, saying, 'Out of Egypt have I called my son.'" (Some skeptics believe Hosea's words in 11:1 were about Israel, and not specific to the Messiah. However, as the Messiah is a representation of all of Israel's redemption and liberty, this interpretive use by Matthew is not incorrect.)

Five miles north of Jerusalem was another small village named Ramah, in the area where the descendants of Rachel (Hebrew *Rahel*) settled. Although Mary and Joseph escaped Herod's order, it was carried out to the horror of those who remained, and every male baby in the area of Bethlehem was killed. This fulfilled the prophecy of Jeremiah 31:15: "A voice was heard in Ramah, lamentation, and bitter weeping; Rahel weeping for her children refused to be comforted for her children, because they were not." The Gospel writer acknowledged this mirroring in Matthew 2:17–18.

After the threat of Herod was over, God arranged for Joseph to have another dream, instructing him to take Mary and Jesus back to Israel (Matthew 2:19–20). Joseph chose a quiet place in Galilee, in a city called Nazareth. The city of Nazareth was named after the Hebrew *neser* ("nay-tzar"), or, "branch." The "Branch" as a messianic term was common wordplay for the prophets, as seen in repeated references earlier on (Isaiah 11:1–9; Jeremiah 23:5; 33:15; Zechariah 3:8; 6:12). Matthew 2:23 recognizes this: "And he came and dwelt in a city called Nazareth: that it might be fulfilled which was spoken by the prophets, 'He shall be called a Nazarene.'" The shoot of Jesse, the holy men had prophesied, would produce a Branch, the Son of David, and He would hail from Nazareth. This was now fulfilled.

Other than the apocryphal or extrabiblical accounts, we know nothing of what Jesus was like when He grew up, other than His mind-boggling trip to the Temple at twelve years old when He met, spoke with, and amazed the most learned rabbis in all of Jerusalem. This account is sharpened with the words of Luke 2:40: "And the child grew, and waxed strong in spirit, filled with wisdom: and the grace of God was upon him," and Luke 2:52: "And Jesus increased in wisdom and stature, and in favour with God and man."

When Jesus grew up, He was every bit the threat to worldly governments that the prophets had said and the Roman leaders were beginning to contemplate…while He was at the same time never a threat at all.

The governments of Jesus' time wouldn't get it.

But two thousand years later, *we* don't really get it, either.

There's a popular bumper sticker here in the States: "No Jesus, no peace. Know Jesus, Know Peace." This is nice and "Christian," but how many of us really *know* Jesus? We may read Scripture, but do we truly comprehend what happened throughout this area of the world just before the Messiah was born?

Remember those Christmas cards and how little they convey about the truth? Well, the same is true of Easter. Our culture doesn't frequently consider whether some of these events and characters represent an accurate portrayal of the Savior on that cross, and in the days leading up to His crucifixion.

It's common scene in Easter plays: the actor portraying Jesus is whipped with a wimpy piece of linen cloth dipped in red food coloring, then he's pulled up by the wrists and fastened to a cross. Scenes later, he emerges from behind a paper-mache rock in front of the tomb after someone has loudly announced it's been three days. In such plays, the person playing Pontias Pilate shrugs and washes his hands of the matter of the execution while an angry mob shouts "crucify him!"… for seemingly no apparent reason other than the contagious nature of anger itself. A more thorough depiction of these events might include the Triumphal Entry event on Passover earlier the same week.

However, despite much scriptural documentation about the days before Christ was crucified, we often miss the significance of specific details due to our cultural disconnect from the world in Jesus' day. There are many things we hear quoted or see in print that we don't fully understand. The only remedy for such a disconnect is to dig into the culture of these matters and place them in their proper historical and cultural setting. In so doing, we gain a fuller understanding of the events that unfolded surrounding the crucifixion.

In the "Intertestamental Period" section of this book, we covered the four hundred years of God's silence. What we did not cover *then*, as it is more pertinent *now*, has to do with the ancient city of Sepphoris, known in historical materials as the "jewel [or ornament] of Galilee."

Most of us tend to imagine Jesus' childhood to be set in a rural area—in a primitive village setting wherein the archaic and ancient ways of the Old Testament were allowed to thrive and were embraced without question. To a large extent, this is true, but it is not the complete context. We hear Jesus was from Nazareth and picture a peaceful setting far from any real commerce. However, something many of us are unaware of is that Jesus grew up within walking distance (approximately four miles[33]) of a prominent city called Sepphoris, a location that, while not mentioned in the Bible at all, is discussed in the ancient Jewish record more often than *any* other city aside from Jerusalem.[34] And, most importantly, this metropolis imposed great cultural influence on the worldview of the people Jesus walked among.

At first glance, Sepphoris appears in historical accounts to have been a Hellenistic town, but the bulk of this influence did not occur until *after* Jesus' death and Resurrection. During His time on earth, Sepphoris was predominately Jewish.[35] This fact is backed by archeological excavations wherein researchers uncovered elements that, for several reasons, confirmed the town's Jewish status. First, the name "Sepphoris" itself is linked to the origin Hebrew *Zippori*, which some scholars state was a city "fortified by Joshua when the tribes of Israel first settled into the Promised Land."[36] While this has not yet been conclusively proven, it does point to Hebrew origin and initial claim of the territory. Additionally, a facility referred to as the "old fort" by rabbis in the Mishnah pointed to a time when the city was predominantly recognized as Jewish, when the ancestry of those rabbis held public office.[37] This segment of the city was constructed during the time of the Seleucid Empire (dated between 200–100 BC) and, when later excavated, held many *mikva'ot*, or Jewish ritual baths, confirming the facilitation of Jewish rituals. Additionally, faunal remains showed "so few pig bones from the Roman era that Grantham [the associate professor of anthropology at Troy State University] concluded that pork was a negligible component of the Sepphorians' diet."[38] This rarity is documented as having been in contrast with the "thousands upon thousands of fragments of animal bones" excavated from the location and available for study. It is also in marked contrast to the 30 percent ratio found in sites dated after Sepphoris' changeover to a Hellenistic setting.[39]

Another indication that the city was predominantly Jewish is its the large number of stone vessels, jars, and bathhouse seats. Because of standards of ritual purity, archeology from Jewish culture produces a larger ratio of stone vessels than pottery, metal, or glass. The residential district of this city yielded more than one hundred such findings. Conversely, what *was not found* speaks volumes as well: The parts of the city dated from before about AD 100 yield no typical Greco-Roman, Hellenistic features such as gymnasiums, pagan temples, cult paraphernalia, chariot-racing coliseums, amphitheaters or theaters; nor do they reveal the presence of pagan shrines, statues, fountains, or typical Roman-designed aqueducts and public bathhouses. Many scholars agree these findings confirm that Sepphoris, during Jesus' childhood on earth, "was a home to a significant Jewish community."[40]

Then, after AD 100, new layers of the city built upon the old manifested many forms of evidence of Hellenistic influence, so we don't say Sepphoris *never was* a Greco-Roman setting; we simply make the case as to *when*. The city was by no means a peacefully uncontested territory. While, before Jesus' time, it was predominantly populated with Jews and their culture, it politically fell under the rule of Roman authority. For those in the city, the Jewish population and the outside Roman authorities were allowed to coexist, so long as the citizens of Sepphoris understood precisely who was in charge. This meant as long as the Jews remained peaceful, they were allowed to continue practicing their cultural traditions and religion. This dichotomy between

Roman authority and Jewish traditional culture at the citizens' level created a type of friction between the general population and anyone who might rise up to antagonize the Romans, thus rocking the boat on their tense but peaceable arrangement. (Consequently, by about AD 60, the Romans had had enough boat-rocking, which was why the city subsequently saw a shift toward increased Roman influence and Hellenistic culture.) As stated, the city has often been called the "ornament of Galilee." However, it must be understood that the term "ornament" doesn't indicate it was merely pretty: The Greek translation of that word, *proschema*, indicates military strategy and an impermeable locale, which was part of the reason opposing forces so often vied to conquer it. Even Josephus called it the "strongest city in Galilea."[41]

Some scholars further point out this was the location Jesus referred to when He said, "A city set on a hill cannot be hidden."[42] It was strategically located, in fact, on a hill overlooking the Bet Netofa Valley, planted in an intrusively managerial location over the major trade route that ran east to west between the Via Maris and the Mediterranean Sea. Because of its locale, it was a coveted site for opposing military forces to engage in battle. The city was within walking distance of Phoenicia, Samaria, Decapolis, Peraea, and other regions near the Sea of Galilee: all areas said in Scripture to have been traversed by Jesus.[43] It was an accomplished metropolis, also one of the prominent Jewish learning centers by AD 100.[44]

At its apex, the city featured upper and lower markets that operated via donkey caravans between the city gate and local and distant towns and villages. Commerce included such goods as grains, flax, breads, herbs, fish (fresh and pickled), all kinds of fresh produce, wine, ceramics, glassware, goods made of fine metals, jewelry, clothing made by skilled weavers and tailors, olives (an expensive ingredient for many uses back then), as well as "cattle...sheep...goat products...basketry, furniture...and perfumes."[45] As such, the location was rich with a constant and unimaginably high number of visits made by experts in their fields of trade. Beyond this range of purchasable goods, a list of public amenities and facilities were also available here, including banks, treasuries, armories, court buildings, and tax processing facilities, to name only a few. The city supported a seemingly limitless list of professions, including masons, farmers, scribes, shopkeepers, teachers, money-changers, fishermen, metal workers, leatherworkers, physicians and medical workers, actors and entertainers, prison security guards, and even prostitutes. (We list these to illustrate the scope of Sepphoris' influence on the nearby region, but recognize some of the amenities included came into play *after* the Hellenistic influence made its full-scale impact, after AD 63. When the city lost the revolt in AD 63–70, there was a change in the minting of coins, wherein Greek and Roman inscriptions became more prominent, moving away from symbolism that was previously Jewish.[46] However, understanding the potential of this metropolis shows its ability to shape its surrounding culture, which is pertinent when considering Jesus grew up a mere four miles away.)

In 4 BC (near the time of Jesus' birth), Herod the Great passed away, after having ruled since 37 BC. Despite Sepphoris' predominantly Jewish population, it still fell within the rule of Roman territory, and Herod used the location as his base of operations for the north. Upon his death, it appeared that a man called Judas, son of Ezekias (or "Hezekiah") of the lingering Maccabean circle who made trouble for Rome earlier on, saw an opportunity for revolt. Gathering a great throng of warriors, he attempted to lead the city in an uprising. Though the Maccabeans of the past had seen some success that led to later peace treaties with Rome, this particular movement was quickly squelched by Roman forces sent on behalf of Roman Varus, governor of Syria. The Romans sacked and burned a large part of Sepphoris, crucifying two thousand rebels and selling thirty thousand others into slavery.[47]

Did you catch that? This happened in (or just after) 4 BC! Scholars typically date Christ's birth to 6–4 BC, so around the same time Gabriel was appearing to Mary and announcing the *real* Messiah's

arrival, men who claimed to be on a mission from God were starting—and failed to win—a revolution. Two thousand people died!
Thirty thousand were sold! The expectations of the Jews were that
these men may have been the Messiah, and each time another one fell,
so, too, did the hopes of the Jews. Whether the rebels ever personally
claimed to be the Messiah (and some of them did) is irrelevant. With
every political intervention, the Jews' (misplaced) hope in a Deliverer
who would come like a super-soldier rose to an all-time high, just to
come crashing down again when their prized "Messiah" died.

Citizens around Sepphoris quickly learned insurgence against
Rome came with a hefty price tag...

Since this occurred near the time of Jesus' birth, and in a city near
His childhood, His culture would have been saturated with stories
of this and other failed rebellions against Rome. Surely individuals
He knew could relay personal stories of loss regarding friends and/
or loved ones who had perished or disappeared during these terrible
events.

And, there were other isolated, sporadic uprisings against Rome
that during this time that were near and partially related to Sepphoris.
For instance, Judas the Galilean—who is identified by Jewish historians
as the same Judas who had led the Sepphoris uprising ten years earlier,
in 4 BC[48]—led a revolt in AD 6 against Publius Quirinus of Syria in
response to newly imposed taxation laws. The movement was met with
brutal force; Judas the Galilean perished along with most of his followers, the remnant of whom was scattered throughout the land.[49]

It would seem to the Jewish populace there were only two sur-
vivable options: 1) submit peaceably to Roman rule, or 2) pray for
a Messiah whom, based on their interpretations of prophecy (Isaiah
42, 61), they were certain would physically, literally, and *politically*
deliver them. Under the mounting pressure of such oppression, they
continued to elevate the idea of a super-hero- or super-soldier-type
Messiah-Deliverer within their culture. (Eventually, in AD 66, the city
rallied an attempt at revolt—the "Great Revolt"—which was over-

turned in AD 70 and was sealed with the destruction of the Temple
and Jerusalem. It was largely after this period that the transition into a
Hellenistic city occurred in Sepphoris. Until then, the Jewish population of this contested, though predominantly Jewish, city had lived
peaceably traditional lives, albeit under the opposing rule of outsiders
such as Herod the Great and his descendants.)

Recalling so vividly—and so recently—the images of two thousand comrades crucified, thirty thousand sold into slavery, and their
great city Sepphoris in ashes, these Jews would have been prompted
to watch for a Messiah whose promised deliverance of God's people
would render them finally free from the very real death threats they
lived beneath daily.

It's not surprising, then, to see that there would be mass conflict
between Yahwism and the worship of Greco-Roman gods.

Culturally, there were deviations between citizens of surrounding
cultures and the Jewish populace for many reasons, but one of the more
glaring sources of dissimilarity was found in the differences in religious
practices. First, the Greco-Roman pantheon consisted of many gods—
each with a designated territory under its control (as hinted at in our
study of the word *logos*). For example, there was Zeus/Jupiter, ruler over
other gods who manifested through thunder and lightning. Demeter/
Ceres was the goddess of agriculture, Apollo was the god of the sun,
Diana was the goddess of childbirth, and so on. Finding these gods was
never hard for their followers; they were seen in their physical manifestations (such as the sun, moon, thunder, etc.) or were believed to be in
their temple. Their appearance was no mystery, as they were visible via
statues, carvings, and other likenesses their followers worshipped. Each
time a person crossed into a new territory (such as mountains, streams,
or agricultural fields), it was understood that he or she had crossed into
the domain of a different reigning god. As such, it was also a common belief that one person aggravating a regional god would provoke
punishment for the entire region. Because of this, religion and worship
carried high political importance. Having one's own personal beliefs

that disputed the beliefs of the population of a region was a rare privilege…and it was only sustained so long as the territorial gods' needs and demands were met.

The God of the Old Testament, however, had, for non-Jews, a mystical quality people at times struggled to understand. There are several reasons for this. For example, He is unrestrained—there is no limit to where His followers can claim to find Him. He is not labeled by any one natural element (such as the sun, moon, or ocean), nor is He related to a certain occurring phenomenon (such as growth of crops, wind, thunder). To outsiders, the Jews worshipped a transcendent and mysterious God who was credited with Creation (Genesis 1:1–5) and could go anywhere He wanted (Jeremiah 23:23–24), interacting with mankind (Genesis 3:9), animals (Numbers 22:28–30), and nature (2 Kings 1:14–15) on any level He saw fit.

In addition, Yahweh is invisible. The Jewish worshippers remained devout without having the benefit of a tangible, visible likeness that could be accredited for His miracles. Conversely, Roman religion (and many others) worshipped their reigning king alongside gods who were revered. In many ancient cultures, the king *was* a god (the pharaohs of Egypt were viewed this way, as well as many Roman leaders after the development of the Imperial Cult). The contrast between this practice and Jews—who refused to worship even the most elevated human political figure in preference of an intangible and invisible god—was often off-putting to those in Roman power who sought admiration.

In addition to this friction between Rome and the Jewish community was the continuing watch for a Messiah. And, the last time the Israelites had seen a real deliverer who was successful in his mission, he had come in the form of Moses. This man had stood in the face of governmental authorities (Pharaoh) and refused to stand down, conveying the words of Yahweh, who delivered His wrath in the form of the plagues. Then, Moses eventually led the freedom event of God's people in a show so miraculous that generations to come would talk of the parting sea, the smoke by day and the fire by night, the Ten

Commandments written by God's own hand, God's provision for His people via sending them manna, and the travels that eventually became their entry to the Promised Land. If history were to repeat itself, then, for Rome, a Messiah's appearance meant certain doom! For Jews, it meant certain political revolution and rescue.

The Messiah had certainly been prophesied centuries earlier. Devout Jews had been anxiously awaiting the Man. So, why didn't they embrace Jesus as the answer to all of their problems?

Ahh… Therein we find a major key to understanding much of the opposition to Christ in the New Testament: It is because the first several false messiahs had been executed. Jesus, before He had the chance to prove Himself—and even in the face of numerous rumors of signs and wonders like the appearance of the star and the magi and the witness of Anna and the shepherds—was discounted because He was seen as just another person claiming to be the Messiah. The anxiously awaiting populace had placed their hopes upon other men before Jesus, only to have those hopes dashed completely. Each had been executed as a symbol of what happens to those who challenged the existing Roman authority.

These men were dead and gone, but *not* forgotten, as their reputation continued to probe the world at the time of Christ with a message: "beware, beware, beware." Even in the face of this, *more* affronts to Roman authority outside of those in Sepphoris appeared to make matters more hostile.

For example, there was Simon of Peraea in 4 BC, a slave of King Herod who stood with great physical stature, a meticulous nature, and bold manner. Upon Herod's death, Simon crowned himself and, with a small entourage, declared himself king. He quickly went about burning the king's palace at Jericho and several royal houses, plundering along the way. He was met by a league of Roman soldiers led by Valerius Gratus—Pontias Pilate's predecessor—who fought with Simon and his followers, scattering the throng and beheading Simon.

That same year, a shepherd named Athronges had the same idea, attempting to claim Judean kingship and leading an insurrection against Archelaus of Rome with his four brothers because the king wouldn't agree to prioritize the reforms demanded by Athronges and his fellow revolutionary leaders. Gratus and Ptolemy captured three of Athronges' brothers, killing and scattering their followers, and the final fate of the would-be messiah himself is unknown. Though Athronges and his brethren were men of strength and fairly organized in their military tactics, they, too, fell...and at a time when the message of Rome would be received the loudest. Scholars acknowledge it was "during the Passover" that the ultimatums of the rebels "reached a feverish pitch," and Archelaus' response was to invade Jerusalem during the holiest week of the year and massacre "thousands of worshiping pilgrims"![50] This bloody and horrendous event was the catalyst for "revolt in every major area of Herod's kingdom."[51]

The aforementioned Judas the Galilean became yet another messianic figure. Besides being a philosopher, he led the rebellion against Rome in AD 6, citing the new taxation akin to slavery. Judas recruited a massive following, including Zadok the Pharisee (who is often brought up in historic literature of this day). Accounts are limited, but Luke recalls a small part of the event in Acts 5:36–39: "After this man rose up Judas of Galilee in the days of the taxing, and drew away much people after him: he also perished; and all, even as many as obeyed him, were dispersed."

A brief overview of Jewish revolutionary movements around this time also shows almost uncountable mutinies developing among a group scholars refer to as "social bandits" (like Robin Hood). These sprang up everywhere, constantly, before and during Christ's life. These and numerous other uprisings consistently plagued the land, resulting in repeated executions of fathers, husbands, and sons whose families were often put to the sword as well to make an example of those who dared to oppose Rome. But no matter how strong and able-bodied these Jewish rebels were, Rome was always stronger, and one revolt after another only led to thicker rivers of blood running through the cities and towns of the oppressed.

We often bemoan the Jews' lack of faith during Jesus' life and ministry years, but we need to understood that seeing a series of would-be messiahs had taught them one lesson well: Stand against Rome—claim to be a "messiah," or even follow one—and the penalty for both you and your comrades will be a brutal death. It also cemented another position in the minds of citizens of the time: If you *are* the Messiah, then you must overturn Rome and get on with it, but whatever you do, don't just make Rome mad without following through, or the price tag will be a brutal one indeed. As Christians, we have the benefit of Scripture and hindsight to illustrate to us the truth of Jesus' Messiahship. We can look back and understand perfectly how it came to be that a world that had watched so devotedly for a Messiah completely missed the mark by not recognizing who Jesus really was. But for those who watched the story unfold on a personal level, the many failed attempts at overthrowing Rome remained too fresh; too many comrades had certainly been killed and scattered or enslaved. Unless they saw a political leader commence in sure-fire acts of war, they remained reserved about placing their hopes upon another would-be.

This was the world Jesus grew up in between His birth and adulthood. He knew very well on a personal level what He was getting into. But to those around Him, it was unclear. By the time He eventually explained who He really was, most would have viewed Him as just another Galilean making claims.

Would He end up like Judas of the Maccabean line?

"Certainly," the Jews' of Jesus' time would have said, "because the death of His so-called forerunner proves it!"

The End of John's Ministry, and the Beginning of the Savior's

As if the stage couldn't be set for more opposition against Jesus, John the Baptist's ministry among the Jews created a hopeful stir that ended with yet another execution.

At the beginning of our reflection of the Gospels, we noted that Mark is the "action writer" of the four. This is shown in his book's first five verses:

> The beginning of the gospel of Jesus Christ, the Son of God; As it is written in the prophets, "Behold, I send my messenger before thy face, which shall prepare thy way before thee. The voice of one crying in the wilderness, 'Prepare ye the way of the Lord, make his paths straight.'"
> John did baptize in the wilderness, and preach the baptism of repentance for the remission of sins. And there went out unto him all the land of Judaea, and they of Jerusalem, and were all baptized of him in the river of Jordan, confessing their sins.

"All" of Judea and those in Jerusalem. Guess what? We did a deep study on this Greek word, *pas*. Wanna know what it means? It means "all." It's crazy, taking such liberty with the Greek here, we know...

See, sarcasm aside, we skim right past it today, and even films tend to show that every time John is out at the river baptizing folks, he has somewhere in the ballpark of twenty guys interested in what he has to say. But by Mark's use of "all" here, we know there were tremendously large crowds. This word doesn't have to be rendered "every single one" in order to represent the vast majority of Judaic attention in this area of the world at the time. Even the *Cambridge Bible for Schools and Colleges* commentary states: "**all the land:** This strong expression is peculiar to St Mark. But it is illustrated by the other Gospels. The crowds that flocked to his baptism included representatives of every class, Pharisees and Sadducees (Matthew 3:7), tax-gatherers (Luke 3:12), soldiers (Luke 3:14), rich and poor (Luke 3:10)."[52] John's gatherings were enormous!

His message was one of extreme repentance as a means of preparing for a coming Kingdom. This mattered more to him in his preaching than any other topic. And this can be expected, since the

Messiah would not be recognized by unrepentant people. John had one job, and he did it well: Prepare the way for the Lord! He generally had one message: The Kingdom of God is at hand!

Unanimously, scholars agree his message was well-received. He did not yet baptize people in the name of Jesus, because he knew well that it wasn't his place. John's baptism looked *forward* to the coming Kingdom, not backward to its inauguration, and it didn't instill within the believers the Holy Spirit, as He had not yet been sent by Christ. Some scholars (including historian Josephus) believe John was copying the proselyte baptism, but the main reason to believe his was unique is because the former Jewish rite was related to ritual cleansing, not to repentance or preparation.

Because Elijah had gone up to heaven in a whirlwind (2 Kings 2:11) and therefore had never truly died, many of the Jews believed the literal Elijah would return—not as a reincarnated being, but as he had been in history. This explains why John the Baptist denied being Elijah (John 1:21), even though he was the very "Elijah-spirited" "voice in the wilderness" that had been prophesied (Isaiah 40:3) and directly identified (Luke 1:17), even by Jesus (Matthew 11:14). The "prepare ye the way for" message was not uncommon in John's time. Actually, it was almost always used of a coming king, and when it was shouted by the king's criers ahead of him on the roads to major cities, the preparations were literal. City officials would see to the reparations of the road and the clean-up of city gates and entryways. For John's audience, it was clear he was announcing the arrival of a king (even if that concept is lost on us today). When Isaiah foresaw the message of John the Baptist in his prophecy (Isaiah 40:3), he alluded to this when he said, "Make straight in the desert a highway for our God."

In the spirit of Elijah he had been equipped with, John's willingness to boldly accuse the pretenders and expose the "vipers," or poisonous snakes in their midst, was very well present in his work, as we see in Matthew 3:7–10:

But when he saw many of the Pharisees and Sadducees come to his baptism, he said unto them, "O generation of vipers, who hath warned you to flee from the wrath to come? Bring forth therefore fruits meet for repentance: And think not to say within yourselves, 'We have Abraham to our father': for I say unto you, that God is able of these stones to raise up children unto Abraham. And now also the axe is laid unto the root of the trees: therefore every tree which bringeth not forth good fruit is hewn down, and cast into the fire."

In other words, God saw the hearts of men, and He would be quick to cut down fakers at the root. No "inheritance of Abraham," blood-line or otherwise, could save them from internal wickedness. (Jesus would also recognize "vipers" in their company [Matthew 23:33], and would use the word picture of cutting down trees that produce bad fruit in His teachings as well [Luke 6:43–45; John 15:1–6].)

That the state of Israel had become so corrupt is clear in John's response to his crowds' panicked questions:

And the people asked him, saying, "What shall we do then?"

He answereth and saith unto them, "He that hath two coats, let him impart to him that hath none; and he that hath meat, let him do likewise."

Then came also publicans [tax collectors] to be baptized, and said unto him, "Master, what shall we do?"

And he said unto them, "Exact no more [tax] than that which is appointed you."

And the soldiers likewise demanded of him, saying, "And what shall we do?"

And he said unto them, "Do violence to no man, neither accuse any falsely; and be content with your wages." (Luke 3:10–14)

Everyone wanted to know: What does one do to repent properly, receive forgiveness, and live in a way that pleases God? John's answer appears in each case to be the easiest and most predictable "fly-straight" responses to us today, but we find in only the job description of the New Testament tax collector quite an underhanded skill. Rome would tax the life out of people (as seen in the rebellions we discussed in the last section). That was true at the highest level. The amount of taxes due constantly fluctuated as provinces were shifting leaders, so the people had no idea how much was really needed for them to remain accountable to the state. The tax collectors would sit at their booths and increase their collections, paying a portion of it to their superiors and pocketing the rest, while the superiors paid only a portion of *that* and pocketed the rest, and so on. The setting back then, of course, wasn't like it is today, when there are well-established paper trails and proofs for those who question the system. So, if a tax collector wanted to inflate his own income on any given day, he could merely pick, at a whim, an amount to be due from the people. It's actually surprising these men would ask John the Baptist for advice in this area, but the simplicity of his answers to questions like these show the true beauty of God's expectations: "It's not hard; just don't be jerks and robbers—give to the needy, care for the poor, share your wealth and abundance, and don't be fake."

"Repent for your past activities" was one part of John's message. The other part was: "Continue living like one whose repentance is sincere." This exhortation to tax collectors, soldiers, and wealthier folk with goods to share is just a tiny example of all the other things John preached about (Luke 3:18).

In Matthew 3:11–12, Mark 1:7–8, and Luke 3:15–18, we see the shift from a message of repentance and righteous living to one of preparation: "I indeed baptize you with water; but one mightier than I cometh, the latchet of whose shoes I am not worthy to unloose: he shall baptize you with the Holy Ghost and with fire" (Luke 3:16).

This "one mightier" was, of course, Jesus Christ…and John was about to be lucky enough to meet Him.

Scholars unanimously agree on two statements: 1) Jesus did not need baptism for "sins," but 2) Jesus' baptism marks the beginning of His public ministry. The event is included in all three of the Synoptic Gospels (Matthew 3:13–17; Mark 1:9–11; Luke 3:21–23).

When Jesus appeared in John's presence to be baptized by his cousin, John was shocked. He said certainly it should be the other way around: Jesus should be baptizing John. Yet, Jesus knew His public ministry and the fulfilling of "all righteousness" would depend on this moment, so John consented (Matthew 3:13–15). Scholars see Jesus' submission to baptism as an example and a way of identifying the people He was about to save:

> The most obvious way in which Jesus' baptism prepares for his mission is by indicating his solidarity with John's call to repentance in view of the arrival of God's kingship. By first identifying with John's proclamation Jesus lays the foundation for his own mission to take on where John has left off. Further, as Jesus is baptized along with others at the Jordan, he is identified with all those who by accepting John's baptism have declared their desire for a new beginning with God…. If he is to be their representative, he must first be identified with them.[53]

Interestingly, some scholars also see Jesus here as submitting not just to baptism, but to a symbolic reenactment of the Israelites' passage through the miraculously parted Red Sea. With Moses, they were freed: a newly liberated people whose shackles were traded in for a renewed focus on the Lord that no pharaoh or king could take away. Now they would see all this in Jesus, also, but in a permanent and superior way. Jesus led His people into the "sea" by example, and through this act He began His Church. Very soon after this, Jesus would make a way to freedom that nobody had ever experienced, and it began the moment that His public ministry began. Understanding this at a deeper level requires leaving behind one's individual concepts and seeing how Israel's history championed those who were more communal in their modelling through actions: Leading by example, Moses fasted and prayed for sins that were not his own. Leading by example, so would Jesus:

> Now when all the people were baptized, it came to pass, that Jesus also being baptized, and praying, the heaven was opened, And the Holy Ghost descended in a bodily shape like a dove upon him, and a voice came from heaven, which said, Thou art my beloved Son; in thee I am well pleased. (Luke 3:21–22)

Throughout the Old Testament, we read many times of the heavens opening as God was visiting mankind, so it's an image well-known among scholars to represent the appearance of the Divine (Isaiah 24:18; Ezekiel 1:1; Malachi 3:10; Acts 7:56; 10:11; Revelation 19:11). In this baptism scene, all members of the Trinity acknowledge the launch of Jesus' ministry: The voice of the Father, the descent of the Holy Spirit, and Jesus standing in the water. Many theologians and academics have weighed in on whether the Gospels describe the Holy Spirit literally turning into a dove (as Luke seems to imply with the words "descended in a bodily shape like a dove"), or if this is merely the only way the writers could have described what the crowds saw, which was something that could be compared to a dove. After paging through probably thirty or more commentaries to try to find the answer, we found that Genesis 8:8–12 (Noah sending out a dove) pops up several times in the discussion. Not many of the scholars saw the symbols *we* did in this connection, though. Most say the dove is a symbol of peace, and then they move on to the next topic. However, we feel it goes further after considering the context of this moment for Noah. This passage from the very first book of the Bible details how Noah, while he was in the boat, sent out a dove. The second time he sent it out, it descended back down to him with an olive branch in its mouth, signaling that land had been found.

Pause and think for a moment: The dove wasn't just a sign the storm was over, although that was true, but it also meant that, after the storm, Noah and his family could to start afresh on a planet with no corruption and no sin! It was the signal of a new era for all of mankind! The Holy Spirit, when He descended upon Jesus in the same form as Noah's little friend, may well have been announcing that, in the Son, there is a fresh, sinless start for all people who wish to follow Christ. (Seriously, why don't other commentators see this?) In Jesus, the storm is over and the troubled waters are at peace, and when we accept the Holy Spirit into our lives, we are a new creation, just like the planet was when it had been rid of evil. That's a picturesque portrayal of our new lives in Christ, which started not at the cross, but at the *baptism*—for the cross wouldn't have meant anything if Jesus hadn't been obedient to the ministry that began on that day.

Wow, that's beautiful…

But it goes much, *much* further. Popular extrabiblical/apocryphal texts called (collectively) *The Testament of the Twelve Patriarchs* (believed by some Jews to have been the last words of the sons of Jacob) prophetically identified this moment. Although we don't have the earliest texts (and therefore don't know the date of their origin), radiocarbon dating has identified several of those we do have to have been written at least a hundred years prior to the time of Christ. Specific to one, parts of the *Testament of Levi*, as well as some footnotes from a later studier of the book, were found among the Dead Sea Scrolls in Qumran cave number 4. Unbelievably, the *Testament of Levi* describes this very moment with Jesus and John. Beginning in chapter 18, verses 1–3 of his work, the writer first identifies Christ and the Jewish system of His day:

> When vengeance will have come upon them from the Lord, the priesthood will lapse. And then the Lord will raise up a new priest to whom all the words of the Lord will be revealed. He

shall effect the judgment of truth over the earth for many days. And his star shall rise in heaven like a king; kindling the light of knowledge as day is illumined by the sun.[54]

By the time of Christ, the priesthood could certainly be interpreted as having "lapsed" (or "collapsed") as the fragmented Jewish world of this time shows. Other than Jesus, no priest in the history of Judaism, from Genesis to today, could ever make known "all the words of the Lord." Nor has there ever been any judge "over the earth for many days" outside of the Messiah. Oh, and that "star" thing? Remember our study of the trip the magi made…

Continuing in verses 6–8, we read from this ancient text a scene that's almost identical to what happened with Christ at this baptism:

The heavens will be opened, and from the temple of glory sanctification will come upon him, with a fatherly voice, as from Abraham to Isaac. And the glory of the Most High shall burst forth upon him. And the spirit of understanding and sanctification shall rest upon him in the water. For he shall give the majesty of the Lord to those who are his sons in truth forever. And there shall be no successor for him from generation to generation forever.[55]

In this passage, we read "the heavens…opened," a "fatherly voice" spoke to Him, and the "spirit" rested upon Him "in the water." There is no question as to whether there was ever a "successor for him from generation to generation." Jesus was the one and only Man who could have performed and experienced the things listed in this apocryphal literature. We believe it's clear that, whether this work is a canonical book or not, someone is obviously referring to the unrivaled Messiah character here, and they described all three members of the Trinity in the way it happened with Jesus.

Most Christians today don't even know this text exists. But

first-century Jews would have understood this "Testament" to be a prophecy of this moment. Thus, the most devout Jews in the massive crowds around Jesus and John that day would have seen this manifestation as an irrefutable sign that Jesus was the Priest the writer of the *Testament of Levi* had looked forward to.

As humble and straightforward as John the Baptist's message was, it was exactly the brand of innocence Israel had lost. No doubt, some of John's listeners who had personally witnessed the uprising of former rebels waited with bated breath to see him rise up against the system, but he never did...

That is, until he *did*.

Whereas many folks in John's day wouldn't dare rebuke the private affairs of a king, John openly criticized Herod Antipas for marrying his brother's ex-wife, Herodias. This bizarre love triangle was complicated enough that we won't address it at length, but suffice it to say John the Baptist was familiar with Leviticus 20:21, which states that it is unlawful and impure for a man to take his brother's wife while the brother still lives. This outburst angered Herodias, who thereafter held a grudge against John (Mark 6:19) and awaited an opportunity to exact revenge against him. Herod Antipas was actually fond of John, having heard his preaching before and enjoyed it (6:20), but pressures from his offended wife led him to imprison John for his unwelcome comments. During Herod's next birthday party among his nobles, Herodias hatched a plan. Her daughter, Salome, danced for the king and his men, after which Herod offered to give her anything she wanted. (By the way, Salome was likely about twelve years old when she danced for her stepfather, according to Mark 9:22, which refers to her as *korasion*, or "girl," suggesting that age. Knowing this makes her "dance"—the Oriental tradition believes it to have been a standard, erotic "dance of veils" [an early striptease]—even more disturbing.) After meeting with her mother, Salome went back to the king and told him her only desire was John's beheading. Herod was "exceedingly sad" to hear this request, but because he had given her his word in front of the guests who were still looking on, he ordered the deed to be done, and John was executed (Mark 6:21–28).

John's undeniable legacy of righteousness will last forever. We can only wonder what he would have thought of Jesus in His coming days of ministry. As history tells, he would not be able to see the ultimate fruition of his baptism moment with Christ. However, now that John's ministry was in the past, Jesus' ministry would be propelled to the foreground.

Temptations in the Wilderness

Following His baptism, Jesus officially got to work in His public ministry, starting with His own testing. His temptation in the wilderness is covered by the Synoptics (Matthew 4:1–11; Mark 1:12–13; Luke 4:1–13). Scholars note the similarities between this event and ancient Israel's years of wandering the wilderness after the Exodus from Pharaoh, suggesting it might be a "new Moses" reenactment (see Deuteronomy 6–8).

First, Jesus fasted for forty days and forty nights. The skeptical response to this—that such a fast would be physically impossible—is easily refuted by the fact that Jesus was led by and filled with the Spirit, which enabled Him accomplish such a feat; in other words, He was sustained by supernatural authority (Luke 4:1), just as Moses and his people had been sustained in the wilderness for the same amount of time (Exodus 34:28).

Second, Satan's words cause some to misunderstand a Greek clause here. The tempter said, "If you are the Son of God…" (Matthew 4:3; Luke 4:3), then followed it with a challenge. The context of this passage, by itself, seems to suggest Jesus might *not* be the Son of God, based on Satan's "if." This, too, can be dismissed easily by understanding that the words of the father of lies would be provoking anyway, but in addition, "if" in biblical context elsewhere can mean "because." For instance, "Wherefore, if God so clothe the grass of the field, which to day is, and to morrow is cast into the oven, shall he not much more clothe you, O ye of little faith?" (Matthew 6:4). There is no question of whether God clothes the grass in this verse. We know this teaching to be saying "*because* He clothes the grass, He will take care of your need as well." This is the same treatment of the clause in Satan's "if." So we should not see these words as bringing into question the validity of Jesus' Sonship (though it wouldn't matter anyway, since Jesus won this game in the end, proving He was who He said He was).

The initial temptation challenged Jesus to turn rocks into bread. The innate sin of this, should He submit to the temptation, would be Jesus using His power to feed the needs of His flesh, which would wreck everything. He answered with a quote from Deuteronomy 8:3: "Man shall not live by bread alone, but by every word that proceedeth out of the mouth of God" (Matthew 4:4).

Seeing that Jesus wasn't as superficial as Satan had hoped, Satan ramped it up.

The next two temptations, appearing in opposite order in Matthew and Luke (to show their differing emphases), were: 1) to throw Himself off the edge of the Temple and call for the angels to save Him; 2) to bow down to Satan just once and receive dominion over all the earth—all that had been placed under Satan's supervision. If Jesus had appeared atop the Temple, *the holy place of the Jews*, He could have called out to the angels in front of all who were gathered there and immediately identified Himself as the Son of God. He could have thrown in a miracle to prove it, landing gently and gracefully to the ground—having been lowered there in the arms of angels—to greet the throng of instant believers. If He had bowed to Satan, He would have had instant charge over all the earth and could have spared Himself the trial, moving immediately into His role as King of all kings, reigning from a throne in a literal fulfillment of the Jewish expectation of the Davidic Messiah. (We can see that these were very real temptations for Christ. Even though He is the Son of God, He was human as we are, and He was tempted in every way we are [Hebrews 4:15]. Being able to escape the destruction of the flesh *and* fulfill messianic prophecy at the same time probably looked very good to Jesus in that moment.)

There are parallels among the temptations, the condemnation, and the victory. If Jesus hadn't been able to endure the hunger at His temptation, He never would have been able to endure the torture of what was to come. Had He worshipped Satan, He would have traded His Kingdom (one not of this world) for a less authoritative one (one of this world). If He had called angels to save Him by jumping over the edge of the Temple, surely they would have when He was on the cross, which would have destroyed the purpose of His appearance.

The Devil brought a game to Jesus in the hopes of swaying Him from His mission, but through His resistance, He had strength to endure not only what He was facing in that moment, but much more in His future:

1. He resisted the temptation to create bread from rocks to survive. Later on, He was condemned by the silence and the cooperation of the regular citizens who were *also* just trying to survive on daily bread. They didn't yet know that He came to be their Bread of Life and to give them Life abundantly, but they someday would, and His resistance to the stones temptation amplifies that link.
2. He resisted the temptation to exploit the forces of heaven by tempting God and calling for angels. Later on, He was condemned to death (in part) by a Jewish system that claimed to be established by God. His death brought about a more direct connection between God and humanity, which included even the most religious of men.
3. He resisted the temptation to receive the earthly kingdom. Later on, He was condemned (in part) by the earthly kingdom. His ministry proclaimed and brought in His own Kingdom.

Christ was tempted by and condemned in each of these temptations, but then he defeated each one as well. This showed His supreme authority over all of secular and religious society. Jesus proved to the enemy that He needed *none* of those things—not sustenance, earthly dominion, or displaying His supernatural power—to conquer and hold sovereignty over all of creation. The pure majesty of how Jesus handled Himself in this situation proves, by itself (at least to these authors) He was the Messiah. Any regular, human mind would be overwhelmed by the lure of giving in to any of these temptations, but especially the last two.

He could have taken a knee to Satan or thrown Himself from the Temple and, in less than five seconds from the act, rule over every single portion of the world under the enemy's control (the entire globe). This would have effectively given Christ the power to send preachers to every city and nation to declare that He was, in fact, the Messiah. This would not only allow Him to avoid the painful circumstances surrounding His crucifixion, but also to enable Him to usher in a *worldwide* kingdom with followers who could serve Him without any doubt regarding His deity. He wouldn't have had to bleed to death and watch as His mother wept for Him. He could have also spared His brethren from their horrifying deaths when they later became martyrs.

Many films depicting Christ frequently portray Him as being constantly somber and sad, bowing His head all the time and refusing to laugh along with His peers because He knew His end was near. He no doubt knew what was coming, but nowhere in the Bible does it suggest our Savior didn't know how to have a good time. He likely enjoyed a lot of good jokes and gave and received many warm hugs—and His laughter probably bubbled up from His belly with the best of them. This kind of camaraderie would have led to close relationships with His disciples and ministerial partners. So, it's hard to imagine a greater temptation than being tempted by the opportunity to save all of them from certain death and anguish and gain the chance to instead promote them to positions as royal advisors and council members of His throne while He spends the rest of His days in the presence of their friendship and love. Jesus *is* love! How He would have loved to immediately bring about brotherly affection and concern in every region the eye could see. He could have enacted healthy reforms not only for His people, but for all people everywhere, sanctioning the very kind of global peace and end to hunger and oppression this world is still desperately struggling to find!

Who *wouldn't* take advantage of this offer? Oh, the things He could have done with this kind of power!

But Jesus knew on an innate and internal level, in His perfect perspective joined together with the Father's, something Satan—and humans everywhere—could not see: the true "power" behind this offer would have, in the beginning and forever, been demonic in origin; it would have stripped faith from the picture. No human would ever have to exercise free will to come to God by faith if the Person they were following was as obvious as this, and the satanic energy that perpetuated the universal inauguration of Christ's "kingdom" would have grown stronger in this deal with the devil. Christ and Satan would have been working *together* for this potential rule, cancelling out the work the alternative cross actually completed in its formidable and permanent defeat over the powers of hell. This is the insight the Son of God had on an eternal level with His Father.

In addition, since the Father is only holy and cannot coexist with evil, Jesus, who was "one with" the Father (John 17), knew this submission to Satan's plans would also sever His relationship with the Father and the Spirit within Him.

What a tragic loss it would have been after all…

Thus, Jesus outwitted Satan—praise the Lord!—ending the temptations with the statement, "Get thee behind me, Satan: for it is written, 'Thou shalt worship the Lord thy God, and him only shalt thou serve'" (Luke 4:8).

In hindsight, we can only be thankful for the personified Wisdom's decisions in these episodes.

Wedding at Cana

Between the temptation in the wilderness and the wedding at Cana, Jesus began to collect a following of disciples. These are the ones who, along with the wedding servants, witnessed the "beginning of [His] miracles" (John 2:11).

Weddings today don't match up to Jewish weddings of Jesus' day, which were celebratory feasts that often lasted seven days. The wine was an important element in the festivities, so running out of it could force the feast to an early close. It has been speculated that Jesus' extra guests may have been the reason the wine ran out early, which is why Mary thought to ask *Him* to fix the problem. It has also been suggested that Mary was a coordinator for the wedding and the responsibility to find more wine fell upon her, which led her to run to Him for help. Either way, there is an often-misunderstood moment in Scripture here, where Jesus, confronted with the last drop of wine, responded, "Woman, what have I to do with thee? mine hour is not yet come" (John 2:4). This is interpreted as if Jesus said, "Woman! What do you want *Me* to do about it!? It ain't My time yet!"

Actually, this verse might often be misjudged based on our culture's perspective of this wording. We hear "woman" at the beginning of a sentence today and assume it will be followed by, "bring me a beer!" But far from the Al Bundy (a character on the sitcom *Married with Children*) tone, this expression—based on its Greek translation—conveys a tone of gentleness and respect. It was an endearing way to address an elder, much like "Madame" in recent history or "Dear Lady" now: "Addressing his mother simply as 'woman,' though abrupt to modern readers' ears, does not imply lack of affection. Jesus addressed his mother in this way from the cross when making loving provision for her care after his death ([John] 19:26)."[56]

Furthermore, what are not recorded in this exchange are the facial expressions of Mary and Jesus, which could reveal a lot of information about their feelings. We don't know how long the time gap was between their words. For all we know, Jesus' comment that it wasn't His time to begin performing miracles may have been a question, as some scholars believe: "My hour has not yet come...has it?" The question wouldn't need to be spoken aloud for it to "linger between them" through eye contact. That's one possibility. Another is that Jesus was bluntly telling her, possibly in a rebuking tone, the timing wasn't right but He would do it anyway because she was His mother. This is unlikely, as the Messiah's "oneness" with God naturally would not lead Him to any waffling about His actions.

But the most probable (and most theologically sound) interpretation of this passage centers not on Jesus' response, but on Mary's implied request. If we imagine that Mary, who had known His true identity from His conception, was hoping to kick-start public acknowledgment of who He was, suddenly it is *her* words, and not His, that can be critiqued. The invisible exchange involving undescribed expressions may have communicated something like this:

Mary: "Hey Jesus, we're out of wine... Think you can, uh, you know, *do* something about this? You and I both know you're the Son of God. Don't you think it's about time *they* knew who You really are?"

Jesus: "Dear woman, it's yet not time for Me to let everyone know that I'm the Messiah. I'm keeping that revelation on the down-low while I gather My disciples. But I will see to your wine problem." (Jesus knew this wouldn't be the "great reveal" of His messianic status, but it *would* be an evidence of it that would help build His case later on.)

Then, Mary, having had no idea what Jesus' soft smile (or whatever it was) may have implied, might have turned to the wedding servants and said, "Do whatever he tells you" (John 2:5).

This interpretation has been championed by commentators almost since the first circulation of the book of John. One commentary by *Holman Publishers* states:

Mary had carried the stigma of Jesus' miraculous birth for thirty years. It was only natural she would want some public revelation that her son was the Messiah. Jesus seemed to be saying, however, "What you expect out of this will not occur yet. I'm on a divine timetable and the revelation of my purpose will not happen today." But God's timetable for the Lamb did allow him to begin giving evidence of his calling by performing this local miracle.[57]

This possibility has been massively overlooked in the modern era and replaced with the concept of rebuke, sometimes by those who view Jesus' "woman" reference to His mother as insolent. After viewing numerous scholarly sources and comparing commentaries, the most reasonable explanation is that Mary, though every bit the innocent and sweet woman the Father chose to bear His Son, was simply human in her understanding of how the Son would be recognized as the prophesied Messiah. She was hoping the wedding could be the moment when He would stand up, arms outstretched, and make the glorious announcement, "Ladies and gentlemen, I am the Messiah, and I am about to prove it by snapping my fingers and making more wine appear—right in front of your eyes!" (or something to that effect). But Jesus knew miracles wouldn't prove anything to the crowd because sorcerers in the land, like Simon of Acts 8:9, were already performing miracles by the powers of darkness (at least they had been, until some or all of their powers were "broken" by the arrival of the star at His birth; see the section "Unbelievable Political Implications of the Magi"). No, just performing a miracle wouldn't have been enough to convince folks of His identity as their Messiah. Perhaps He even knew that, in the future, when He would heal the possessed, blind, and dumb man in front of the Pharisees, they would say He had done so by the powers of "Beelzebub the prince of devils" (Matthew 12:22–37). Maybe Jesus' thoughts included the "miracle" that occurred when Pharaoh's men had *also* turned the water into blood as Moses had done (Exodus 7:14–25). In order for Jesus to establish Himself as the embodiment of the Messiah, His hour was not yet at hand. He would help with the wine issue, but discreetly, in such a way that "the ruler of the feast had tasted the water that was made wine, and knew not whence it was [didn't know where it came from]," perhaps assuming the bridegroom had produced wine—and had saved the best for last (John 2:9–10).

But while most people weren't aware of Jesus' subtle and inconspicuous act, the disciples definitely noticed: "What Jesus did here in Cana of Galilee was the first of the signs through which he revealed his glory; and his disciples believed in him" (John 2:11). This plays into a striking parallel: Both wine (Isaiah 25:6; 55:1; Joel 3:18; Amos 9:13) and feasts (Matthew 8:11; 22:1–14; Lk 13:29; 14:15–24; Revelation 19:7–9) are signs of the coming Kingdom, which will be better than the old Kingdom (Mark 2:21–22).

One last issue must be addressed maturely in regard to the nature of the "wine." (It is one of the most highly debated subjects in recent history among believers, and if we can help some by sharing what we feel is going on here, then we'd like to take a moment now to do so.) A number of folks argue that Jesus didn't create an alcoholic beverage, but unfermented grape juice. This claim is based on a) the immediacy in which the beverage was consumed (it therefore hadn't been given ample time to ferment), and b) the Greek translation of the word "wine" used here, *oinos* (John 2:9–10) which could refer either a fermented or non-fermented drink. This approach greatly reassures those who see any consumption of alcohol as a sin, based on the many warnings in the Word against being a drunkard. To them, it's puzzling that God in the flesh would make, then serve, a substance that could cause a partygoer to become intoxicated.

The first statement we wish to make on this subject is that any people who make their conclusions *responsibly*, meaning by studying the languages and context, should be commended, regardless of what they deduce. Far too many Christians, even those who are well-meaning, hear one teaching on the subject and, without consulting the Bible or attempting to exegete the Scriptures properly, repeat that teaching to others in a way that either endorses or condemns the consumption of alcohol. This can be dangerous, as it may encourage someone who struggles with alcohol abuse to find justification for continuing to do so, *or* it might unnecessarily come across as judgmental to someone who uses it in moderation. Scholars, too, have at times found this particular issue such a worthy and provocative topic that they've set aside their professionalism by slandering those who don't agree with their stance. So, no matter what we personally believe about this miracle at Cana, it's important to maintain loving tact in discussions. Remember that, if trusted academics, historians, researchers, and lingual experts can't even agree, then we likely won't know the "right" answer on this side of eternity. In this matter, as in all matters that leave room for various interpretations, we should be willing to admit when there's something we simply don't know.

That said, here are a few facts that may help with your studies:

The issue of how soon the beverage was consumed is, in our respectful opinion, a non-issue. Yes, party guests with empty cups might have immediately depleted the wine barrel, but if Jesus was powerful enough to turn water into grape juice, He would have been powerful enough to turn it into wine without having to create something and then stave off the feasters for several months for it to be fully prepared.

As for the translation matter, it's true the Greek word *oinos*—which derives from the Hebrew *yayin*—can refer to either fermented or nonfermented beverages. In some places in Scripture, the context is perfectly clear. For example, in the first book of the Bible, we read: "And he drank of the wine [*yayin*], and was drunken; and he was uncovered within his tent" (Genesis 9:21). Obviously, the context of this verse, which describes a very drunk and stumbling man, shows that *yayin* can certainly refer to juice from the vine that has been fermented and therefore potentially intoxicating. And in the New

Testament, we see *oinos* also used this way: "It is good neither to eat flesh, nor to drink wine, nor any thing whereby thy brother stumbleth, or is offended, or is made weak" (Romans 14:21). Again, the context of someone being caused by a fellow believer to sin could only be referring to alcoholic wine, as "grape juice" would not cause anyone to "stumble."

Also, we do have a Greek word in use that refers specifically to new wine: "Others mocking said, 'These men are full of new wine [Greek *gleukos*]'" (Acts 2:13). Those who believe the water was turned to wine, not grape juice defend their position with reasoning that goes something like this: "If Jesus merely created nonalcoholic 'grape-ade,' why wouldn't the Word say He turned water into *gleukos* ["sweet wine"]?"

Actually, as Acts 2:13 stipulates (that drinking this could still cause drunkenness), the Greek word *also* refers to a kind of wine with intoxicating properties. The difference is not in which one contains more alcohol, but in how this drink is made. "New wine" —*gleukos*—is more literally translated as "sweet wine." In fact, it's from this Greek term that the English word "glucose" is derived (meaning a form of naturally produced sugar in fruit and in the human bloodstream that's later transformed into energy.) The Greeks and Romans had a practice of covering a jar with pitch (a tar-like substance) and placing grapes within it that had not yet been completely trampled or pressed. This airtight container was then either submerged in water or buried in the sand for as little as six weeks or as long as several months. The end product was therefore believed to be just as alcoholic as standard table wines, but it had preserved more of the sweetness and flavor of the original grape. This beverage, too, appeared in the Old Testament (Isaiah 49:26; Amos 9:13), although its process may not have been the same as that of those in the Greco-Roman era. So, either way, the existence of this word fails to prove anything on either side of the debate.

The answer may not be found in the study of a single word, as is often the case in the Bible...but it *may* be found in the context of the whole passage. Read the following and note that the term is the same in every instance:

> And when they wanted wine [*oinos*], the mother of Jesus saith unto him, They have no wine [*oinos*]....
>
> Jesus saith unto them, "Fill the waterpots with water." And they filled them up to the brim. And he saith unto them, "Draw out now, and bear unto the governor of the feast." And they bare it.
>
> The key to this passage is not in what the servants handed the ruler of the feast, it's in his response: At the beginning of a feast, everyone sets out the good stuff, and when everyone's had plenty, they set out the cheap stuff. But *this* bridegroom (the ruler of the feast thought it was the groom who replenished the wine supply) saved the best for last. In other words, whatever they were consuming at the beginning of the festivities is the same as what they were consuming on this round, with one difference: this stuff was better; it was "good." We have little choice but to accept that Jesus turned the water into whatever was served the guests early on.

With that in mind, the only way we can deduce that Jesus made grape juice is to reason that grape juice was what they had been drinking from the onset of the feast. But again, context cancels that conclusion. Here's why: The very reason someone (the groom or anyone else) would serve the best stuff first and switch to "that which is worse" later is because, after having consumed so much alcohol by that point, the guests wouldn't be able to tell the difference between what was in their cups at first and the substandard refill later. (This can happen early on. It doesn't mean anyone would have to be drunk not to recognize the quality of the beverage handed to them.)

Moreover, much can be said about what a "ruler of the feast" was. In other translations, the phrase is rendered "master of the feast," which is a more literal wording. Far from where our imagination might go with a term as grand as "master," this doesn't indicate a hoity-toity, wealthy man who makes it his business to frequent all the best local parties in the New Testament. As the cup-bearers to the kings of the Old Testament were those who tasted the wine before the kings did to spare them of potential poisoning, the master over the feasts in the New Testament tasted the food and drink to ensure quality. Consider it against today's phrase, "master of ceremonies." That doesn't denote a true "master" of anything; it simply means a supervisor or planner. Wedding celebrations in the times of the New Testament, for generally all people groups in that culture (Jewish or otherwise), included regular table wine that *did contain* alcohol. So, in light of the context, this fermented wine is likely what was served.

But that's not to say any of those attending the Cana wedding were getting drunk, either. Those who prefer to believe Jesus created grape juice find it tough to imagine Jesus being surrounded by wild partygoers; surely He wouldn't be a part of or contribute (wine) to such an inebriated group of revelers. The truth is, He didn't, and that, too, can be proven by understanding the master of the feast also served as somewhat of a room monitor. If someone at one of the shindigs was to become intoxicated, it was the master's duty to cut that person off from imbibing further. If anyone was getting out of hand, the master would even go as far as breaking a glass. As this narrative describes nothing more than the master's approval of the miraculously supplied beverage, we can breathe a sigh of relief that none of these guests were drunk, but instead were drinking in polite moderation. (In case you're wondering, there were absolutely stronger drinks in that day, wine being mild in comparison. Note that Jesus didn't turn water into one of those alternatives.)

Furthermore, this isn't the only time God's holy and authoritative Word presents the balanced consumption of wine in a positive light. Ecclesiastes 9:7 says, "Go thy way, eat thy bread with joy, and drink thy wine with a merry heart; for God now accepteth thy works." Elsewhere, the Bible says the natural growth of the grape of the ground was specifically created for our enjoyment: "He causeth the grass to grow for the cattle, and herb for the service of man: that he may bring forth food out of the earth; And wine that maketh glad the heart of man" (Psalm 104:14–15a). Amos 9:14, a prophecy linked to the context of God's future blessings for the righteous, states: "And I will bring again the captivity of my people of Israel…and they shall plant vineyards, and drink the wine thereof." In Paul's first Pastoral Epistle, 1 Timothy (5:23), the apostle instructed Timothy to take some wine in addition to his water to soothe a chronic illness he suffered: "Drink no longer [just] water, but use a little wine for thy stomach's sake and thine often infirmities." In strong language, *Jamieson, Fausset, & Brown* believe "God hereby commands believers to use all due means for preserving health, and condemns by anticipation the human traditions which among various sects have denied the use of wine to the faithful."[58]

Those who believe drinking *past* the point of moderation is wrong are, however, correct, as our focus should be on the work of the Spirit more than on partying: "And be not drunk with wine, wherein is excess; but be filled with the Spirit" (Ephesians 5:18). The bottom line of the lesson we can take from the wedding narrative is this: If, for you, that means abstaining from all intoxicating liquids, we thank you for your obedience. If you studied this issue on your own and conclude it's okay to drink alcohol, we likewise thank you—both for your temperance and your self-control. Either way, all of us would benefit from being delicate in how we discuss these issues with members of our family of believers. We don't have to always agree in order to be united in the same Gospel work.

This brings us to the real purpose of Jesus' miracles. Believe it or not, though His miraculous works did benefit the recipients, Jesus' ultimate goal was not *only* to show mercy to the lucky ones bestowed with His grace. Once we understand this principle, it may explain why we don't see many miracles in today's time!

Miracles of Jesus

We often hear sincere prayers in our contemporary Christian world for a supernatural actions such as healings, changes in the weather, or interventions from God in areas of need. In fact, it happens frequently. How often do such pleas result in the outcome hoped for? Not every time, at least in the experiences of these authors.

Here's a question that can help provide clarity in all of this before we begin discussing the rest of Jesus' miracles: How often do the prayers like those just mentioned include the words "so You might be proven/glorified"? Sometimes, maybe. But how often do these prayers take place in a setting where, for many, Jesus is a brand-new concept?

See, that changes everything.

This word study we're about to present might be one of the greatest apologetics (argument) regarding why our prayers for miracles aren't always answered affirmatively, even when we offer them with the grandest levels of human faith. Bookmark this page and highlight it, because the current absence of God's intervention in a New-Testament, storm-calming, make-the-blind-see-again fashion is an enormous reasons for atheists' disbelief—which, tragically, many of us can't refute with much more than a weak, "God works in mysterious ways" response. (Don't take that wrong. There *are* times this is the appropriate answer. Isaiah 55:8–9 makes it clear that God's ways are mysterious to us. However, unfortunately, it has become a short, pat, abused cop-out response to explain away every "failed" prayer, excusing Christians from having to tackle a tough subject.)

The Greek word translated "miracle" in the New Testament is almost always *semeion*, or "sign," and *semeion* is regularly used in conjunction with *teras*, or "wonders." (Another similar term is *dynamis*, translated "mighty works" or "power." Though these don't mean exactly what *semeion* and *teras* do, the context of Scripture is clear that they accomplish the same goal.) Scholars acknowledge what we often miss:

Miracles in the New Testament are often referred to as *signs and wonders*. This is key [see that?: *key*, meaning of paramount importance!] to understanding the purpose of Jesus' supernatural acts of healing, spiritual deliverance, control of nature, and raising of individuals from the dead. The Gospels present these miracles as signs of Jesus' rightful authority as King over the natural realm. The words of Jesus, including His announcement of the coming of God's kingdom, are substantiated by His performance of miraculous deeds. Thus *the miracles served a specific and designated purpose*—to prove that Jesus is King and that God's kingdom over which He rules is now immediately accessible, operating on earth. Jesus'…miraculous deeds demonstrated the authenticity of this Kingdom and the legitimacy of His claims to be its King [or Messiah]. Only the legitimate Ruler of such a government could exercise such a degree of control and authority over its elements.[59]

Going deeper, the *Lexham Theological Wordbook* states *semeion* is the object or occurrence that makes it possible to recognize something important that's otherwise ambiguous or unknown, and it goes on to say: "This basic sense is attested in the [New Testament], as in the instance where Judas' kiss serves as a sign (*semeion*) revealing Jesus' identity to the men tasked with seizing him (Matt 26:48)."[60] Without Judas' "sign" of the kiss, the Roman soldiers wouldn't have known who to arrest. Thus, the kiss "proved" Jesus was the One they were after.

Miracles in the New Testament were, therefore, ultimately not for the benefit of the recipients, though that was an obvious side effect. It was a "sign," literally an indicator or marker, that the Savior was among them and was who He said He was. The reactions of the beneficiaries bolstered this, as they would transform from quiet beggars or afflicted individuals to loud proclaimers of what had been done for them.

Knowing this, we should really question the motive behind our prayers today. If we ask for miraculous intervention from a place that isn't—in any way, shape, or form—intrinsically connected to our hope of proving the Messiah to others who can observe the miracle and come to believe in His sovereignty, then our intent does not line up with the purpose of the miracles we read about in the Bible. And even when pointing others to Him is, in the fullest way, our intent when we pray, we have to consider whether the people of the area we live in are familiar with Jesus. Those in the Western world usually do know of Him, even though they reject Him. Also remember when Jesus was asked to show the Pharisees a sign, He responded by saying only a wicked generation would ask for such proof (Matthew 16:4). He didn't say this because their request was inherently wicked, but because He knew their *motives* were wrong. They were familiar with Jesus in a human-flesh, person-to-person way that we can't be today, but they, too, rejected Him. When the motive behind asking for miracles isn't pure, He isn't willing to perform parlor tricks for our amusement. From there, we must be willing to admit whether, if the prayer is answered the way we wish, we would hurry to spread the Good News as did the beneficiaries of the New Testament miracles. If we don't meet these requirements to the fullest, then we, ourselves, become the benefactors of the miracles we're asking for…which is, when traced to the very root of motive, a selfish request.

In the earliest days of Defender publishing company (known as "Anomalos" at the time), we released a book, *God Sent Me Back*, about a Nigerian pastor, Daniel Ekechukwu, who was raised from the dead in 2001 after perishing in a car accident. This book has since been taken out of print, but we remember how astonished our production staff was by the colossal mountain of evidence that supported the incident. (Note the author was writing on behalf of the man who had come back from death, which challenges the idea that Ekechukwu was exaggerating his own story.) This pastor had been dead for three full days, his body in the morgue. The book included corroborated interviews and documents from the mortician who wrote up and signed his certificate of death and saw to the administration of embalming fluids. Pictures included in the publication showed graphic before, during, and after photos of the wreck, as well as the "Lazarus" moment when Ekechukwu rose again after his body had been taken to a Reinhard Bonnke crusade. Bonnke's Christ for All Nations ministry went on to produce a documentary of the incident. If all that transpired after this event was that the Nigerian man returned home and spent the rest of his life in peace and privacy, it would be a beautiful description of God's grace...but that would not fulfill the ultimate, point-to-Christ *purpose* of the miracle, and thankfully that's not what he chose to do. Instead, he rose and dedicated the rest of his life to telling as many people as he could about the miracle he had experienced in an area of the world where witchcraft and voodoo (and other world religions) often hold people in a tighter, more demonic grip than in the highly Christianized West.

Miracles do happen, but not with the same rate of frequency and saturation as they did in the New Testament period, when Jesus had just appeared on the scene, when the world had no idea of who He was or whether the whispers about Him being the Messiah were true. When Jesus walked the earth, He was a new idea, a new answer to the question of which power on earth was more authoritative than all others amidst sorcery and satanic energies that were alive and well up to His appearance. Had He merely stated with empty words that He was the Son, but refused to show signs that validated those declarations, then He would have been no more impressive in the history books than all the other revolutionaries who came before Him, like Judas the Galilean.

Though it may not be the answer we want to hear, miracles were and are about *God*, not us, and He knows the secret depths of our motive and our hearts, as well as the future, and therefore has the divine right to see whether our miracle will produce the harvest that supports the sign in the first place.

But doesn't the Word say "by His stripes we are healed"?

Yes, but it's not a physical healing we are promised; plus, don't miss the emphasis of this verse (despite it being so often misquoted) is in the *past* tense.

In 1 Peter 2:24, we read, "by whose [Jesus'] stripes ye were healed." The key word here is "were." This verse is an echo of a prophecy in Isaiah 53:5–6 that clearly points to a then-future physical wounding for the sake of spiritual healing. Note the clarification in brackets:

> But he [Christ] was wounded [physical wound] for our trans-
> gressions [for our sin], He was bruised [physical wound] for our
> iniquities [again, for our *sin*]...All we like sheep have gone astray;
> We have turned every one to his own way [fallen away from God;
> not a physical illness]; And the Lord hath laid on him the iniquity
> of us all [the Father has laid upon the Son the sin of the world].

Nowhere in this passage did Isaiah point to a physical element. The only treatment of anything physical is that *Jesus* was physically wounded for the sake of our transgressions/iniquities.

We frequently assign 1 Peter 2:24 to a promise of bodily heal-ing, but that can't be the meaning of this Isaiah verse based on the Greek word behind "you were healed," *iaomai*, which is used in the common aorist verb, or past, tense. Peter was using Isaiah's prophecy to acknowledge a fulfillment—that the work of Christ on the cross paved the way for a *spiritual* healing for all on the day He died. As are the common rules of context, this is also shown in the very next verse, 1 Peter 2:25: "For ye were as sheep going astray; but are now returned unto the Shepherd and Bishop of your souls." The emphasis here is unmistakably about the *soul*.

Yes, but "where two or more are gathered—"

Wait a sec... There is also a common misunderstanding about Matthew 18:20: "For where two or three are gathered together in my name, there am I in the midst of them." Many of us, as sincere as we may be, take this Scripture out of context to say that we can claim literally *anything* in the name of God/Jesus, and so long as two or more others are present and the request fits with biblical teaching (and by extension, God's will as outlined in the Word), it will be done. But this verse's context (starting with verse 15), regards conflict among church members. Jesus explained that if our "brothers" (fellow Christians) "trespass thee" (sin against us—and note that this is a *sin* against us, not merely "offending" us), we are to take the following steps:

1. Speak privately with the individual who sinned against us. If the person will not listen:
2. Take one or two other "witnesses" to have further discussion with that person. This doesn't mean we should take along those who "witnessed" the sin, as the context is a personal conflict and not a judicial/legal one in which "witnesses" would provide testimony. Instead, we should be accompanied by people who know what sin is and what it's not. If the offender still won't listen:
3. Tell the "church." Some scholars interpret this to indicate the whole church, as in making a church-wide statement, while others interpret it to mean the leaders of the church, but either way, the purpose is not to pass judgment and gang up on the offender, but to bring him or her back to the fold and completely restored with the fellowship. If the offender, however, *still* will not listen:
4. He or she should be removed from the church and treated as a pagan or tax collector—as a foreigner to the disciples.

This radical removal is a response to a sin that goes above and beyond personal hurt feelings, as the context of the next verses stipulate regarding forgiving a person "seventy times seven." An example of extending this kind of forgiveness is in the parable of the king who forgave the debts (Matthew 18:21–35). If we allow the popular "where two or more" interpretation to lead, then we're not only forced to believe anything we ask for will be granted, but we also must admit that God's presence is *not* found in the presence of just one Christian.

In other words, this interpretation asserts that He requires that two or more people be in attendance before He will grant His presence or a miracle. Both of these teachings are heretical. Also, the Greek word translated "gathered" is *synegmenoi,* and it means "united," not just people occupying the same physical space. In proper New Testament context, "united" people are integrated for the cause of spreading of the Gospel, not for any kind of personal gain. The bottom line: Where two or more are united for the purpose of sharing the Gospel, God will honor decisions to deal with, and possibly remove, troublesome congregants, assuming those actions are made slowly, methodically, maturely, and with the offender's restoration as the goal.

Yeah, but…my pastor said we don't have healing or whatever we need because we don't ask for it. So if we ask—

Hang on… Yet another abused verse that looks like it might be promising answers to prayer comes from James 4:1–4, often shortened to "you have not because you ask not," as if that applies to anything we might ask for. The true context of the verse is, ironically, *also* about church conflict, as the whole passage shows:

> From whence come wars and fightings among you [believers in the early Church]? come they not hence, even of your lusts that war in your members? Ye lust, and have not: ye kill, and desire to have, and cannot obtain: ye fight and war, yet ye have not, because ye ask not. Ye ask, and receive not, because ye ask amiss [meaning "you ask with the wrong motives"], that ye may consume it upon your lusts. Ye adulterers and adulteresses, know ye not that the friendship of the world is enmity with God? whosoever therefore will be a friend of the world is the enemy of God.

It's unfortunate so many drop "you have not because you ask not" in the air like a promise, because the verse after it speaks of not getting what we ask for because we ask out of selfish or vain motives ("that ye may consume it upon your lusts"). The believers James was addressing in his letter were making the mistake of assuming their earthly bless-ings (their relationship with the world) would justify spiritual-holiness competitions among members.

More often than not, the words of the Bible do not promise specific outcomes. As stated earlier, the Israelites interpreted the Deuteronomic "retributional justice" system to be a constant prom-ise, not a general guideline. This led to confusion every time someone met what they believed to be "pointless" suffering. For example, when Jesus healed a man who was blind from birth, as recorded in John 9:1–12, the disciples asked, "Master, who did sin, this man, or his parents, that he was born blind?" To them, the man couldn't be blind simply because he came into the world with an affliction. But, "Jesus answered, 'Neither hath this man sinned, nor his parents: but that the works of God should be made manifest in him.'" The man had been born that way so God could be glorified in the healing.

This also *does not mean* God is oblivious to our needs or doesn't wish to bless His people, even to the point of miraculous intervention. Here's one instance—again as a guideline, not a promise—that we can ask for what we need and expect those needs to be taken care of:

> Ask, and it shall be given you; seek, and ye shall find; knock, and it shall be opened unto you: For every one that asketh receiveth; and he that seeketh findeth; and to him that knock-eth it shall be opened. Or what man is there of you, whom if his son ask bread, will he give him a stone? Or if he ask a fish, will he give him a serpent? If ye then, being evil, know how to give good gifts unto your children, how much more shall your Father which is in heaven give good things to them that ask him? (Matthew 7:7–11)

The Gospel of Matthew commentary brings this into focus, rightly emphasizing that the requests of believers should be based on *need* only, and not on preferences or luxury: "In [Matthew] vv. 25–34 the focus was explicitly on need rather than desire, and here too the son's requests are for basic food, not for luxuries.... The 'carte blanche' approach to petitionary prayer does not find support from the NT as a whole."[61] The commentator goes on to explain that there are circumstances when "the door" is *not* opened to those who knock, citing Matthew 25:10–12 and 7:21–23 as examples. Likewise, he says Matthew describes instances in which prayers are not answered, citing 6:5 and 6:7, as well as Jesus' own prayer in 26:29 just before His arrest.[62]

Again: If our eyes remain on the goal of spreading the Good News of Christ through the power of the Holy Spirit, many prayers are often answered in the positive (God knows when it's not). The result of such prayers can lead the lost to Christ. This is why, though we in the West may not see many amazing miracles, certain Christian missionaries in the Majority World report them all the time. In one of her earlier college classes, Howell read of a long list of astounding miracles that occurred in Muslim countries through a practice some call the "power encounter," all occurring as recently as between 2013–2019. Christian missionaries boldly go to this territory to tell everyone they meet that Christ is more powerful than Allah and that they, the precious unbelievers whom God loves, can have that power shown to them by merely asking Christ to intervene for them in some way. These missionaries also teach about signs and related motives of the askers. Because of these prayers, many have been healed from physical ailments, have had dreams of Jesus probing their minds during slumber, and have even been freed from the intensely oppressive response of their culture after their conversion became public (unheard of in Muslim countries!). Jesus is then glorified as the sole reason behind their miracles—and all this in a region where folks have yet to widely accept Him as Savior.

As a last word on Matthew 7:7 (as well as on its counterpart, John 16:24), we must keep in mind that humans—though finite and faulty—are made in the image of God, and we can learn one thing from this: A relationship with God is *comparable* to our relationships with other people. (Note we didn't say it's "the *same as*.") Like children, when we ask for something God, in His infinite wisdom, knows is not what we need, we may not understand why His answer is no. If your child asks for a poisonous snake, both of you might banter about the request, your child never fully accepting your reasons for turning him down. When we read that we can ask "any thing" in Christ's name and He will give it, the "thing" we ask for must still be within the will of God (compare John 14:14 with John 6:38, then compare them both with 1 John 5:14). What is the ultimate will of God? That Christ might be glorified…thus bringing us back to the beginning of this whole study: that the answered prayer would be a *semeion*, or "sign" of Christ in some way.

This quick search through the Scriptures on prayer is meant to *encourage* readers who have heard the dreaded "no" or "wait" as an answer to a prayer, and to bring back into focus what the miracles of Jesus were *for*. If you've been praying for a miracle, don't stop praying! Just consider adding to your prayer the intent to use that miracle as a sign of Christ's deity whenever and wherever you're given the chance. Then, if your prayer is answered the way you had hoped, follow through with your promises.

Jesus' many miracles documented in the New Testament aren't even close to the whole story, either. John's Gospel made that clear when he wrote: "And there are also many other things which Jesus did, the which, if they should be written every one, I suppose that even the world itself could not contain the books that should be written. Amen" (21:25). But here's a list we can remember and praise Jesus for (beginning with His second miracle, because His turning water into wine has already been discussed).

Jesus Christ:

- Healed an official's son at Capernaum (John 4:43–54).
- Delivered a man in Capernaum from an evil spirit (Mark 1:21–27; Luke 4:31–36).

- Healed Peter's mother-in-law's fever (Matthew 8:14–15; Mark 1:29–31; Luke 4:38–39).
- Cast out devils and healed the sick of many—on the same evening as Peter's mother-in-law was sick with a fever (Matthew 8:16–17; Mark 1:32–34; Luke 4:40–41).
- Instructed fishermen to lower their nets, producing a miraculous catch after an all-day fishing attempt rendered nothing on Lake Gennesaret (Luke 5:1–11).
- Cleansed a man of leprosy (Matthew 8:1–4; Mark 1:40–45; Luke 5:12–14).
- Healed a centurion's paralyzed servant in Capernaum (Matthew 8:5–13; Luke 7:1–10).
- Healed the paralyzed man who was lowered from an opening in the roof over the room where Jesus was (Matthew 9:1–8; Mark 2:1–12; Luke 5:17–26).
- Healed a man's withered hand on the Sabbath (Matthew 12:9–14; Mark 3:1–6; Luke 6:6–11).
- Resurrected the son of a widow in Nain (Luke 7:11–17).
- Calmed a storm over the sea (Matthew 8:23–27; Mark 4:35–41; Luke 8:22–25).
- Cast demons into pigs (Matthew 8:28–33; Mark 5:1–20; Luke 8:26–39).
- Healed a woman with an issue of blood (Matthew 9:20–22; Mark 5:25–34; Luke 8:42–48).
- Resurrected the ruler Jairus' daughter (Matthew 9:18, 23–26; Mark 5:21–24, 35–43; Luke 8:40–42, 49–56).
- Healed two blind men (Matthew 9:27–31).
- Healed a mute man (Matthew 9:32–34).
- Healed a crippled man at Bethesda (John 5:1–15).
- Fed five thousand (plus women and children) with five loaves of bread and two fish after healing the sick among them (Matthew 14:13–21; Mark 6:30–44; Luke 9:10–17; John 6:1–15).

- Walked across the water (Matthew 14:22–33; Mark 6:45–52; John 6:16–21).
- Healed many from sickness in Gennesaret as they touched His garment (Matthew 14:34–36; Mark 6:53–56).
- Healed a demon-possessed daughter of a Gentile woman (Matthew 15:21–28; Mark 7:24–30).
- Healed a man who was both deaf and mute (Mark 7:31–37).
- Fed four thousand (plus women and children) with seven loaves of bread and "a few little fishes" (Matthew 15:32–39; Mark 8:1–13).
- Healed a blind man at Bethesda (Mark 8:22–26).
- Healed a blind-from-birth man by spitting on the ground and making a healing ointment from mud (or "clay") (John 9:1–12).
- Delivered a boy from an unclean spirit (Matthew 17:14–20; Mark 9:14–29; Luke 9:37–43).
- Drew the amount of money due for the Temple taxes from the mouth of a fish (Matthew 17:24–27).
- Healed and delivered a blind, mute man possessed by demons (Matthew 12:22–23; Luke 11:14–23).
- Healed a woman who had been crippled for eighteen years (Luke 13:10–17).
- Cured a man from edema (or "dropsy") on the Sabbath day (Luke 14:1–6).
- Cleansed ten people from leprosy on His way to Jerusalem (Luke 17:11–19).
- Raised Lazarus from the dead in Bethany (John 11:1–45).
- Healed a blind man, Bartimaeus, in Jericho (Matthew 20:29–34; Mark 10:46–52; Luke 18:35–43).
- Caused a fruitless fig tree on the road from Bethany to wither and die (Matthew 21:18–22; Mark 11:12–14).
- Healed a soldier's ear after Peter cut it off the night of Jesus' arrest (Luke 22:50–51).
- Resurrected Himself from the grave/tomb (Matthew 28:11–15, 18).

- Appeared in a room "with closed doors" (in other words, He walked through a wall) where His disciples had gathered after His crucifixion (John 20:19).
- Appeared to His disciples after His crucifixion, instructing them to lower the net on the other side of the boat, resulting in a huge catch after a tiring day of catching nothing (John 21:3–11).
- Vanished from thin air without an explanation (Luke 24:31).
- Repeatedly appeared to many individuals and gatherings to produce "many infallible proofs" after His crucifixion (Acts 1:3–4).

Almost all these miracles, signs, and wonders were performed in front of multiple witnesses, and some were amid gatherings of hundreds or thousands. One particular sign took place in front of three disciples only, and they were asked not to tell anyone "till the Son of man were risen from the dead" (Mark 9:9).

(Jesus' popular self-reference, "Son of Man," appears more than eighty times in the Gospels. The most obvious underlying meaning we see *today* of that name is that God would one day appear in human form, looking like any other "son" who has ever come from any other "man [human male]," as Jesus did. But that wasn't necessarily the interpretation of the Jews. After the effects of Maccabean revolt [circa 140–36 BC], the Jews began to reinterpret the "Son of Man" from Daniel 7 as a more mystical, eschatological [end-times] character who would rise up in the last days with a literal, physical Kingdom of God and rule over all the earth. Therefore, this "character" would be different from all others, so "Son of Man" implied an eternal Person who embodied perfection from the Most High. He would be the most pious of Sages. But the Jews also believed this Being would, as an eternal Person, be a heavenly Being incapable of physical death, and that He would not "appear" as a human until His *Parousia*, or "Final Advent" [what we understand to be the Second Coming].[63] Either way, there is a definitive cohabitation of divine qualities alongside human qualities in one, which cannot point to anything besides an Incarnation. So Jesus, God Incarnate, in His choice to refer to Himself as this Being, wasn't only positioning Himself as the eschatological ruler of a future earthly Kingdom, but He was also showing that there would be a "First Advent" [the disciples were witnessing this now] and a "Second Advent." The First Coming would provide an answer to the problem of sin—substitutionary atonement: a "removal" of sin instead of a "covering" of it like in the Mosaic Law— which would eventually lead to the Second Coming, the culmination of all things in the end of all time. In this reference, however, Christ identified Himself as the fulfillment of the Man Daniel saw in his vision.)

Jesus had an opportunity to take Peter, James, and John with Him up to "a high mountain" (scholars believe it was Mt. Hermon, Mt. Miron, or Mt. Tabor) to pray. It was there that the miracle of the Transfiguration occurred (see Matthew 17:1–8; Mark 9:2–8; Luke 9:28–36). "And [Christ's] raiment became shining, exceeding white as snow; so as no fuller on earth can white them [meaning no expert in clothing could have bleached them that white]" (Mark 9:3), "and his face did shine as the sun" (Matthew 17:2). Moses and Elijah appeared "in glorious splendor" (Luke 9:31) to speak with Him about His coming departure from Jerusalem. Moses was the supreme deliverer of God's people prior to Christ, and his presence represents the entire Old Testament Law. Elijah was the supreme prophet, as well as Jesus' forerunner (Malachi 4:4–6). In this trio, Israel's past (Moses), present (Elijah), and future (Christ) are in view. Once again, a voice from heaven from the Father recognized the bright and shining Son: "This is my beloved Son: hear him" (Mark 9:7).

With Christ's end goal of "signs" in mind, we need to recall that He wasn't just proving He was the Son of God so He could accumulate worshippers and disciples. In every case, each *semeion* He performed pointed to His central message of teaching: The Kingdom of God is here! Book of Acts exegete F. F. Bruce concurs:

The miracles of Jesus were not mere "wonders"; they were "mighty works," evidences of the power of God operating among the people, and "signs" of the kingdom of God—"the powers of the age to come," in the language of Heb. 6:5. "If it is by the finger of God that I cast out demons," said Jesus on one occasion, "then the kingdom of God has come upon you" (Luke 11:20). And the generality of those who saw his mighty works agreed: "God has visited his people" (Luke 7:16).[64]

Proof was offered to those with ears to hear and eyes to see (Matthew 13:9–16), and not just to glorify Jesus, but to support His message, His *teaching*, that the Kingdom of God was, finally and forever, at hand.

HIS Kingdom?! This Guy Has to Go!

When a newly known, up-and-coming rabbi from Galilee named Jesus started getting attention, most people within the Jerusalem elite were immediately on guard. While He seemed to have a flawless understanding of Scripture, He also spoke like a radical—a dangerous thing to do in a community under tight Roman oppression. His revolutionary "Kingdom of God" talk was both ambiguous and groundbreaking. For the Jews who had been subject to enslavement or harsh governmental rule for centuries, such talk could mean a victorious takeover of earthly kingdoms, or the provocation of doom by opposing forces that would quickly remind Jews of their place.

And yet, "this Jesus guy" seemed to speak with authority and have all the answers. In His Sermon on the Mount (Matthew 5), He spoke of a place where: the downtrodden would inherit a kingdom; the sad would be comforted; the meek would inherit the earth; the hungry and thirsty would find satisfaction and righteousness; the people who were brave enough to show mercy would see it reciprocated; the peaceful would be close to God; and the persecuted would be vindicated. Such a kingdom would make the most successful and progressive government of any the world had ever seen. Everything was a reversal of the norm. Over and again in this "Kingdom" teaching, Jesus made "replacement" sayings: "You've heard it written…" followed by, "But I say to you…" Though, for scarcely appearing, wisdom-fed Jews, it was a sign that the New Contract was replacing the Old (see brief synopses of these immediately under the "Old Testament" and "New Testament" major headings in this book). For Roman and religious-spirited Jews, a man was growing to replace the old world government and civilization with a new system. To anyone without the knowledge we have today, it sounded as if He was saying the "poor" will get the kingdom (Matthew 5:3); the "meek" will "inherit" (read: "take over") the earth (5:5); the "persecuted" (those whom the Romans oppressed) are those whose kingdom is heaven's (read: "the persecuted will rise up against oppressors and establish earthly kingdoms to match what God has planned"; 5:10).

It certainly would not align with how Rome, *or* the Jews, liked to run things, which made this type of talk dangerous. Rome saw that if this radical Man could actually back His claims, then there was a new kingdom coming wherein the peasants got to rule things. So earthly religion and politics were *both* threatened by Him.

As for the Jews, many ignored Him at first, then became increasingly off-put by Him. Whispers about His teaching were reaching the privileged and influential religious men, and they didn't like some of the things they were hearing. Whereas His intent was to show an internal matter of heart in His words on adultery, the divorced listeners in His gathering (and there were many, as a Jewish man needed only hand a paper to his wife to make it legal for him to kick her out and move on) would see the following words as a direct attack against their spiritual and cultural integrity and identity: "It hath been said, 'Whosoever shall put away his wife, let him give her a writing of divorcement': But I say unto you, That whosoever shall put away his wife, saving for the cause of fornication, causeth her to commit adultery: and whosoever shall marry her that is divorced committeth adultery" (Matthew 5:31–32). Certain words would have landed on

His listeners' ears as a doctrine of violence or revolutionary action if they applied it literally: "And if thy right eye offend thee, pluck it out, and cast it from thee... And if thy right hand offend thee, cut it off, and cast it from thee" (5:29–30). With only the "filter of warning" activated over the ears of those who were present, Jesus' new ideas resembled those of a cult leader. As reports kept spreading across Palestine, it was clear He was beginning to get a little too bold. Jesus said He didn't come to destroy the Law, but to fulfill it (what?!), but, as His following statement would suggest to the unlearned listener, "fulfillment" equaled the current "heaven and earth system passing away" (5:17–18). Christ's statement about how we must be more righteous than the "Pharisees and scribes" to enter heaven (5:20) would have provoked any listeners who may have been high-ranking Jews.

Many Jews of Jesus' assemblies heard His "Kingdom of God" teachings, but didn't understand their full implications. (Unfortunately, this trend continues today. The concept of God's Kingdom, to many, has become an ambiguous collective of moralistic teachings. These folks fail to truly grasp the notion that *this* is the very reason Jesus came to earth: to usher in a Kingdom wherein man can live free of sin, abundantly, and infused with supernatural power and victory while living in continual communion with our Creator because the barrier of sin is removed by the soteriological [salvational] work Jesus accomplished. To them, these are pretty ideas we can all dream about, but their primary focus remains on the practical and material amenities human life requires. For example, someone may recognize that Jesus came to provide salvation [initiating His Kingdom], but he or she often reduces His work to the facilitation of material wants and needs. Similarly, the "power of God" is often misunderstood to be the rights by which we claim material goods or wealth.) For the people who were listening to Jesus in His own time, the Kingdom concept likely was somewhat well accepted, but the audience largely missed its meaning then, remaining focused on *when* Jesus planned to overturn the Roman Empire and become the political leader of the world. The Old

Testament Messiah of David's lineage would reestablish the Davidic monarchy, wouldn't He? Passages such as Isaiah 24:23—"when the Lord of hosts shall reign in mount Zion, and in Jerusalem, and before his ancients gloriously"—didn't they foretell of a literal, earthly kingdom the Messiah would rule? Didn't the prophet mean it when he said in Zechariah 14:9 that the Lord will be "king over all the *earth*"?

What the Jews thought Jesus would be is covered in the "Jewish Expectations" section of this book (under the heading "Intertestamental Period"), but as a reminder: See what *The Life of Christ in the Synoptic Gospels* author Mike McClaffin explains regarding this perception held by the Jews of this time:

> At least part of the tension between Christ and the Jews was that His teaching on the Kingdom did not match their expectations, and this ultimately led them to reject him. Looking back on the Davidic kingdom made them long for the restoration of the conditions that had existed during the greatest period of their history. Then Israel had exercised great power, and her people had lived in relative peace and been their own masters. Foreign domination was unthinkable. Therefore it was easy to see why Jews longed for the day when these conditions would be restored... Whatever else might happen, of this they were sure: *the Messiah would come, and foreign rulers would be overthrown.*[65]

Unfortunately, the Jews operated under the assumption that the kingdom would be a physical one, as the "Davidic" emphasis implied to them. They just couldn't fully grasp that Jesus had a bigger Kingdom as His primary focus, because the tangible and visible kingdom of rulers had the attention in their daily lives. We know today Jesus didn't come to overturn the worldly government (although that happened, too, as Roman history attests that all this political unrest greatly intensified after His death); He came to shift the focus of mankind *from* their earthly troubles by engaging them in a Kingdom that would carry them always, even after their lives on earth had ended. Yet, it is unfortunate that this message wasn't then (or now) fully received by many, since it is the central theme of Jesus' teachings during His ministry on earth: "[T]he term *kingdom* appears a total of 121 times in the synoptics."[66] Clearly a teacher as important as God, Himself, coming to earth in the flesh would be carrying a vital message, yet people missed the central point.

Jesus Himself explained this in His parable of the sower. Ironically, as He described humanity's inability to understand the Kingdom of God, He was also describing the different types of people within the entourage who would acquiesce to and even encourage His own execution: "When anyone heareth the word of the kingdom, and understandeth it not, then cometh the wicked one, and catcheth away that which was sown in his heart. This is he which received seed by the way side" (Matthew 13:19). His meaning was that some would hear of the coming Kingdom and misunderstand its meaning, leaving them vulnerable to being misled by the enemy. He then went on in subsequent verses (v. 20–23) to explain that others would understand what was being explained, but they would be unable to withstand the persecution, and for this reason, would hide. Others would perceive truth, but would sell out for things such as riches and social comfort.

Furthermore, as He described the Kingdom He was bringing to the earth, He explained in shrouded, parabolic language that it wouldn't look the way people had imagined. In Matthew 13:31–32, we read: "Another parable put he forth unto them, saying, 'The kingdom of heaven is like to a grain of mustard seed, which a man took, and sowed in his field: Which indeed is the least of all seeds: but when it is grown, it is the greatest among herbs, and becometh a tree, so that the birds of the air come and lodge in the branches thereof.'"

In this, He was explaining that the Kingdom doesn't come from a seed that appears mighty and fortified; but rather its beginning is humble and not seen as having great strength. However, as it grows, it becomes stronger, hardier, and more resilient than those otherwise assumed would see greater growth or success. Further, this unpresuming origin eventually becomes a source of nourishment, nesting, and stability for those who gather in its branches. One would think likening an earthly-kingdom-conquering establishment to a seed would connect its origin to a more robust seed than Jesus' example. Instead, He explained that it would be the "least of all seeds": an origin they would never suspect. This is one of many ways Jesus described His Kingdom in a way quite opposite of what people were expecting.

(One important clarification: It's true that, while Christ was among us in human form, His Kingdom was "not of this world," as He repeatedly taught [both in direct statements as well as descriptions of a Kingdom that couldn't be interpreted as an earthly one]. It is also true that, while Jesus was here, as well as in this very day, the "god of this world" is Satan [2 Corinthians 4:4; 1 John 5:19; Ephesians 2:2; John 14:30; and many others]. One might ask why some premillennial theologians [premillennialism is discussed in the Revelation study in volume 3 of this set] would believe the coming Millennial Reign to be a literal time when Christ's Kingdom becomes a literal and earthly one. Doesn't that contradict everything He taught? Actually, no, it doesn't, because of the transference of power that occurs in the future, as described in Revelation 11:15: "And the seventh angel sounded; and there were great voices in heaven, saying, 'The kingdoms of this world *are become* [have transferred to] the kingdoms of our Lord, and of his Christ; and he shall reign for ever and ever.'" So this "Kingdom seed" wasn't only planted for a great harvest during Christ's time in the first century [when the Kingdom was not of this earth and therefore not a true threat to Rome]; it was also planted for a Kingdom that would rise in the very last days, the end times. The little mustard plant would spring into full blossom just after the earth as we know has been severely shaken to its core by the events of Revelation… Everything about Yeshua's Kingdom of God message that emphasized the internal would be finished at the cross. There was another, physical, literal Kingdom of God coming as well, but it would not transpire until the Second Coming of Christ [more on this later; tuck it into the back of your thoughts for now as we continue].)

In addition to mounting tension over the mismatch between expectation and delivery, teachings that described the Kingdom of God or Kingdom of Heaven were formerly understood to refer to a realm that belonged to God the Father, Yahweh, the great "I AM" (Exodus 3:14), the *Jehovahjireh* (Genesis 22:14) of the Old Testament. But there was Jesus claiming that *that* Being and He were Father and Son: "I and my Father are one" (John 10:30). This created a point of contention for devout Jews who—for a variety of reasons ranging from righteous indignation to malevolent ulterior motives—became suspicious of how such a claim might be true. Upon what—or whose—authority, did Jesus make a statement like that? It would certainly be blasphemy if made by one who didn't truly hold such status, yet Jesus boldly said He was a shareholder in all the sovereign authority the people had previously attributed only to their God the Father of the Old Testament.

The Jews of Jesus' day demonstrated their holiness with external symbols and practices, including their clothing (Matthew 23:5; Mark 12:38; Luke 20:46). Despite Jesus' grandest efforts, both secular and religious crowds couldn't let go of their belief that the *external* Kingdom was Christ's focus. It wouldn't be until after Paul's time that nearby regions would have such writings in circulation as: "For the kingdom of God is not meat and drink; but righteousness, and peace, and joy in the Holy Ghost" (Romans 14:17).

The Kingdom of God called for different obligations for its inheritors than any earthly kingdom would mandate upon worldly inhabitants. Citizens of God's Kingdom, listeners often thought, have a duty to: keep the heart pure (which is true; Matthew 5:8); keep the mouth pure (also true; 12:36); deny one's own earthly self (true when the temporal life distracts us from the spiritual life; 16:24); be willing to self-mutilate (obviously a misunderstanding based on hyperbole in Christ's teaching—meaning we would prioritize spiritual cleanliness over the physical body; 5:29–30); show mercy always to everyone (always true; 5:7); be willing to be persecuted without retort (accurate of all ages who follow Christ; 5:10); "hate" one's family (a teaching that really means to prioritize Christ over family; Luke 14:26); "carry one's own cross" daily (to live spiritually; 14:27); be watchful and prayerful (true of both the kingdom and Kingdom; 21:36); and recruit others into this system (which must have sounded quite bizarre under an Authority who could rule with force; Matthew 28:19). As we can see, just as the "Jewish Expectations" section showed they got some things correct and not others, Jesus' audiences only comprehended a limited number of His statements, while they misconstrued other teachings.

These "crazy ideas" just went on and on, and it wasn't just Jesus' theology that made religious leaders mad, it was also His fearless willingness to lead religious practices on a public level that dug under their skin like an irritant no ointment could cure.

Throughout His ministry and teaching, Jesus was "above the rules," having "the audacity" to "work" (read: "heal") on the Sabbath (Matthew 12:9–14; Mark 3:1–6; Luke 6:6–11; 14:1–6), going on to claim the Sabbath was made to benefit people, not the other way around (Mark 2:27–28)! In that Jewish culture, females weren't considered to be equals to men, and they certainly weren't allowed to learn theology, but Jesus taught women theology in their own homes, saying the practice was good and could not be taken away from them (Luke 10:38–42); females were segregated in the "women's court" of the Temple (where the treasury was housed), and Jesus regularly visited that area (Mark 12:41).

To make matters worse, Jesus upheaved religion as traditional Jews knew it by overhauling the way it intersected with culture. He broadened eligibility for Kingdom entrance to include *Gentiles*—those rascals! He diminished the importance of time-honored rituals, disregarded the status or perceived "holiness" of the highest of institutional religious leaders, and brought church *to the street*! He enraged religious leaders and their condescending, pious-appearing, elbow-rubbing political counterparts by promising the lowliest individuals in society an inheritance in the Kingdom (Matthew 5:3–12). People could now minister and be ministered to without having to first pay the Temple fees, buy a sacrificial animal, build a reputation among the religious elite, etc., which stomped on the lucrative worship commerce the Sanhedrin had built, usurping their religious control, as if God had cut them and their "hoops" out of the process of religion and relationship with Him. And, the fact that it was working could only mean "this man worked via blasphemy and evil spirits" (or so they accused in 12:24–37). To add insult to injury, Jesus revealed that their Law (including Oral Tradition) not only was incomplete, but that He, Himself, will be the fulfillment of that Law (5:17). This invalidated their religion as it had been known, amending it with the new and additional terms that religion without Christ, Himself, had become insufficient. Essentially, Jesus flipped their religion upside down. Legalism had been pushed aside while Jesus asserted Himself as the new way to God (John 14:6). Not only would the Kingdom *not* be a physical, governmental monarchy that would rule the world with an iron fist, but the intangible, spiritual territory was now open to non-Israelites as well.

Jesus' revolutionary approach to religion was a game-changer for those whose power had been amassed through the day's religious systems. In many ways, this increased His infamy: He went from being only an enemy of the state to being an enemy of the religious institution as well. Those who previously had status suddenly did not, while those society looked down upon were now elevated. *And*, because Jesus changed the criteria for entering the Kingdom (inviting Gentiles), it seemed that the most deviant scoundrels would gain access with preference over many who believed themselves righteous: "Verily I say unto you, that the publicans and the harlots go into the kingdom of God before you" (Matthew 21:31).

Jesus' approach to sacred matters was always "come one, come all," which stung like a bee to the holy men. Jesus had taken the Church outside the synagogue or Temple and to the people of the "filthy" roadways, had performed healings, and even forgave sin (Matthew 9:1–8, Mark 2:1–12). These actions (and others) all made access to God available to the common people without their having to play the institution's games, and their way of life was threatened. The religious leaders accused Him of operating by the power of demons (Matthew 12:22–37); He responded by *continuing* the theme of "His Father, in heaven," claiming to be the Son of God (John 10:30).

And just when it couldn't get any worse (or so they thought), Jesus marked Himself, *literally*, as King.

Pause.

Imagine this scene…

It's hot inside, while the sun outside is beaming and inviting over the yellowed stones of the Jerusalem walls. You're a young child who has been asked by your parents—Hebrews like their parents before them—not to leave the house and to stay by the window. You have it in mind to obey them explicitly when quite suddenly you overhear two familiar, well-educated local rabbis conversing down a brick alleyway in what sounds like a fit of hysterics. One is quoting Scripture, speaking rapidly and claiming the demonstration occurring down the road this very day could actually be a fulfillment of the words of the Hebrew prophet, Zechariah. Driven by extreme curiosity, you arch your neck out the window as far as you can reach, but the other rabbi is just out of sight. Without considering the consequences—and driven by an insatiable curiosity—you slip from your seat by the window and run outside to see what's going on.

In the faraway distance, you can hear shouting, but you can't make out any words. Through the back end of the alleyway, you see people running in the direction of the commotion. The second rabbi is scolding the first, making uncharacteristically harsh accusations against the first rabbi's faulty logic. He waves his arms about, pointing in the direction of the distant crowd, asking why, if this "Yeshua" is legitimate, there doesn't appear to be any accompanying military to help Him conquer their oppressors. The first rabbi shakes his head, muttering something about prophecies and insisting this "Yeshua" resembles them all.

I have heard this before, you think in your young mind. *Zechariah the prophet spoke of a humble colt carrying a future king.*

As the rabbis continue arguing, your mother bursts from the open door to your home. At first, she's angrily bellowing at you about your disobedience, but stops short just as a small crowd of folks rush past the alley, making no mind of your mother as she is bumped by several of them. Her expression turns from one of fury, to wonder, then to surprise as she turns to listen to the noise in the distance. Grabbing your hand, she escorts you around the corner to a long set of stairs overlooking an enormous throng of citizens, many you recognize as fellow Jews in your area of Jerusalem.

Beyond them is a gentle-looking man riding a colt in the direction of the Temple. People around him are taking off their outer layers of clothing and throwing them anxiously to the ground in front of him so his small, humble mount can walk atop them. Others are rapidly cutting branches from the trees and tossing them farther down the path in the same manner (Matthew 21:8). On both sides of the forming trail, people press in with palm leaves in their hands, similar to those that your neighbors carry during the Feast of Tabernacles (John 12:13; see also Leviticus 23:40). You vaguely recall a lesson from your father regarding this particular leaf being a symbol of triumph and victory, an act of homage to a king.

"Who is this?" your mother asks a few women nearby, pointing at the man in the center of the procession (the question was asked in Matthew 21:10).

The eldest turns quickly toward her, appearing to be either excited or startled, saying, "This is Jesus, the prophet of Nazareth of Galilee" (this answer was given in Matthew 21:11).

You glance at your mother to see if the news is good or bad, but she remains merely bewildered as she follows the women down the long steps and closer to the multitudes. The shouts become clearer:

"Hosanna to the Son of David! Blessed is He that cometh in the name of the Lord; Hosanna in the highest!" (the praise given Jesus in Matthew 21:9).

As the words sink in, your mother's eyes widen. She raises a hand over her mouth and shakes her head.

"Mother?" you inquire nervously.

In a tone you have heard many times, one your mother uses when she's forcing herself to remain calm, she answers, grabbing you firmly by the shoulders. "Run. Summon your father, immediately."

In obedience, you dash back to your house, yelling for your father before you even reach the door. He emerges with concern wrinkling his brow and, just like your mother's did, his countenance shifts from worry to disorientation as he sees a growing number of his companions hurry past without giving him a second thought—unusual for a man with your father's prominence in the community. Gesturing for him to follow, you grasp his hand as you lead him back to your mother, who is now standing nearer to the bottom of the steps as she tries to see through the mass of heads in front of her. As your father sees the enormous gathering and hears the expressions of adoration ringing in the air from a few trusted, learned men, one of his hands slowly comes to rest on your mother's shoulder while the other clasps more tightly around yours than ever before. Largely oblivious to the implications of the event and feeling a bit nervous, your eyes dart to your father's for reassurance, but he doesn't return your gaze. He is looking intensely onward at the man on the colt, breaking his stare only to observe the outbursts from those around him who have joined the recitation about the Son of David and something regarding Nazareth.

"It cannot be," he says. "Yeshua? Is not he the son of that carpenter?" (a question asked in Matthew 13:55 and Mark 6:3).

The rabbis from the alleyway appear in your peripheral vision, the first offering a swift answer to what your father had evidently overheard.

"Yes!" he answers loudly, with pride and excitement, straining to be heard in the growing volume of the noise around him. "He is the son of a carpenter, but it matters not. This is the prophesied Son of David. For His works have gone before Him, and those who have eyes to see will recognize the fulfillment. This is that which was spoken of by the prophet Zechariah. Hosanna in the highest! Behold, upon the colt he rides! The day has come!"

The second rabbi from the alleyway approaches, shooting a cold glare at the first.

"Foolishness! Gather your wits about you! This man is no king! I care not how many men approach him waving the palm or other branches!"

You watch as your father takes in the words of both teachers, who until this moment had never disagreed as far as you know. The tension between them is rising and your father, against his typically bold nature, only shakes his head. At first you expect him to dismiss it all as rubbish and escort his family back home, but his hesitation is enough proof to you that he is actually deliberating the testimony of the first rabbi.

Could this man on a colt truly be a king?

In an instant of anticipation so strong it defies description, you risk the wrath of your mother and father and break away from them, ignoring their call for you to return and weaving your way through the crowd to get a better view. For what seems like an eternity, you duck, sidestep, and squirm through what feels like an endless sea of bodies until, at last, you're standing at the front edge of the fray, only a stone's throw from the man on the colt.

Thoughts buzz through your mind as you take in the bizarre scene. A king would be surrounded by officials, soldiers, servants, women, gold, riches, and spectacle, not commoners... His entrance into Jerusalem would no doubt be a grand display of wealth and power...yet this man isn't the slightest bit ashamed by his lack of such grandeur. He almost resembles a servant, himself, though he sits straight, confident, and regal in his modest robe, like a great leader, in ironic juxtaposition to his surroundings.

The voices crying "Hosanna!" are now almost deafening. You bring your hands to your ears, but your eyes don't move from the rider.

As a meager child, and therefore largely unversed in the synagogue teachings, you can't imagine you would ever be important enough for the rider to look your way. But suddenly, he does.

The impression is instant, and somehow, you know it's a connection you will never forget. There is a kindness in his eyes that inspires deep warmth within—and the smile he offers somehow tells you he is open to being approached by little ones who would be considered an imposition to most important adults (Matthew 19:14)—but beyond that, there is something else...

As the rider bores into your soul with a mere gentle gaze, an impression of his authority and truthfulness boils up from your spirit. In an instant, you know.

This Man is the King!

Readers, can you only imagine?

The Triumphal Entry of Christ into Jerusalem (Matthew 21:1–9; Mark 11:1–10; Luke 19:28–38; John 12:12–15) was—for believers in and followers of Christ—the grandest and most comforting announcement in the history of Jerusalem. For unbelievers, skeptics, and the "holy men" whose corrupted hearts made a self-serving game of Yahweh's religion, this was a brazen show put on by a "blasphemer."

It is easy to miss the significance of this moment in history. Jesus was, in this very moment, fulfilling a very important prophecy from Israel's history: "Rejoice greatly, O daughter of Zion; shout, O daughter of Jerusalem: Behold, thy King cometh unto thee: he is just, and having salvation; lowly, and riding upon an ass, and upon a colt the foal of an ass" (Zechariah 9:9).

The educated Jews in the assembly who knew of prophecy would have recognized this. On that day, these observers had to either believe in Jesus as Messiah or see His daring gesture as sacrilege. Because Jesus did not appear to be overthrowing earthly governmental powers, the conclusion for many Jews quickly became that He was a false messiah—thus a blasphemer, a *pretender*, another "Judas the Galilean" of days gone by.

To the commoners in the crowd, Jesus' entry showed Him as their Champion and Savior. In ancient tradition, when a soldier went to war and was victorious, he would make a triumphal reentry into the city—known as a "parade of triumph"—carrying His spoils of war.[67] When such a warrior was entering a defeated city and claiming it as his own territory, the preexisting king and cohorts would be stripped of their throne, power, and royal garments, and sometimes they were even executed publicly. The conqueror would then claim or install the role of king and receive the keys to the city. Public response fell into two categories: celebrate and embrace the new king, or become part of the defeated population (and be enslaved, executed, etc.).

Jesus had endured the temptation in the wilderness and emerged victorious. This triumph solidified (not that there was ever any doubt!) the fact that He was ready, capable, and resolved regarding the final, brutal battle ahead. He was there established as the victor, riding as Champion through the streets of Jerusalem, announcing Himself as the conquering Warrior and soon-to-be-crowned King.[68] The public response involving palm leaves indicated their acceptance of Him. However, His wilderness conquest had been a spiritual one, and His announcement as King, Champion, and Savior staked His claim in the unseen realm as well. This was His announcement to the crowd of "regular Joes."

In His announcement to Rome and Israel that a new King had arrived via a Triumphal Entry, He was not only carrying out a prophecy and announcing Himself Victor, He was also reenacting an important Old Testament parallel. Toward the end of David's reign, as the king grew old, his son, Adonijah, attempted to exalt himself as David's successor (1 Kings 1:5). He did this without consulting advisors or his brother, Solomon (verse 10), despite the fact that God had told David his *immediate* reign would continue through Solomon (1 Chronicles 22:9–10). After some intervention from Nathan, the prophet, and Bathsheba, one of his wives, David was made aware of Adonijah's political tactics and swore Solomon would be his successor (1 Kings 1:24–30). David then handed over his personal mule to Solomon and ordered his son to ride it to Gihon, where he would be proclaimed and anointed as the new king of Israel. From there, he was to ride in a procession to *Jerusalem*, where he would sit on David's throne and officially claim kingship (1:33–35). This order was obeyed, and during the march toward Jerusalem, the accompanying entourage played music and celebrated so loudly that from a distance it sounded like a great uproar (1:38–41). (All the while, Adonijah's group was unaware of what was going on; they remained so until the noise of Solomon's parade caused them to investigate the source of the hubbub.)

Don't miss the significance of this: The kingdom of Israel had eagerly awaited the announcement of the new king. The contested throne had sat empty, waiting for its new champion to take his seat on it. Then, majestically, the answer came riding in on the royal donkey. It didn't matter who attempted to contest the throne or upon what grounds—there was no altering the *truth* of precisely who would reign.

The arrival of Solomon—the biological son of David—at Jerusalem was a historic moment when God's "anointed one" (as kings were often called) was officially established as the king over Yahweh's people. The arrival of Jesus—the fulfillment of the prophesied Son of David—at Jerusalem was *the* historic moment when God's Anointed One was officially and forever established as the one and only King over the Father's people!

The King of all kings. He came riding in on a donkey and an entourage followed Him, rejoicing, proclaiming: "Hosanna to the Son of David: Blessed is He that cometh in the name of the Lord; Hosanna in the highest." They praised loudly enough to catch the attention of every other competing governmental power. Just as Solomon peacefully reclaimed a contested throne by riding into Jerusalem on a donkey, Jesus boldly, yet *peacefully*, rode into Jerusalem, and made the statement: "I am the true, Anointed One, the Son of David, and I'm here to reclaim the contested spiritual territory of this world."

The revelers and believers couldn't be more thrilled! They simply couldn't believe this was finally happening!

…But the religious leaders and unbelievers couldn't be more insulted. They, too, could not believe this was happening. It was likely in this moment that several began to hatch a plan to kill Him. Yet, Jesus wasn't done ruffling feathers—not by a long shot. Nor would His cheerful waves last long. He was now arriving at His Father's holy city…and He would *not* be happy to see how the Pharisees, Sadducees, scribes, and Jewish elite were running the Temple. He went as far as to storm in and say so without batting an eye.

You see, Zechariah had prophesied that, one day, "there shall be no more the Canaanite in the house of the Lord of hosts" (14:21). Canaanite, in this context, referred to traders. Hezekiah and Josiah made the Hebrews' holy places sacred again (2 Kings 18:4; 2 Kings 22:3–23:25), and no Jew would question such a thing—the act or the one who carried it out—from the scrolls of the past.

But it was a completely different picture having this "impudent" Jesus of Nazareth carry it out like He did (Matthew 21:12–13; Mark 11:15–17; Luke 19:45–46; John 2:13–22). When He found out the outer courts of His Father's house of prayer had become a marketplace, He was furious! That was the *only* area the non-Jews were allowed to worship in. The squawking of the manhandled birds, the scuffling about of the cattle, the bleating of the sheep, and the voices of men calling out from their booths—all of this noise was permitted by the most highly respected Jewish leaders because of their blatant disregard for those who weren't lucky enough to have been born and raised Jewish. (It would be similar to someone charging into a local church in the middle of a sermon or prayer-hour with a circus every Sunday.)

Surprisingly, this was only one tiny part of the problem, though.

All the commerce of this area of the ancient world operated with the Roman currency, but those coins featured the faces of pagan rulers and were not worthy to exchange in the house of God. The Temple, however, required an offering (a tax, really) of Jewish money for its services (Exodus 30:11–16). A Jew would arrive with his family, give a moneychanger his Roman money, and for a hefty fee, he would receive Hebrew coins with which he would pay the Temple tax. Over time, this money-changing "convenience" had become a lucrative scheme that rendered the religious leaders as being guilty of the same atrocity as the tax collectors in that they were pocketing (for themselves or their supervisors) more money than needed for the exchange. Yet, it goes further: Those who brought their own animals had to pass the "perfection inspection" at the Temple's entrance prior to offering the sacrifice. A wicked trade trick developed wherein the inspectors would declare any animal (no matter how spotless) unfit for sacrifice. Then they would make a grand sum of money by reselling their own sacrificial sheep to the poor men whose animals were deemed unworthy. Then, the con men would wait until heads were turned and would escort the "unfit" sheep to the back of the pen, selling it as "fit for sacrifice" to the next victim. Additionally, the people traveling from afar for the Passover found their trip to be very difficult to take with animals along for the ride. So, in the interest of profit, religious leaders set up a marketplace with "perfect" animals and moneychangers *right there* in the outer court of the Temple. The noise was deafening at Passover time, and the corrupt dealings—the financial profit raked in from the worship of God—on God's property was an offense both to Yahweh (Exodus 22:21; Leviticus 19:34), as well as to His Son, who observed this "marketplace" trickery in person.

Isaiah 56:7 states: "Even them [foreigners] will I bring to my holy mountain, and make them joyful in my house of prayer: their burnt offerings and their sacrifices shall be accepted upon mine altar; for mine house shall be called an house of prayer for all people." The joy of the Lord was on this prophecy, imagining a day when Jerusalem's Temple would be a place of honest worship for all who wanted to commit their lives to the Father, including foreigners and Gentiles. His Temple, then, would be known to all as a "house of prayer."

Jeremiah 7:11 states: "Is this house, which is called by my name, become a den of robbers in your eyes? Behold, even I have seen it, saith the Lord." This rebuked those who were abusing Temple worship in the Old Testament by oppressing the poor. God, through Jeremiah, called these men "robbers." Yet this was the same grievance the Jewish leaders were guilty of when King Yeshua came to the Temple just after His Triumphal Entry.

Jesus made a whip out of cords (John 2:15) and shamelessly marched into the Temple courts, overturning tables and running both the animals (sheep, cattle, and doves) and the moneychangers from their booths, saying, "My house shall be called of all nations the house of prayer? but ye have made it a den of thieves!" (Matthew 11:17). By using the contrast of a beautiful picture in Isaiah and the reproach of oppressors in Jeremiah, Jesus didn't *just* run around throwing furniture and coins and shooing away the animals of a corrupt sacrifice scheme. He threw a word dagger at every Jew in His vicinity, using Old Testament words that would *sting*. He accused the Temple brethren of turning their backs on God's hopes for a place of prayer and worship while spitting on His sovereignty as they tyrannized the destitute. That was about as colossal of an affront to Jewish leaders as any of them had seen in multiple generations.

And, if some interpreters are correct, Jesus did this *twice*!

John 2:11–12 might describe this event as happening shortly after the wedding at Cana, and it notes Jesus was confronted by Temple leaders during the cleansing event (John 2:18). The Synoptics describe it as happening just after the Triumphal Entry during the Passion Week, and Jewish leaders confronted Jesus the next day (Matthew 21:17–23). (Also, only John mentions a whip of cords.) So, either John's wording can be interpreted to mean the same time as the Synoptics, *or*, Jesus actually drove the moneychangers, thieves, robbers, crooks, and animals out on two occasions. (We can't be sure either way, but if it was, in fact, two cleansings, Jesus would have been seen as even more of a blight by these debased men.)

Jews ran to challenge Jesus, asking for a sign to show them whose authority He was working under that allowed Him to do these things (John 2:18). His answer came as a shock: "Destroy this temple, and in three days I will raise it up" (2:19). John's Gospel immediately explains that Jesus "spake of the temple of his body" (2:21), but the pious men didn't get it: "Forty and six years was this temple in building, and wilt thou rear it up in three days?" (2:20). Someday soon—someday just around the corner from then—a lot of people would "get it."

Most films depicting this scene tend to present it as a moment when every single jaw drops and people are startled. However, the poor folks among the crowd that day likely cheered and spurred Jesus on. Scholars are nearly unanimous in asserting that the wealthier Jewish classes were accustomed to this sort of treatment and it didn't faze them much. The lower-class Jews, however, put in a lot of time and effort to be in Jerusalem every year, and each time, they were taken advantage of in a way that no prior preparation or arrangements could prevent. No matter how kosher (lawful) their sheep, the unscrupulous inspectors would still find flaws in them, refusing them entry into the Temple unless they sold the animal for half what it was worth and purchased one of the blessed "approved" animals for two or three times what it was worth. (No doubt some were aware that their "flawed" sheep were being escorted to the sale pen for the next guys to buy as "perfect.") Jesus, in this scene, wasn't just a madman to *everyone*. To some, He was a hero, and that likely wouldn't have settled well with those He found in need of reproach.

And it would definitely be brought to the attention of the high priest!

By now, Jesus was making the wrong people angry…and when He drove the mob from the Temple, He was making a strong statement:

"Religion as you know it is over!" Not only did this anger the religious leaders, it also made them insecure that their carefully crafted world was changing.

Considering the delicate religio-political relationship between the Sanhedrin and Rome, this would put the priests on guard.

And this Jesus wasn't just any Johnny-come-lately. This Man had the power to heal, and cast out devils, and He even had the audacity to tell people their sins were forgiven—an act only carried out by God or the gods before His time. Who did this guy think He *was*? It likely caused many to wonder: Is this *really* the Messiah? Or is He only the latest to provoke Rome into retaliation? Will He, just as Simon of Peraea, Athronges the Shepherd, Judas the Galilean, and so many others, *also* fall victim to Rome's cruelty?

As Jesus' teachings, healings, miracles, and other interactions began to gain attention, local authorities became aware of Him. And, the more He spoke of the Kingdom of God, the more He was cast as a potential political rebel. While this marked Him by local authorities as a character to watch closely, it deemed Him among the civilians as one who could show with proof that He could accomplish what He said (which was why He did gain a great following).

However, when such talk was not accompanied by political action, it served at times to breed resentment among the crowds. They wanted Rome gone—and if this wasn't possible, then it was better not to provoke Rome in the first place. Jesus' talk regarding His Kingdom was accompanied only by peaceful promises—none outlining victorious warfare, and when He was questioned about it, He answered in ambiguous tones about it "not being of this world."

What was *that* about? That wasn't at all what the Jewish men had been telling everyone the Messiah would be!

With these and nearly countless other examples, Jesus made people nervous by just about everything He did, because He *acted* like the Messiah, but He was not pulling the political deliverer act. People didn't like the negative attention being drawn to their area, *unless* the person drawing such attention was going to make good on the promises of delivering Jews from Rome. It was an earth-shatteringly important "do it or don't" moment because of the inflammatory and seemingly confrontational teachings of Christ's Kingdom.

Then, in the midst of this, Jesus raised the dead (Matthew 9:18, 23–26; Mark 5:21–24, 35–43; Luke 7:11–17; 8:40–42, 49–56; John 11:1–45).

The buzz throughout the region of this event was the very, *very* last straw...

These acts were completely undeniable, and rumors spread all over the place *fast*. Teaching radical ideas, calming seas, or healing people was one thing, but the words that came out of Christ's mouth when raising the dead set the stage for His execution. When Jesus was told, "Lord, if thou hadst been here, my brother [would not have] died" (John 11:21, 32), His response was, once again, that it had been done for the glory of God (11:40). In other words, "This happened because God is going to show you *His* power—right here, right now, not through Rome, not through the synagogue, but through *Me*."

Whoa... The resident "rabble-rouser" had crossed a line for the last time. He had authority over life and death, and it wasn't benefitting either the Jews or the Romans! What's worse, if He was as powerful as being able to call a soul back into its body, He might actually have the power needed to conquer Rome after all!

Jesus had done what no other rebel before Him could do: prove Himself to be a completely unpredictable wildcard. And He took it all to the maximum, trumping all prior "would-be" messiahs who talked a lot of talk and even conjured political rebellion, but who were ultimately proven to be...just men. Yeshua of Galilee had now ascertained He had unlimited supernatural power at His command. Romans who weren't worried about saving the religious institution didn't seem to care where His power came from. If, like the Pharisees said, His source was demonic, it made little difference to them, so long as He was actually holding the power of the unseen realm in His hand.

With the raising of Lazarus and others, what would stop Jesus from going against the state, then the Empire, with unlimited armies of men who, once killed, could be easily resurrected and fully restored for other rounds of battle?! Even Rome was beginning to think this guy had to go… And this made the religious leaders very, *very* happy indeed.

But wait.

If He *was* that powerful, who would be the unlucky sap who had to take Him down? How would he go about doing it?

Tension Builds Toward Execution

Those plotting the death of Jesus were already taking notes as to who knew Him and who could be trusted to betray Him. Meanwhile, Jesus remained free, teaching about the Kingdom in clear parables He, Himself, frequently interpreted (if or when His listeners were confused). Many of Christ's stories ended with a statement such as, "As [these characters have done], so will the Father do for you," or, "If [this character did that], how much more so will the Father do for you?" Jesus was in every way a Prophet of Yahweh, but He understood that many seekers needed more than just mysterious words.

Early on, Christ was always surrounded by twelve men who became the group of disciples we hear about most often. These twelve certainly weren't His only followers, but were the ones who became apostles, leaving everything in their natural lives to follow Him because they believed so much in His identity as Messiah. Some of the men should have been, in any other setting, natural enemies. For instance, a tax collector (Matthew) and a Zealot (Simon) normally would never occupy the same dinner table, but an encounter with the personal Jesus changed all of that. Even while Christ still lived, the Gospels explain, these disciples went into the surrounding cities or back to their hometowns and preached the message of Christ to all who would listen; further, they healed the sick, cured the afflicted, and produced many miracles and signs of the Christ (Matthew 11:1; Mark 6:12–13; Luke 9:6).

Jesus had already, many times, warned His disciples of His upcoming death (John 1:29; 2:19; 3:14; Matthew 9:15; 10:38–39; 12:39–40). To make Himself more clear, He told them again, and in no uncertain terms (Matthew 16:21–23; Mark 8:31–33; Luke 9:22). He knew down to the very last detail what was coming down the pike, explaining these details "openly," including those about His own Resurrection:

> And he began to teach them, that the Son of man must suffer many things, and be rejected of the elders, and of the chief priests, and scribes, and be killed, and after three days rise again. And he spake that saying openly. (Mark 8:31–32)

A short time later, Jesus reiterated these predictions, once again explaining to His disciples that His death was nigh (Matthew 17:22–23; Mark 9:30–32; Luke 9:43b–45): "For he taught his disciples, and said unto them, 'The Son of man is delivered [betrayed] into the hands of men, and they shall kill him; and after that he is killed, he shall rise the third day'" (Mark 9:31). But, each time Jesus tried to tell the twelve what was to become of Him, "they understood not" (Mark 9:32).

That Jesus was correct in His prophecies is not only clear to us *now*, it was clear to many *then*. In fact, though the plot against Jesus had begun earlier in His public ministry, as early as John 5:18, we read of the Sanhedrin's official stance: "Therefore the Jews sought the more to kill him, because he not only had broken the sabbath, but said also that God was his Father, making himself equal with God." When Jesus arrived in Jerusalem for the Feast of Tabernacles, members of the general public were picking up on the rumors: "Then said some of them of Jerusalem, 'Is not this he, whom they seek to kill?'" (John

7:25). Despite this, Jesus maintained a fearless face toward the public, even going to the Temple courts to teach (John 7:14). (And everyone who heard His teaching repeatedly left His presence in astonishment, saying He spoke with extreme authority [Matthew 7:28–29; Mark 1:22; Luke 2:46–47]. However, there were always some who believed His words originated from someplace dark [John 7:21].)

Nevertheless, despite the rumors of murder and execution, Jesus' following continued to grow, and everywhere He spoke or taught, murmurings of who He was and what He was doing echoed behind Him. This led to the first attempt at His arrest:

> The Pharisees heard that the people murmured such things con-
> cerning him; and the Pharisees and the chief priests sent officers
> to take him. Then said Jesus unto them, "Yet a little while am
> I with you, and then I go unto him that sent me. Ye shall seek
> me, and shall not find me: and where I am, thither ye cannot
> come." Then said the Jews among themselves, "Whither will
> he go, that we shall not find him? will he go unto the dispersed
> among the Gentiles, and teach the Gentiles? What manner of
> saying is this that he said, 'Ye shall seek me, and shall not find
> me: and where I am, thither ye cannot come'?" (John 7:32–36)

Those who had come to arrest Jesus ended up leaving empty-handed and perplexed. But on the last day of the Feast of Tabernacles, Jesus would say something damning. With a loud voice, Jesus cried out to a crowd: "If any man thirst, let him come unto me, and drink. He that believeth on me, as the scripture hath said, out of his belly shall flow rivers of living water" (John 7:37–38). One might wonder what the big deal was—why *this* statement would curl all toes that weren't curled already.

First, this was a fulfillment of Ezekiel 47:1–10, which had spo-ken of a River of the Water of Life that would flow from Jerusalem to the surrounding regions—that is, the spread of the Gospel of

Christ, which was developing now in their presence. This passage of Scripture was featured in one of the ceremonial readings of the Feast of Tabernacles.

But another passage—one *also* featured during the Tabernacles observance—was also fulfilled: "Living waters shall go out from Jerusalem" (Zechariah 14:8).

Whether the religious leaders completely understood that or not, however, one thing they did catch was the connection between Jesus' declarations of being "Living Water" on the same day as their messianic water-pouring ritual, followed by His boldly identifying Himself as the very Light the Feast of Tabernacles foreshadowed. Allie Anderson, coauthor of *The Messenger*, makes short work of this conundrum for us:

At the time Jesus walked the earth, on the last day of the Feast of Tabernacles, also called *Hoshanah Rabbah* (meaning "The Day of the Great Hosanna"), something called the ritual of water pouring took place.[69] This was a petition for God to send the Messiah to save/deliver them. The water pouring was also an act of faith, as the rainy season had not yet arrived. Thus, this offering was as a statement of faith that God would send adequate rain in the upcoming months, but its deeper meaning was a supplication for the forthcoming Messiah, and the life-saving deliverance that He would bring with Him. The ritual consisted of one priest using a golden receptacle to retrieve water from the Pool of Siloam, which he then delivered to the High Priest in the Temple. The contents would then be emptied into a basin which sat below the altar, which signified the Messiah's coming.

Meanwhile, nearby priests blew shofars as onlookers waved palm leaves and sang the praises of the Most High God. These traditions draw from Isaiah 12:3 and 44:3: "Therefore with joy shall ye draw water out of the wells of salvation," "For I will pour water upon him that is thirsty, and floods upon the dry ground: I will pour my spirit upon thy seed, and my blessing upon thine offspring."...

It was on *Hoshanah Rabbah* that "Jesus stood and cried, saying, "If any man thirst, let him come unto me, and drink. He that believeth on me, as the scripture hath said, out of his belly shall flow rivers of living water" (John 7:37–38). In other words, while those in the Temple poured water in petition to God to provide the blessing of rain in the upcoming seasons and to send the Delivering Messiah, Jesus stood in the midst of them and explained to them that the answer to their prayers had *already* arrived. Likewise, this was His way of explaining to them that while the waters of this earth (even those drawn from the Pool of Siloam) were temporary and fleeting, His was the true water of life which would forever satisfy.

Unfortunately, we see in the following verse that only some of them *truly* heard His message: "But this spake he of the Spirit, which they that believe on him should receive: for the Holy Ghost was not yet given; because that Jesus was not yet glorified" (John 7:39). Of those who understood His message, many began comparing prophetic lineages and birth-origins to what they knew of Him in attempt to discern His true identity. Jesus, later (that is to say, later the same day on a *Hebrew* calendar, but by modern Gregorian day-counts would be considered the afternoon of the following day), *also* took ownership of another unique aspect of this feast's elements.

The Lighting of the Temple

Another factor associated with this feast was the Temple Lighting. Because people would make a pilgrimage from miles around and then reside in temporary booths which were built on-site for the week of this feast, the entire area would be lit with tens of thousands of burning torches which illuminated the entire city of Jerusalem. The Temple was filled with golden lampposts which were lit, and other illuminations were located all throughout the town. All of this radiance signified the Light of the forthcoming Messiah (Isaiah 49:6). The glow held an ambient factor which became known as the "lighting of the Temple." Since the entire city would be filled with torches of walking travelers, it illuminated a residual luminosity which could be seen from a distance. Jesus, after a night spent amongst these burning torches, said to those around Him, "I am the light of the world. He who follows me shall not walk in darkness, but have the light of life" (John 8:12). Many modern readers overlook the significance of these statements made by Jesus (His being the Water and the Light) because they don't catch the implications of such a statement within the cultural setting of the feast. Because of lack of cultural understanding, they often miss that Jesus essentially stood among the populace and told them that He was *the very answer they were looking for*: the cool drink to quench all thirst, and the brilliance that would never leave them in the darkness.[70]

Furthermore, while the priest was pouring the water, he would quote the prophecy from Isaiah 12:3: "Therefore with joy shall ye draw water out of the wells of salvation." The rock (or Rock) in the wilderness that sprang forth water was on the minds of the Jews. Jesus was linking Himself both to the wells of eternal salvation *and* to the Exodus account, when God's people were freed from the dictatorship of Pharaoh. (Later, Paul would write that "all our fathers...drank of that spiritual Rock that followed them: and that Rock was Christ," confirming Jesus was, in fact, the Rock in the wilderness, and now we see He was/is the Water as well [1 Corinthians 10:1, 4].) The reaction of the crowd shows just how close Jesus is to the time of His capture:

Many of the people therefore, when they heard this saying, said, "Of a truth this is the Prophet." Others said, "This is the Christ." But some said, "Shall Christ come out of Galilee? Hath not the scripture said, 'That Christ cometh of the seed of David, and out of the town of Bethlehem, where David was?'" So there was a division among the people because of him. And some of them would have taken him; but no man laid hands on him. (John 7:40–44)

No longer were the multitudes appearing only outside Jerusalem. Jesus brought belief inside the city, to the *very door of the Temple*, in the middle of rich ceremony about a Someday Messiah, and people were seeing something within Him and His words that helped them recognize He was every bit the fulfillment He claimed to be. The people were "divided" about Him because not all of them knew His lineage; He was known publicly as a Galilean. It would only be a matter of time until everyone found out that He was, in fact, from "Bethlehem, where David was."

As far as the officers who "would have taken him" but didn't, they would answer to the Pharisees immediately after the event. When asked why He wasn't arrested then and there, the officers reported that they were stunned because no man before Jesus had ever spoken like Him (John 7:45–46).

Our precious Yeshua had certainly been in a "challenge-and-riposte" position many times prior (for instance, His healings on the Sabbath: Matthew 12:10; Mark 3:2; Luke 6:7; review the subsection called "The 'Word'" to revisit this public challenge). But on this particular day and event, things ramped up quite a bit. As Jesus was quietly teaching in the Temple the morning after His "Living Water" comments, the Pharisees and scribes burst in with a woman, standing her in their midst (probably roughly handling her, scholars believe), and said, "Master [or Teacher], this woman was taken in adultery, in the very act" (John 8:4). Their eagerness is made clear by their repetition. Nobody needed to hear she had been "taken in adultery" *and* "in the very act" to believe she had been caught. We can almost imagine the "aha!" look in their eyes and the grin across their conniving lips as they went on to question the Savior: "Now Moses in the law commanded us, that such should be stoned: but what sayest thou?" (John 8:5). Do you hear the same "nanny-nanny-noo-noo" tone these authors do? It's like kids on a playground: "Teacher, the principal said that if anybody was caught doing what she just did, they would be expelled. But what do *you* say? Huh? Man I can't wait to hear *this*…"

According to the Law, if a couple was found to be involved in this crime against fidelity, both the man and the woman were to be stoned to death (Leviticus 20:10; Deuteronomy 22:22). Throughout the years, almost all scholarly sources visit the same question: Where's the guy? The answer, apart from the obvious (we have no idea where he was), is that the scribes and Pharisees didn't give a hoot where he was. Nor would they have been as interested in this woman if she wasn't providing the means for a potential entrapment of the resident Messiah.

All who were present, no doubt, were on the edges of their seats as they waited to hear what Jesus would say to this. On one hand, if He told the religious leaders to stone her, it would go against everything loving the Messiah had stood for and taught about, while simultaneously marking Himself as one who would *dare* consider Himself capable of exacting capital punishment—a privilege only the Romans had the legal right to carry out. The Romans would have loved that, as it would have immediately usurped their authority and allowed them to then pursue Him criminally. On the other hand, if He told them *not* to stone her, He would be going against the Mosaic Law (which He came to fulfill, though that work was not yet complete). Either answer He gave would be lacking, and finally, they would have Him right where they wanted Him!

Challenge and riposte. Game, set, match. Go!

Yet, they were outmatched.

Jesus stooped down and wrote something with His fingertip on the ground, and then told His audience: "He that is without sin among you, let him first cast a stone at her" (John 8:7).

In that short string of words, He beat them at their own game.

Again.

As for what Jesus wrote with His fingertip, nobody has ever known for certain. However, considering the most recent "offensive" statement about Jesus being the "Water" the day before, and the way the religious men had forsaken God by this time, many scholars have guessed He may have referenced Jeremiah 17:13: "O Lord, the hope of Israel, all that forsake thee shall be ashamed, and they that depart from me shall be *written in the earth*, because they have forsaken the Lord, the fountain of living waters" (emphasis added). If this is in fact what He wrote (or even if it was a reference to it His audience would have recognized), then it would have been seriously, grievously convicting. The words "written in the earth" can also be translated "written in the dirt." Jesus was essentially writing in the dirt with His finger, and the allusion would have been clear: These men had "forsaken" God and Israel, and they would be "ashamed" for also forsaking the "Living Water" to whom they had just rushed to ensnare.

Some in the crowd felt immediate conviction, and from the eldest to the "last," they dropped their stones and walked away (John 8:9). They didn't even take the woman with them (once again showing their concern was not for her, but for tricking Jesus). Jesus knew what they were up to, and He responded in the woman's favor without going as far as dismissing her sin. In the beautiful, loving way Jesus often spoke, He simply told her, "Go, and sin no more" (8:11).

Now, before we assume Jesus outwitted these men only by logic and grace, keep in mind Deuteronomy 17:7 stipulated that the first stone was to be thrown by the *witnesses* of the adulterous act, while 22:22 stated both parties to be stoned. Before Jesus' last, merciful words to the woman, He asked where her accusers were, and she admitted they were not present (John 8:10–11). Had Jesus, in His majestic oneness with the Father, already known her witnesses were not also among her accusers? If so, then we can assume He already knew they would never be allowed to execute her according to the Law anyway, and it was also obvious that the man who was also guilty was nowhere around, cancelling lawful execution on two accounts. This renders His reaction even more compassionate, as He made her case about love and redemption rather than standing up in the crowd and demanding they proceed to produce witnesses and the other offender (which they may have been able to do, but either way, it would have forced her already humiliating adultery case to drag on longer).

Jesus went on with His teaching, once again declaring Himself the Son of God, to the chagrin of the Pharisees who were still looking for every opportunity to have Him arrested. For what must have been the hundredth time, He told His listeners He would have to depart from them, but again, they didn't understand. It was in this very conversation that He said, "Before Abraham was, I am."

If this sounds like broken English to you, that's because it is. Jesus used a past-tense term, "was," followed by the present-tense, "am." Here's what many Christians today miss: God's "unspeakable name" (the Tetragrammaton)—the name that would someday be transliterated into "Yahweh" or "Jehovah"—was "I AM." This was the name Yahweh used to identify Himself to Moses at the site of the burning bush (Exodus 3:14), and scholars generally agree it refers to the Father's eternal, omniscient, omnipresent nature. In other words, "Before Abraham was ever born, I was and am God." Whether or not we recognize it now, any devout Jew in Jesus' gathering at the Temple would have instantly caught the significance of the expression.

Not only that, but the name was *unspeakable*! The Jews believed it was such a holy utterance that no mere human would ever be allowed to say it audibly. So, in one fell swoop, Jesus not only said something aloud that would have been more offensive to these unbelievers than a preacher dropping the F-bomb during a sermon today, but He also did so *while* claiming to be God in the flesh!

Man oh man, Jesus was bold...

In the very next verse, we read the unbelieving Jews amidst them picked up stones and readied themselves to kill Him on the spot, but Jesus slipped out of the Temple and went to heal a blind man on the Sabbath (John 8:59–9:7). At that scene, while the Pharisees were busying themselves with pelting the blind man with questions and trying to discover a loophole to pave the way for Jesus' death, Jesus continued to teach and gather His followers, sending seventy of them out to heal the sick and preach to the surrounding regions that the Kingdom of God was near (Luke 10:1–16).

After Jesus taught His disciples how to pray, He was accused of casting out a demon by the power of Beelzebub (Luke 11:15). Those in the assembly who wanted to provoke Him further said He must produce a sign. Every beautiful miracle Jesus had performed up to this point had been a "sign" (refer back to our section "Miracles of Jesus"). Now, quite unbelievably, they were demanding more. This wasn't because a sincere seeker was present, but because they were fixed upon their unbelief. Yet another "sign" to these people would not prove anything further, and Jesus knew it. His response to them was that the only sign *they* would see was "the sign of Jonah the prophet. For as Jonah was a sign unto the Ninevites, so shall also the Son of man be to this generation" (11:29–30).

In the upcoming act of death, burial in a tomb, and Resurrection on the third day, Jesus would fulfill every way the prophet Jonah had foreshadowed Jesus. As the "sign unto the Ninevites" was Jonah appearing from the "belly of a great fish" after three days, the "sign unto the unbelievers" would be Jesus appearing from the "belly of the tomb" after three days.

Herod Antipas was, not surprisingly, informed of the commotion surrounding the Messiah, and Jesus' name therefore became "well known" to him. In his heavy misinterpretation of the news, the king thought Jesus was the resurrected John the Baptist (Matthew 14:1–2; Mark 6:14–16; Luke 9:7–9). Some of Herod's servants were disciples of Christ as well (Luke 8:3), so it's likely he felt intimidated by Jesus' popularity. Not surprisingly, a few folks rushed to tell Jesus that Herod planned to kill Him (Luke 13:31). (The messengers were Pharisees, and it's unclear whether they were supporters of Jesus who truly wanted Him to hide, or if they were in with Herod on some scheme to get Him back into Jerusalem sooner.) Jesus' response is telling: "Go tell that fox that I will keep on casting out demons and healing people today and tomorrow; and the third day I will accomplish my purpose. Yes, today, tomorrow, and the next day I must proceed on my way. For it wouldn't do for a prophet of God to be killed except in Jerusalem!" (Luke 13:32–33; NLT [New Living Translation]). He knew His own end already, and had been warning His devotees for months about that reality. Then, He heard the king was officially hunting Him down and acknowledged that His execution *would* be carried out, but it would be done in Jerusalem—a detail no regular humans would know in advance of their own death, nor could they ever have the authority to arrange on their own, or His, behalf.

In addition, Jesus called Herod a "fox." This was a term the Jews used when referring to a man whose worldly pursuits were cunning and sly, but ultimately worthless in light of eternity. It was a major insult in a day when language about a king and "god" of the Imperial Cult should have been worshipful and doting. Jesus' unwillingness to acknowledge Herod's majesty was a serious insult. Yet, far from responding with an aloof or uncaring reaction, Jesus wept for the state of Jerusalem (Luke 13:34–35).

After Jesus had raised Lazarus, which, as previously stated, caused the stir that sealed Christ's fate:

[M]any of the Jews...believed on him. But some of them went their ways to the Pharisees, and told them what things Jesus had done.

Then gathered the chief priests and the Pharisees a council, and said, "What do we? for this man doeth many miracles. If we let him thus alone, all men will believe on him: and the Romans shall come and take away both our place and nation."

And one of them, named Caiaphas, being the high priest that same year, said unto them, "Ye know nothing at all, Nor consider that it is expedient for us, that one man should die for the people, and that the whole nation perish not."...

One unusual detail that's easy to misunderstand is why, at the time of Christ, there were two high priests. This was not a Jewish decision. When the Jews elected a high priest, that man maintained that seat until death. Annas had been acknowledged as high priest from AD 7–14. Then the Romans displaced him, and Caiaphas (Annas' son-in-law) was appointed; he held the position from AD 18–36. But, in the Jews' opinion, Annas was still the reigning high priest, so in the trial of Jesus, Annas—who held supreme power in the Jewish community and no power politically—both high priests would be involved.

The irony of Caiaphas' words about "one man" dying for "the whole nation [who would therefore] perish not" is not lost on the modern audience. When he spoke them, he no doubt expected that Jesus would be the sacrifice for the better of all, though he didn't know Jesus' death would be the spiritual activity that would accomplish an eternal benefit for souls even outside his own "nation."

Following His Triumphal Entry into Jerusalem, Jesus heard a group of Greeks were looking for Him, and His favorable response showed His willingness to die even for those who don't belong to the nation of Israel: "The hour is come, that the Son of man should be glorified... Now is my soul troubled; and what shall I say? Father, save me from this hour: but for this cause came I unto this hour" (John 12:23, 27). When Jesus, in this heartfelt moment, asked the Father to glorify His own name, "Then came there a voice from heaven, saying, 'I have both glorified it, and will glorify it again.' The people therefore, that stood by, and heard it, said that it thundered: others said, 'An angel spake to him'" (12:28–29). Jesus explained the voice was for *their* sake (12:30), so they might see the end of the Son of Man and know it was what God intended despite the gruesomeness of what was necessary for His work.

As He taught in and around the Temple during His last week, He was again challenged by religious leaders regarding His authority. He rose to the occasion with His own challenge and riposte, and once again won, leaving them with nothing further to say (Matthew 21:25–27; Luke 20:6; Mark 11:32). He proceeded to teach three (terrifying) parables regarding the Kingdom implications of those who reject Him as the Son of God (Matthew 21:28–22:14; Mark 12:1–12; Luke 20:9–19).

In the face of continual threats, Jesus rose again and again in boldness, refusing to be intimidated by the circumstances He knew would come before the week was out. This obviously angered the religious leaders, who responded by setting a series of traps (Matthew 22:15). Each trap was a syrupy, lovey-dovey, innocent-sounding, and civilly worded question designed to stump the Teacher, and each one of them failed.

First, a group of Pharisees and spies of Herod asked Jesus if taxes should be paid to Caesar (Matthew 22:15–22; Mark 12:13–17; Luke 20:20–26). Had Jesus said "no," He likely would have been arrested by Herod's spies on the spot and executed immediately. Had He supported taxation, it would have gone against everything He had been teaching about alliance to a spiritual Kingdom (a concept people were still unsure of, but were willing to hear more about). "But Jesus perceived their wickedness, and said, 'Why tempt ye me, ye hypocrites?… Render therefore unto Caesar the things which are Caesar's; and unto God the things that are God's,'" so they once again walked away in defeat (Matthew 22:18, 21–22).

Second, the Sadducees, who did *not* believe in a resurrection beyond the grave of Sheol, came with a riddle: A woman marries a man and does not have children, so, as per the Mosaic Law, after the woman's husband dies, the brother of the deceased takes her as his own, yet she does not produce offspring for him, either. Seven times this woman marries into this family of brothers, and there is never a child. Therefore, in the resurrection beyond Sheol, whose wife of the brothers would she be? (Matthew 22:23–33; Mark 12:18–27; Luke 20:27–40). The Sadducees weren't even remotely interested in a real answer because they didn't believe in any of it anyway, but if Jesus said the woman would be a wife to all of them, it would indicate an incestuous scenario in heaven that defied the Mosaic Law. Jesus once again stifled their games by explaining the assignment of husbands and wives does not carry on into the afterlife. Then He warned His listeners regarding this kind of word-gamey religious abuse: "Beware of the scribes, which desire to walk in long robes, and love greetings in the markets, and the highest seats in the synagogues, and the chief rooms at feasts; Which devour widows' houses, and for a shew make long prayers: the same shall receive greater damnation" (Luke 20:46–47).

Third, an expert of the Law from within the circle of the Pharisees asked Jesus which of the Lord's commandments was the most important. Note the scribe didn't ask which one of the "Ten" Commandments, but which was most important out of *all* of the commandments (Matthew 22:34–40; Mark 12:28–34; see also Luke 10:25–27). This single question would have covered more than six hundred commands from the Old Testament, along with seemingly countless laws that had been intermingled with Jewish life from the Intertestamental Period forward. Absolutely any commandment Jesus could have chosen from this list could have been argued to be less important in some way than another, but Jesus was aware of the intent to trap Him. In His answer, He quoted from Deuteronomy 6:4–6, the *Shema Yisrael,* which was the "our God is one" statement the people of Israel wrote and placed above their doors and on their properties following the Exodus, and the Jews of Jesus' day still read it daily. Its pinnacle was, itself, a commandment: "And thou shalt love the Lord thy God with all thine heart, and with all thy soul, and with all thy might." Obedience to this one directive, Jesus knew, would essentially drive one to accomplish obedience to them all, together. However, He took it a step further, showing from the command of Leviticus 19:18 that second only to loving God is to "love thy neighbor" as much as one loves one's self. He finished by explaining: "On these two commandments hang all the law and the prophets" (Matthew 22:40).

The crowd of followers couldn't have been more pleased to see that the greatest and most pious minds of their day could not pull one over on Christ. Jesus used this moment of unadulterated attention upon Him to warn His audience not to ever become like those who had tried to entangle Him in terminological snares (Matthew 23:1–36; Mark 12:38–40; Luke 20:45–47). His rebuke was brave, indeed, as He went as far as to say: "Woe unto you, scribes and Pharisees, hypocrites! for ye compass sea and land to make one proselyte, and when he is made, ye make him twofold more the child of hell than yourselves" (Matthew 23:15). (By this, Jesus meant: They go to great distances to convert someone to their religion, and when they've succeeded, they've made him twice a child of hell than themselves because of their hypocritical religion.)

As Jesus' righteous anger mounted, He identified that He was not the first prophet these "vipers" and "snakes" had killed, and then ramped up the future reality of His death by prophetically acknowledging that others would die for His name:

Ye serpents, ye generation of vipers, how can ye escape the damnation of hell? Wherefore, behold, I send unto you prophets, and wise men, and scribes: and some of them ye shall kill and crucify; and some of them shall ye scourge in your synagogues, and persecute them from city to city: That upon you may come all the righteous blood shed upon the earth, from the blood of righteous Abel unto the blood of Zacharias son of Barachias, whom ye slew between the temple and the altar. Verily I say unto you, All these things shall come upon this generation. (Matthew 23:33–36)

As soon as the crowd broke up, Jesus continued to teach and instruct those who would listen regarding the future, including His words about a day when He would come *again* to this earth upon the clouds, though no man would know when (Matthew 24:29–31, 36–46; Mark 13:24–27, 32; Luke 21:25–27). Then He taught disciples how to be ready for that day through four more parables (Matthew 24:42–25:30; Mark 13:33–37; Luke 21:34–36). With that, the final preparations for death were in place, and Jesus began to submit Himself to that end: "And it came to pass, when Jesus had finished all these sayings, he said unto his disciples, 'Ye know that after two days is the feast of the passover, and the Son of man is betrayed to be crucified'" (Matthew 26:1–2).

> Then one of the twelve, called Judas Iscariot, went unto the chief priests, And said unto them, "What will ye give me, and I will deliver him unto you?" And they covenanted with him for thirty pieces of silver. And from that time he sought opportunity to betray him. (Matthew 26:14–16)

Jesus sat with His disciples to a legitimate Passover Seder meal. (For those who are curious about the timing of all these events and the apparent "contradiction" of days, please note that Jesus was a Galilean and, therefore, He followed the Galilean calendar, not the Judean one. This would have placed His meal in the evening a whole twenty-four hours prior to the Passover meal that most other Jews followed. A very well-researched and thorough treatment of these events is covered in *The Messenger*.)

He explained it was now His body, which would be broken for all, and His blood, which would be shed for all. This "communion," as stated in our reflection of Exodus (volume 1 of this series), wasn't new to the Jews. Prior to Christ's birth, it had been known as the ritual of the *afikomen*, when an unleavened cracker would be split into pieces, hidden somewhere dark, located after the meal, and shared among the Jews of a single household as a way of looking forward to the Someday Messiah. This time, however, Jesus did not instruct that the *afikomen* be hidden. Instead, He took the bread, broke it, and announced that the Passover and all of its symbols were fulfilled in Him: It was now His body and blood that would forever replace the lambs of the Passover. By choosing next to wash His disciples' feet, He set the example for all to follow in becoming lowly servants for others (John 13:12–20).

While they were eating, Jesus dropped a bomb: "Verily I say unto you, that one of you shall betray me" (John 13:21). The disciples were puzzled; who could among these devoted followers could possibly do such a thing? Jesus explained to John and Peter that the betrayer would be identified as the one to whom He would give a dipped morsel. Dipping a piece of food in the sauce served at Passover, He then handed the morsel to Judas, instructing him that what he was about to do needed to be done quickly. With that, Judas slipped out into the night to take word to the enemies of Jesus (John 13:27, 30). The price he was paid for this information was thirty pieces of silver.

Later, Judas—out of guilt—returned the money to the religious leaders. The silver, which became tainted as blood money, was used to buy the potter's field as a burial ground for foreigners.

In this, the prophecy of Zechariah 11:12–13 was fulfilled:

"If ye think good, give me my price; and if not, forbear." So they weighed for my price thirty pieces of silver. And the Lord said unto me, "Cast it unto the potter: a goodly price that I was prised at of them." And I took the thirty pieces of silver, and cast them to the potter in the house of the Lord.

The events that followed occurred rapidly…

Trial and Death

Taking His men to the Garden of Gethsemane, Jesus prayed to His Father, in a desperate and human tone that was rare for the Christ, that if there was any way to spare Him from impending death, He would take that other route. But in the tone that captured His divinity, Jesus submitted to the will of the Father (Matthew 26:30–46; Mark 14:26–42; Luke 22:39–46), knowing what *must* be done for the salvation of all. As His disciples continued to fall asleep as a result of the late hour, Jesus prayed over and over the same prayer. Three times He prayed "the same words":

> "O my Father, if it be possible, let this cup pass from me: nevertheless not as I will, but as thou wilt." And he cometh unto the disciples, and findeth them asleep.... He went away again the second time, and prayed, saying, "O my Father, if this cup may not pass away from me, except I drink it, thy will be done." And he came and found them asleep again.... And he left them, and went away again, and prayed the third time, saying the same words. (Matthew 26:39–44)

Before long, He was joined by an angel who comforted Him (Luke 22:43–44), but alas, it did not change Jesus' fate. Jesus *would* die for the sin of mankind, and His trial would start right then! "And while he yet spake, lo, Judas, one of the twelve, came, and with him a great multitude with swords and staves, from the chief priests and elders of the people" (Matthew 26:47).

Judas used a kiss as his means to betray his best friend and Messiah. Peter began to retaliate with force, cutting off the ear of one of the servants to the high priest, but Jesus healed it on the spot and submitted to the arrest (Matthew 26:47–56; Mark 14:43–49; Luke 22:47–53; John 18:1–12).

Next, Jesus would be tried in the most fraudulent trial documented in human history—fraudulent not just because He was innocent, but because the legalities in place to ensure a fair trial were cast aside in the interest of getting Him killed as fast as possible in order to do away with the threat He posed against both Jewish and Roman ways of life. Let's reflect briefly on what transpired, and then we will revisit the injustice of the civil proceedings as outlined in the Mishnah.

In the middle of the night, Jesus was taken first to the high priest, Annas, to be tried, as the Jews believed it was he who truly stood as the first Jewish legislator. When asked what His teachings had been about, Jesus told Annas and the other officials to redirect their questions to His followers, as they knew very well what He had said. This answer was perceived as insolent, and Jesus was stricken across the face by a nearby officer. Jesus responded by asking why He had been hit: If it was because His teachings were evil, then they should present evidence; if it wasn't, what was the justification for violence? (John 18:19–23). As was often the case when Jesus spoke to those who opposed Him, they were silent in response and dragged Him, still bound, to Caiaphas (who was likely located in his own wing of the same palace).

The chief priests, along with the leaders of the Sanhedrin, had been busy searching for evidence against the Lord, but they repeatedly found none. Desperate, Caiaphas sank to the low point of accumulating witnesses to provide false testimony, and although "many" agreed to this scam, their pathetic claims didn't agree with one another. Finally, two men stood and testified that Jesus had threatened to tear down the Temple and rebuild it in three days, but even their stories didn't match up (Matthew 26:59–60; Mark 14:55–59). When Jesus didn't immediately respond to His accusers, the high priest charged Him under oath of the Living God to answer, once and for all, if He was, in fact, the Messiah, the Son of God. Jesus answered straightforwardly, in truth, and with yet another nod to His future return: "I am: and ye shall see the Son of man sitting on the right hand of power, and coming in the clouds of heaven" (Matthew 26:62–64; Mark 14:61–62). The audience was, no doubt, familiar with the prophets (even if, like the Sadducees, they didn't believe in the prophets' words and writings). Therefore, those present during Jesus' conversation with Caiaphas would understand Jesus' quote from Daniel 7:13 referring to "one like the Son of man [who] came with the clouds of heaven."

Caiaphas tore his garment (an action conveying the Jewish court's pronouncement of blasphemy), he and followed up by accusing Jesus of blasphemy verbally, noting that with this level of impudence, there was no more need for witnesses. (Caiaphas must have loved that, seeing as his "witnesses" had proved to be nothing more than an embarrassment minutes prior.) Caiaphas asked the crowd if they agreed, and they responded favorably to his allegation of blasphemy. Jesus was then spat on, blindfolded, and punched, while mockers cried out, "Prophesy unto us, thou Christ, Who is he that smote thee?" (Matthew 26:65–68; Mark 14:64–65; Luke 22:63–65).

The sun was rising as Jesus was led in to face the Sanhedrin. Once again, they asked if this Man who stood before them was really the Christ. "And he said unto them, 'Ye say that I am.'" That was all they needed to hear. The whole assembly agreed this "criminal" had committed His last crime. Everyone agreed that He should to be put to death (Matthew 27:1; Mark 15:1; Luke 22:66–71). All that stood between Christ and the cross now was the approval of the Roman state.

Pilate, who stayed in Jerusalem during the feasts, was situated in the palace built for the governor. (Scholars note that since this wasn't Pilate's usual Caesarean home, he may have been staying in the old palace of Herod the Great, making sense of how this back-and-forth trial could have all happened in a very short time.) This secular and ritually unclean place would "taint" the cleanliness of the Jews, so they remained outside while they conversed about the fate of Jesus. Pilate asked what He had done, and the answer was insufficient, so the Roman governor told the Jews to judge Jesus according to their own laws. They protested, explaining they had no authority to execute a criminal, but it was clear that Pilate wasn't going to be bothered with a Jewish matter until it became a Roman one. So the leaders of the crowd upped the ante, saying Jesus was "perverting the nation, and forbidding to give tribute to Caesar, saying that he himself is Christ a King." Pilate still found no fault in Jesus, and said as much, so Christ's accusers "were the more fierce, saying, 'He stirreth up the people, teaching throughout all Jewry, beginning from Galilee to this place.'"

Pilate then invited Jesus inside and away from the crowd, asking Him directly if He was King of the Jews. Jesus answered affirmatively that He *was* a King, but that His Kingdom was "not of this world." He summarized His Kingship and the purpose of His entire earthly existence in a single sentence: "To this end was I born, and for this cause came I into the world, that I should bear witness unto the truth." Pilate exited the room, confirmed that Jesus was a Galilean, and sent Him to Herod, the leader of that jurisdiction (Matthew 27:2, 11–14; Mark 15:1b–5; Luke 23:1–7; John 18:28–37).

Herod couldn't be more excited at first. He had been after this Jesus fellow for a long time. When He was brought in, Herod could hardly contain himself, believing naively he would be able to see a "show" of this Man's works. But Jesus wasn't exactly what Herod anticipated, and after the ruler questioned the silent Lamb for slaughter, he became bored and disenchanted by the lack of the magical miracles he'd hoped to see. Determined to get some entertainment value out of Jesus, Herod and his men dressed Jesus in an elegant, royal robe, and mocked Him. When they tired of this, too, they sent Jesus back to Pilate for a second round (Luke 23:8–12).

Pilate called together the chief priests and local leaders and once again said he found Jesus had committed no crime. Meanwhile, a feast custom allowed for the release of one Jewish prisoner annually. When Pilate asked the crowd if they wanted Jesus or the "murderer" Barabbas released, it's likely he was hoping the laymen of the gathering would cry louder for Jesus than the religious leaders, silencing the chief priests and releasing Jesus by popular demand, but surprisingly, they cried for Barabbas. Pilate's intent, likely influenced by his wife's message detailing a disturbing dream she had regarding how he should have nothing to do with this precious Jew, shifted toward releasing Jesus, though He would receive a harsh punishment. All the louder, the crowd demanded, "Crucify him!" Pilate, feeling the intense weight of his decision could have unending political ramifications later, went forward with his plan and had Jesus brutally, mercilessly scourged. During the ordeal, Jesus was flogged between bouts of mockery as Pilate's men bowed before Him, stripped Him, crowned Him with thorns, spat on Him, dressed Him in royal garments, and undressed Him again. Pilate brought Jesus out one final time, showing the Jews the King they would only ever fail to recognize. Rather than be moved to grant clemency by the sight of a bloodied, beaten, innocent Man, they threatened Pilate by telling him that he would be seen as an enemy of Caesar if he didn't comply with their demands. As the growing din of the crowd and their increasing threats proved to be the beginning of an uproar, publicly and literally, Pilate washed his hands of the whole affair (literally, using a basin in front of them all), released Barabbas, and sent Jesus to be crucified (Matthew 27:15–30; Mark 15:6–20; Luke 23:13–25; John 18:39–19:16).

Jesus was then en route to Golgotha (the "Place of the Skull"), carrying His own cross until His physical strength gave out and Simon of Cyrene stepped in to carry it the rest of the way. Multitudes followed Him, some wailing in emotional agony, while two other condemned criminals made their way alongside Him on the Via Delarosa (a path called "Valley of Suffering"; Matthew 27:31–34; Mark 15:20–23; Luke 23:26–33a; John 19:16b–17).

After the Roman soldiers drove nails into His hands and feet and erected His cursed cross of shame, Jesus said to His Father, "Forgive them, for they know not what they do." Pilate, against the wishes of the Jews, had a placard placed above Jesus' head that read, in three languages, "This is Jesus of Nazareth, the King of the Jews." Onlookers sneered and mocked; one criminal, upon believing Jesus was indeed His Savior, was promised by Christ that he would inherit Paradise that day. Jesus' clothing was divided among the soldiers, and they cast lots for the remaining undergarments (Matthew 27:35–44; Mark 15:24–32; Luke 23:33b–43; John 19:18–27).

This fulfilled the messianic Psalm 22:18: "They part my garments among them, And cast lots upon my vesture," while the entire death scene fulfilled Isaiah 53:10–12:

Yet it pleased the Lord to bruise him; he hath put him to grief:
When thou shalt make his soul an offering for sin, He shall
see his seed, he shall prolong his days, And the pleasure of the
Lord shall prosper in his hand. He shall see of the travail of his
soul, and shall be satisfied: By his knowledge shall my righteous
servant justify many; For he shall bear their iniquities. Therefore will I divide him a portion with the great, And he shall
divide the spoil with the strong; Because he hath poured out his
soul unto death: And he was numbered with the transgressors;
And he bare the sin of many, And made intercession for the
transgressors.

While nearing the end of His life, Christ quoted Psalm 22:1: "My
God, my God, why hath thou forsaken me?" Drink was brought to His
lips, and He drank the wine vinegar, lowering His head and saying, "It
is finished.... Father, into thy hands I commend my spirit" (Matthew
27:45–50; Mark 15:33–37; Luke 23:44–46; John 19:28–30).

In this, Psalm 69:21, "They gave me also gall for my meat; And in
my thirst they gave me vinegar to drink," and Psalm 31:5, "Into thine
hand I commit my spirit," were fulfilled.

In that very moment, over in the Temple, the veil (that Mary *may*
have had a hand in weaving; see the section titled "Mary") separating
the common people from the Holy of Holies was torn from top to
bottom. An earthquake rumbled the grounds to the point that rocks
split in two. These signs terrified the centurion and those with him,
who thus believed in the testimony of Jesus; others merely beat their
chests in grief and walked away while Mary (the mother of Jesus),
Mary Magdalene, and Salome (mother of James and John) watched
on (Matthew 27:51–56; Mark 15:38–41; Luke 23:47–49).

The soldiers broke the legs of both the other offenders to quicken
their death, but when they came to Jesus, they discovered He was
already dead, so they pierced His side to be sure, and water and blood
flowed from the wound.

Thus, Exodus 12:46, Numbers 9:12, and Psalm 34:20 were fulfilled, which stated that no bones of the sacrifice would be broken. Zechariah 12:10 was also fulfilled, which said the messianic sacrifice for the atonement of all sins would be pierced:

> And I will pour upon the house of David, and upon the inhabitants of Jerusalem, The spirit of grace and of supplications: And they shall look upon me whom they have pierced, And they shall mourn for him, as one mourneth for his only son.

With Pilate's permission, Joseph of Arimathea obtained the broken and bleeding body of our Lord (Matthew 27:57–58; Mark 15:42–45; Luke 23:50–52; John 19:31–38) and placed Him in a new tomb where no other body had previously been put to rest; a giant stone was rolled in front of the entryway (Matthew 27:59–60; Mark 15:46; Luke 23:53–54; John 19:39–42).

Injustice of the Trial: Ultimately Intentional

Not every scholar interprets the timeline of trial and death as we have. Though the tweaks to chronology are minor (for instance, some believe Jesus was taken first to Caiaphas, and *then* to Annas), the ultimate outcome of the events have been reported faithfully.

Many believers have argued that the trial of Christ was fraudulent from the beginning, noting *hundreds* of infractions by religious leaders, and quoting from a variety of ancient legal documents…but not all of those documents were in effect by the time of Jesus. As sincere and well-meaning as these believers are, when this enormous list is circulated among contemporary researchers amidst a wide range of lawyers who dutifully compare their knowledge of the court system with what the Jews were up to in the first century, the claims that Jesus' trial was unfair are discounted entirely. When these same lawyers write full-length books showing how Christians are wrong, it makes what Jesus went through look fair by comparison. This is why, if the question of a fair trial is brought up at all, it must be done in a way that's relevant not to what Jewish laws had shifted to become *after* Jesus' trial, but what they were at the time of His arrest. (This is why we've included on our list only *some* of the same infractions Google-searched articles online cover.)

We have chosen to focus on the Mosaic Law, as it was "elaborated and extended in the system which grew up after the return from Babylon,"[71] therefore, *far* before Jesus was born to Mary. *The International Standard Bible Encyclopaedia* (*ISBE*), in a section titled "Jesus Christ, Arrest and Trial Of," we find that many elements of the trial were wrongfully carried out. This source goes on to explain the Jewish legal system at the time of Christ was established even before the formation of the Sanhedrin, and was carried on by those officials throughout the first two centuries of the Christian era, when they were then codified in the Mishna by Rabbi Judah and his Jewish associates at the beginning of the third century. The *ISBE* goes on to say: "It is generally conceded by both Jewish and Christian writers that the main provisions, therein found for the protection of accused persons...were recognized as a part of [trial proceedings] in the time of Annas and Caiaphas."[72]

No witnesses or evidence: To begin with, a capital punishment trial, according to the laws cited in Deuteronomy, always had to involve two or three true witnesses (19:15). In the trial of Jesus, several witnesses stood in front of the high priest and blabbed, probably just to say they were a part of something exciting. However, *none* of those witnesses could keep his story straight; none of their accounts aligned with the others, and the religious leaders went out of their way to seek "false witnesses" against Jesus (Matthew 26:59–60; Mark 14:55–59). Even back in those days, this kind of bogus witness testimony would be dismissed. After also eliminating the Jewish leaders whose testimonies would have been biased, Judas is left as a single "witness" to what Jesus was being accused of. Technically speaking, Judas' testimony wouldn't be considered legitimate since it was obtained with a blood-money bribe. Remember, no legitimate hearing was held to address Christ's crimes. We never see in these biblical accounts any scenario in which a judge presides over court while testimony is given and evidence is presented in front of a balanced and impartial jury. Even if criminal evidence against Jesus did exist, it was never—not once, *ever*—presented to any court in a timely manner. Nor did there appear to be a single defense party who represented Christ. We know that as far back as when the book of Job was written (as mentioned in volume 1 of this series, scholars often consider Job one of the first books of the Bible ever written) that the concept of a "defense attorney" existed in ancient Jewish culture.

Browbeating judge: Further, "no prisoner could be convicted on his own evidence; it was the duty of a judge to see that the interests of the accused were fully protected."[73] None of that applied with Jesus. The concept of a preliminary investigation was not implemented at the time, and the legal proceedings began with an open court. Thus, *all* of the evidence against a criminal "was that which was disclosed by the evidence of the witnesses."[74] As stated, there were no legitimate witnesses in the trial of Christ. The high priest knew this, but he pressed Jesus into convicting Himself. Jesus *could not*, under any circumstances, be convicted based on His own responses to the line of questioning, but the judge attempted it anyway. When it failed, he "rent his garment" and cried "blasphemy," using his status to propel the case forward illegally.

Improper timing of the trial: Proceedings related to criminal trials were, in no uncertain terms, to take place during the day. If a case did drag on into the evening (many did), then they were to adjourn for the day and resume the next morning (or the next "business" day, if the following day was a feast day or the equivalent). Jesus, however, was arrested in the garden at night, and the trial commenced immediately rather than beginning the next day, as mandated.

Infraction of "same-day verdict" rule: If the criminal was acquitted, that verdict could be announced on the day of the trial. If the criminal was found guilty, though, the verdict was to be announced on the following day—and again, these decisions were only legally binding if they occurred during regular court hours.

Infraction of a rule mandating closed-court: Without a preliminary investigation, the high priest's interrogation of Jesus in a private setting, as outlined in John 18:19, was not a part of an official Jewish trial. It could not be taken in good faith for an appropriate proceeding, and was therefore an attempt at "entrapping Jesus into admissions that might be used against Him" at the subsequent trial at the Sanhedrin.[75] Jesus' response to this line of questioning showed that He was well aware anything He said could and would be used against Him in the coming days, so He referred His questioner to His "witnesses"; He knew that was the way to begin. The reaction to His redirection of the question was a (literal) punch to the face, which our source calls "an outrageous proceeding" the judge on the scene should have rebuked, had the trial been fair. By no means should this private-court setting in the middle of the night been allowed, and violence was also prohibited at this point in the hearing. (Jesus recognized this, which is why He asked the leaders to present evidence that justified their allowance of physical aggression [John 18:19–23].)

Sanhedrin infraction of rule regarding "new council": When Jesus was taken to stand before the Sanhedrin, many new faces were in the council that had not been there the night before. The trial, if fair, should have started completely over with the "witnesses" from the previous investigation speaking in front of these new council members. Jesus, who had already been found worthy of the death penalty, was questioned again as to whether He was the Messiah. He replied, "*You* say that I am," which wasn't technically an admission and therefore wasn't a legally justifiable cause for the sentence of death. Throwing official standards out the window, "[the members of the Sanhedrin] said, 'What need we any further witness? for we ourselves have heard of his own mouth,'" and proceeded without any witness testimony to enlighten the council members who were new to the case (Luke 22:66–71).

In summation: "The Jewish trial of Our Lord was absolutely illegal, the court which condemned Him being without jurisdiction to try a capital offence…. Even if there had been jurisdiction, it would have been irregular, as the judges had rendered themselves incompetent to try the case, having been guilty of the violation of the spirit of the law that required judges to be unprejudiced and impartial, and carefully to guard the interests of the accused."[76]

Though a few legal experts have, since Christ's trial, written lengthy works explaining in sharp detail why everything was fair, these claims are discredited by the Jewish laws in effect *in that time*, under the very justice system implemented by the Sanhedrin. Jurisprudence was irrefutably absent from the proceedings that condemned Jesus to suffer and die. Thus, He wasn't just "executed," He was "murdered."

However, as believers, we can see the hand of God working behind the scenes of human operations to bring to pass what was ultimately the will of the Father in all things. Jesus died for our sin, and since He truly *was* the Messiah, the only way to convict Him would have been to disregard judicial standards and incriminate Him in the most faulty and illogical ways. It's the only way this otherwise completely innocent and guiltless Man would end up on the cross…for all of us.

And now, the Gospels draw to a close with quite a story, indeed!

The difference between Jesus and all the other would-be messiahs boils down to one major element: Jesus didn't stay dead like the rest of them.

No.

Jesus came back!

Resurrection, Posthumous Appearances, and the Closing of the Gospels

Just as promised, regardless of all the missing justice in the system that contributed to His death, Jesus arose on the third day after He was buried.

Though today we view "a day" as a twenty-four-hour period, the Jews, Greeks, and Romans did not. In their form of counting (and by extension, Christ's words regarding His rising), Jesus could be murdered on day one, remain in the tomb on day two, and rise on the "third day."

Pilate arranged for guards to be placed at the entrance of the tomb. According to laws regarding dereliction of duty in that day, being asleep while the tomb was tampered with would have been immediate grounds for execution, so these guards had every reason to stay awake to ensure nobody would steal Jesus' body.

The stone in front of the tomb was sealed. Commonly, when we think of this episode, imagine a giant, round, disc-shaped stone, likely because of the presence of the Greek word *kulio* in the narrative. That term can be translated as "rolled," which denotes an item with a circular shape. However, in the Second-Temple era, Jewish burials did not follow this method, so that's likely not what was blocking the entrance to Jesus' tomb. Amos Kloner, a specialist in Hellenistic, Roman, and Byzantine archaeology and a professor at Bar-Ilan University in Israel, states the Greek word *kulio* can also mean "dislodge," "move back," or simply "move."[77] The stone in front of Jesus' tomb, he explained in 1999, was far more likely to be the standard burial stone of the day: it would have been shaped like a cork. Imagine a kind of mushroom-shaped rock on which the "stem" was the same size as the door, fitting like a puzzle piece into the opening and extending a couple of feet inside the tomb. From outside the tomb, the rock was seen to protrude from the opening another foot or so around the door's outline. A wax seal would have then been placed between the doorway and the overlapping lip of the bulge, bleeding into the entrance and "gluing" the stone into place.

This is another layer of evidence supporting the idea that nobody, outside of a group of soldiers with proper moving equipment, could simply "heave-ho" and roll the stone away. It's likely that the writers of the Gospels, in referring to the stone having been "rolled," were actually describing the nearly impossible "uncorking" miracle performed by an angel who then sat atop it like it was a flat chair (it's more difficult to imagine the angel "perching" on a circular disc).

Yet the stone *was* moved, even while the guards watched the angel of God do his work. When the ground shook and the mighty angel popped the rock out of the way like it was nothing, the guards fainted (Matthew 28:1–8; Mark 16:1–8; Luke 24:1–9; John 20:1).

When Mary, the mother of Christ, and Mary Magdalene made their way to the tomb, they found it empty. Two "men" (angels) in glittering, white garments stood beside them. Their response to the arrival of the women is, in hindsight, somewhat humorous: "Why seek ye the living among the dead? He is not here, but is risen: remember how he spake unto you when he was yet in Galilee, Saying, 'The Son of man must be delivered into the hands of sinful men, and be crucified, and the third day rise again'" (Luke 24:5–7). In modern English, their words could be reworded to say, "What are you doing looking for the Living One here, at a gravesite? What did you girls *think* you were going to find here? He's alive, obviously! He already told you back in Galilee that He would be murdered, but would raise to life on the third day. Don't you remember that?"

The women *did* remember, and after being instructed to go and tell the remaining eleven disciples the news (Mark 16:7) they quickly gathered their wits and ran from the scene to inform the others that someone had taken Jesus' body. (Despite the angels' words, the women were still dealing with doubt.) Not surprisingly, most assumed these poor women were merely hallucinating or beside themselves in grief, so they didn't believe their news. Peter and John, however, wanted to see for themselves, so they hustled like the wind to the tomb. Inside, they found the burial linens, but no body. (In the book *Afterlife*, by Donna Howell, Allie Anderson, and Josh Peck, a very responsible and breathtaking case is made for the legitimacy of the Shroud of Turin as Christ's burial cloth. If you are like many readers who have felt as though this subject was never given proper scientific attention— or if you feel it's a subject primarily for Catholics—you may want to pick up a copy. Many skeptics have made glaring errors in their research of the relic, and, unfortunately, many faithful "Shroudites" have reported details about it that sound inspiring and miraculous, but are easily debunked by science. In *Afterlife*, Howell, Anderson, and Peck account for the forensic facts about the cloth while uprooting the inaccurate reports of recent history. It's a short, to-the-point read with no fluff, and the case for the Shroud is convincing. It has already been a faith-building tool for many readers, including many skeptics, who have provided feedback letting us know that, whether or not the Shroud is the legitimate burial cloth of Christ, we handled the topic reliably.)

The disciples returned home, but Mary Magdalene stayed at the tomb, wrestling with her emotions and weeping. As she went in to gaze at the empty cavity in the rock, sat two angels—one at the head and one at the foot of where Jesus had been laid. The angels asked Mary why she was crying, and she said, "Because they have taken away my Lord, and I know not where they have laid him" (John 20:13). At that moment, she sensed the presence of another, and spun around to see Jesus. He was so immersed in the luminescence of His risen glory that she didn't recognize Him right away. Jesus asked why she was crying and who she was looking for, and, mistakenly assuming He was the gardener, she said again she was in pursuit of the body of Jesus.

Without a big explanation, and without any theological lessons or complicated diatribes, Jesus simply said her name: "Mary." With that one word, she recognized her Lord and Savior, shouting "Master!" (John 20:16). The biblical account doesn't go into detail, but we can imagine she was overwhelmed with questions and possibly asked them aloud. It's also possible Jesus provided some answers, but next we read that she ran back to tell the others, who, *again*, did not believe her (Mark 16:11).

The guards, meanwhile, hastened to tell the chief priests what had happened. This moment in the story is hugely important. Had there been any chance the tomb had been tampered with by anyone other than an angel, the guards surely would have been executed. The chief priests, who had made easy work of Jesus' trial, would have been able to sentence these men to death with as little as a quick jaunt over to see Pilate or Herod. But, after listening to the guards' accounts, the priests instead bribed them with a giant sum of money to lie about what they had seen. If the story were to reach the governor, the priests said, they would protect the guards from harm. We know the soldiers went along with the plan because they lived long enough to spread the lie: "So they took the money, and did as they were taught: and this saying is commonly reported among the Jews until this day" (Matthew 28:15). A number of other questions abound about this woven tale: If the guards had been asleep when the disciples had supposedly stolen the body, then how could the guards have known *who* did the deed? If the guards had *not* fallen asleep, then why didn't they stop the tomb-robbers? Furthermore, if dereliction of duty carries a death sentence, then surely stealing the body under the watch of the Roman guard would also be a crime punishable by death. So how could the disciples have gotten away with it? Why weren't they persecuted? These questions and countless others make the theory that the body was stolen look ridiculous. Be that as it may, most of the Jews of Jesus' time through, at least, the day the Gospel of Mark was written believed this version of the story.

Nevertheless, Jesus continued to materialize, alive and well, in front of people all over the place, showing that His "third day" prediction had been fulfilled. After appearing to Mary, He met two men on the road to Emmaus (Mark 16:12; Luke 24:13–16), and they ran back to Jerusalem to tell the disciples (Luke 24:33–35). (These were the two who recognized Jesus by the breaking of the bread (*afikomen*). It's true that would not have been the Passover feast, but that hadn't kept Jesus from breaking the cracker in a way that identified Him as the Lamb whose body and blood had replaced the previous sacrificial lambs.) While His disciples were still discussing this event behind locked doors (for fear of the Jews: John 20:19), Jesus suddenly appeared among them, standing in their presence while they ate. Terrified, and believing they were looking at a ghost, Jesus said, "Why are ye troubled? and why do thoughts arise in your hearts? Behold my hands and my feet, that it is I myself: handle me, and see; for a spirit hath not flesh and bones, as ye see me have" (Luke 24:38–39). Then, as casual as ever, Jesus asked if they had any meat. When they offered a piece of broiled fish, He took it and consumed it while explaining:

> These are the words which I spake unto you, while I was yet with you, that all things must be fulfilled, which were written in the law of Moses, and in the prophets, and in the psalms, concerning me.... Thus it is written, and thus it behoved Christ to suffer, and to rise from the dead the third day: And that repentance and remission of sins should be preached in his name among all nations, beginning at Jerusalem. And ye are witnesses of these things. And, behold, I send the promise of my Father upon you: but tarry ye in the city of Jerusalem, until ye be endued with power from on high. (Luke 24:44, 46–49)

As detailed in the book of Acts, the men followed these instructions about waiting in Jerusalem until they would be empowered from on high. Meanwhile, Luke's account winds down to a grand finale. The last words of his Gospel preview the Savior's Ascension to His place at the right hand of the Father:

> And he led them out as far as to Bethany, and he lifted up his hands, and blessed them. And it came to pass, while he blessed them, he was parted from them, and carried up into heaven. And they worshipped him, and returned to Jerusalem with great joy: And were continually in the temple, praising and blessing God. Amen. (Luke 24:50–53)

But this isn't quite the end for the other three Gospel books.

After Jesus left His followers, Thomas (one of the remaining eleven apostles) walked in and heard what he had missed. Earning forever the name "Doubting Thomas," he declared that unless he saw the nail prints in the Savior's hands, ran his finger along the site of the wound, and "thrust" his hand into Jesus' side, he would not believe (John 20:25). For a second time, Jesus evidently walked through a wall or locked doors. He appeared to Thomas a week later and invited the doubter to do precisely what he had wanted. Jesus said: "Reach hither thy finger, and behold my hands; and reach hither thy hand, and thrust it into my side: and be not faithless, but believing.... Thomas, because thou hast seen me, thou hast believed: blessed are they that have not seen, and yet have believed" (John 20:27–29).

At the Sea of Tiberius, Jesus appeared again to the disciples, this time specifically to "Simon Peter, and Thomas called Didymus, and Nathanael of Cana in Galilee, and the sons of Zebedee, and two other of his disciples" (John 21:2). They had been fishing all night and had caught nothing. Jesus, who was standing on the shoreline about a hundred yards away, told them to lower their nets once more, on the right side of the boat. Believing they were following the advice of a distant stranger, they obliged, likely with the intention of showing the "stranger" his counsel would do no good. But when they did as he said and lowered the nets again, they made such a catch that they couldn't even reel in all the fish. John told Peter, "It is the Lord," and Peter jumped instantly into the sea and swam to meet Him. As the boat arrived behind Peter minutes later, they saw Jesus by a fire and holding some bread. He instructed them to join Him for a meal, and they did so without hesitating (John 21:1–14).

This is the last episode of Jesus' life John described in his Gospel. John, the "disciple that Jesus loved" (a self-reference used often throughout his entire book), concluded his whole account with this:

And there are also many other things which Jesus did, the which, if they should be written every one, I suppose that even the world itself could not contain the books that should be written. Amen. (John 21:25)

Matthew's Gospel also draws to a close at about this point, but not before Jesus presents the Great Commission. Again, Christ appeared in Galilee to the eleven, and He left them with these final words before He departed from them physically:

> All power is given unto me in heaven and in earth. Go ye there-fore, and teach all nations, baptizing them in the name of the Father, and of the Son, and of the Holy Ghost: Teaching them to observe all things whatsoever I have commanded you: and, lo, I am with you always[s], even unto the end of the world. (Matthew 28:18–20)

With a final "Amen," the Gospel of Matthew concludes.

In the final verses of Mark, we read again of this same appearance of Jesus, His parting words, and the nature in which He left:

> [Jesus said:] "Go ye into all the world, and preach the gospel to every creature. He that believeth and is baptized shall be saved; but he that believeth not shall be damned. And these signs shall follow them that believe; In my name shall they cast out devils; they shall speak with new tongues; They shall take up serpents; and if they drink any deadly thing, it shall not hurt them; they shall lay hands on the sick, and they shall recover."
>
> So then after the Lord had spoken unto them, he was received up into heaven, and sat on the right hand of God. And they went forth, and preached every where, the Lord work-ing with them, and confirming the word with signs following. Amen. (Mark 16:15–20)

Acts 1:3 indicates that when Jesus appeared to many people over the period of forty days, it was with "many infallible proofs" while "speaking of the things pertaining to the kingdom of God." Even in His glorified, posthumous state, Jesus was still teaching about the

Kingdom of God. First Corinthians 15:5–8 gives yet another account of Christ's appearances, one of which involved a group of *five hundred* people!: "And that he was seen of Cephas [Peter], then of the twelve: After that, he was seen of above five hundred brethren at once; of whom the greater part remain unto this present, but some are fallen asleep. After that, he was seen of James; then of all the apostles. And last of all he was seen of me [Paul] also" (1 Corinthians 15:5–8). This reference to James was in regard to Jesus' half-brother, and his life was changed forever as a result. He went on to become a major leader in Jerusalem, dying a martyr's death like the rest of the apostles who so believed in His Sonship they willingly perished in the most brutal ways…just to spread the word.

Or, rather, just to spread the *Word*.

Christ's work, as carried on through His apostles and disciples of the early Church, is far from over…

Acts

THE LONGER (BUT STILL OFFICIAL) title of the book of Acts is "The Acts of the Apostles." A short overview or outline of the work reveals it as the account of the "acts" or "works" not just of those labeled "apostles," but also of the disciples who made it their entire lives' work to build the early Church. The book covers much travel, church-planting, discipleship, and martyrdom, as many men and women died for the sake of their Savior. It picks up where the Gospels end, at the Ascension of Christ, followed by the crucially important Day of Pentecost. In the same way we did not have to look for how Jesus "appeared" in the Gospels—because they were all about His earthly life—we don't have to try hard to see Him in Acts, because it's all about the massive, almost overnight expansion of His Church.

Luke, the "careful historian" who wrote the Gospel with the same name, is the author of the book of Acts as well. There has been much debate regarding who he wrote it to, as the first verse states: "The former treatise have I made, O Theophilus, of all that Jesus began both to do and teach" (Acts 1:1). The "former treatise" refers to his Gospel. The word *theophilus* means "dear to God," and many have suggested it simply refers to *any* Christian (all, of course, would be "dear to God") rather than to a man with that name. (Whether it is one person or a generic address, "Theophilus" is mentioned in Luke 1:3 as well).

The modest opener launches straight into the account of the Ascension, with Jesus instructing His followers to wait for "the promise of the Father." Jesus then explained exactly what that "promise" was:

> For John [the Baptist] truly baptized with water; but ye shall be baptized with the Holy Ghost not many days hence....[and] ye shall receive power, after that the Holy Ghost is come upon you: and ye shall be witnesses unto me both in Jerusalem, and in all Judaea, and in Samaria, and unto the uttermost part of the earth. (Acts 1:5, 8)

Jesus didn't have fair witnesses toward the end of His earthly life, but now He was building a heavenly army of saints that would absolutely wreck the world's system in a permanent and beautiful way. These saints would never die out, from generation to generation they would live on, even until the end of the world, preaching, teaching, prophesying, and embodying the true, righteous witnesses of the continuing "case" of Christ on earth.

After our Lord told His disciples about the promise of the Father:

> [W]hile they beheld, he was taken up; and a cloud received him out of their sight. And while they looked stedfastly toward heaven as he went up, behold, two men stood by them in white apparel; Which also said, "Ye men of Galilee, why stand ye gazing up into heaven? this same Jesus, which is taken up from you into heaven, shall so come in like manner as ye have seen him go into heaven." (Acts 1:9–11)

Psalm 110:1 was therefore fulfilled: "The Lord said unto my Lord, 'Sit thou at my right hand.'"

We love it when the angels speak in Scripture! The questions they ask show us how finite, temporal, and curious human nature is. Just like with Mary Magdalene at the tomb, angels are here again asking what could be a humorous question: "Why are you guys standing here looking at the sky? What is it you think you're going to see?" It's one of many "LOL" moments we can glean from Scripture.

In any case, these were the last words Christ spoke upon the earth. ...Or *were* they? (Stay tuned!)

The disciples returned to Jerusalem and obediently remained there, waiting for the promise to be fulfilled. They stayed, united together in prayer and supplication, in an important location: the Upper Room. Listed among this gathering are: "Peter, and James, and John, and Andrew, Philip, and Thomas, Bartholomew, and Matthew, James the son of Alphaeus, and Simon [the Zealot], and Judas the brother of [or "son of," in some translations] James...with the women, and Mary the mother of Jesus, and with his brethren...(the number of names together were about an hundred and twenty)" (Acts 1:13–15). Though we can't be certain where this Upper Room was, many scholars and archeologists believe they have located it, deeming it to be upstairs in the home of John Mark's mother (see Acts 12:12), as well as the site of the Last Supper. The Holy Land Experience theme park in Orlando, Florida, before it closed, featured a built-to-scale model of this room where tourists were welcome to go inside, pray, worship, and even sit at a replica of the table where Jesus broke bread with His disciples the night of His arrest. It was hard to imagine a hundred and twenty people gathered in such a small place because, the day we authors visited it, only about seventy people were in our tour group, and even though we tried to put space between each of us since we were strangers, the room was still pretty crowded. (Unfortunately, this park is now said to be closed for good, not having survived the economic impact of COVID-19. But one thing we will stress about its glory days: We had a phenomenal and otherworldly time there! After our visit, a newcomer to the cast was given the role of Jesus and some have said he took his part perhaps…a little too seriously. Stories circulated that the actor was arrogant, both in and out of character. That is *not* the experience we had. The one who played our "Jesus" was humble, sweet, and sincere, and when he wasn't in character, he prayed for folks on the street "in Jesus' precious and holy Name." We are saddened by the news the park has closed, and we can only pray it will reopen someday. Meanwhile, the Bible museum that it housed was pretty hard to take in at times. In fact, Donna Howell and Allie Anderson were in tears at one point, after being told that what they were seeing on a Bible they were looking at wasn't a coffee stain, but blood. It was that of an early martyr who had been forced to look at God's Word while he was beheaded hovering over it. The blood had turned a dark brown over the years. It was a sobering reminder that we are blessed to be here, in the States, where we're [at least currently] free to read the Word of God without fear of persecution. If you get nothing else from this three-book series, we pray you'll walk away with a prompting to thank the Lord—in the midst of political and social upheaval and increased secularization of our society—that His Word is still accessible to us in this era.)

After Jesus ascended to the right hand of the Father, Peter addressed those 120 present in the Upper Room with a fairly significant problem: The "twelve" were now the "eleven" because of the loss of Judas the betrayer. When Peter said, "Men and brethren, this scripture must needs have been fulfilled, which the Holy Ghost by the mouth of David spake before concerning Judas" (Acts 1:16), he was referring to David's words of Psalm 41:9: "Yea, mine own familiar friend, in whom I trusted, Which did eat of my bread, Hath lifted up his heel against me." In John 13:18b, we read that Jesus said, "I know whom I have chosen: but that the scripture may be fulfilled, He that eateth bread with me hath lifted up his heel against me." Frederick Bruce, author of the celebrated and well-known *The Book of the Acts* commentary often used as a textbook in universities, explains: "The total of twelve was significant: it corresponded to the number of the tribes of Israel, and may have marked the apostles out as leaders of the new Israel (cf. Luke 22:30 par. Matt. 19:28)."[78] But there's more to it than that.

Peter went on to explain that Judas, who hung himself, ended up disemboweled; the potter's field came to be known as "the field of blood" (1:18–19). He then stated: "For it is written in the book of Psalms, Let his habitation be desolate, and let no man dwell therein: and his bishoprick let another take" (1:20). This reference to the Psalms actually points to two verses: "Let their habitation be desolate" (Psalm 69:25a); "And let another take his office" (Psalm 109:8b). In other words, let the dwelling place of enemies (Judas' field) be deserted and forgotten, and let another, worthy man replace the man who was lost (Judas). This, then, is the key justification for finding a replacement for the twelfth apostle. Peter noted (Acts 1:21–22) two qualifications for one to be called an apostle: He must have been 1) taught personally by Jesus for many years, and 2) a witness of the Resurrected Christ. (Scholars note there is within this list a third implied qualification: a man had to be personally called by Jesus for His work.) Two men among them met these qualifications: Barsabas and Matthias. So, those gathered prayed for God's guidance in choosing which man should be chosen for such an important role, and then they cast lots. This is how Matthias became the twelfth apostle.

Luke wastes no time hurling the reader into action from this point. In the very next scene, we are thrust into rushing winds and tongues of fire. *This* was the "promise of the Father" the early Church was waiting for.

Day of Pentecost–Not Your Average "Sunday School" Interpretation!

The Day of Pentecost is documented in Acts 2. As most are aware, this was the day the Holy Spirit fell upon those gathered in the Upper Room; afterward, they ran into the streets preaching the Gospel in new languages they had never learned, leading to the most intense Church-growth event of history: "And when the day of Pentecost was fully come, they were all with one accord in one place. And suddenly there came a sound from heaven as of a rushing mighty wind, and it filled all the house where they were sitting. And there appeared unto them cloven tongues like as of fire, and it sat upon each of them. And they were all filled with the Holy Ghost, and began to speak with other tongues, as the Spirit gave them utterance" (Acts 2:1–6).

This was done to fulfill the prophecy: "I will pour out my spirit upon all flesh; and your sons and your daughters shall prophesy… And also upon the servants and upon the handmaids in those days will I pour out my spirit" (Joel 2:28–29).

Peter then "lifted up his voice" to the crowd and identified that the Holy-Spirit outpouring on the Day of Pentecost was "that which was spoken by the prophet Joel" (Acts 2:14–16). (It's interesting that we have an account of women rushing to preach the Gospel in this account! We know the Spirit fell on all who were gathered in the Upper Room, and that included women [Acts 1:12–14], so this is an early proof of women preachers being established by the Spirit, Himself. More to come on this subject soon.)

Some of what we'll focus on in this section will be taken from our "Pentecost" study in *The Messenger*.[79] However, to keep things easier to read, we will not be using block quotations for lengthy excerpts as they were in the original.

First, we must understand the background of Pentecost.

Beginning with the wave offering of the barley firstfruits each day for seven weeks, the Israelites observed the "Counting of the *Omer*." (An *omer* is one tenth of an *ephah*, and an *ephah* is equivalent to a bushel of dry goods, like grain or barley.) This involved the blessing—"Blessed are You, Lord our God, King of the universe, who has sanctified us with His commandments and commanded us to count the Omer"—followed by the number of the day: "Today is the first day of Omer"; "Today is the second day of Omer" and so on. The end of this seven-week counting lands at precisely forty-nine days.

The following day, then, makes fifty, which is what the Greek word *pentecost* means; the Feast of Pentecost takes place on the fiftieth day. This is why there is no official observance date. Nevertheless, it falls in the early days of the Hebrew month Sivan, which, on our Gregorian calendar, overlaps the second half of May and the first half of June. This counting ritual bridges the Feast of Firstfruits to the Feast of Pentecost (or "Feast of Weeks").

There are many names for the Feast of Pentecost, the alternative "Feast of Weeks" being the most referenced. However, the nature and practice of this feast has earned it several other titles worth mentioning: "Feast of Harvest," "Day of Firstfruits," and "Latter Firstfruits." The first wheat crops (not to be confused with the barley of the last feast) would be harvested and the first two loaves of bread baked from that yield would then be presented to the Lord in a wave offering. The offering of these "firstfruit" loaves is the reason behind the many names of this feast or festival.

Unlike the bread prepared during the week of Passover, the two loaves of bread for the Feast of Pentecost are to be baked with leaven. The flour for these loaves must be the finest, not just in quality, but in its preparation: It is to be sifted repeatedly until it is completely separated from any course material.

Prior to the diaspora (the scattering of the Jews), this feast was an acknowledgment of dependence upon God's providence in the abundance of wheat for their daily bread, a thanksgiving toward Him for the harvest, and a day to remember when the Torah was given to the people. After the diaspora, when Jews were no longer united to celebrate the same land harvests as they were all over the known world at that time, the agricultural roots of the feast faded and the focus became heavily the delivery of the Law on Mt. Sinai.

With that in mind, it's important to note the delivery of the Law at the base of that mountain was "the inauguration of the Old Testament church."[80] The Day of Pentecost in the book of Acts is the inauguration of the New Testament Church, and the parallels are, well, for

lack of a better word: astonishing! We almost always view the "thunder and lightning" at Sinai and the "wind and tongues of fire" from
Acts as two unrelated, separate phenomena, but when we dig a little
deeper, we see the latter strictly parallels the former in a supernatural
expansion and completion. What we're about to tell you is nothing
new to the scholars; they've been writing about these connections and
links for two thousand years. However, this information has been all
but lost from today's mainstream pulpit, and its significance is crucial
to understanding not just the event of Pentecost for the apostles, but
also exactly what that "power from on high" did for them.

Read the full account of the first occurrence in Exodus, paying
special attention to what is said about thunder and lightning:

> And it came to pass on the third day [this would be 6 Sivan on
> the Hebrew calendar[81]] in the morning, that there were thun-
> derings and lightnings, and a thick cloud upon the mount, and
> the voice of the trumpet exceeding loud; so that all the people
> that was in the camp trembled.
>
> And Moses brought forth the people out of the camp to
> meet with God; and they stood at the nether part of the mount.
> And mount Sinai was altogether on a smoke, because the Lord
> descended upon it in fire: and the smoke thereof ascended as
> the smoke of a furnace, and the whole mount quaked greatly.
>
> Here we stumble upon an awkward translation that, sadly,
> dampens what actually occurred that day. The Hebrew words
> *qowl* and *baraq*, represented here as "thunderings" and "light-
> nings," mean something different than what the English trans-
> lation suggests.

See, *qowl*, first and foremost, means "voice," "sound," or "noise,"
and this is the translation used almost every time *qowl* appears
elsewhere in the Word. As one quick example (of which there are hun-

dreds): "Did ever people hear the voice [*qowl*] of God speaking out of the midst of the fire, as thou hast heard, and live?" (Deuteronomy 4:33).

Actually, in (*qowl's*) 506 appearances in the Bible, *only two instances* are translated "thunderings," and both are right at this spot in Exodus. In a few other places, the English renders *qowl* as the more generic "thunder," but it's likely the translators met the same challenge as here in Exodus, choosing a weather term because it's the closest English terminology they had to choose from.

Here's the problem… In almost every place where "thunder" (or "thunderings," "thundered," etc.) is chosen as the appropriate English swap-out for a Hebrew word that truly means "voice," the scene in question is of God displaying extreme vocal power from the heavens in a way as can be *seen* with human eyes. Exodus 20:18 explicitly states that "all the people *saw* the thunderings [*qowl*]." It's linguistically awkward to "see" a "voice," so the translators, whose job is certainly unenviable at times, chose what they felt was the closest English alternative. Thunder is loud, comes from the heavens, and can be terrifying, but because of the rolling clouds and other weather phenomena accompanying it, it can also be *seen*, which makes it at least a decent place-holder when a narrative literally describes something indescribable (such as "seeing" a "voice"). Additionally, there is a historical association between "voice" and "thunder" in literature, though it's more poetic than literal. For instance, if you were to read the following sample sentence from a fiction novel—"'That's it! I've had enough! I'm warning you!' the large, angry man thundered"—you would know "thundered" was being used as an adjective to describe the character's volume and intensity—obviously not anything related to weather. This, too, may have played a part in why the translators chose "thunderings" instead of the more accurate reference to a speech experience, because we know for certain God's shout was more than just a gentle speaking engagement.

This *qowl* describes a roar so loud, so rushing, and so atmospherically encompassing that there are no accurate one-word trade-outs from Hebrew to English.

Imagine screaming at the very top of your lungs, bloody-murder style, and your voice doesn't even register as a sound above the intense reverberation of the atmosphere. Your own loudest, blood-curdling shrieks of terror are completely muted under the waves of sound coming from heaven. God's declaration rumbles the ground around you, sinks into your skin, and makes you feel as if you will vibrate away, disintegrate away, without ever even being touched by any force other than that of His voice. It's that kind of permeating sound that digs into your very soul and never leaves. It's the voice of the Lord—spoken in volumes so loud and authoritative that it causes earthquakes (Exodus 19:18) all around you—who is about to give His nonnegotiable Ten Commandments to live by. The sound issuing from heaven is from a Creator who has the power to crush all of His own creation with a mere shout; it is a sound that says He *will* be taken seriously.

Don't think we're sensationalizing. The Israelites at the foot of Mt. Sinai who had just heard God's *qowl* were convinced they would all be killed if He used His strong voice to speak to them again (Exodus 20:19b: "let not God speak with us, lest we die"). But in addition, we can look at what God's intense, *qowl*-from-heaven shout did in a similar set of circumstances we read of in 1 Samuel 7:10: "And as Samuel was offering up the burnt offering, the Philistines drew near to battle against Israel: but the Lord thundered [*ra'am*; Hebrew "roar"] with a great thunder [*qowl*] on that day upon the Philistines, and discomfited them; and they were smitten before Israel." On a purely technical level, this should read: "the Lord roared with a great voice from heaven."

If you "go there" all the way in your imagination, then you're probably taking the same thought journey the translators did when they placed themselves into the narrative to choose the most suitable English word for the Mt. Sinai episode in Exodus. A translator's responsibility isn't just to replace each foreign word with an English one, but to understand, study, and respect the *context* in which each word or phrase is used throughout the whole native work (the Bible, in this case). What else, *in English*, besides the word "thunder" comes from the heavens and is visible, loud, and potentially frightening enough to confuse multitudes and strike entire armies dead? In this case, "thunder" wasn't the worst possible choice.

However, amiability to the translators aside, *it was not the most accurate choice.*

All the Hebrew says about the supposed "thunderings" is that a "voice" came from God, Himself, as He descended on the mountain, and that the Israelites "saw" it.

Just to be perfectly clear: *There is no reason in the Hebrew to believe thunder was a part of the display of God's power on Mt. Sinai on the day the Law was given!*

In the end, as grammatically awkward as it is to say "the Israelites *saw* a *voice*," that is the true meaning, and this will become clear after reflecting upon the larger picture. As to what the voice *looked* like, put a pin in that thought for a moment while we hone in on the "lightnings."

The Hebrew word *baraq* can certainly be used in a sentence to mean "lightning," but only because its root definition indicates something extremely bright, like a flash of light. By itself, translators may have chosen to say "bright lights" or "flashes of light" were seen coming from the sky, but because of the word's agreeable association with "lightning" elsewhere in ancient Hebrew—*and* because, by now, the translators had probably already agreed to make *qowl* read "thunderings"—it made sense to make this second, observable phenomenon a part of an erratic weather pattern. Again, however, "lightning" just doesn't completely capture this word.

In fact, this term is used in other passages that don't even have the first thing to do with lightning or storms, such as the following, where *baraq* appears as a flash of light upon a sharp blade: "If I whet my glittering [*baraq*] sword, and mine hand take hold on judgment; I will render vengeance to mine enemies, and will reward them that hate me" (Deuteronomy 32:41); "It is drawn, and cometh out of the body; yea, the glittering [*baraq*] sword cometh out of his gall: terrors are upon him" (Job 20:25). For the word *baraq*, the "light reflecting off of a sword," along with other similar uses, are more abundant throughout the Old Testament than "lightning." Besides just the numerous "sword" and "spear" allusions (see Ezekiel 21:15, 28; Nahum 3:3; Habakkuk 3:11) *baraq* also refers to the brightness of a flame, like from a lamp or torch (Ezekiel 1:13).

Fortunately, the "lightnings" of Sinai don't solely rely on our ability to analyze just *baraq*.

After the delivery of the Ten Commandments to the people, this supernatural phenomenon was still going on, but, in an unexpected and bizarre turn of events, the Hebrew words aren't exactly the same, nor are they quite where we expected them to be: "And all the people saw the thunderings [*qowl*], and the lightnings [*lappiyd*]" (Exodus 20:18).

Wait a second… What is *lappiyd*? Where did that word come from, and why is rendered "lightnings" here, when back in Exodus 19:16 "lightnings" was *baraq*? Were the "bright, flashing lights" from before morphed into something new now?

First of all, please note the Hebrew word for "fire"—meaning *any* regular reference to fire, from what belongs on an altar to what engulfed the burning bush, to what roasts meat, and so on—is *'esh*. Here, suddenly, the "lightnings," or *lappiyd*, refers to a sort of fire, but it's a specific enough kind of fire that it prompted the Hebrew author to steer around using the most common *'esh*. As noted, *baraq* means a bright flash of light. Here, in the same context as *baraq*, with an identical "lightnings" translation treatment later, the word *lappiyd* describes the evolution from mere flashes of light to bright flashes of fire!

The Hebrew *lappiyd* means "torch" (or "lamp"), which is how it is translated most often in the Old Testament (Genesis 15:17; Judges

7:16, 20; Job 12:5; 41:19; Isaiah 62:1; Ezekiel 1:13; Daniel 10:6). Consider the context of this word as a tool: The Hebrews would have had hundreds of useful purposes for regular fire in the middle of the day in the sunshine, such as cooking, forging, cleansing, etc. However, they wouldn't have had use for a torch in broad daylight. In proper context, a "torch" or "lamp" are tools that burn brighter than their surroundings.

There is a certain peculiarity about this word, however, that appears fairly consistent. Not only does *lappiyd* indicate a fiery flame, but, at times, this flame appears to have a life of its own, like a kind of floating, animated symbol, as it does here: "And it came to pass, that, when the sun went down, and it was dark, behold a smoking furnace, and a burning lamp [*lappiyd*] that passed between those pieces. In the same day the Lord made a covenant with Abram, saying, Unto thy seed have I given this land, from the river of Egypt unto the great river, the river Euphrates" (Genesis 15:17–18). As recorded in Judges 15:4–5, Samson tied a crude hunk of burning wood between two foxes over and over again, eventually setting about three hundred foxes with these *lappiyd* "firebrands" into the corn stalks of the Philistine fields. This fiery scene isn't the only one that depicts a wild, out-of-control brush fire caused by *lappiyd*. Nahum once compared *lappiyd* torches to pure chaos, when he prophesied that the chariots in the streets of Nineveh would violently rage and thrash about and "justle one against another in the broad ways: they shall seem like torches [*lappiyd*]" (Nahum 2:4). In Zechariah, the image is that God will "make the governors of Judah like an hearth of fire among the wood, and like a torch [*lappiyd*] of fire in a sheaf; and they shall devour all the people round about, on the right hand and on the left: and Jerusalem shall be inhabited again in her own place, even in Jerusalem" (Zechariah 12:6).

In context within Scripture, *lappiyd* looks almost feral, untamed, unmanageable, at least out of human control, and at times even autonomous or self-governing. In other words, the account in Exodus is not talking about a regular, everyday, run-of-the-mill fire, and it certainly isn't referring to lightning. According to the witness of the Hebrew author, what started as bright, flashing lights (*baraq*) became, by the end of God's delivery of the Ten Commandments, bright, flashing fire (*lappiyd*)!

To sum up what we've looked at so far: The account of this moment in Exodus never actually mentions thunder at all. The Israelites "*saw* a voice," and it was the one and only powerful voice of God. How they "saw" a sound has yet to be addressed. Then, we stopped to reflect upon another fact: The lightning they witnessed was never lightning, but a bright, flashing light (*baraq*) that rapidly evolved into a flashing fire (*lappiyd*) sometime between God's arrival at Sinai and His finalizing of the commandments. And, after viewing the context of the words *baraq* and *lappiyd* to how they're used in other parts of the Bible and studying the way it was described, it's fair to say this light/fire was probably moving around of its own (God's) will.

At this point, it might look like we have more information about the lightnings that weren't really lightnings than we do about the thunderings that weren't thunderings. What was really going on with the *qowl* shouting from heaven?

Here's the glue. Ready?

When we study the sentence structure of the description of the phenomenon in Exodus 19:16 in Hebrew, *without all the modern English additions for flow*, we arrive at: *boqer qowl baraq*. That's it. That's all the Hebrew says. In a literal, word-for-word, initially nonsensical reading, *boqer qowl baraq* means "morning voice light." It is from these seemingly vague three Hebrew words that we were given the English, "In the morning there were thunderings and lightnings." Similarly, Exodus 20:18: *'am ra'ah qowl lappiyd*. Once again, the literal, word-for-word rendering is "people saw voice torch." This was where we received, "All the people saw the thunderings and the lightnings."

Don't miss this.

The Hebrew never suggested "and" in the original formation of the sentence. The translators inserted the "and" (as well as other words) as they did in countless other passages to ensure the sentence made sense. It's all a bit Tarzan-style—"morning voice light," "people saw voice torch"—without the smoothing that occurs during the translation process. Unfortunately, unless the translators are correct, even the tiniest word like "and" can disjoint the original story.

We're not reading about two separate phenomena. The Hebrew doesn't say the *baraq* and *lappiyd* were "in addition to" the *qowl*, it says the *baraq* and *lappiyd* "were" the *qowl*. In English, the Israelites didn't "see a voice" *and then also* "see lights/fires"; they "saw a voice *appearing as* lights/fires." Go back to the bare-bones, Tarzan version, and imagine inserting not words but just the punctuation that didn't exist back then. It might look like this: "Morning; voice-light." "People saw voice-torch."

The voice manifested as fire!

All this time we've been confused about how a "voice" can be "seen" is finally explained, because we now have the physical manifestation of God's voice as these flickering, bright flames appeared all over the mountainside.

Dr. Juergen Buehler, physicist, chemist, and president of the International Christian Embassy Jerusalem (ICEJ), painted what these authors believe to be a striking word picture of this moment The teachings of the rabbis on this area, Buehler explains, is that "every word God spoke that day was like the stroke of a hammer on an anvil. With each stroke on the anvil, which was Mount Sinai, sparks...of fire flew outward."[82] How appropriate a web this weaves between the *qowl*, *baraq*, and *lappiyd*... God's voice, like sparks, shooting out with every reverberating boom of the Law.

But this visual, especially for those who are learning about it for the first time, does raise a few questions: Why would God, Himself, appear as smoke and fire all over the mountain, while His voice—declaring the Ten Commandments for the first time—appeared as flickering, glinting flames that grew in intensity as He spoke, described in such a way as to travel about? Why were the little flame-lights so animated…if they even were? And what was the purpose of any of this?

Perhaps some of the earlier Torah commentary experts would be of help to us now.

The Midrash, the Jewish community's most respected Scripture commentary, compiled by celebrated rabbis (sages) between AD 400 and AD 1200, is alive and well on the subject of the "thunderings" and the "lightnings." These rabbis observed a great number of related verses in addition to the geographical spread of God's appearance worldwide as outlined in the Word, and they came to a most interesting connection, starting at Mt. Sinai and spreading outward. Observe what the records say in Midrash, "Shemot Rabbah" (Hebrew, "Great Exodus") 5:9, regarding the visible voice of God in Exodus 19:16 and 20:18:

> This is that which is written (Job 37:5), "God thunders wonders with His voice"—what is it that He thunders? When the Holy One, blessed be He, gave the Torah at Sinai, He showed wonders of wonders to Israel. How is it? The Holy One, blessed be He, would speak and the voice would go out and travel the whole world: Israel would hear the voice coming to them from the South and they would run to the South to meet the voice; and from the South, it would switch for them to the North, and they would all run to the North; and from the North, it would switch to the East, and they would run to the East; and from the East, it would switch to the West, and they would run to the West; and from the West, it would switch [to be] from the heavens, and they would suspend their eyes [to the heavens], and it would switch [to be] in the earth, and they would stare at the earth, as it is stated (Deuteronomy 4:36), "From the Heavens did He make you hear His voice, to discipline you." And Israel would say one to the other, "And wisdom, from where can it be found" (Job 28:12). And Israel would say, from where is the Holy One, blessed be He, coming, from the East or from

the South? As it is stated (Deuteronomy 33:2), "The Lord came from Sinai, and shone from Seir (in the East) to them"; and it is written (Habakuk 3:3), "And God will come from Teiman (in the South)." And it is stated (Exodus 20:18), "And all the people saw the sounds (literally, voices)"…[83]

Huh… So, according to this explanation, God's voice "went out" to the north, south, east, and west, all over the world. There was not one area—from Sinai to the opposite point on our round planet—that anyone could go to escape His message.

Why the multiple light/fires, though? God, the Creator of the universe, whose voice can kill entire armies with one utterance, could have just talked really loud, right?

Uh-huh. He could have. But our creative Father chose this method for His *tongues* to reach everyone on the globe…and it wasn't the only time He would do so.

If these Jewish scholars whose commentary paved the way for Old Testament understanding for the last several thousand years are correct, and we *can* see that God's voice manifested all over the globe, then we humbly seek a deeper understanding if we're to believe there is a New-Testament, Christ-centered fulfillment of the Day of Pentecost (or Feast of Weeks).

See, it wasn't just a spectacle of voice, lights, and fire. Rabbi Yochanan, a first-century sage, in his Midrash commentary on the Sinai account in Exodus, notes: "The voice would go out and divide into seventy voices for the seventy languages, so that all the nations would hear [and understand]."[84] Maybe when Yochanan wrote this he was inspired by Psalm 29:7: "The voice of the Lord divideth the flames of fire"!

You caught that, right? It's about being *multilingual.*

If the Midrash is correct: God's voice came from the heavens over Mt. Sinai, manifested in bright flashes of fiery light and divided into all known languages of the world at that time. Then His voice traveled all over the globe so that all people might hear and understand His words…*all on 6 Sivan*, the very first Day of Pentecost, exactly fifty days from the first Passover in Egypt.

Remember, these rabbis are *Jewish*. Their consideration of what was occurring at that point in Exodus is naturally no respecter of any story in Acts 2 of the New Testament; that's a "Testament" of the Messiah they don't believe in. Far be it for any contributor to Midrash commentary to attempt to show through Jewish theology that the Old Testament Mt. Sinai tongues/languages event foreshadowed the New Testament Mt. Sinai tongues/languages event. A truly Jewish rabbi would likely be more interested in wanting to show the *dissimilarities* between Jehovah on the mountain and the Comforter Jesus promised to send!

Yet, as most Christians know, the book of Acts, chapter 2, tells: On the Day of Pentecost, fifty days after Jesus had sat at the Last Supper and instituted communion instead of Passover, the same day all the Jews were wrapping up the Counting of the Omer on the Hebrews' 6 Sivan, the Holy Spirit descended on Christ's followers. When He did, bright, flickering "tongues of flame" descended from heaven and hovered over the men and women there, who proceeded to file out into the streets, speaking in all the known languages of that day…so that all men might hear God's words and understand.

This time, unlike the last time, the message wasn't about the Law, but about Jesus Christ, the Messiah who came to fulfill the Law (Matthew 5:17–20).

…And *this* time, unlike the last time, God's words would be directed and received by both Jews and Gentiles.

Before we get into that too far, let's read what happened in Acts 2 directly from the Bible. Tragically (but not surprisingly), some of its potency is lost in translation:

And when the day [Feast] of Pentecost was fully come, they were all with one accord in one place. And suddenly there came a sound from heaven as of a rushing mighty wind, and it filled all the house where they were sitting. And there appeared unto them cloven tongues like as of fire, and it sat upon each of them. And they were all filled with the Holy Ghost, and began to speak with other tongues, as the Spirit gave them utterance. (Acts 2:1–4)

To begin with, the "sound" mentioned in "there came a sound from heaven" was not just a noise. This is the Greek word *echos*, which appears in only a few places in the Word. In one of those occurrences, Luke 21:25, it's translated to "roar"! In Hebrews 12:19, it's used in conjunction with *salpigx* to refer to the very trumpet blast "which signals the Second Coming"![85] Then, oddly, over in Luke 4:37, after Jesus cast a demon out of the man in Capernaum, *echos* is translated as "fame": "And the fame [*echos*] of him went out into every place of the country round about."

So far, from only within the Bible, it looks like this word could mean a roar, a blast-signal of God's appearance, or the spreading recognition of God's power. See what we mean? It's *so* much more than just "a sound."

And, you know, that's quite interesting, considering the context of Acts 2:2 in comparison to the Sinai account. Could it be the "sound from heaven" that fell upon the great city of Jerusalem on that Feast of Pentecost day was a terrifically loud roar from the mouth of God; His own blast signaling the arrival of God in the Person of the Holy Spirit; the power of His voice going out from Him and ahead of Him, spreading the word of His imminent, soon-arriving, fame and glory?!

Man that's beautiful!

Wouldn't it be almost too good to be true if we could find a solid link showing the Greek *echos* was used in literature of this time directly and irrefutably to mean "voice"? Seriously… Wouldn't that really nail down the first parallel between God's *qowl* on Mt. Sinai and the sound here in Acts?

Actually, that *is* a definition of this word, and proof isn't difficult to find. Not only is this Greek term and its variants used to mean "voice" by writers at the time of Christ—such as in the academic medicine textbook *de Materia Medica* ("On Medical Material") by the Greek physician Pedanius Dioscorides[86]—thanks to the scholarly authors and editors behind the *Greek-English Lexicon* by Oxford, we now know *it referred specifically to the voice of God* in the LXX (Septuagint) Bible translation[87] (again, the LXX was the *Greek* Bible studied at the time of Christ!).

Our iron is hot. Let's strike again, shall we?

Next on the list is "rushing," which is from the Greek, *phero*.

Just as "thunder" wasn't necessarily the *worst* word that could have been chosen from the Hebrew for *qowl*, "rushing" isn't necessarily the worst choice for *phero*, as the immediate context does describe something happening rapidly ("And *suddenly* there came..."). Nevertheless, just as "thunder" wasn't accurate there, "rushing" isn't accurate here. As just about any lexicon or study tool will indicate, *phero* means "bring," "carry," or "bear."[88]

As just a few of countless examples, here are four verses—each from one of the four Gospels—that use *phero*:

- "He said, 'Bring [*phero*] them hither to me'" (Matthew 14:18).
- "'Shall we give, or shall we not give?' But he, knowing their hypocrisy, said unto them, 'Why tempt ye me? bring [*phero*] me a penny, that I may see it'" (Mark 12:15).
- "And bring [*phero*] hither the fatted calf, and kill it; and let us eat, and be merry" (Luke 15:23).
- "Every branch in me that beareth not fruit he taketh away: and every branch that beareth fruit, he purgeth it, that it may bring [*phero*] forth more fruit" (John 15:2).

It's quite a leap, from "bring" to "rushing." Right? The latter of these terms is detached from any identifiable driving force and almost sounds random, chaotic, or even accidental. There's nobody involved in it. The former, to "bring" or "carry" something, is personal, intentional...it almost rings from the page like a gift, no? Though either one can ultimately be interpreted to acknowledge the wind as God's handiwork, considering the colossal significance of what was taking place in both physical and spiritual realms in that moment, saying God "brought" or "carried" the wind allows for intention and specificity directly from the Divine.

It probably goes without saying by this point, but we will say it anyway: A person has to try, *hard*, to see the distant, detached, impersonal word "rushing" in this place instead of what is more apparently meant here, which is the act of the Holy Spirit carrying something.

What, exactly, is He carrying, though?

Remember how the "thunder and lightning" at Mt. Sinai wasn't really thunder and lightning, and how it wasn't two phenomena but rather one, and its corresponding description? Recall how, in English, there likely wouldn't have been any way of knowing that based on how our language bleeds off the page? Well, this moment is similar in that it will require readers to be open-minded in challenging some age-old concepts and imagery. It's surprisingly dissimilar, however, in that even the English—*when read carefully*—by itself dispels the most common misinterpretation of this verse in all of Christendom.

Here it is again, Acts 2:2a, in English. Pay attention to every single word: "And suddenly there came a sound from heaven as of a rushing mighty wind."

If, in that reading, you came up with the Holy Spirit "bringing" or "carrying" anything other than a *sound*, you might want to go back and read it again. Let us explain.

The time-honored, and frankly *gorgeous*, visual of the powerful winds is all over the place in our church curriculum and charts, religious media, historical paintings, books, and even various Christian retail products. We hear about the "rushing mighty wind" from the pulpit with such excitement—how it came bursting through the windows and doors into the Upper Room, swirling around the followers of Christ, whipping about their robes and hair, alerting everyone that something big is coming... Sometimes the retelling even involves the apostles being lifted up from the floor!

As inspiring as it is, however, the "wind" idea we all have isn't what the Greek originally described. If it were, then a few issues would have to be addressed. To name only one: The adjective translated into English as "mighty" here is the Greek word *biaios*, which surprisingly means "violent."[89] In other words, if this wind was a literal, physical, and purely natural element, then we are told here the gentle Comforter sent a "violent" wind to tear through the city on the day He arrived. But imagining the Holy Spirit sending danger to the disciples He's about to bless is odd. For as many words in the Greek language as there are that would have conveyed *both* might (or power) *and* safety in the presence of the Lord, *biaios* kinda sticks out like the proverbial sore thumb here.

Why not just "mighty" by itself? Why "violent"? If Luke was only attempting to tell the readers the wind was "strong" or "mighty," a number of more appropriate terms could have been used...*and* they were terms he already knew and used! Why wouldn't Luke have chosen *dynatos*—the literal Greek word for "mighty" or "powerful"— here, like he did elsewhere (Luke 1:49; 14:31; 18:27; 24:19; Acts 2:24; 7:22; 11:17; 18:24; 20:16; 25:5)? Why did he suddenly break character in Acts 2:2 and depict God as the sender of perilous weather conditions?

Actually, scholarly opinions about this section of Scripture are fairly unanimous: Luke wrote "violent," and "violent" is precisely what he meant, but he wasn't describing a "wind," he was describing a "sound." Technically, the wind didn't exist in any way other than as a basis for comparison. For many readers, this is a huge surprise. So long has the literal wind on the Day of Pentecost in the New Testament been ingrained in our concepts that it's hard to let go of the whooshing, sweeping, dust-in-the-air ideas. But *Thayer's Greek Lexicon* is the first of many sources we can point to fairly quickly that will dispel this. According to *Thayer's*, the comparative Greek adverb *hosper*, translated "as" here in the cluster "a sound from heaven as of a rushing mighty wind," is a word meaning something that simply "stands in close relation to what precedes," therefore representing a direct comparison in Acts 2:2, "i.e., just as a sound is made when a mighty wind blows."[90] Scotland's finest New Testament scholar and former chairman of the Tyndale Fellowship for Biblical and Theological Research, Ian Howard Marshall, acknowledges this in *Acts: An Introduction and Commentary*, pointing out that the grammatical relationship between the Greek *pnoe* ("wind") next to the aggressive *biaios* is "that of analogy—a sound *like* that of wind."[91] Leading academic and Fellowship of the British Academy award-winning professor of divinity at England's University of Durham, Charles Kingsley Barrett, states in *A Critical and Exegetical Commentary on the Acts of the Apostles* that "Luke is confining himself to a vivid *natural* analogy... There was a noise *like* that made by a powerful wind."[92]

To recap so far: 1) The disciples of Christ were all together "in one accord"; 2) God personally ushered, carried, and delivered to them the sound of His voice—a *roar* so powerful and commanding that it sounded to those assembled like a howling, violent wind.

Next: Not only do the followers of Jesus *hear* the voice of God like a wind, they *see* the voice as it manifests as "cloven tongues like as of fire, and it sat upon each of them." But note that "cloven" here is a bit misleading in English because of our familiarity with phrases like "cloven hoof," which refers to one object with a "split" shape in it. The "cloven" reference is from the Greek *diamerizo* ("divided"), which describes when God's voice descended, split apart into many "tongues," and then "each person present was touched with flame."[93] Again, this is the wonder being referred to in Psalm 29:7: "The voice of the Lord divideth the flames of fire."

Then, of course, comes the question scholars have sometimes taken an unexpected turn on: whether "tongues" describes the shape of the flames in comparison to the bodily organ, *or* more simply, "languages." Technically, the Greek *glossa* is used for both the body part as well as the speech it makes, so it could be either. However, despite the somewhat convincing argument for the former by some astute language experts (that Luke was saying the flames were "tongue-shaped"), it seems the more complicated conclusion to make. The context of the very next verse—"and began to speak with other tongues, as the Spirit gave them utterance"—is clearly in reference to spoken languages, and generally no one in academia argues with that. Since the context and application are therefore the same, it's safe to agree with the vast majority of scholars on this one and stick to the following deduction: "Tongues," *both in verse 3 and in verse 4*, in reference to "languages," which renders what readers may have, before our reflection on Sinai, thought was awkward: "And there appeared unto them [divided languages] like as of fire, and it sat upon each of them. And they were all filled with the Holy Ghost, and began to speak with other [languages]."

A couple more quick thoughts on this area of Scripture before we wrap this up: First, the words "all with one accord" have caused speculation. What, exactly, were the disciples in harmony about? Most scholars and commentators link this to the close-proximity instance of "one accord" in Acts 1:14, where there is a direct description of what they were doing together: "These all continued with one accord in prayer and supplication, with the women, and Mary the mother of Jesus, and with his brethren." These authors particularly like the way *Benson Commentary* says it:

The word [Greek *homothymadon*], rendered **with one accord,** implies that they were united in their views, intentions, and affections, and that there was no discord or strife among them, as there sometimes had been while their Master was with them. Doubtless, they were also united in their desire and expectation of the baptism of the Holy Ghost, **the power from on high,** which Christ had promised them; and in praying earnestly and importunately for it whenever they met together, which it appears they were in the habit of doing daily.[94] (Emphasis in original)

They were all praying together, but it's likely they were praying specifically for the power from God to assist them in the Great Commission, since that is what the Holy Spirit does. Take note of this, because it is a crucial point in "The Church Age," which is what the Feast of Pentecost represents. And don't misunderstand this to be an argument for speaking in tongues, as these authors truly believe that matter is between the believer and God. We want to stress that, just as the Holy Spirit came to the disciples on 6 Sivan in what was likely the year AD 33 with languages of fire, He can come upon any and all believers with the gifts of the Spirit they've been equipped with for Great Commission work today, so long as every believer is praying in expectation for that.

Consider again Acts 2:1–4 in light of all we've reflected on. Based on the original languages and contexts and the consistency of God's nature from the Old Testament, we will suggest a contemplative, dynamic wording of this passage:

And on 6 Sivan, during the Feast of Pentecost, the disciples of Christ were all gathered together in one place, supporting one another and agreeing with one another in prayer [probably for the "power from on high"]. And suddenly there came a voice, roaring from heaven like a violent wind, and the sound filled all the dwelling place where they were sitting. And the disciples saw the voice from heaven divide into many languages, looking like fire, and the fire sat upon each of them. And they were all filled with the Holy Ghost, and began to speak with other languages, as the Spirit gave them utterance. (Acts 2:1–4)

Hey readers… Remember that time on Mt. Sinai when God's voice physically manifested as a bright fire, then split up and went out to all the world so every man would know and understand His Law?

Yeah. He did *that* again.

The "fiftieth day" (Pentecost) from the deliverance of Egypt, when the Law (the *Old Covenant*) united the nation of Israel under the will of God while on Mt. Sinai, was a literal, moment-for-moment parallel of the "fiftieth day" (Pentecost) from the death of Christ and deliverance from the confines of sin, when Jesus fulfilled the Law down to the letter and united Jew and Gentile (the *New Covenant*) as a new people under the grace of God while on Mt. Zion.

Most folks who have little to no familiarity with the feasts aren't aware of this connection, but once we see it, we can't "unsee" it without extreme effort. The resemblance between the two events is no coincidence.

Barrett recognizes this comparison without hesitation: "Luke is accumulating features characteristic of theophanies...[like the] descriptions of the giving of the Law on Mount Sinai: Exod. 19:18."[95] Marshall is likewise convinced: "A flame divided itself into several *tongues*, so that each rested upon one of the persons present.... And again we are reminded of Old Testament theophanies, especially of that at Sinai (Exod. 19:18)."[96] Dr. Richard Booker of *Celebrating Jesus in the Biblical Feasts* notes this wonderful Old Testament/New Testament connection as well:

> The English translation [of the Sinai event] says all the people witnessed the thunderings and the lightnings. Jewish scholars believe that the people actually "saw the voice of God" coming out of the mountain in tongues of fire....
>
> The first Pentecost was at Mount Sinai when God wrote His words on tablets of stone. Yet, the Lord promised there would be a time in the distant future when He would write His laws on the fleshly tablets of their hearts. (See Jeremiah 31:31–34.)...
>
> And let's not leave out a very important rabbi, Southern Evangelical Seminary's pride and Word of Messiah Ministries' president, Dr. Sam Nadler, who also acknowledged in his book, *Messiah in the Feasts of Israel*:

Luke, who wrote the book of Acts, was trained by his mentor Paul to understand the work of God in Messiah from a Biblically Jewish frame of reference. Luke depicts the events of Acts 2 as a second "Mount Sinai experience." When the Law was given, there was fire and noise as God descended on Mount Sinai (Exodus 19:18–20). When the Spirit was given there was fire and noise as well (Acts 2:2–3). The rabbis comment in the Talmud that when the Torah was given at Mount Sinai, "Every single word that went forth from the Omnipotent was split up into seventy languages for the nations of the world." When the Holy Spirit was given, men from every nation spoke in other languages as the Spirit enabled them.[98]

And many of the classic commentators, at the time of their writings (circa 1820–1850 on a lot of them), wrote as if God's manifestation in both the Old Testament and New Testament Pentecost was a foreshadowing followed by fulfillment. As one example from *Benson*: "It is computed that the law was given just fifty days after their coming out of Egypt, in remembrance of which the feast of pentecost was observed the fiftieth day after the passover, and in compliance with which the Spirit was poured out upon the apostles, at the feast of pentecost, fifty days after the death of Christ."[99]

It's really no wonder scholars concluded that the Acts 2 episode was a direct fulfillment of what God started on Mt. Sinai. The parallels are seemingly endless, including many we haven't even covered well enough to do great justice. Take a look at this list, which isn't even close to exhaustive:

- Both demonstrations of God's power involve tongues of fire and multiple languages so that all mankind will hear and understand the message of God.
- Both events took place on the Feast of Pentecost, and on 6 Sivan.

- Both events involved a theophany—that is, a visible manifestation of the Lord.
- Both events marked the delivery of a Divine Covenant: In Exodus, it was fifty days after the Israelites completed the threshold covenant with the lamb sacrifice; in Acts, it was fifty days after Jesus became the ultimate Lamb Sacrifice.
- In Exodus, Israel as a nation was established; in Acts, Christianity was established.
- Exodus 24:13 calls Mt. *Sinai* the "mountain of God." Isaiah 2:3 calls Mt. *Zion* the "mountain of God." Both the Old Testament (Old Covenant) tongues-of-fire event at Sinai and the New Testament (New Covenant) tongues-of-fire event at Zion took place on "the mountain of God," though they are over three hundred miles apart.
- In Hebrew, the word *towrah* ("Torah"—the Law), as it derives from the root *yarah*, means "teach." John 14:16 refers to the Holy Spirit as the "teacher."
- In Exodus, we read about the inauguration of the Old Testament Church; in Acts, we read about the inauguration of the New Testament—and current—Church.

Again, the list goes on. Studying these two occurrences side by side as we have done flags another hundred or so deeply theological parallels that blow the mind. If this book were *just* about the Jewish feasts, we would be tempted to devote another hundred pages on Pentecost alone. Alas, we don't have space herein to accomplish that…but what do you readers say? One more for the road?

Woohoo! This next one is the *best*!

In Exodus 32, just after the Mt. Sinai Pentecost demonstration when the idolatry-forbidding Mosaic Law had been given to the Israelites, God's chosen people had the audacity to create and worship a golden calf. Moses delegated the tribe of Levi, who had *not* turned their backs upon the Lord like the others, to carry out the unfortunate task of making an example out of the idolaters. "And the children of Levi did according to the word of Moses: and there fell of the people that day about three thousand men" (Exodus 32:28). These authors wonder if this particular travesty was in Paul's mind when he called the Law the "ministry of condemnation" (2 Corinthians 3:7–9).

Flip forward a heavy heap in the Word. Just after the Holy Spirit's Pentecost demonstration, the disciples ran to the streets to preach that "God hath made the same Jesus, [who was] crucified, both Lord and Christ" (Acts 2:36). Here's what happened next:

> Now when they heard this, they were pricked in their heart, and said unto Peter and to the rest of the apostles, "Men and brethren, what shall we do?"
>
> Then Peter said unto them, "Repent, and be baptized every one of you in the name of Jesus Christ for the remission of sins, and ye shall receive the gift of the Holy Ghost. For the promise is unto you, and to your children, and to all that are afar off, even as many as the Lord our God shall call." And with many other words did he testify and exhort, saying, "Save yourselves from this untoward generation."
>
> What a glorious, gracious turnaround! At Sinai, three thousand people died under the Old Covenant. In the book of Acts, three thousand were saved because of the message of the New Covenant!

Folks, this *is* "the Church Age" that fulfills the old Feast of Pentecost. Jesus fulfilled it by sending the Spirit He promised to send, and now, with the Spirit's gentle, personal, and patient help, we believers are empowered by the Holy Spirit to take God's story to the ends of the earth in every language, just like the followers of Christ did in the book of Acts. What a privilege!

Early Church Initial Growth

So, the apostles and disciples rushed all over the city, speaking in other languages as the Holy Spirit gave them utterance and preaching the Gospel of Christ. After quite a bit of confusion regarding this phenomenon, Peter stood before the crowd of listeners and explained that this was not, as they believed, an unexpected occurrence. Not only was this event one the Lord, Himself, promised would take place, the prophets Isaiah and Joel saw it coming from time immemorial as well. God prophesied through Isaiah: "I will pour my spirit upon thy seed, And my blessing upon thine offspring" (44:3b). God had also spoken through Joel:

> And it shall come to pass afterward, That I will pour out my spirit upon all flesh; And your sons and your daughters shall prophesy, Your old men shall dream dreams, Your young men shall see visions: And also upon the servants and upon the handmaids. In those days will I pour out my spirit. And I will shew wonders in the heavens and in the earth... And it shall come to pass, that whosoever ["whosoever" includes Gentiles] shall call on the name of the Lord shall be delivered: For in mount Zion and in Jerusalem shall be deliverance, As the Lord hath said. (2:28–30a, 32a)

On the Day of Pentecost, *all this* was fulfilled. With conviction, Peter then spoke about the shared guilt of the Messiah's death, which was necessary for the Resurrection, and then explained that this was a foreordained act of God as acknowledged by David (Acts 2:29–36).

Acts 2:5 mentions "devout Jews." Commentator C. K. Barrett states that, from its onset, the Christian church has been "a universal community [including] 'pious men' of every kind (cf. 10:34, 35)."[100] The receptive crowd recognized the supernatural nature of the miracle immediately (2:6–12). Though *some* mocked the apostles/disciples for being drunk, upon hearing Peter's sermon, mockery had disappeared and in its place were conviction and concern (2:37). Mass repentance led to a glorious baptism, and the saving of three thousand souls who were added to the fledgling church (2:41).

Such boldness! On one hand, Peter had to be willing to be bold as he shouted out such convicting, punchy words to the crowds. His sudden confidence (a noteworthy shift since Peter allowed fear to own him the night he denied Christ) in proclaiming the Gospel is inspiring. On the other hand, it is only by the empowering of the Holy Spirit that the otherwise-fearful Peter would be so bold. (We have access to the same Spirit today, and He is only one "ask" away from being as available to each of us as He was for Peter on that Day of Pentecost. What intensely God-glorifying miracles could/would happen through us today if we grasped onto that same boldness in the streets?!)

Another moment of early Church growth is found in Acts 2:42–47, when the recent converts form a fellowship community and church in Jerusalem and establish "the four essential elements" that would forever help to define "the religious practice of the Christian church": teaching, fellowship, the breaking of bread, and prayer.[101]

The faith, itself, was brand new—Christianity had never existed before. This assembly would have involved men of diverse backgrounds as well. Some of these believers no doubt would have felt some level of anxiety about joining the very movement/religion that had angered religious leaders to capture and torture Christ...and many would face scorned family members who didn't share the same affirmation and conviction about the Messiah (perhaps not unlike what Muslims face under the same circumstances today). Nevertheless, as is clear through the entire book of Acts, everything was communally shared, including both material goods (such as possessions and land) and immaterial belongings (such as faith, emotion, joy, excitement, etc.), creating a new religious/familial setting for everyone. This bond, driven by the Holy Spirit and the power of the Gospel, engendered receptive, teachable, and passionate Christians who were eager for growth.

(As a lesson that can apply to us today: In this New Testament model, we don't need a full band, sound equipment, ushers, or velvet offering bags to achieve a church service as legitimate as it is anywhere else at any other time in history. We can [and should] practice teaching, fellowshipping, communing, and praying both inside *and outside* those buildings the increasingly secularized world is coming to disdain.)

Following this, over and over again, Acts accounts for many lives who were saved, well beyond the three thousand who were saved on that day (those who created the first Christian Church in history [2:41]). The vast majority of the book of Acts is a description of where these men and women went and what they did to fulfill the Great Commission. Just as repeatedly, as hands were laid upon new believers, the equipment of the Holy Spirit frequently landed upon them, and they spoke in other tongues as well—Jews and Gentiles alike. Many were healed and delivered from demons just as they had been while Jesus had walked the earth. As yet another lesson for modern times, this was never done simply because God smiled upon His servants, but because the Lord's servants bathed themselves in prayer, supplication, and unity among believers.

One particularly "loud" example (that has stretched forth to speak to us today, even as our children sing Sunday school songs about the healing) occurs in the beginning of Acts 3: Peter and John went to pray at the Temple, during the "ninth hour" (the hour of prayer). A group of men carried a man who had been lame from birth to the "Beautiful Gate" (3:1–3).

There is a reason for this name: The gate literally was beautiful. (And women will be touched to know it may have been the "Nicanor Gate, as it is called in the Mishnah, leading into the Court of the Women"![102]) Josephus wrote of this particular part of the Temple being covered in "Corinthian brass" and adorned with extra beauty:

Now nine of these gates were on every side covered over with gold and silver, as were the jambs of their doors and their lintels; but there was one gate that was without [the inward court of] the holy house, which was of Corinthian brass, and greatly excelled those that were only covered over with silver and gold.... Now the magnitudes of the other gates were equal one to another; but that over the Corinthian gate, which opened on the east over against the gate of the holy house itself, was much larger; for its height was fifty cubits; and its doors were forty cubits; and it was adorned after a most costly manner, as having much richer and thicker plates of silver and gold upon them than the other. These nine gates had that silver and gold poured upon them by Alexander, the father of Tiberius.[103]

The lame man was carried to that gate every day to beg for alms. When he saw Peter and John there, he asked for money as usual, but money wasn't what the apostles had in mind. When Peter said, "Look on us" (Acts 3:4), the poor man looked upon them, expecting an affirmative response to his request. But then:

Peter said, "Silver and gold have I none; but such as I have give I thee: In the name of Jesus Christ of Nazareth rise up and walk." And [Peter] took [the crippled man] by the right hand, and lifted him up: and immediately his feet and ancle bones received strength. And he leaping up stood, and walked, and entered with them into the temple, walking, and leaping, and praising God. And all the people saw him walking and praising God: And they knew that it was he which sat for alms at the Beautiful gate of the temple: and they were filled with wonder and amazement at that which had happened unto him. (Acts 3:6–10)

See how quickly these events caught the attention of observers? And these were no ordinary men of the street, like some of the accounts in Acts describe. These were folks who had seen this lame man every single day begging for alms at the gate, those "pious men" whose primary goal was to submerge their mind, body, and soul into the depths of Jewish theology, customs, practice, culture, and worship. The narrative goes on to explain:

> And it came to pass on the morrow, that their rulers, and elders, and scribes, And Annas the high priest, and Caiaphas, and John, and Alexander, and as many as were of the kindred of the high priest, were gathered together at Jerusalem. And when they had set [Peter and John] in the midst, they asked, "By what power, or by what name, have ye done this?"
>
> When the crippled man bounced up, walking, leaping and praising God, righteous men who frequented the Temple were the first to see that the Man who had been crucified had surely sent His followers some kind of power to enable them to perform miracles as He had done. Even if Jesus had not visited them personally, His presence was still with them as proof of His claims. In a way, this healing would be the best example of this reality. But on the other hand, this very healing may have been what angered the Jews and Romans all the more, leading to intensified persecution of Christians in the first century. As history does tell, the deaths of the martyrs were...well, they were *so* bad we can't discuss them at length and still call this book "family friendly." The details are so gruesome they make our previous study about sex in the Songs look muted.

But despite, and against, all odds, Christianity continued to expand across Judea, the neighboring regions, and the uttermost ends of the earth, as Christ had said was possible. Many of these accounts have conclusive endings, showing exactly where and when the new Christians traveled to new locations and planted churches, despite the threats from Roman leaders that anyone caught teaching about Christ's Kingdom (on earth or otherwise) would receive the death penalty.

In Acts 6:1–7, the Jerusalem church got too large to manage its own charity/food distribution, and the hungry widows became the victims of a communication error. The twelve apostles acted fast, delegating and laying hands on seven men (one of whom was Stephen, who was soon to be martyred) to take over the food distribution, which freed the apostles to return their full focus to prayer and teaching. By verse 7, it is clear that communication and smooth operations were restored, and the church was greatly increased. The audience in Acts 6:1–6 is the same eager, united church discussed earlier, working together in the interest of keeping the teachings of Jesus alive and well. However, in verse 7, something astonishing happens when the new level of organization contributes to a large number of Jewish priests joining the family! Though some commentaries suggest "priests" should be read simply as "Jews," others say "priests" refers to "ordinary priests" who did, in fact, serve in higher positions, including some in the Temple.[104] This meant they a) may have been harder to convert because they had preexisting theological ideas, *but* b) had more experience in watching how a church should be managed.

Perhaps something about the apostles incorporating structure made the new Christian church appear less chaotic to the experienced priests.

Had the enemy gotten his way, the grumbling between believers that erupted from the food-rations issue would have been the end of the church. But by the power of the Holy Spirit, weak humans found the strength to rise above their squabbles and implement an organized strategy to correct the problem. (A spiritual truth drawn from Acts 6:1–7 is that, if a church wishes to be relevant and effective for the lost, it requires organized, Spirit-filled leaders to work together in a respectful and organized way, while they remain flexible enough to respond to problems as they arise.)

The church in Jerusalem steadily grew, sometimes by the thousands (see 4:4; 5:14; 6:1, 7; 8:4), and sometimes through persecution. The stoning of Stephen (6:8–8:1) and the scattering of Jews essentially launched preachers into action all over Judea and Samaria. The harder the persecution during this time, the more a sense of unity, spiritual family, and charity served to feed the disciples with more zeal…until persecution became a catalyst for growth. In the face of opposition, Christians fearlessly spread the Gospel (8:4–5). A colorful portrayal by Professor Kenneth Gangel of Dallas Theological Seminary reads: "Picture them as they run for their lives, grasping what few possessions they could take with them…. See them praying for deliverance [and] courage to be faithful to their Savior and to proclaim his message effectively wherever they went."[105] The threat of death and execution wasn't going to stop these mighty men and women touched by the strength of the Gospel message of Christ; it only served to send them out to the far ends of the earth in a manner that would fulfill the Great Commission in their time!

Philip—the key player whose name was the only one recorded in Acts 8:4–8, 12—went to Samaria, empowered by the Holy Spirit, healing the lame and casting out demons from the possessed in the Name of Christ (8:4–8, 12). The relief from pain, suffering, and bondage had the entire city erupting with joy (8:8), to the point that many men and women in the region believed in Christ and were baptized (8:12). Philip's audience was made up of crowds who were eager and in one accord, their attention "aroused by [the miracles] they heard and saw…which acted as a confirmation of his message."[106] (Though this passage represents an audience that is brand-new to the Christian faith, even well-versed believers today could learn something from their eagerness. If we would only press in to Jesus with similar zeal, excitement, and togetherness as the crowds before Philip [refusing to be apathetic; 8:6], we would no doubt see *acts* similar to those the Holy Spirit performed through Philip.)

Acts chapters 10–11 tells the story of Cornelius of Caesarea, whose conversion triggered the extension of the Gospel message to *everyone*, no longer just the Jews. The new faith was already causing a rift between the Jews—nonbelievers against believers. In the midst of this vulnerable reformation, another challenge arose when some believing Jews still clung to countless customs/traditions of Judaism, including circumcision.

Cornelius was in the Gentile city of Caesarea when an angelic visit led him to summon Peter in Joppa. Peter, *before* Cornelius' men arrived, had a vision of his own, the later interpretation of which illustrated that Gentiles—like Cornelius—can be equal inheritors of salvation (10:9–15, 28). Peter went to Cornelius in Caesarea and witnessed to the "many" who were gathered in his home (10:27). The Holy Spirit fell upon the entire assembly and, to the amazement of the Jewish Christians, they all spoke in tongues (10:44–48), which irreversibly marked the inauguration of the Gentiles into the family of God.

The church growth in this instance is thereby not only numerical, but it involves a spiritual growth also, as the church matured into a new diverse Jew/Gentile family and took on a new attitude of acceptance and love.

The entire household of Cornelius was made up of devout, God-fearing folks (10:2). As such, they were well primed and ready for spiritual increase. By the time of Peter's message, more people had arrived (10:24, 27), though nothing specific is said about their spiritual life until it's noted that they spoke in tongues. (This shows sensitivity to, and an eagerness to cooperate with, the Spirit.) At the onset of Acts 10, Cornelius was not a Christian—nor was he a Jew, a proselyte, or a pagan (because he was a "God-fearer"). "Gentile" might *technically* appear a compatible term in that Cornelius was a non-Jew, but since "Cornelius believed in the God of the Jews and was committed to honoring him from a sincere and submissive heart,"[107] "Gentile" seems off-kilter now.

Some things never change. In that day, the religious-spirited sharks had their labelling games. Today, we have ours. The cliques and labelling games the Church participates in are destructive and divisive: not what we want the lost to see. Whether it's inside the Body (interdenominational squabbles) or is ostracizing those outside, it harms the mission Jesus has asked us to carry out. A Pharisee would have written off Cornelius for not getting circumcised and identifying as a proselyte. How many modern Corneliuses do we shun for not jumping through our own (Pharisaic) hoops?

Cornelius, for a moment, broke all the boxes our human-created labelling games fit into. We should, too.

If Jesus Really Was Who He Said He Was—Yikes!

Recall some of the would-be messiahs who stood against Rome just before Christ's birth and during His childhood. In Acts 5, John and Peter had been arrested, but an angel released them from jail and they proceeded to the Temple the next morning to preach. The religious leaders discovered it and were terrified that the news of the men's supernatural release would spread, so they sent officers to confront the apostles right where they taught and bring them to the Sanhedrin for trial. As John and Peter stood before the council, the council reminded them they were not to teach in Christ's Name: "Did not we straitly command you that ye should not teach in this name? and, behold, ye have filled Jerusalem with your doctrine, and intend to bring this man's blood upon us" (5:28). The apostles answered, "We ought to obey God rather than men" (5:29). The council then determined Peter and John (and those with them) would be killed, but Gamaliel—a doctor of the Law and a man of great reputation—stood up in a defense that has been as timelessly true as the Gospel: If Jesus was just another would-be, like Theudas or Judas the Galilean, Gamaliel said, then His death would eventually cause His followers to scatter and His movement would fizzle. If He was who He said He was, that would mean anyone who stood against Him was standing against God!

Some scholars don't find this to be good advice, because, if radically applied during all eras, the Church moving forward would never stand against false teaching under the assumption that it would simply die out. Politely, we disagree, landing somewhere in the middle on the issue: Though a strong stance against false teachers in the fold is a *must* for a healthy Body (and therefore teaching should not be dealt with via irresponsible assumptions), Gamaliel was *not* suggesting that we twiddle our thumbs and wait for God to strike down everything that doesn't line up with His doctrines. Gamaliel merely said that if a movement is of God, it will thrive regardless of anything mankind does to oppose it, but if it is not of God, it has no chance of maintaining its own momentum throughout future times. Even the end-times, one-world-order church under the Antichrist will grow to encompass the globe, but it will still die out and rain death upon its followers. No good advice from the mouths of men should be applied recklessly, but Gamaliel's logic here is sturdy, and that very reasoning freed the apostles in this instance.

For the souls who were saved in the days following their release, it was a miracle that John and Peter were let go to continue their Gospel work. Nevertheless, tragically, every one of the apostles—and countless numbers of disciples (both who are mentioned in Scripture and the precious lives of those who aren't mentioned in the Word)— would die martyrs' deaths. As stated prior, the leaders of this fledgling Church were the twelve (Matthias replacing Judas), and just under them were many empowered disciples who, just like their superiors, gave their whole life to the message of Gospel for both Jew and Gentile.

Oh yeah, and there was that one guy who became…a thirteenth apostle!?

Wait… Could there *be* such a thing?

Paul: His Background, Conversion, and Ministry

One man was hated by the early Christians at first, and he avoided them like the plague. But later, he would become hated among the Jews when the risen Jesus made yet another personal appearance. This was the man who would go on to be credited as the author of thirteen (possibly fourteen) books within the New Testament!

His Greek name was Paul, but his Jewish name was Saul, possibly after King Saul, Israel's first king. Saul was the son of a Pharisee (Acts 23:6), which likely contributed to his evident legalism in the beginning of his biblical role. He hailed from the tribe of Benjamin (Philippians 3:5), which meant he was born into a tribe known in Israel's history as great warriors. When Saul was young, he had developed a trade skill. Similar to Jesus, who was a carpenter, Saul was a tentmaker. Though we can assume this particular skill played little part of his life during his years as a Jewish sage of the Law working directly under Gamaliel (Acts 22:3), and as he was establishing himself as a great and zealous leader of the Jews (Galatians 1:13), he would later use his tentmaking to fund his ministry (Acts 18:3). Another important ability Saul developed while he was young was to fluently speak Greek, Hebrew, and Aramaic. (All three of these were common languages of his day and in his area of the world. This multilingual capability would make him an expert in communication, which would be vital for what God called him to do later on.) His familiarity with Greek culture, customs, religions, and ancient proverbs and writings (Acts 17:28; Titus 1:12) made him not only able to communicate but to also understand those he would minister to. In addition to all of this, Saul was legally a Roman citizen (Acts 22:28), giving him extra clout with Rome than fellow non-citizens, and very few of his religious associates could claim such a divergent background. (When he and Silas were jailed in Acts 16, they were not given the same fair trial a Roman citizen could expect. They were beaten and jailed on the spot, and when Saul brought up his citizenship, it was to the shock and dismay of those who had enacted punishment based on his appearing to be a mere Jew, so they scrambled to make him feel respected [16:37–39]. And again, in Acts 25:11–12, Saul appealed to Caesar for supreme justice—a right given to only a Roman citizen. It's therefore no wonder Saul was chosen for the work he was given in the Divine plan of our Lord. It's clear God had His hand on His servant from the beginning!) As his character in the New Testament is almost always referred to by his Greek name, we will hereafter call him "Paul."

Paul's physical appearance is noted in the mid-second century *Acts of Paul*. Far from the tall, lanky, intimidating man with a brooding face and a brow of judgment, hovering over his quill like we see in classic paintings, Paul was actually short, bald, possibly bow-legged from horseback riding, and had a kink in the bridge of his nose. A man named Onesiphorus, a resident of Iconium, met Paul on the way to the city and it is then that Paul is described as "a man small of stature, with a bald head and crooked legs...with eyebrows meeting and nose somewhat hooked, full of friendliness."[108]

Paul first appears in Acts as an advocate of the stoning of Stephen, who was "a man of...the Holy Ghost," "filled with faith and power," and "did great wonders and miracles among the people" (Acts 6:5, 8). The synagogue where Stephen angered the Jews is not mentioned specifically. However, the description of "the synagogue of the Libertines, and Cyrenians, and Alexandrians, and of them of Cilicia and of Asia" (6:9) gives us some tracking power. Paul, being "a Hebrew born of the Hebrews" (Philippians 3:5), may have chosen to attend a place of worship where the services were conducted entirely in his native, Hebrew language. But in Acts 22:3, Paul speaks of himself: "I am verily a man which am a Jew, born in Tarsus, a city in Cilicia." The mentioning of Cilicia in both Acts 6:9 and 22:3 possibly infers that Paul (and therefore his direct Jewish mentor, Gamaliel) were regular attendees at the synagogue where Stephen ran into trouble.[109]

Stephen, like Peter and John, stood before the Sanhedrin in trial for teaching about Christ's Kingdom, or, as the religious leaders accused, speaking "blasphemous words against Moses, and against God" (6:11). And, like Christ, Stephen could not be found guilty for anything he had actually done, so the Sanhedrin appointed "false witnesses" (yet again) to testify against him (6:13). At this moment, Stephen's face became like that of an "angel." This is, at first, an ambiguous description, but scholars have dissected the terminology here and compared it to similar phrasings in other Scriptures (2 Samuel 14:17; 2 Samuel 19:27; Genesis 33:10; Exodus 34:29–30; 2 Corinthians 3:7, 13; Revelation 1:16; Matthew 17:2). The consensus shows that, most likely, Stephen's face had a literal glow as well as a solemn, calm countenance of faith. Paul, *also*, had this look about him at one point, if the account of Onesiphorus of Iconium in *Acts of Paul* is accurate: "And he saw Paul approaching...for now he appeared like a man, and now he had the face of an angel."[110]

Stephen's self-defense before the council revisits the history of Israel and their failure to follow Moses (a good defense considering he was being accused of speaking blasphemy against that very man). He illustrates how the Jewish nation had always been guilty of rejecting the forefathers and the Spirit that guided them (7:2–53). While the council gnashed their teeth at his words, Stephen looked upward to heaven and saw Christ: "Behold, I see the heavens opened, and the Son of man standing on the right hand of God!" (7:56). This was a direct reference to both Psalm 110:1 ("the Lord said unto my Lord, 'Sit thou at my right hand'") and Daniel 7:13 regarding the "Son of Man" coming on the clouds of heaven. But scholars also connect this vision of Stephen's to that of Ezekiel:

> Now it came to pass in the thirtieth year, in the fourth month, in the fifth day of the month, as I was among the captives by the river of Chebar, that the heavens were opened, and I saw visions of God.... And above the firmament that was over their heads was the likeness of a throne, as the appearance of a sapphire stone: and upon the likeness of the throne was the likeness as the appearance of a man above upon it.... This was the appearance of the likeness of the glory of the Lord. And when I saw it, I fell upon my face. (Ezekiel 1:1, 26, 28)

Evidently it *was* the Son of Man, this Jesus, whom Ezekiel had seen so many years ago...

What a magnificent fulfillment! (And there will be another in Revelation!) But the Jews were not as excited as we are to hear Stephen speak of these things. It so angered the chief priests of the Sanhedrin that Stephen was stoned on the spot. This is where Paul comes into the story:

Then they cried out with a loud voice, and stopped their ears, and ran upon him with one accord, And cast him out of the city, and stoned him: and the witnesses laid down their clothes at a young man's feet, whose name was Saul. [In a formal execution, witnesses would take off their outer robes and lay them at the feet of the supervisor of the act. This being Paul heavily suggests that he was the key leader in Stephen's death.] And they stoned Stephen, calling upon God, and saying, "Lord Jesus, receive my spirit." And he kneeled down, and cried with a loud voice, "Lord, lay not this sin to their charge." [This is extremely similar to Jesus' final words on the cross, "Father, into Your hands I commit My Spirit" (Luke 23:46) and "Father, forgive them; for they know not what they do" (Luke 23:34).] And when he had said this, he fell asleep.

And Saul was consenting unto his death.

And at that time there was a great persecution against the church which was at Jerusalem; and they were all scattered abroad throughout the regions of Judaea and Samaria, except the apostles. And devout men carried Stephen to his burial, and made great lamentation over him.

When men and women were arrested for preaching in the Name of Christ, the punishment was death. Therefore, Paul was directly responsible for a great many martyrs. He personally burst through the doors of humble homes belonging to early Christians and had them carted off to prison where they would be tried, convicted, and executed for their work in the Kingdom of Jesus. And this was not just "a few Christians here and there in the area of Jerusalem." Later, Paul would write that his anger against Christians was so exceedingly hot that he pursued them well beyond the traditional borders of Israel and into "foreign cities" (26:11). Scholars believe Paul's zeal was equal to the Maccabeans.[111]

But back in Acts 9:1–2, we see that Paul was "breathing out threatenings and slaughter against the disciples of the Lord" when he went to the high priest and asked for official documents allowing his persecution of those who had fled from Jerusalem to Damascus so he could bring them back to the Sanhedrin for trial. The high priest granted his request, and Paul left straightaway to spread his own message: You can't run, you can't hide, and if you've been marked as one who follows the Gospel, you will face death.

On the way there, a great light from heaven surrounded him, and an authoritative voice spoke, saying, "Saul, Saul, why persecutest thou me?" (9:4). Again, scholars note: "There are affinities between [Paul's] conversion experience and Ezekiel's inaugural vision."[112] Paul asked who the Speaker was, and Jesus answered, "I am Jesus whom thou persecutest: it is hard for thee to kick against the pricks" (9:5). This reference to "kicking against the pricks" (or "goads") was an old Greek proverb. A "goad" was a stick with a sharp, iron protrusion connected to the oxen during plowing to urge them forward. If a stubborn ox kicked against it in protest, it would only cause injury to the ox, but it wouldn't stop the forward motion of the plowing process. Christ's words here were letting Paul know that resistance to the Gospel movement was futile, and that the only one he was hurting by persecuting those who were willing to die for the sake of Jesus was himself.

Paul asked the Speaker what he must do, and he was sent to Damascus to await further instruction. When he stood and opened his eyes, he was blind, but those who were travelling with him, who also heard the voice, led him into the city (9:6–8).

When Paul arrived, three days passed while he remained blind in the home of a man named Judas. Jesus then came to a believer named Ananias and told him where to find Paul. Christ instructed Ananias to minister to Paul, despite Ananias' reservations at the mention of the name of this persecutor, saying, "Go thy way: for he is a chosen vessel unto me, to bear my name before the Gentiles, and kings, and the children of Israel: For I will shew him how great things he must suffer for my name's sake" (9:15–16). Ananias obeyed, and when he laid hands on Paul, "scales" fell from his eyes (9:18). (The "scales" have been the subject of much debate. However, in the apocryphal book *Tobit* [3:17; 11:13], a similar account seems to explain that this was a filmy substance that fell—an expulsion of the "grey haze" that often covers the eyes of the blind.) Paul rose up, was baptized, and immediately started preaching the Gospel in the local synagogues, to the amazement of all who heard this radically saved convert (9:18–22).

Recall that there were three (two directly stated and one implied) qualifications for one to be called an apostle. He must be: personally called by Christ (as Paul just had been); taught by Christ (as Paul would then be during his time of isolation [Galatians 1:1–19]); and a witness to the Resurrected Messiah (as Paul had been on the road to Damascus). Therefore, fresh with the power of Christ and the Holy Spirit infused in his very being, Paul was empowered for what would become one of the greatest ministries in world history…the office of the thirteenth apostle, who wrote most of the New Testament!

However, there was a distinct difference between Paul and the other apostles. Paul would become the world's first—and the grandest example—missionary. His multilingual, multicultural background qualified him to reach Jews and Gentiles alike ("to bear my name before the Gentiles…and the children of Israel" [Acts 9:15]) in a way that many only-Jewish or only-Gentile ministers would never be able to.

Donna Howell, in her earlier college years, came face to face with a modern Paul (though this humble man would scarcely describe himself in such a manner!). His name was Otto Kaiser, and though he went to be with the Lord peacefully in his sleep on May 25, 2021, the entirety of his adult life prior to that day was as a servant to our Savior all over the world, though he spent most of his days right here in the States. His "tentmaking" manifested as a professor of biblical and theological studies, and he corresponded with believers globally through his international networks.

Sometime in mid-2017, Howell's work had been graded through long-distance, correspondence learning by Professor Otto Kaiser in a class on Islamic religion (therefore, they had never met in person). Howell had a question about the comments he had left in the margins of one of her papers. When she emailed him for clarification, she expected the standard, short response in a couple of business days. When a week had passed without response, Howell assumed he was too busy to get back to her, and because her inquiry was not of crucial importance, she decided to let it go. Imagine her surprise when she checked her post office box the next day and found a hand-written, *seven-page* letter from the professor detailing his logic behind every single one of his comments to her?! Such a gesture was overwhelming. Howell pored over that letter for several days, touched to the core that this busy man would spend so much time addressing her simple needs. It was more than humbling, this example he had set, and the time he spent to make sure she knew precisely all she had to regarding the historical spread of Islam in predominantly Muslim-centric countries. (This reminds us of how much time Paul also spent handwriting letters in response to many early-Church issues.)

Later that week, Howell and her husband, James, visited her college to drop off several more cases of *Redeemed Unredeemable* (a book she co-wrote with Thomas Horn in 2014 that tells the stories of seven notorious murderers' post-incarceration conversion stories the prison ministries department of the college had distributed to the students who had begun their Bible studies in detainment). In a chance meeting, Howell bumped into Professor Otto at the base of the elevator. As they waited for the door to open, Otto—instead of standing in awkward silence—smiled widely and boldly stretched out his hand to meet her. After a brief introduction wherein Howell acknowledged that she had been his most recent student, his eyes lit up, and he asked her to come visit his office. When they arrived, Howell noticed his office shelves were packed with an unimaginable number of missionary materials, including expert analyses of nearly every world religion, especially Islam (and these books would, upon his death, be donated to the library at Global Initiative and the Asia Pacific Theological Seminary at Bagio, Philippines).

This chance meeting led to lunch at a buffet in town, where Donna, James, Otto, and his wife, Edith, broke bread together and talked about the mission field, followed by Otto and Edith laying hands on Donna and James in the parking lot to pray over their future in ministry. It was a meeting the Howells will never forget. To this day, it is frequently brought up in conversation, and this missionary couple is remembered as the most gracious hosts of an unplanned lunch they insisted on paying for!

On their way home, Donna and James thought about these friendly people and marveled at their dedication. Donna immediately saw the similarities between Otto and Paul—a missionary who, by the power of the Spirit of God, was supremely dedicated to not only teaching his students about the doctrines of Christ and how they differ from dominating local religions, but to discipleship following those lessons. Otto, like Paul, refused to mentor his students with a quick, pat answer. Instead, this professor took advantage of the time he had on earth to pour himself heart and soul into those who sought his council so their takeaway would be an eternal one bathed in growth and Christian maturity.

Years before Otto married, he had prayed that the Lord would send him a missionary wife with whom to share his life of godly servitude, and God brought him Edith. Their child was named—of all names—Paul. As only a very recent update to the lives that have been touched (through the continual work of Edith) since his passing: In July and August of 2021, Edith kept in touch long-distance with 886 people from all over the globe. Out of that number, 539 people gave their hearts and lives to the Lord, and in only two months! Edith, in her September 2021, "General Prayer Letter # 139" newsletter through the college, writes: "[God] gives me *songs of joy* for each one I correspond with... I keep a record of all those I correspond with and pray over them that God will raise up an army for the Lord in these last days." This source goes on to report: "...the responders [are] telling us that we have presented the Gospel to 45 million individuals in 242 countries and territories. In the last few days I have corresponded with those from Morocco, Liberia, South Africa, Nigeria, Ghana, Cameroon, Philippines, Uganda, Ukraine, Zimbabwe, Pakistan, Bangladesh, Papua New Guinea, Kenya, and Nepal." That is quite the list from just a "few days"! And that's hardly all Edith has to report of the work she and Otto were committed to. During the pandemic lockdown in India, students associated with this couple's work planted an average of three churches per day! Modestly, Edith writes that this is only possible through the prayers of those who support this beautiful ministry.

Paul certainly set the standard, didn't he? His ministry was marked with the utmost love for all people (Romans 9:1–4; 2 Corinthians 11:28–29; Philemon 12–19). Despite his legalistic past, after he was touched by his encounter with the Risen Christ, he was blessed with an unparalleled servant's heart (Acts 21:17–26; 1 Corinthians 9:19–23; 2 Corinthians 6:3–10), and he "ran his race" (served the Lord in the area he was called) with incomparable diligence (1 Corinthians 9:24–27; 2 Corinthians 11:23–33; Philippians 3:13–14).

It is to his writings that we will now turn, as well as those other early Church letters written by his contemporaries. A few more details of Paul's missionary journeys will be brought up in these studies.

The Epistles

EARLY ON, WE WOULD LIKE to share a crucially important statement with the readers regarding our treatment of all books from here forward (including Revelation): Though we have truncated the entire message of most of these books, we are *not* translators! We chose to have four or five different translations open for each book (always the KJV, and the others varied) while we earnestly focused on every verse, attempting to capture the true message behind them responsibly so we could squash down and reiterate the bulk of the content for you. For example, if the original Greek said the definite article "the" in a certain spot, and we said "a" in our summary—or if Revelation said "scarlet" and we write "red"—we are not attempting to provide the readers with new, Holy-Spirit inspired material that contradicts the Word. Also, when something has been stated already, we may choose not to say it again, even though the Bible repeats certain words and phrases for emphasis. Instead, we are hoping to simplify and give the book's message in a general way that newer readers can understand and mature readers can be refreshed in taking in.

Up to the Gospels, the purpose of this work was to show how Christ "showed up" in all of the biblical books. Then, "finding Christ" in the Gospels was a no-brainer, as they are all narratives of His life and redemptive sacrifice of the cross, followed by His Resurrection and appearances afterward. Acts was equally obvious, as it outlined His Ascension, the fulfillment of the Holy Spirit He promised to send, and the growth of the early Church as a result of that Day of Pentecost event. (It was also an introduction to Paul).

So, where does Jesus "appear" in the Epistles? Is it not just a random collection of old letters?

Mature believers know the answer to that immediately. Every one of these books points to what individuals within the Church Body should now be doing with their lives to continue following Christ, after conversion. In that way, they are all about Him, and nothing but Him.

The Epistles are somewhat similar to the Wisdom literature. There are a few major differences, such as the fact that the Epistles are letters to specific people and congregations in operation during the formation of the early Church, while the Wisdom literature was for a more general audience. But generally speaking, the Epistles provide much guidance on the subject of how to live a pleasing life unto God, so they share a comparable spirit and purpose. Because these letters were all written for the members of the fledgling Church while it sprouted its initial roots, they will be treated together, as the Wisdom books and the Prophets were.

It's crucial to understand before proceeding that these letters were not just "howdy" notes from believers to fellow churches—even though many include warm greetings. Much to the contrary, with few exceptions, they were often undiluted and harsh rebukes that corrected major issues plaguing the early churches in Judea and the surrounding regions. That's not to say the Epistles were written like a wagging finger that arrogantly chides, "You oughtta know better than that!" They *didn't* know better, and that was the point, but the writers of these messages also knew they couldn't take the opposite approach of so much acceptance or toleration that it would produce a lenient attitude leading to blasphemy in the Church, so the "voices" behind the letters are often stern: Early church members were praised for their faith, but then they were firmly redirected toward proper religious practice wherein their faith led to sacrilege. This is why the Epistles fall into the category of "didactic literature" (writings with the central purpose of teaching; in a biblical context, this term refers to instructions on morality).

Many new Christians, even in modern times, don't know any better than to rush in and, with well-meaning zeal, practice forms of worship that are sometimes inherently heretical. Here's one way to look at it: Allie Anderson of SkyWatch Television often says, "Even a group of folks who have no science or religion at all in a faraway culture can observe the natural elements—rain, astrological phenomena, the harvest, etc. If you leave them to their own devices, eventually they will be found worshipping the ocean because of the mystery of the tide." This has been shown to be true throughout ancient history. If you can imagine taking a group like this and thrusting them into the Gospel scene, you can sort of see the kind of folks the Epistles were addressing. That's not to say they didn't have very developed theologies of their home cultures, as we know from our studies up to this point in the book that we are primarily dealing with Jewish, as well as Greco-Roman pantheonic, religions. But the similarity is found in how unenlightened the world was about this new "Christianity" at the time of its early formation (called "the Way" at the time), and sincere believers were making quite a mess of theology based on what they had believed for centuries prior. For instance, the letters written to Pastor Timothy were dealing with issues in Ephesus, where the Artemisium, the temple of Artemis/Diana (daughter of Zeus/Jupiter, twin sister of Apollo), was erected. The Ephesians believed she was "top goddess," or that there were no other gods above her. Mystery cults, magic rites, and strange sexual-religious practices were in abundance surrounding

this goddess. Gentile men and women (but especially women) therefore brought a lot of pagan ideas into their worship of Christ simply
because they didn't know any better. So Paul, through his recipient,
Timothy, had to respond to the situation like an emergency, rushing
in and saying the equivalent of, "Guys! Guys! You're all so sweet, and I
know you mean well, but *we Christians* don't conduct worship of the
Christ in that way!" Then another church from another city would
have a similar problem, and he would speak up again: "No wait! You
don't understand! That's not what *we* do! You have to leave that in
the past!" Before long, Peter, James, Jude, and the author of Hebrews
were also addressing similar issues. Without these letters, many of the
churches that began just after the stoning of Stephen and the scattering of the Jews would have suffered a tremendous efficacy failure, and
for that reason, we certainly couldn't live without these paramount
warnings in our congregations today!

That said, there are a *ton* of interpretational differences throughout the Epistles. That's true for all of the Word, but it can be especially
true for these letters. That's because we're reading personal memos,
written by one person to another (or by one person to a congregation). It's a bit like peeping into someone's emails or private texts.
(Note that no "postal service" was in effect at this time. Mail couri-
ers served the government, only. Therefore, personal "mail" like the
Epistles had to be hand-delivered by friends or work associates, and
many times, the letters did not land at the intended designation. This
makes the Epistles even more precious and rare!) At times, details are
left out for readers because both the sender and the recipient knew
what was being discussed. In cases like this, all we can do is guess
about what's missing. (This is a major issue for the Corinthian letters
and the correspondence to Timothy, which are frequently assumed
to be, in part, prohibitions against women teachers and preachers
in the church. We will address more about this later, using Howell's
Handmaidens Conspiracy to assist us with a few excerpts, but that's
at least one specific example to think about moving forward.) But

that does not mean the Epistles are any "less" biblical than any other books of the Bible. The information gleaned from this ancient mail has been more useful than any other part of Scripture when it comes to how believers should live in every era following Christ's Ascension, and what churches across the world should consider the standards for worship gatherings for all eras of time.

Regarding such "gatherings," it is likewise important to remember exactly where these meetings took place. Christians were heavily persecuted during these times, and there was no such thing as walking down a couple of blocks to "try out a new church" when believers were uncomfortable. Worship took place in hidden locations and in the homes of congregational leaders. As such, when quarrels broke out among believers (which happened a great deal, as these letters show), the only choice they had was to work it out maturely. This may sound like a bad deal, but because of those squabbles we have the Epistles to teach us (in all times) how to find solutions to difficulties in relationships. Persecution also united the brethren in desperation for survival.

As noted, Paul wrote thirteen books in the New Testament. Those were Romans, 1 and 2 Corinthians, Galatians, Ephesians, Philippians, Colossians, 1 and 2 Thessalonians, 1 and 2 Timothy, Titus, and Philemon. (Some scholars [although it appears they are among the minority] believe Paul also wrote the letter to the Hebrews, which could bring his number to fourteen total New Testament books. These authors do not come to this conclusion, however, as we will briefly address later.) As Paul was a church-planter all throughout Acts, his writings address congregations or pastors that he, himself, began, and thankfully he was committed enough to stick with these individuals for discipleship and continued growth. Conveniently, Paul's books are included in the canon all in a row immediately after Acts, so as we just visited his story at the end of our reflection on that book, we can shift from what he did to what he wrote without interruption. From there, we will consider the other New Testament writers, who contributed

Hebrews; James; 1 and 2 Peter; 1, 2, and 3 John; and Jude. (Revelation is not an epistle, and, as the last book of the Bible, it will be considered on its own in our final study.)

Note Paul's works can be divided thus: soteriological (salvation) letters (Romans, Galatians, and 1 and 2 Corinthians); "Prison Epistles" (those he wrote while incarcerated: Ephesians Philippians, Colossians, and Philemon); eschatological letters (the studies of the end times; 1 and 2 Thessalonians); and "Pastoral Epistles" (those he wrote to pastors; Titus and 1 and 2 Timothy).

(As a final note before we launch: Without doubt, these documents apply to us as Christians of today. However, to preserve the "feel" of the New Testament era—while we both read summaries of the letters as well as historical and cultural backgrounds that required their writing—we are preserving the author's voice as it speaks to the first recipients. For instance, instead of saying, "Paul says we should live wisely," we say, "Paul explains to the Corinthians that they must live wisely." It is an "author and recipient" relationship that fits the framework of this book. When a teaching is related to a particular city's issue, and therefore that changes whether or not we should apply the advice today, those exceptions are either so obvious they don't require explanation [such as Paul's instructions to greet Priscilla and Aquila, two folks we cannot greet in modern times], or are addressed in our voice with an explanation of what was going on at that time that is not occurring in ours. Otherwise, assume that when an Epistle writer instructs the early Church to do something, he is speaking to all Christians of all times.)

Romans

OBVIOUSLY, AS THE NAME of the letter implies, this congregation would have been located in Rome. The literature contains words that clarify the congregation was brand new to the doctrine of the Risen Christ, and even some of the Jewish roots behind it, which means that Paul's audience would have been primarily Gentiles, with Jews as a minority audience.

Some scholars believe that the expelling of Jews from Rome mentioned in Acts 18:2 would prove there were no Jews among the congregation of Rome at the time Paul wrote this letter. However, a deeper look at when the Jews were allowed to return to Rome helps us understand that although they left for some time, the expulsion event was short-lived. Thus, Jews would have influenced the church in the beginning, maintained contact through their dismissal from the area, and, within less than three years, they were back. Paul irrefutably addressed a tension between the Hebrew nation and the Gentiles in much of his letter—a bit of a "who worships better" question captured well in his instruction to Gentile readers to "boast not against the branches" (Romans 11:18), the "branches" being the Jews, who were the root of the Christian system. This indicates that even if the Jews were not physically present amidst the brethren, they were still a part of the congregation in spirit and must not be involved in a holiness competition.

Paul, subsequent to his conversion, did not have the opportunity to personally travel to the church in Rome prior to writing his letter, but he had heard of it. In fact, the things he had heard were actually very good (Romans 1:8)! But as the Romans were so young in the faith, there was much they did not understand regarding heavily theological concepts, so they were in need of illumination. A central theme of this book is salvation through grace and our faithful response to it. As such, it is considered to be one of Paul's four "soteriological" letters. A secondary theme is that of justification by faith. (It was this very book [verses 1:17 and 8:1] that led Martin Luther to oppose the Roman Catholic Church with his *justificatio sola fide* or "justification by faith *alone*" doctrine, which eventually triggered the Protestant Reformation. Readers who hope to someday be apologists should acknowledge that Romans 9–11 also holds the passages that certain Reformed theologians [like John Calvin] interpreted to support the doctrine of predestination, leading to the Calvinist denomination. Though we will not address predestination in this section, there are many fair arguments against that theology, and it should be stated on record that these authors do not agree with the doctrine of predestination.)

Romans covers the plan of salvation throughout Israel's history, showing that God had always intended to provide salvation through a Lamb whose blood provided the ultimate sacrifice for sin. The Law or Old Contract was not enough to provide total justification, Romans collectively teaches.

There is a "road map" to salvation that's often used; it's called "Romans Road." A more appropriate phrasing would be "Romans Road to Salvation." Perhaps you've heard of it, due to its enormous popularity. It frequently appears in tracts that originate from Christian organizations with sidebar commentaries or Bible studies as well. In essence, the Romans Road is comprised of a set of verses that explain on the most basic level the existence of sin and our very simple response to it in order to be saved. New believers can read these verses, or "walk this road," and be led to Christ with the assurance of a guaranteed salvation (assuming they are sincere). Without the distracting ellipses (the "dot, dot, dot" that represents omitted material from a manuscript), the following is the total message of this "road":

> For all have sinned, and come short of the glory of God. For the wages of sin is death; but the gift of God is eternal life through Jesus Christ our Lord. But God commendeth his love toward us, in that, while we were yet sinners, Christ died for us. That if thou shalt confess with thy mouth the Lord Jesus, and shalt believe in thine heart that God hath raised him from the dead, thou shalt be saved. For with the heart man believeth unto righteousness; and with the mouth confession is made unto salvation. For whosoever shall call upon the name of the Lord shall be saved. (Romans 3:23; 6:23; 5:8; 10:9–10, 13)

For the sake of academic comparison (and because parts can be difficult to understand in the KJV), here is the same collection of verses from the NLT:

> For everyone has sinned; we all fall short of God's glorious standards. For the payment of sin is death, but the free gift of God is eternal life through Christ Jesus our Lord. But God showed his great love for us by sending Christ to die for us while we were still sinners. If you openly declare that Jesus is Lord and believe in your heart that God raised him from the dead, you will be saved. For it is by believing in your heart that you are made right with God, and it is by openly declaring your faith

that you are saved. For everyone who calls on the name of the Lord will be saved.

Whereas no true Christian would ever question the validity of this "road," Paul said more to those followers of Christ than simply, "Have faith and be saved." Romans—the longest Epistle—heavily stresses the importance of righteous living. In fact, a fairly unanimous opinion of scholars is that the book of Romans includes the most thorough teaching of righteousness in the New Testament. The letter teaches that blamelessness before God doesn't come by accident or by merely believing in a doctrine, but through a thriving, *active* faith in Jesus that goes deeper than external expressions of piousness (10:3).

Early on, after explaining the need for righteousness and its sovereign origins, Paul went on to express the innate human need for righteousness. Every person who has ever lived has a deep core of sin within that must be cleansed, and this purification rests in the simple act of submitting to Christ and His Gospel. In chapter 2 Paul made the statement: There is no excuse for sin; nobody can escape the judgment that it brings on his or her own, and this is true for the Gentile as well as the Jew. In the chapter following, he visited the Jewish ways of life and pointed out that no ritual or custom, such as circumcision, could purify the heart. All within mankind are by nature slanderers, bringers of war and destruction, feeders of the flesh, and disobedient to conviction. So, who can boast? The Jew? The Gentile? The Roman? The man who follows the Law? The man who does good deeds? "Nay: [none can boast] but by the law of faith. Therefore we conclude that a man is justified by faith.... Is he the God of the Jews only? is he not also of the Gentiles?" (3:27b–29a).

Jesus didn't die "for the Jews," "for the Gentiles," *or* "for the Romans," despite the tension created by attitudes of superiority between those groups. His redemption brought the same opportunity for every man, woman, and child to come to the light through His sacrifice, no matter their race or cultural background. Even Abraham, the very patriarch of Israel, Paul said, was not counted as righteous by works. If he had been, then he could boast, but that's not the plan God put in place for man. Abraham was counted as righteous before God because of his *faith* (4:1–3), even before he was circumcised (4:10). In this same way, Abraham was the forefather also of those who come to Jesus just as they are, not in outward show, but from internal transformation (4:11–12). Anyone—meaning *anyone*—who embraces and applies this truth will be guaranteed to receive the free gift of salvation (4:16). When all looked hopeless for Abraham to have a son, he still believed in the promises of God, which established him as righteous, and this is the example the Romans should all follow. It was for both his own benefit and theirs that this story lived on as a model for the Romans to believe in the promise of Christ's sacrifice for their sin, and who "was raised again for our justification" (4:18–25).

Being justified in our faith brings peace and hope even during trials, because hard times produce good character (5:3–5). It would be one thing if Christ had come to die for just the "good" people, but He came for the sinners, and that beautiful message is one the Romans could be sure would save them from all condemnation. God sent His Son as the Savior of mankind while we were enemies of God, and now, because of the Son, we are considered the friends of God (5:6–11). Every man since the time of Adam has sinned, and because of the sin of Adam, all perish. But through the Sinless One, Jesus the Christ, we have victory over the snares of sin (5:12–17). "For as by one man's disobedience many were made sinners, so by the obedience of one shall many be made righteous" (5:19). The Law was given to show mankind what sin *is*, and though it didn't stop people from being corrupt, God's grace through this arrangement of salvation made the new system of eternal life more abundantly merciful (5:20–21).

By now, you can see the pattern Paul used to express the efficacy and limitlessness of the Gospel: God does not favor Jew over Gentile, or vice versa; all are doomed alike, or saved alike, through the act of faithfulness, which is shown in godly behavior. He went on in chapter

6 to stress that sin brings death, and we need to commit to living in submission to the guidelines of righteousness—in Christ, the power of immorality is broken. Chapter 7 states that although the Law is useful for revealing degeneracy, the idea that service to the Law creates moral virtue is incorrect. Even Paul, himself, struggled with the sin nature. He wanted to do what was right, but he kept making a mess of things. The answer to such struggle is found in Christ, who doesn't demand constant perfection, but in whom lies all forgiveness and a consistently fresh start.

Chapter 8 contrasts the flesh with the life the Spirit brings. God literally predestined this freedom from condemnation, and nothing on this earth can separate us from the love of God if we accept salvation. In chapter 9, Paul addressed the stumbling of the Jews—simply being a son or daughter of Abraham did not automatically make them sons or daughters of God. Wouldn't God be sovereign enough to implement His own system of grace? Yet He knew, as He spoke through Isaiah, that only a remnant of the Jews in the end would find their way. In chapter 10, Paul expressed how even the Scriptures showed the difference between Law and faith, and showed both the Jew and the Gentile to be equal inheritors of the gift that faith brings. Not all of Israel would be lost, he said in chapter 11, and just as Jews were not the elite, Gentiles should not believe themselves to be better than the children of Israel. Therefore, he stated in chapter 12, we should *all* present ourselves as a living sacrifice, modelling our lives after Christ: holy and blameless; truly loving; refusing to hate; holding tightly to all that is good; honoring others; working hard; remaining confident in hope; being determined to stay faithful during troubles; praying always; assisting brethren in never-ending hospitality; blessing our persecutors; rejoicing with those who are happy, and weeping with those who are sad; enjoying the company of others; avoiding the egotistical idea that we have all the answers; denying the temptation to seek revenge; living in a peaceful way; and conquering evil through intentional acts of goodness. We must always respect our authorities, chapter 13 teaches, and while time is running out, it is crucial to remember that love fulfills God's law.

Readers can feel the "pulse" of Paul's letter slowing down at the beginning of chapter 14. He has taught so many lessons already, and his letter is almost finished. But Christians cannot follow all the instructions of this letter and still squabble amidst themselves over menial things. Believers who think they know more than their neighbors and are willing to pursue such meaningless endeavors only show themselves as foolish as those who judge another master's servants. What one does to honor God (such as choosing a certain "holy" day to worship or eating only "clean" foods) is that person's own business. It simply isn't worth fighting about. We will all be judged in the end, so we should never cause a brother or sister in the same faith to fall or stumble over something negligible. The one who ignores his own convictions is guilty of sin, while the one dedicated to doing what he or she thinks is right before God is blessed, and we should be willing to see that. (What Paul was *not* saying here is that we can continue to do what we think is right, even when that idea contradicts what the Word of God says. He debunks that in this same letter; 5:19; 12:1–2; 13:1.)

In the second to the last chapter, Paul brought it home: We are to live to please others, for this is the witness of Christ. This does not mean we shouldn't help others find their way if they are struggling, but that we should live in complete harmony, allowing petty disputes and differences to die in the central cause of Gospel work.

Paul then addressed his reason for the letter: He already knew the recipients were aware of its contents, but they needed a reminder, a sharpening of the truth. Then, he discussed his plans to travel in person to see them as soon as he could.

Chapter 16 presents Paul's closing greetings to the believers, several of whom he named specifically. The final verses of the book contains a warning to avoid people who have no interest beyond causing division in the Body: "Mark them which cause divisions and offences contrary to the doctrine which ye have learned; and avoid them. For they that are such serve not our Lord Jesus Christ, but their own belly; and by good words and fair speeches deceive the hearts of the [innocent]" (16:17–18). From there, he signed off through his scribe, Tertius (16:22).

Before we wrap up Romans and move on to Corinthians, there are three women from the book of Romans we would like to take a moment to highlight: Phoebe, Junia, and Priscilla. As you will see in the following paragraphs, these women were not only beloved leaders of the Church in their time, but Paul publicly commended them for this work (which supports the idea of women's ability to be leaders in the Church in *our* time).

Paul's very own writing is the source of today's prohibitions against women teachers, preachers, pastors, deacons, and many other leadership positions within Christianity. But those prohibitions are not sourced from his original writing (stay with us for a minute). We will take a brief look at these three women leaders here, and then, in our following studies (primarily 1 Corinthians and 1 Timothy), we'll address the "trouble verses" that led to the interpretations against women leaders.

(If you're wondering why a project that shows Jesus in every book of the Bible would address this issue, the answer is bulging over the cup here: Women are equal inheritors of the Great Commission charge, and when their power and ability is limited by misinterpretations of the Word, they are not carrying out that call on their life. Another reason is that it's one of the most hotly debated topics in today's Church, and if we can help some folks in this work on both sides [women and men], we want to.)

In the closing statements of Romans, Paul said: "I commend unto you Phebe [or "Phoebe," the deliverer of the letter to Romans] our sister, which is a servant [*diakonos*] of the church which is at Cenchrea" (16:1). Typically, "servant" in the New Testament is the Greek *doulos*. The different Greek word *diakonos*, here used of Phoebe, literally translates "deacon." When the Bible was translated to English in the

KJV, in an overwhelming *twenty-three* other instances, the translators chose to use "deacon" or "minister" in place of this Greek word. A deacon or minister, in New Testament context, was always, without deviation, a mature leader of the early Christian Church in biblical contexts. Yet because this verse was referring to a female during a time when most scholarly work was approached through a male-dominated culture, translators of the KJV chose "servant" as the word to describe Phoebe. (It's very likely this was not done on purpose, but as a means of truly trying to preserve Paul's intent in a day and age when translators were still approaching Pauline literature through the traditional patriarchal lens. Note that the KJV was translated in the year 1611. Many lingual experts who transferred what they read into a second language would have naturally, and innocently, chosen "servant" instead of "deacon" because, at that time, it was unthinkable for a woman to be a leader. However, the freedom for women that Christ brought and Paul documented in the Word of God should be prioritized above anything that happened over fifteen hundred years later when the KJV was released.)

Because this is such a new idea to some readers, we will offer a few proofs from scholars here:

[From F. F. Bruce's *Romans: An Introduction and Commentary* by InterVarsity press:] She was a *diakonos*, "a fellow-Christian who holds office in the congregation at Cenchreae" (NEB); in a church context the word should be rendered "deacon," whether masculine or feminine. That the duties of a deacon could be performed by either men or women is suggested by 1 Timothy 3:11, where "the women" are to be understood as "deacons" (like the men of verses 3–10).[113]

[From the *New Bible Commentary: 21st Century Edition:*] [With the official-sounding addition *of the church of Cenchrea* it is more likely that Paul is identifying Phoebe as holding the office of "deacon" (see Phil. 1:1; 1 Tim. 3:8, 12; many understand 1 Tim. 3:11 as a reference to female deacons).[114]

[From *The Bible Knowledge Commentary*:] Phoebe…was Paul's emissary to deliver this letter, so he wrote officially, **I commend to you our sister Phoebe.…** Phoebe was **a servant of the church in Cenchrea.…** The word *diakonon*, "servant," is used for the office of deacon.… Use of the word with the phrase "of the church" strongly suggests some recognized position, a fact appropriate for a person serving as Paul's emissary.[115]

[From the sixth volume of *Romans* by Broadman & Holman Publishers:] Her designation as a **servant**…not *doulos*, bondservant, but *diakonos*…implies a position of responsibility in the church at Cenchrea…[116]

Phoebe's official position in leadership is also shown in Paul's very next words: "That ye receive her in the Lord, as becometh saints, and that ye assist her in whatsoever business she hath need of you: for she hath been a succourer of many, and of myself also" (16:2). The word "succourer" derives from the Greek *prostatis* (sometimes translated in ancient literature as "patroness"). *Prostatis* is formed from the prefix *pro*, "before," together with the verb *istemi*, "to stand." In other words, "to stand before" (or "over") others, like the word "overseer." A "patroness" had much authority in the world at this time, and *prostatis* regularly identified church leaders.[117] But even without all this word study, the context of Paul's statement is clear, as this letter was sent to the superiors of this congregation in Rome: "That the leaders receive Phoebe well and *assist her* in whatever she needs." Why would Paul ask male chiefs of an early church to obey, support, or aid a woman if females were not allowed to be leaders, themselves? The answer is simple: He wouldn't.

Therefore, we have no choice but to see in Paul's writing the appointment of a female *diakonos*, or, "deacon/minister."

Junia is mentioned in Romans 16:7. The name is feminine. Paul wrote, "Salute Andronicus and Junia, my kinsmen, and my fellow-prisoners, who are of note among the apostles, who also were in Christ before me." Though responsible academia has restored her to her proper identity as a *woman*, early Latin translators thought Paul's words about her here were so lofty that they had added an erroneous "s" to the end of her name, making her "Junias," as that one letter functioned to "masculinize" some names in Greek. (Martin Luther's Bible commentary, a famous and widely distributed work, helped solidify the idea that Junia was male. Thankfully, most translations in the 1980s corrected this, and most Bibles today use simply "Junia.") That said, there is absolutely no record of any instance of the male name "Junias" in Greco-Roman history.[118] Since we know this person was female, our attention now goes to said "lofty" words of Paul: "of note among the apostles."

This phrase could be interpreted two ways: "she is *known by* the apostles," as in they were familiar with her, or, "she is *one of* the apostles." It's the difference between whether "of note among" is exclusive or inclusive, grammatically speaking. Some of the celebrated, historical, and scholarly names who openly wrote of Junia as "a woman apostle" were: Origen, Jerome, Hatto, Theophylact, Peter Abelard, John Chrysostom, Ambrosiaster, Theodoret of Cyrrhus, John Damascene, Haymo, Oecumenius, Lanfranc of Bec, Bruno the Carthusian, and Peter Lombard (and this is in no way an exhaustive list).[119] (Note that some who hear this teaching quickly determine that it is feminist doctrine. That statement does not take into consideration the fact that the overwhelming majority of folks who have concluded Junia's female apostleship are today, and were throughout history, *male* scholars. John Chrysostom, himself, one of the most important early theologians and Church fathers, famously wrote: "O how great is the devotion of this woman that she should be counted worthy of the appellation of apostle!"[120])

Early on, the question forms:

How are there more than twelve apostles? I thought that was a sacred number… I mean yeah, Paul was technically the thirteenth, but his was a special case.

There appears to be more than just one "special case," here. The Greek word for "apostle," *apostolos*, means "delegate," "messenger," or "one sent with orders."[121] The Bible also directly refers to Barnabas (Acts 14:14), James (Galatians 1:19), and Silas and Timothy (1 Thessalonians 2:7) as "apostles" as well, bringing the number to seventeen, even without counting Matthias as additional when he replaced Judas. The qualifications of an apostle (that we've already outlined twice—in the story of Paul's conversion and the appointment of Matthias) could have technically applied to more people. In fact, under those same requirements, Mary the mother of Christ, Mary Magdalene, Salome the disciple, and many men alongside them could have fit the bill, as they all followed Jesus, learned from Him, and witnessed His resurrected form. (We don't know enough about this mysterious figure, Junia, to say whether or not she was there with Him from the beginning.) Nevertheless, we do see in Acts that Peter reestablished the twelve, an important number, so it could be that there were twelve "main apostles," and the rest of them were servile to those. (If this is true, then either Paul really was a "special case," or he, too, was subservient to the "main" apostles, and internal biblical evidence does not appear to support that conclusion. In fact, Paul rebuked Peter in Galatians 2:11–19. That said, we are not offended by the idea that "main authority apostles" could have been "twelve plus Paul." No matter how we assign who has the top spot here, the focus is on whether Junia could have been "one of them" [not merely "known by them"] who earned the title just as Barnabas, James, Silas, and Timothy did.)

As to the "known by" or "one of" interpretations, it boils down to the Greek *en* (English "among"). This term is "a primary preposition denoting (fixed) position (in place, time or state)."[122] *Thayer's Greek Lexicon* teaches that the first meaning of *en* is "I. Locally; 1. of Place proper; a. in the interior of some whole."[123] In the case of a person, it identifies a member of a group. To say it refers to an *outsider* of that group who is simply appreciated by them is not likely. The KJV also translates *en* as "in" 1,902 times and "among" only 117 times. Additionally, PhD professor of biblical studies, Linda Belleville, considered this term not just as a word-study, but also in context of its usage in the New Testament writings. Her conclusion was that, in Greek, the "primary usage of *en* and the plural dative (personal or otherwise) inside and outside the NT (with rare exceptions) is inclusive 'in'/'among' and not exclusive 'to.'"[124] Her deduction—based on a rather extensive and meticulous sweeping over Greek nouns, plural nouns, genitive personal modifiers, dative personal adjuncts, and the variations/comparative senses of the language in use during the New Testament times—was that Paul's words "bear the inclusive meaning 'a notable member of the larger group.'"[125]

Eldon Jay Epp, male scholar and author of *Junia: The First Woman Apostle*, is a powerhouse in the world of exegesis. His master's degree in Sacred Theology through Harvard University is only one of his many educational triumphs. He is author of *The Theological Tendency of Codex Bezae Cantebrigiensis in Acts*; *New Testament Textual Criticism: Its Significance for Exegesis*; *Studies in the Theory and Method of New Testament Textual Criticism*; and *Perspectives on New Testament Textual Criticism*. It's clear both by his works and his reputation among academia that he is well known for true, exegetical, nonbiased studies of the original Greek language. In each of his available works, Epp has expounded upon the importance of accuracy within biblical interpretation, and his knowledge of the various formations of Greek words throughout history is astounding.

In the conclusion of his book on Junia—after spending well over a hundred pages specifically on the study of the Greek texts, their variations throughout history, the "weigh-in" from numerous scholars, and the cultural implications of it all—Epp states:

> Therefore, the conclusion to this investigation is simple and straightforward: there was an apostle Junia. For me, this conclusion

is indisputable, though it will not, I fear, be undisputed… But far more significant and regrettable is the unnecessary alienation of women that has taken place and continues in many quarters of the church.…

As one final thought on Junia, we will quote from *The Handmaidens Conspiracy*, from which we have borrowed some of the material you'll read throughout this section:

> Another significant detail that argues for Junia's role as an apostle relies on the reader's willingness to acknowledge the profound burdens she carried and the work Paul attributed to her. Once we take a moment to consider the enormous implications of Paul's reference to her as a "fellow-prisoner," we begin to see a boldness that most women of her day wouldn't have been able to conceive.… She didn't allow her gender or social status to stand in her way of spreading the Gospel alongside Paul. She didn't fear persecution or imprisonment, she *embraced* it as a necessary evil in the fight of getting the story into the hearts of as many listeners as possible no matter the consequence. Any other woman in her position might have [chosen to focus on the duties of women at that time], and it would have been a choice that her culture would have supported since women were not expected to don their sandals and march throughout the territory as a minister. But nothing would stop Junia from doing the same work as Paul while she ministered alongside him. It's as if she said, "If you boys think you're alone in this, you're mistaken. I may be a woman, but I believe so passionately in the message of Christ that I will follow the Great Commission if it kills me. If Paul is willing to journey into the wickedest cities and confront thousands of years of pagan culture in the name of Christ, then

I'm willing, too. If Paul is committed to throwing his own safety and comforts out the window in trade for seeing souls come to the saving grace of Christ, then I'm committed also. If Paul is beaten, I will be beaten alongside him. If Paul is thrown with his gaping wounds into a freezing prison cell, I will be thrown in as well." She was *with* Paul; she spread the word of Jesus *with* Paul; she suffered as a prisoner *with* Paul. If Paul had written about her actions as immoral or inappropriate because of the fact she was a woman, then her zeal to share the work [would have likewise been immoral or inappropriate to the apostles she was "of note among" in this verse]. Yet that's not how he wrote of her. Much to the contrary, her choice to become a "fellow-prisoner" led Paul to instruct others to welcome her as a distinguished servant of Christ "among the apostles."

Wait a second... What was that about Priscilla being a pastor or preacher? Where does the Bible say that?

That name pops up at the end of Romans, too. Priscilla is yet another female leader about whom Paul stated: "Greet Priscilla and Aquila my helpers in Christ Jesus: Who have for my life laid down their own necks: unto whom not only I give thanks, but also all the churches of the Gentiles" (16:3–4).

Priscilla's authority as a minister of the Gospel is mentioned in Acts 18:24–26, which states that she, alongside Aquila, corrected the theology of the "eloquent" Jew Apollos:

Apollos was documented in this section of Acts as a man "mighty in the scriptures," "instructed in the way of the Lord," and "fervent in the spirit," so this speaks highly of Priscilla's influence: She...took Apollos aside and "expounded unto him the way of God more perfectly."...

But maybe Aquila was really the one "expounding" and correcting Apollos' theology while Priscilla stood beside them smiling and nodding... Right?

No, not really... Evidence points to the opposite, actually.

It was customary in New Testament times for men to have the first position in nearly everything, as they were the central focus in society. When someone introduced a group with both men and women present, the introduction would begin with the men and end with the women. However, in Romans 16:3, Paul writes to the Gentiles of Rome, "Greet Priscilla [some translations say "Prisca"] and Aquila...." *Ellicott's Commentary for English Readers* notes this peculiarity: "It is rather remarkable that the wife should be mentioned first. Perhaps it may be inferred that she was the more active and conspicuous of the two."[128] *Maclaren's Expositions* also notes this oddity: "Did you ever notice that in the majority of the places where these two are named, if we adopt the better readings, Priscilla's name comes first?... Now, such a couple, and a couple in which the wife took the foremost place, was an absolute impossibility in heathenism. They are a specimen of what Christianity did in the primitive age, all over the Empire, and is doing to-day, everywhere—lifting woman to her proper place."[129] *Bengel's Gnomen* commentary, yet again, comes to the same conclusion: "The name of the wife is put here before that of the husband, because she was the more distinguished of the two in the Church."[130]... At the very least, we know the Bible says that when the act of correcting Apollos' theology occurred, "they," Aquila *and* Priscilla, carried out the act. Priscilla was at least her husband's equal—and likely the leader, in this moment.

The question is then raised of whether Priscilla was an "official" pastor in the early Church...

The historical etymology of the word "pastor" dates to circa 1325–1375; likewise, the word "preacher" dates to 1175–1225.

Both words derive from Latin originally, so he couldn't have referred to her that way even if the duties of Priscilla's work were a precise match to that office…. We cannot conclude that Paul [didn't view her as a pastor] just because he did not use a modern, Western word to introduce her—especially when the word modern ministers are looking for didn't exist at the time…. [Much is cut from this area that is very relevant to the discussion of women "pastors" in the New Testament. We are handling this briefly, but *Handmaidens* goes on to say:]

With a severely condensed approach, we will touch on a few more of Paul's words regarding women in his forthcoming letters—not to rile any readers who are opposed to women serving as leaders in the Church (that is very much *not* our goal here), but in hopes to free those ladies from what they believe to be spiritual injunctions against serving in leadership positions so they can launch into ministry. For now, however, we will move on to the intense disorder of the city of Corinth, the congregation that was the audience of Paul's next Epistle. (For those interested in further discussion on women of the Bible, including many details about what God created them to be from Genesis forward, we recommend the book *Handmaidens Conspiracy* by Donna Howell for a more thorough approach to the subject.)

In closing: The message of Romans is as alive today as it was then. The Spirit who guided these verses knew the teachings therein would be timelessly missiological (pertaining to missionary work), and that's true on both an international and local level. Just as the Jew is not better than the Gentile, nor the other way around, if a Muslim walked into our congregations today, would we boast? Let's be honest, here. Please actually consider what is being asked: *Would* we think ourselves "better" than those who haven't yet found "the Way"? Is God not *also* the God of that Muslim? Or, if we feel called to Haiti as a missionary and meet up with a woman deeply entrenched in voodoo, would we treat her the same way as we would treat the Christians in the group? Or would we be standoffish and cold to her and warm to the others? Certainly, if we clothe ourselves in a haughty attitude of superiority, we are not "pointing anyone to Christ" as this breathtaking, brilliant letter of Paul's illustrates. Thank God, in every literal way, that it was included in the canon so we can continue to be reminded of virtues that, though commonly known in modern times, would be lost in history if it didn't exist.

1 and 2 Corinthians

BEFORE WE BEGIN, we would like to point out that 1 Corinthians is one of our longest Epistle studies for two reasons: 1) it appears early on the list and therefore requires some breakdown of content that comes up in subsequent letters; 2) it is highly regarded as one of the easiest books to misinterpret. For instance: Paul's reference to "uncomely body parts" have made many in today's Church believe they are one of the unlucky believers to whom a lesser important gift or job was given by the Lord for their work in the Kingdom. After looking at what Paul actually said in the *Greek*, we see he was never assigning "uncomely parts" in the first place. He was rebuking those who did, and then he followed that rebuke by explaining that the believers who feel their role in the church is less important should actually be lifted higher and given honorary, privileged distinction among the rest of the Body. That's only one example of a few things we plan to break down and give attention to. Once we have, we will not have to explain it again in later letters, which will understandably be shorter.

In 1 Corinthians 5:9, Paul referred to an earlier letter he had sent to this church, instructing them to separate themselves from participants in sexual sin. This means, technically, "1 Corinthians" would be, had all the letters been preserved, "2 Corinthians." Then, in 1 Corinthians 16:5–8, Paul explained that he planned to visit them soon. This stopover eventually did take place, and following that trip, Paul wrote another letter that is lost to us; it would have been "3 Corinthians," if we had it. We don't know what that document said, but we know its contents, complete with ruthless admonitions, caused a lot of sorrow for both Paul and his audience, because in 2 Corinthians 2:4 and 7:8, he made reference to the tears he had shed in composing it. Chronologically, that would make "2 Corinthians" actually "4 Corinthians." The order goes:

1. Lost letter
2. 1 Corinthians
3. Lost letter that created much grief
4. 2 Corinthians

Because we know at least two of the letters are gone, some scholars acknowledge the very real possibility that there may have been others as well. But this should not cause us concern. Dr. Michael Heiser—our close personal friend, master of multiple biblical languages, and key theologian behind Logos Bible Software for several formative years—addresses this issue. He notes that believers are sometimes afraid that a "missing letter" would give the impression that the Bible's current canon is incomplete, or worse, flawed. Nevertheless, Heiser emphasizes, God is not limited by "circumstances of history," and this human fear results not from the state of the canon, but from our own finite ideas of how biblical inspiration works. We see "inspiration" as "a string of momentary supernatural writing sessions" instead of God using His Spirit to guide regular men to communicate with their own languages, personalities, and choice of words.[132] But the principles of biblical interpretation negate the concept of "mechanical dictation," which claims the writers fell into a sort of trance (Heiser calls this a "holy spell") and had no control over what they wrote.

To the contrary, Heiser writes, the Spirit influenced the writers of the Word through "circumstances of providence" in order to produce what God felt was "necessary for posterity" (success in future generations). Therefore, Heiser concludes, inspiration is a matter of providence, *including the development of the canon*, which gives us just what we need for the revelatory Word of God to mankind—nothing more and nothing less. His conclusion to the matter is simple: "We owe both the writers and God a debt of gratitude for giving us the Word of God" as we have it.[133]

Paul was the founder of the church in Corinth, and after he planted it, he nurtured it with follow-up discipleship and watched it grow for about eighteen months. This shows that Paul did not just get the church up and running and then take off. He was familiar with the troubles that plagued the congregation and, when he wrote them later, his words showed his personal understanding of them as a fledgling body. Scholars and theologians are familiar with the background of this unholy city, but in casual conversations, we have discovered that many Christians (even those who are mature in the faith) find much information about this city to be new to them. With that said, we'll outline the occasion for Paul's letters.

About a hundred and fifty years before Christ, Corinth—a city named after the currant grapes that grew wildly in its area—had been destroyed by the Romans, but it was rebuilt and fully restored by Julius Caesar, established circa 46 BC (about a decade before Paul's letters were written). In Paul's day, this would have meant the city was still new enough to be the glittering pride of Rome, while old enough to have worked out the kinks of reconstructing the foundations of civilization. It was, without doubt, one of the largest and most famous locations on the world map.

Corinth was the capital city of the Achaian province (Greece's biggest territory), and it was protected by the Acrocorinth: a mountain that stood nineteen hundred feet high. Upon this mountain sat a temple of Aphrodite, the Greek goddess of love. Further down was the temple of Melicertes, goddess over the sailors. Poseidon, the god of the sea, also had his own temple stationed conveniently within this area, as well as Apollo, Hermes, Venus, Fortuna, Isis, and a sanctuary dedicated to Demeter. Nearby were worship sites to Ashtarte and Baal of the Canaanites, Bacchus (the god of fertility and wine), and the mother goddess, Cybele. The island of the Peloponnese was physically connected to the Greek mainland about three hundred feet above the deepest canal in the world by a land bridge called the "Corinthian Isthmus." Smaller canals intersected in this area to expedite shipping endeavors. Such features drew a massive amount of trade overseas, making Corinth a "world trade center" of its day—a constant beehive for international and commercial activity.

During the eras of the Persian and Peloponnesian wars, soldiers came from Corinth to band together with the Greek military. As such, it's not a surprise this was one of the chief locations of powerful Roman government. The population is not an easy issue to nail down, as it fluctuated as a result of travelers throughout the territory. However, research into this inquiry shows that there were anywhere between one hundred thousand and six hundred thousand residents at any one time.

Every other year, the Isthmian Games took place in Corinth, which was a festival of both music and athletic competition (like our Olympics). While the festivities were not all religious, many were, and the reigning god most greatly honored throughout the duration of these celebrations was Poseidon.

At the time of Paul, pagan worship was prolific. History books acknowledge this as a time of great revival for the Greco-Roman pantheon. Commentaries on the Corinthian letters (and others written around this area and time) theorize that this activity was a direct result of spiritual warfare. Christ had just recently come to earth, the Holy Spirit had fallen on believers and empowered them spiritually, the Church was growing *fast*, and a possible reaction of the enemy was to use his own disciples to sharply increase paganism. Within all this commotion in the spiritual realm, we see a heavy upsurge of religious syncretism (the blending of multiple religions into one). Although not all Hellenists would fit into this example, one popular movement of syncretism in the Hellenistic Period was to adopt portions of Judaism, Christianity, Greek and/or Roman pantheonic religions, and beliefs from Oriental mystery cults (like Gnosticism) and mesh them into one new religious system. It was an early form of spiritual postmodernism that manifested into a "pick-and-choose," "all-you-can-eat-buffet" style of worship that allowed a person to reap the benefits of multiple convictions. (If you're thinking this sounds like an oxymoronic faith that cancels itself out because some religions contradict others, that's precisely what it was. Some would find this kind of practice surprising and question the logic of one who participates in it, due to its obvious, intrinsic failure. Nonetheless, syncretism is positively rampant in the world today, even within Christianity. Donna Howell and Allie Anderson wrote a book about this very subject called *Dark Covenant*. In it, they discuss all the signs and symptoms of a religiously syncretized system in the Western Church and how it is paving the way for the future success of Antichrist's one world order/religion. So the contamination of faiths that plagued the area of Corinth in Paul's day is still thriving, and it will again in the end.) Thus, massive crowds of people from all over the ancient world would end up in Corinth for everything from business trips to vacations and beyond. As Corinth was such a nucleus of industry, it's not hard to imagine how travelers could go there with great, awe-inspiring tales of their own religious experiences in faraway lands and perpetuate this problem.

In addition to the many religions taken into to Corinth, an average of one thousand prostitutes serviced the cult of Aphrodite in the temple of the goddess. Some of these women were called *hetairai*, who were of the upper class and stuck to maintaining more long-term relationships with the same men. The other category of prostitutes was the *pornai* (this is where we get the English word "pornography"), lower-class women who professionally functioned in a way more closely resembling what we think of prostitution today: they were simply a kind of "overnight companions." Whereas the affluent *hetairai* were often well-educated, the *pornai* were mostly illiterate. The *hetairai* were courtesans to the wealthy and the elite; the *pornai* were available for anyone, anytime, as long as their "suitors" had money. *Handmaidens Conspiracy* teaches of the *hetairai*: "They were richly dressed, articulate, heavily painted, schooled in oratory skills and rhetoric, and every hair was in the right place as they flitted about society and 'owned' every room they entered.... As such, their social standing and cultural status were consistently respected in a locality where such sexual activity held precedence and equaled blessings from the gods...."[134] The very fabric of Corinthian society was woven around their service. (This is not to insinuate they had any kind of political power [they weren't allowed to vote, for instance], but they remained socially influential.)

Whether it was for a male traveler who had just come into one of the local seaports or for a permanent resident of Corinth, these women were available for hire to do something completely foreign to our concepts of prostitution today: They "divined" oracles (visions, revelations, prophecies, etc.) of the gods and delivered them to their paying clients through orgiastic worship at the temple. As alarming and grotesque as this sounds, it probably goes even further than anything we might imagine (and yes, at times, these sorts of "worship" included incest). This is a family read, so we will not go into detail, but suffice it to say it was believed that the body of a prostitute was the "conduit" through which some of the gods spoke to men. A man would pay one of these women to escort him down to the temple, clothing was removed in a room packed with...*activity*, we will say, and then their act of copulation would amplify into external signs of frenzy that would likely be compared to demon possession today. (Is it really that hard to believe how many people were possessed during Christ's ministry in light of these facts?) At some point during or after the event, the women would speak oracles, and the male would receive it as his "word" from whichever god or goddess he was appealing to.

Though Church leaders eventually put a stop to this "hobby," somewhere around the time of Paul, "holy weddings" involved this kind of debauched "reveling" in intense magnitude, involving family members of the bride and groom together in public sexual parties.[135]

The Archeological Museum of Ancient Corinth today features an attraction called, "Asklepieion, the Healing Sanctuary," which houses many body parts shaped from terracotta clay. These formed parts were, in ancient times, offered to the god of medicine, Asklepios and his daughter, Hygieia, at the shrine dedicated to them in Corinth, by pilgrims who suffered an affliction and sought healing. (Sometimes they were brought by pilgrims who had already experienced a medicinal healing and the parts were an offering of gratitude for a job well done by Asklepios.) Though the display certainly exhibits arms, legs, torsos, and heads (and sometimes miniature full bodies), there are almost as many private body parts in the attraction as there are in the rest of the categories together, showing that Corinth was probably a site of early infestations of sexually transmitted diseases. (Please be careful looking this up on the Internet around children, as the images are explicit!)

Corinth was so well known for its sexual perversion and immorality that, in regions well outside the city, a man or woman who earned a bad reputation (especially in relation to being promiscuous with one's body) earned him or her the title of a "Corinthian," whether the individual had ever visited there or not.[136]

This religiously syncretized and sexually perverted world was the cesspool in which Paul launched a Christian church... His audience, one commentator says, was a "mongrel and heterogeneous population of Greek adventurers and Roman bourgeois, with a tainting infusion of Phoenicians; this mass of Jews, ex-soldiers, philosophers, merchants, sailors, freedmen, slaves, trades-people, hucksters and agents of every form of vice...."[137] Establishing a church in a city like this was great news! But it would be unfathomably hard to maintain, and the follow-up care in the interest of discipleship would be a tedious mountain of a task.

Word reached Paul, while he was stationed in Ephesus (and building/discipling the church that would require the letters Ephesians and 1 and 2 Timothy), that these young saints were quarreling over many things. Division and the eventual dissolution of this congregation looked probable. One central argument among the saints was regarding how a worship service and the sacraments should be conducted. Unlike believers around the world today, there was no "New Testament" they could pick up at a local bookstore to help them sort out their differences, and with the Gospel in its infancy, an unpolluted message of Jesus was nowhere on the horizon without Paul's help.

The content of 1 Corinthians shows that the congregation was not insusceptible to the lifestyles of those around them. Paul had a lot to correct, and the situation was nothing less than the direst of crises. Not only were some of these Christians (maybe even some with Jewish roots that had been guided by Hellenism in recent years) regularly participating in the very kind of disturbing "temple worship" just discussed, the assembly was: tolerant in its response to incest; suing each other in the pagan/secular courts; attending church in lewd attire and profaning the sacraments; arguing even during services, causing major disruptions; distorting the doctrinal teachings of Christ's Resurrection; and a whole menagerie of other demoralizing issues.

With this background firmly established, let's look at an overview of the letter.

Paul begins with warm greetings, exhorting his readers to embrace unity (1 Corinthians 1:1–11). Following this, he rebukes the believers' constant arguments (1:12–17), and then explains that God's wisdom is superior to that of the world's. The cross looks like such foolishness to unbelievers, including sages, orators, scribes, and rhetors (teachers and participants of rhetoric and debate). To God, however, the grandest wisdom of the world is destroyed and made foolishness, itself (1:18–25). The believers of Corinth were not strong, mighty, wise men of noble birth, but weak, low, and despised. Yet, through Christ, they experience not only true wisdom, but righteousness, sanctification, and justification. Therefore, the man who absolutely must boast should boast in what the Lord has done for him (1:26–31): "God hath chosen the foolish things of the world to confound the wise; and God hath chosen the weak things of the world to confound the things which are mighty" (1:27).

Paul goes on to admit that when he first came to Corinth to begin the church, he completely abandoned rhetoric of wisdom, debate, and lofty words. In fact, he was terribly weak, even to the point of trembling in their midst as he preached. Any good thing that came from him was a result of the Holy Spirit carrying his message, and as a testimony to the Spirit's power, Paul's inarticulate words were a success. But these Christians had to remember that God's secret and hidden wisdom is so far above the powers of mere natural men to comprehend (chapter 2): "Even so the things of God knoweth no man, but the Spirit of God... For who hath known the mind of the Lord, that he may instruct him? but we have the mind of Christ" (2:11b, 16).

Just as babies are fed with milk, these new believers were infants in Christ, so they were not ready for the "solid food" of a more mature Christian when Paul visited them before (3:1–2). Why was there so much dissention among believers? Paul asks why, when their shared goal is growth in the Gospel, do some of these people say, "I follow Paul," while others say, "I follow Apollo," as if that is going to accomplish anything? Isn't this all just silly games humans play? What leverage does name-dropping like "Paul" and "Apollo" have for them? After all, these were just the names of servants of Jesus, like the Corinthian congregation. Paul "planted" the church, and Apollo "watered" it, but God is ultimately responsible for how it was growing. The planters and waterers are nothing compared to the Grower (3:3–9). Paul laid the true foundation for this church, which was Jesus Christ. Anyone who builds upon it could do so, though there would be some whose work is not helpful, and all of that will be sorted out and judged in the end, each man according to his work (3:10–15). As believers, the Corinthians were the new "temples" of God, and the Holy Spirit resided within them. As such, they must remain holy, for if they don't, they would face destruction (3:16–17). These believers needed to be sure that none of them fooled themselves into thinking they were wise in their age. The ones who thought themselves to be wise in this world must become what that same world will see as a fool, incorporating God's true wisdom (3:18–21). "Whether Paul, or Apollos, or Cephas, or the world, or life, or death, or things present, or things to come; all are your's; And ye are Christ's; and Christ is God's" (3:22–23).

In chapter 4, it becomes clear that some members of the Corinthian congregation were questioning Paul's authority. Using court terms, he makes it clear that he doesn't answer to them, but to God, the Judge of the true court. He goes on to describe the ministry of the apostles, showing their characteristic humility and servitude, and further clarifies that he is not out to shame anyone, but to act as a father over his wayward, bickering children. They shouldn't have any reason to go against him after all he had done for them, but in fact, they should attempt to model their own lives after the example set by the apostles. These arrogant people, when Paul next comes to visit, will not prove themselves by words but by the power of their actions.

Paul here shifts gears, and his writing spares no person's feelings...

"It is reported commonly that there is fornication among you, and such fornication as is not so much as named among the Gentiles, that one should have his father's wife!" (5:1): not even the *Gentiles* would condone this behavior as these Corinthians were—and the Corinthians were proud of it! Why in the world weren't they mourning such an act as taking one's own father's wife to the bedroom (5:2)?! (A stepmother is in view here. Scholars almost unanimously believe that even though Paul immediately instructs that this congregant should be excommunicated for this illicit affair and the bragging he had done afterward [5:2], Paul's rebuke would have acknowledged if the report he had received had regarded a mother-son relationship.) Paul is not physically present, but he is present in spirit with the Corinthians, and the only option for this offender is that he be delivered to "Satan for the destruction of the flesh" (or sinful lusts; 5:5).

As harsh as this sounds, there is redemption in this undertaking. If a man is sent away from the church, he will be delivered into the sphere of Satan and begin to long for the purity of that which was lost in godly fellowship:

> The contrast between a present experience of the things of Satan and the nostalgic recollection of the things of God might cause a revulsion of feeling and conduct, the fleshly lusts being destroyed.... At the final day of judgment [Paul] expects to see the disciplined offender among the Lord's people.[138]

The second half of Paul's instruction about excommunicating the incestuous man reads: "that [this offender's] spirit may be saved in the day of the Lord Jesus."

The fact that these Corinthians were glorifying incest was "not good," Paul said. Didn't these believers know that a little yeast (a representation of sin in Israel's history) would spread through the whole lump of dough? This reaction to the man's iniquity was like the yeast, leavening them together in a great lump of sin. Therefore, the sin must be purged from their midst and become purified (5:6–8). Paul had written to them before, warning them not to associate with, or endorse, sexually immoral people in this way. But now, he instructs them that they cannot have anything to do with "any man that is called a brother be a fornicator, or covetous, or an idolator, or a railer, or a drunkard, or an extortioner" (5:9–11). It's not about those *outside* the church, but those on the *inside* who should be the concern of the brethren, and they must purge all evil from within them (5:12–13).

And what on earth is this report that Paul has received that righteous men of the church are suing each other in the pagan courts of unbelievers? Christians will someday judge even the angels, so it is crucial to be proper judges over things in this life. Defrauding others in the Body is below them (6:1–8). Why couldn't they understand that the unrighteous will not inherit the Kingdom of God that Christ taught about?

> Know ye not that the unrighteous shall not inherit the kingdom of God? Be not deceived: neither fornicators, nor idolaters, nor adulterers, nor effeminate, nor abusers of themselves with mankind, Nor thieves, nor covetous, nor drunkards, nor revilers, nor extortioners, shall inherit the kingdom of God. (6:9–10)

This list describes some of the members of this congregation, before they were cleansed, sanctified, and justified in Christ and the Spirit of God (6:11).

Oh, sure, sexual immorality might be *legal*, but it was certainly not helpful, and it had the power to dominate the lives of these people (6:12). The Corinthians would say, "Food is for the belly, and the belly for food." Paul responds that "God shall destroy both…. Now the body is not for fornication, but for the Lord; and the Lord for the body" (6:13):

> Eating is a natural activity, and [the Corinthians] held that one bodily function is much like another. [They believed that] Fornication is as natural as eating. Paul rejects this…. God did not design *the body* for *sexual immorality* as he did *the stomach* for *food*. Rather the connection is between *the body* and *the Lord*.[139] (emphasis in original)

Didn't these believers know their bodies were members of Christ? Should these members of Christ be joined with a prostitute? Of course not! Or, were they not yet aware that those who join with a prostitute become "one" with her? It's even written in Scripture that "the two shall become one flesh" (Genesis 2:24). In contrast, the man who is joined to the Lord becomes one with Him in spirit. For this reason, these Corinthians must run from sexual immorality, as that is a sin against one's own body, which is the temple of the Holy Spirit. Christians are not their own; they were bought with a price, so the body should be used only in ways that glorify God (6:14–20).

However, the report Paul received did note that some extra pious believers took this idea to the extreme, believing "it is good for a man not to [even] touch a woman" (7:1). Paul responded by alerting his readers of good principles in marriage: Because of the sexual temptation in their area, getting married would be a good idea for many of them, and their conjugal rights should be shared and celebrated. Neither a husband or wife has full authority over his or her own body—each belongs to the other. Some should remain single, if they can, but between getting married and burning with passion, marriage is the better path (7:2–9). Paul then addresses the sensitive issues of separation and divorce (7:10–16), advising the Corinthian believers who are facing such issues how to proceed in those conditions.

Clearly, the issue of circumcision plagued this church as well. It appears that, once again, members were arguing whether this physical mark upon God's people in the past was still necessary. Paul's reaction made short work of the issue, advising that men should serve just as they are, living with whatever their conditions were in this area from their calling forward (7:17–24). (Paul continues in his offering of marital advice regarding virgins and widows in verses 25–40. In context, his words make it clear they had asked him a question about whether they should marry, considering the sexual immorality of their culture, and if they did, whether celibacy could or should be a part of that union.)

In chapter 8, Paul addresses food offered to idols and liberates his audience from having to investigate everything they eat. Idols aren't real anyway, he reminds them, so they needn't fight about that issue. However, if someone in their midst considers these foods to be so important that it may cause them to stumble if they see a brother eating in that way, doing so flippantly in disregard of their spiritual maturity would be sinful. (As an important note regarding the other Epistles, as well as the later letters to the churches in Revelation: Paul is not saying everyone is free to eat whatever they want. He explicitly teaches that if eating food connected to idolatry hurts fellow believers' faith in any way—if there's even a possibility it might damage a Christian's spiritual health—they should refrain from eating it. All he has technically freed them from is having to shame a friend by going into his home and asking awkward questions about where the food came from. Keep this in mind, especially during the epistemological and prophetic words of Christ to the seven churches in Asia Minor in Revelation 2–3).

On the tail end of that thought, Paul only appears to switch subjects into a defense of his own apostolic decisions. Chapter 9 has confused many folks in this way. However, digging into research on this chapter reveals he isn't just defending himself at random. He is essentially surrendering certain rights he has had as an apostle all along to set the proper example:

> Paul has been dealing with the strong who asserted their rights even when that harmed others [like those who eat the meat offered to idols in the previous chapter, even when it hurts their faith and becomes a stumbling block]. He has told them that this is wrong. He now proceeds to show that he himself… practises what he preaches…neither he nor any other believer should assert Christian liberty to the detriment of others.[140]

But, while he's on the subject, idolatry has been a major factor in Israel's history. Although Paul doesn't say it outright, we can almost imagine a line between chapters 9 and 10 that says, "Don't think, just because you can eat meat without investigating its links to idolatry, that idol-worship is okay. Remember what happened in Israel's history?" Chapter 10 revisits how Israel fell repeatedly under the foolish assumption that God's people could flirt with other gods when they should have been faithful. If someone invites one of these believers into his house and offers him meat, they don't have to—as the Corinthians were—start asking awkward questions regarding where the meat came from. "If any of them that believe not bid you to a feast, and ye be disposed to go; whatsoever is set before you, eat, asking no question for conscience sake" (10:27). If a believer can give thanks for the food placed in front of him, and if he can then enjoy it, why would he *then* be condemned for eating it (10:30)? "Whether therefore ye eat, or drink, or whatsoever ye do, do all to the glory of God" (10:31).

Because of so much indecency in the area, the believers of Corinth also lacked balance in understanding how decent they should look when going to church. Paul addresses the culture of their day and instructs them to appear with their head and hair in ways that make them publicly identifiable as wholesome believers (11:3–16). (Note that, after reading all the background on Corinth and the prostitution in and around the temples, certain appearances *in that day* [not ours] were considered perverse [like a woman allowing her hair to be uncovered]. Paul's intent here is not to define a normative, absolute behavior for all men and women of all times, but to address the fact those who are attending church should look like they're attending church, not a pagan temple of prostitution. In Ephesus, there was an issue about "braids," and when we reach our study of 1 Timothy later, this principle will be further illustrated.)

Communion, Paul now turns to, is *not* being conducted how it ought. Paul even says they are doing more harm than good by practicing communion how they were.

Though some readers will already know this, many are unaware the sacrament Christ instigated as a replacement of the *afikomen* matzah-breaking ritual at the end of Passover was not intended to be one sip and one bite, like we practice in churches today. That's not to say that what we do in modern times is disrespectful, either, as it still captures the heart of our Lord's instruction to "remember" what He had done. But because believers in the New Testament held church services in the homes of believers, the sacrament was a full feast, a complete meal spread, and it was originally called the *agapai*, or, "love-feasts" (Jude 1:12). Having a "potluck" style meal would have been more difficult for the early Church; people couldn't merely pack a slow cooker into their wagons and plug it into the wall of a back room until after service. So, eventually, when the "feasts" were taken into more public meeting locations in areas more tolerant of Christianity, they became truncated: one sip of wine and one bite of an unleavened cracker. The transition from the love feast into a short sacrament observed with the reading of Scripture in church buildings happened gradually, and according to Justin Martyr, even though Christianity wasn't legalized in a widespread way until the fourth century, this shift may have occurred in some areas under the radar as early as the second century. In any case, at the time of the Epistles, the love feast wouldn't have looked anything like what it does today. "Communion" or "the Lord's Supper," for the Corinthians, would have been a gathering hosted by a homeowner who oversaw assembling a large volume of food. Additionally, as the New Testament *agapai* title suggests, the entire purpose of coming together (apart from remembering Christ) was to see "the love of Christian for Christian as seen in their sharing the one loaf."[141]

The latter part of chapter 11 very clearly responds to a report that the Corinthians were treating the Lord's Supper as a free meal ticket, scarfing down food before others had a chance to share in it. Such an act is selfish and cannot possibly be what Christ intended when He gave His sacred order to "do this in remembrance of me" (11:17–26):

When you meet together, you are not really interested in the Lord's Supper. For some of you hurry to eat your own meal without sharing with others. As a result, some go hungry while others get drunk.

Paul is madder than a provoked hornet, and his words do sting:

Wherefore whosoever shall eat this bread, and drink this cup of the Lord, unworthily, shall be guilty of the body and blood of the Lord. But let a man examine himself, and so let him eat of that bread, and drink of that cup. For he that eateth and drinketh unworthily, eateth and drinketh damnation to himself, not discerning the Lord's body. (11:27–29)

Some have (erroneously, we believe) interpreted these verses to the extreme, believing people must be super-saved (pardon the sarcasm) in order to be worthy of the cup of the Lord. If believers partake of communion and have any unconfessed sin, they will drink their own damnation...the "blood" of Christ is *that* holy. That's not at all a responsible conclusion considering the context. As we've just read, the Corinthians were abusing communion: The poor among them who would likely not get a meal from anywhere else were being shoved aside while these "wild-animal Christians" were devouring everything, gorging themselves and getting drunk! It is true that we should examine ourselves (our motives and our internal holiness) before we partake of communion, because it *is* a sacrament (a sacred thing). But the idea that our very soul is threatened if we aren't perfect at the time we partake is rubbish, since nobody other than Christ, Himself, is perfect. Scholars universally acknowledge that the abuse of communion Paul found to be contemptable was the "breakdown of *koinonia*,"[142] the "Greek word meaning 'fellowship, partnership, a sharing in'...particularly by sharing in 'the breaking of bread' (Acts 2:42)."[143] (The idea that our souls hang on the balance of a Dixie cup and an oyster cracker on Sunday is universally dismissed. We hope this clarification has freed a few precious folks who were influenced by a more condemning interpretation of these verses!)

We now arrive at the "spiritual gifts" section of 1 Corinthians. Paul identifies nine personal "gifts of the Spirit" that were poured out on believers initially at Pentecost, and, many scholars think, subsequently on every person at the time of conversion. He stipulates that "there are diversities of gifts, but the same Spirit. And there are differences of administrations, but the same Lord" (12:4–5)—meaning nobody should assume they will receive all of the gifts, but those "administrations" (jobs) we are individually called to fulfill will be strengthened by the Spirit's gifts that complement our calling and service:

1. *The Word of Wisdom*
2. *The Word of Knowledge*
3. *Faith*
4. *Gifts of Healing*
5. *Working of Miracles*
6. *Prophecy*
7. *Discerning of Spirits*
8. *Tongues*
9. *Interpretation of Tongues* (12:8–10)

The debates that stem from this doctrine are also, like the ones regarding the subjects of head coverings and communion, quite numerous. Depending on the denomination (and the extremity to which its teachings are applied), verses in chapter 12 are interpreted as anything from, "You're not saved if you don't speak in tongues" all the way to "the gifts of the Spirit were for the first century only, while the Church was being built, and they no longer apply." The former is the typically the "radical Pentecostal view," while the latter is referred to as the "radical cessationist view."

We believe the gifts were, as Paul wrote, "given to every man to profit withal" (12:7), and that "every man" means just what it sounds like: not *just* those in the first century. Put simply, we adhere to the interpretation that the gifts of the Spirit are alive and well today, and at least one (and often more than one) is available for every seeker. (Also relevant to this topic is that a person can be given a true gift, even when that gift is not always in operation. This sounds obvious initially, because everyone knows that a person who speaks in tongues on Sunday isn't likely going on Monday to order a cheeseburger through a drive-through window by speaking in tongues; a prophet will have regular conversations; a discerner of spirits is not going to "see a spirit around every corner"; and so on. But quite frequently, if a person does not operate in his or her gift for a while, they make the mistake of assuming that gift is gone. This is a mistake! Especially when it's assumed the gift has ceased because of "hidden sin" or the like. If you or a friend have faced this feeling of wondering why you "used to have the word of wisdom" [or whatever the gifting] and "now you don't," remember: It is the *Spirit* who prompts the use of these gifts! He may choose to refrain from prompting the gifted for a particular season, just as He likely would at the drive-through window of a fast-food joint, but it isn't always because someone has done something wrong. When in doubt, ask Him before you ask someone whose harsh advice could leave a lasting imprint.)

Another interpretational issue rears its head at this point, varying from, again, the extremes: "the Spirit gave only *nine* gifts; the Word says it, I believe it, and there will only be nine forever" to "anything a man is good at is a gift from the Spirit because He operates beyond the closing of the New Testament and is relevant today." We're not exactly sure why 1 Corinthians 12:8–10 gets all the attention in the modern Church, but it does, and at overwhelming levels. The idea there are only nine gifts is easily dismissed because two more gifts are listed a few verses later:

1. Helps
2. Governments (12:28)

This is in addition to a few we see in Romans we're placing in this study as it's relevant to the subject of gifts. Paul's first book in the Word includes an additional list called, in most circles, the "grace gifts":

1. Prophecy
2. Ministry
3. Teaching
4. Exhortation
5. Giving
6. Ruling
7. Mercy (Romans 12:6–8)

Also, nowhere in Paul's address does he even state that there is a specific number. In fact, when the Greek is studied, the context supports the idea that he was listing those he wrote about as mere examples of a much larger list. Therefore, of the two approaches (whether there are nine gifts or an unlimited number of gifts), we swing with the latter, *but with much caution.* The Holy Spirit would never prompt or empower us to do anything that doesn't expressly align with the rest of the Word. Recent research shows that 18 percent of professing evangelicals in the West (and this number is currently growing) believe the Holy Spirit can empower, or direct, a Christian to do something the Bible expressly forbids.[144] (This may appear to be a small number, but it's just under *one-fifth* of the Western Church, and, therefore, it is alarmingly high!) If a woman feels she is given the gift of dancing, for instance, the Holy Spirit might empower her to dance in the way David "danced with all his might before the Lord" (2 Samuel 6:14), but He wouldn't be instructing her to use that gift by wearing skimpy clothing and dancing provocatively in front of her fellow church members.

Who would do such a thing? you ask.

We know it's a shock to some, but we've seen this very act. Donna Howell, Allie Anderson, and Tom Horn were present in a church a number of years ago when Cathy (not her real name) was given this very "gift," and her dancing with tambourines and ribbons was, at first, very worshipful. We have no doubt she began boldly expressing herself directly to the Lord with pure intentions. Cathy was middle-aged, but she had taken good care of herself and was physically fit. It didn't take long before men in the congregation were paying more attention to her worship activity during the song service than they were on their relationship with the Lord or their own families. Their wives started side-glancing nervously at Cathy about this time, but overall, the assembly remained civil. Slowly, over time, Cathy's clothing got a little tighter and more revealing as she noticed the attention she was gaining, and her tambourine-shaking grew louder. What had been a small "dance corner" at the back of the sanctuary eventually included the whole aisle and the front altar area. Eventually she began to dance on the worship stage where the band played. It was clear from Cathy's conversation and history that she was new to the Body of Christ and there should have been some early intervention by church leaders to help her understand this "David-style" worship so it wouldn't get out of control. Nevertheless, to avoid hurting her feelings, nobody said anything, and by the time our work there was done and we moved on to the next ministry, Cathy was dressing in mini-skirts with hems so high and tops so low that her undergarments frequently made cameo appearances while she swooped, swung, and dipped her body about the whole assembly (including between members of the worship team on stage). Compliments about her dancing flooded in from the men, and what was initially her own personal worship became her weekly performance that drew glowing reports and handshakes all around after she presented her latest number. Cathy, as well as many married couples, left the church shortly after that. We don't know why, but we suspect that her "gift" ended up causing distress for everyone.

Donna and Allie attended a women's conference a few years ago that was presented by a major organization. Throughout the weekend, a young dance group performed on stage in what are commonly called "human videos" (music-video-style choreographies that act out a story through the expression of the body). All of the presentations were powerful and tear-jerking, but the dance they performed on the subject of human trafficking will remain in Allie and Donna's memory forever as one of the most fittingly chilling reenactments of what victims of that heinous crime face. Due to the subject matter (sexual slave trade), it's clear that the motions would have to be carried out with delicacy. The choreographers were mature and sensitive in their expressions, and though the scene played out in a way that was *emotionally* graphic, the movements the girls carried out were well done. Imagine Donna and Allie's surprise, then, when the main song-service leader introduced the gathering to "kinetic worship" (dance with flags in a sort of "color guard" approach), and by the end of the weekend the performance had morphed into a full-blown belly-dance wherein the leader danced using pelvic thrusts and gyrating against the poles of the flags. In the same conference, there were two expressions of the same gift; one was anointed, as evidenced by its careful treatment and effect, and the other was nothing short of madness. (We're not familiar enough with "kinetic worship" to know if this is the typical outcome or not; we mean no offense to those who carry it out tactfully.)

If you have this picture in your head, then the issue Paul was addressing with the Corinthians comes into clearer focus.

Cathy and the flag dancer should probably be viewed more as examples of gifts being used inappropriately than as raising the question of whether the Holy Spirit gave them a gift for this special expression of worship in the first place. One who argues that "dance" cannot be a gift of the Spirit's because it is not listed in the Bible cannot have seen the human-trafficking video we saw (we're telling you, that was one of the most moving visual aids we've ever seen about a subject that is otherwise difficult to deal with from the average pulpit!). A shrewd understanding of computer-aided graphics and design isn't listed in Scripture, nor is playing the electric bass (strictly speaking), but there's no doubt in our minds that James Howell was, seemingly from out of *nowhere*, empowered to rock both without a shred of training. He trapped himself in a basement for a few short months, sharpening both skills nobody in his family had ever dabbled with, and is now a head graphic designer of SkyWatch Television and Defender Publishing as well as a total beast on the guitar when Joe Horn's band ministers at fundraisers and Christian rallies. These expressions of James' "worship" are an enormous blessing to the Body! His testimony is one example of hundreds of thousands showing that the Holy Spirit can and will enable us to minister to others with gifts not named in the New Testament. So long as the gift in question a) does not contradict moral teachings of Scripture and b) ultimately serves the Lord, we authors believe the Spirit is as alive today as He was in the first century, and therefore isn't limited to what opportunities and technology applied at that time. For certain, at the very least, there are more than "nine," like we've showed above, as Scripture lists eleven just in 1 Corinthians, alone.

Getting back to the letter: Verses 12 through 31 address Paul's word-picture of the "Body" of Christ. The Christians in Corinth were in excessive competition to see who had the better gift. This had escalated (as chapter 14 will show) to the point that the worship service was becoming more about disorderly contests than ministry to the lost. Many readers of 1 Corinthians see chapters 12–14 as three or four unrelated topics, but they are actually one thread making a very useful, and single, point. In order for Paul to give an answer to this holiness war between congregants, he had to 1) teach that we are supposed to be dissimilar in our giftings (chapter 12); 2) emphasize that all of our contributions to ministerial practice should only be motivated by love (chapter 13), in order to; 3) avoid improper expressions of our gifts (like what's happening in chapter 14). Let's look at this breakdown further.

First, he explains that we are diverse and this is intentional. In comparing us to parts of the human body, he proficiently demonstrates how silly it is for one person to envy another person's gift:

For the body is not one member, but many. If the foot shall say, "Because I am not the hand, I am not of the body"; is it therefore not of the body? And if the ear shall say, "Because I am not the eye, I am not of the body"; is it therefore not of the body? If the whole body were an eye, where were the hearing? If the whole were hearing, where were the smelling? But now hath God set the members every one of them in the body, as it hath pleased him. And if they were all one member, where were the body?…the eye cannot say unto the hand, "I have no need of thee": nor again the head to the feet, "I have no need of you." (12:14–19, 21)

In order to fully grasp the depth of what Paul is teaching here, we must consider not only the absurdity of this word-picture, but the *impossibility* of this kind of rivalry within the human body. It's preposterous to imagine that a kneecap would be jealous of the tongue's ability to taste. Again, it's not even possible that the kneecap would be capable of thinking that way. That's Paul's whole argument here. Christians not only shouldn't compete because it's wrong, but they should be *so* motivated by loving each other and others that competition becomes as unfeasible. It should never occur to them in the first place to desire what the Spirit has given someone else, because it takes the operation of the whole to accomplish effective bodily movement and function.

With that said, Paul goes on to teach that some human body parts that appear to be weak or less honorable are actually the most important to our health, and it is to those areas we must give special attention and protection: "And those members of the body, which we think to be less honourable, upon these we bestow more abundant honour; and our uncomely parts have more abundant comeliness" (12:23). "So God has put the body together such that extra honor and care are given to those parts that have less dignity" (12:24b; NLT). By this, again in human-body terms, Paul is elegantly referring to "reproductive and excretory organs."[145] Yet, it's probably not what contemporary readers are thinking... We should remember that this is a metaphor, and it requires a mature approach.

The apostle is not here assigning any men or women of Corinth to consider themselves as "low" as one of these organs, and sometimes folks in our modern culture sees these verses to be more explicit than Paul intended. Before proceeding to show how Paul is actually saying the opposite of what it sounds like to *us*, we must begin by explaining why these parts were not offensive to the original audience: Remember that this is the city where people produced terra cotta representations of their reproductive organs and left them at the altar of Asklepios without blushing. They attended family weddings and engaged in orgiastic displays. Folks were not at all surprised when a man and woman would go "worship" with their bodies at the local temple, igniting an ecstatic oracle with frenzied speech, bodies thrashing, eyes bulging, and so on. Scholars are well aware that this kind of behavior was "universally accepted" in this culture as an outward show of "the divine spirit within them."[146] On the Day of Pentecost, the disciples were preaching the Gospel on the streets with so much enthusiasm that some in their audience thought they were drunk (Acts 2:13). This no doubt had resulted in supporting the concept that "the more intense my public worship is, the more spiritual I am." The new and virtuous practices of Christian gifts in appropriate use appeared dull. Paul is here showing it is not ecstatic behavior, but a constant, steady expression of love (using Holy Spirit giftings to that end) that shows one's true personal spiritual maturity. By comparison to *their* culture (not ours), he uses the body parts that were a part of pagan worship to purify religious concepts that had become radically perverted. To us, we read his remarks and think, *Why did he go there?* But to Corinth, these parts required a lot of protection and care to avoid sickness and disease—this was merely a common subject the apostle used to drive home his goal in an irrefutable way.

For instance, those who spoke in tongues could stand in the congregation and utter mysteries, marking themselves as the holy men of the assembly or the "beautiful part." If another man sat and prayed in faith (gift number 3 in 1 Corinthians 12:8–10 pages back), his "spiritual show" was quiet and sober by comparison, marking him as an "ugly part" to the confused Corinthians. In the end, though Paul used creative language to get there, none of this had to do with the human body at all (and most definitely not the reproductive organs). The metaphor shows that the quiet, praying man who looks like one with "less dignity" (12:24) is not only just as important to the Body of Christ as the former man, but he requires *extra* covering and protection (12:22–23) by the other "parts" around him. From Joe Horn's *Everyday Champions*, we read:

> The take-home thought from this: Paul is not identifying *any* roles within Christ's corporate Body as shameful or ugly ("less honorable"; "uncomely"), nor is he suggesting there would be an appropriate circumstance for that kind of branding. He is identifying an attitude problem ("which we *think*" [12:23]; "to be of opinion") that results in support roles being viewed as unappealing or less important. If anything, Paul's words here should be seen as a gentle rebuke followed by a confident redirect.
>
> The word *peritithemi*, translated here [12:23] as "bestow," literally means "to put on" (such as a piece of clothing; see Matthew 27:28), or to "surround" with something protective (such as a hedge or fence; see Matthew 21:33)....[147] Paul isn't saying we should give those in support roles the biggest trophies or the loudest applause; he is saying we should *clothe* them in something. It's a figurative and poetic way of commanding that these supporting roles, whom the narrow-minded Corinthian Christians *opine* to be "less honorable" or "uncomely" (detestable, unappealing), must be under a metaphorical covering—one that should be *provided by the rest of the Body*. Paul said "*we* bestow," not "God will bestow," so this is one of those verses that requires action from *us*, fellow Christians. But what is this clothing?...

Paul is *in no way* suggesting that people in support roles should be shamefully hidden away, since the surrounding verses—as well as his references of clothing in *honor*, which is the opposite of shame—dismiss that as a possibility.

Contrarily, when we consider both the culture at the time of Paul's writings and the internal evidence within Scripture, we see that a person's clothing had the potential of identifying him or her with honor, glory, and even royalty...and *sometimes* it could mean all three of those things, like the "glory" or "splendor" of King Solomon, the richest human ruler in the ancient world, when he was compared to the "clothed" lilies (as referenced in Matthew 6:29). In biblical times, if the garment of a man was his glory, and if it reflected his standing with the Lord (such as being clothed in "salvation" in Isaiah 61:10), then to be "bestowed" (clothed; surrounded protectively) with clothing so handsome that it brings "abundant honor" would be a great reward, and that would place upon the seemingly "uncomely" parts all the more "abundant comeliness."

Do you see what just happened? It's all there in one verse. Those "ugly" support roles suddenly became quite beautiful... Paul's clothing analogy shouldn't be related to shame, but to *privileged distinction* [!!!]. It relates more appropriately to "badge of honor" in our culture's lingo today than "hide it; it's ugly." [See that? Paul never actually said that any part was "uncomely"; he said that this was the immature assumption and attitude of the Corinthians!]

However, though Paul isn't suggesting certain people should be hidden for shame, he is allowing the natural cause and effect of "putting on" clothing to mean that body parts under garments are naturally more concealed (more protected; less visible) than others. Paul is acknowledging that some, because of their giftings, are in the limelight, while others are more anonymous, and *neither position is bad. Both* are a natural result of being members of the same Body that intrinsically *cannot* be made up of members who all have the same giftings, or else, Paul says, we amount to nothing more than a giant eyeball (1 Corinthians 12:17).

But we, as Christians, should always be willing to go out of our way to give supporting members of the Body the attention, care, honor, glory, and protection they need to function optimally.

Thanks to this excerpt from Joe Horn's book (*Everyday Champions* is centered on the gifts of the Spirit and their function within Christ's body), we now see that Paul is doing the opposite of what some readers think. He is not using graphic "reproductive organ" language to put down certain members or make their role less grand. Nor is he, as is popularly taught today, suggesting some of us will be given ugly jobs in ministry and our way of dealing with that disgrace is to simply accept that we contribute to the function of the whole, so we must grin and bear it. He is protecting those in Corinth who appear to their fellows as unspiritual, lifting them up to a place of honor and shaming anyone who don't agree! To specific Corinthians, the attitude was such as to assign less "ecstatic" members to a part no more important than a ghastly terra cotta offering at the local shrine. Paul answers with a collective, "How dare you?!"

Don't you just *love* the Word of God when it's fully understood? It breathes life abundantly in every culture and era! It's so comforting knowing Paul wasn't suggesting that any one should accept the fate of being an "ugly part" of the Body...

Turning to the next chapter (13), Paul continues his address of the gifts with the motive of love. By itself, when divorced from its context, this chapter still teaches timelessly constructive advice on what love is and how it manifests. But in its true context, it's not simply an explanation of love, but an exhortation to use the gifts in the previous chapter to love God and others. If this is truly how the Corinthians agree to proceed, then the holiness competitions would cease.

Chapter 14 is a severe scolding to the Corinthians... It may not look that way to modern audiences, but Paul spares no feelings when he says: "If therefore the whole church be come together into one place, and all speak with tongues, and there come in those that are unlearned, or unbelievers, will they not say that ye are mad?" (14:23). By "mad" here, he doesn't mean angry, he means absolutely, off-their-rocker nuts, insane, *crazy*. For reasons we've addressed about "ecstatic worship" and misinterpretations (or rumors) of what had happened on the already enormously famous Day of Pentecost (when believers spoke in tongues for the first time), Corinthians believed that speaking in tongues was the best of the gifts. Here, Paul describes a hypothetical day when everyone in the church comes together in their usual, competing manner, and the whole assembly is uttering mysteries (like oracles). If a lost soul wanders in, they will leave and never come back, believing that the members are just as eccentric, wild, and fanatical in this "new religion" called "Christianity" as they were in the local prostitution temples (minus the "worship" going on in those places). In no way can this contribute to the work of the Gospel, which is the Church's chief goal. In the second half of chapter 14, Paul settles the matter once and for all, explaining precisely how a worship service is to be held: in an orderly way, each with his or her own gift, and in the interest of growth for all (including the overlooked but crucial gift of the *interpretation of* tongues; 14:26–40).

By now, after reading about what the women were up to in this city, the context of the much-feared, women-prohibiting verse should be better understood: "Let your women keep silence in the churches: for it is not permitted unto them to speak; but they are commanded to be under obedience as also saith the law" (14:34). Paul can't be referring to an absolute silence for all times, as he said in his letter already that women were allowed to pray and prophesy in the church (11:5). In 12:28, Paul ranks "teachers" (including preachers) *below* the prophets with a counting system: "And God hath set some in the church, first apostles, secondarily prophets, thirdly teachers, after that miracles, then gifts of healings, helps, governments, diversities of tongues." No gift is held higher than that of prophecy, Paul writes: "I would that ye all spake with tongues but rather that ye prophesied: for greater is he that prophesieth" (14:5). By this order, if we're playing the same competition games as the Corinthians, a woman who prophesies would outrank a male teacher. (We're *not* playing that game, and we're not ranking anyone. We're simply showing that the "silencing" of women here, when applied to the extreme that it often is in today's culture, creates this very brand of division that this entire letter rebukes!) Let us consider an excerpt from *Handmaidens* that helps solidify this even more:

> The word "law" from Paul's words, "as also saith the law," is the Greek *nomos*. It is the same word used in reference to the Mosaic Law, and even *Strong's* [*Concordance*] acknowledges that. However, to the New Testament culture, apart from the Mosaic Law, it meant "1. anything established, anything received by usage, a custom, a law, a command A. of any law whatsoever."[149] There are only three possibilities for what "law" Paul might have been referring to here: 1) the Mosaic Law; 2) the law of the land; and 3) generically a law amidst the people, such as "anything established" or "a custom." The first of these can be ruled out immediately, because nowhere in the Mosaic Law does it give this regulation. The second can likewise be ruled out immediately because, in Corinth, women were allowed to make all kinds of noises wherever they wanted to. (Not to be crude, but their voices were heard in the temples of the pagan gods in extremely loud and sexual ways, and that was the norm for this society.... Historical evidence[s]...also rule out that there had been a "law of the land" for women's silence within this vicinity.) This leaves only the third potential interpretation, and in

an age when Judaizers were treating oral tradition (read: "anything established," "custom," "any law whatsoever" [that the legalistic and Pharisaic circles believed]) as "law," such a conclusion is quite plausible. Therefore, this "law" was not one given by God but by mankind, and it was to this authority Paul was appealing (not one that we are held to today). (Note that some Bibles reference 1 Timothy 2:11 in the margins, suggesting that Paul's words in that verse, "Let the woman learn in silence with all subjection," is the "law" that Paul's referring to. But since 1 Timothy was written *after* 1 Corinthians, as historical evidence shows, this reference of "law" could not have anything to do with 1 Timothy.)…

…[C]ertain members of today's Church still interpret 1 Corinthians 14:34–35 to mean total silence (with…exceptions regarding "prophesying," which, ironically, is a form of teaching as well), to the full and literal extent of its meaning, under extreme application, to every audience and reader, throughout all time, in every culture, in every society, in every circumstance, throughout the universe, and into perpetuity. The question is not *whether* Paul was condemning a woman from speaking in a church; the question is *when*…

We know that Paul allowed for women to speak in the church, because he said as much when he: a) acknowledged the gifts of the Spirit—the word of wisdom, the word of knowledge, faith, healing, the working of miracles, prophecy, the discerning of spirits, tongues, and the interpretation of tongues—to be poured out upon men and women alike, just as it was on the Day of Pentecost involving "the women" in the upper room; b) acknowledged these gifts to be carried out *in church* under proper, non-chaotic circumstances; and c) discussed the proper head covering for a woman praying or prophesying in church (11:5). When he did place limitations on who was allowed to say what, and when, he repeatedly included the men in those limitations (as is peppered throughout chapter 14). Everything clearly points to the notion that Paul didn't want [women] speaking aloud at inappropriate times....

In the group, "for it is not permitted unto them to speak," the word for "speak" here is the Greek *laleo*, which simply means "to talk." Paul could have said the women are not permitted to preach, teach, sing, praise, worship, prophesy, address, discourse, expound, advise, lecture, advocate, persuade, and so on and so forth, because...he had *thirty* [Greek] words to choose from in his native tongue that would have been more specific to the type of activity he was censuring. Instead, however, he chose "talk," which cannot be seen as a binding commandment in all circumstances, because he already said women can pray and prophesy (11:5).

Additionally, from within the lexicology (the study of word usage) and grammar subsections of the textbook, *The Biblical Role of Women*, by New Testament Greek homiletics expert Dr. Deborah M. Gill and theological seminary professor Dr. Barbara L. Cavaness Parks: "The tense of the verb *laleo* is not the most common tense (the aorist) but the less common Greek tense (the present) that emphasizes linear (ongoing) action. Thus, it is better translated 'to *keep* talking.' Paul is saying in verse 34, '[Women] are not allowed to keep on talking,' and in verse 35, 'It is disgraceful for a woman to continually chatter in church.' The kind of verbal action indicates that it is not women's vocal participation but the perpetual disruptive rumble of noise that is disallowed."[150]

Now imagine you're visiting the ancient church at Corinth—or any church, for that matter—and you see a sign above the entryway that says, "Please don't talk in church." Without having to deeply analyze what we're being asked to do and in what language, we all know that "don't talk in church" means "don't be disruptive." By saying women are not permitted to *laleo*,

Paul was saying that women are not permitted to keep talking while the service is in session. As to why Paul would have laid this foundation of behavior for only women and not men, it requires understanding the cultural shift taking place at this time....

[S]uddenly, a new age was dawning for this new belief system called "Christianity."...

Specifically to Corinth, however, thanks to the *hetairai* and *pornai* prostitutes who had already formed an entire cultural acceptance of women who shared "enlightened" opinions and beliefs regarding spirituality and theology [from their oracles], the Christian women in Corinth would have been especially chatty in their newfound [Day-of-Pentecost] freedom. The *hetairai* and *pornai* had...paved the way for women to...assert themselves with questions, tongues, and other less-than-ideal utterances. Whether the Christians in this church were prostitutes, Jewish converts, Gentile converts, travelers, or simply curious women wandering in from the street (and there is historical evidence to suggest a mixture of these, since Corinth was such a beehive of commercial trading), they would have walked into a building with confident, well-educated, vocal woman seeking theological answers.

What Howell explains elsewhere in her book is the concept that these women's unholy oracles were one of the only rights the women of Corinth would have had, since women were so overlooked in that culture (they were not allowed to vote, be witnesses, or establish themselves as experts in science, medicine, or anything else). It's reminds us of the old proverb, "if you give [her] an inch, [she'll] take a mile." What the women in Corinth *could* do was tell a man what "the gods" wanted him to know, which naturally positioned them (or so they thought) as those who could challenge religious teachers of their time. This they did *during services*, as the context of this letter shows.

Paul is putting women (and especially wives, as the Greek indicates) in their place. These details could be argued forever (and maybe they will be), but the absolute bottom line is this: Paul writes that the gifts, including teaching and preaching, are to be exercised in church by recipients referred to in the Greek as *anthropois*: "people," meaning both genders. *Anthropois* is where we get our English word "anthropology," which, as you're likely already aware, is the study of people in ancient cultures. It has always referred to men *and* women. So the apostle's silencing women here in a state of disruptive emergency wherein the "utterance" of a woman could have been obscene should be kept in the proper, Corinthian context.

So, what you're saying is that we can throw that verse out because it no longer applies?

Not one bit. *When these same circumstances of Corinth apply today,* the warnings of Paul apply today. Let us say this another way: When one of today's churches starts to resemble the church in Corinth—when a well-meaning and sincere but disruptive group of people are committing the same sins Paul rebukes here—then Paul's advice should be sought to fix that issue. One grievance that we'll mention again in our reflection of 1 Timothy is the inconsistency of scriptural application among the churches today. A pastor might say a woman cannot preach or teach, because it's a natural usurpation of the authority of a man (as interpreted from 1 Timothy 2:9–15). This same pastor, as is our experience, has no problem seeing females of all ages wearing their hair in braids in church, even though "braids" are *also* a prohibition of Paul's—and not only in "Pauline literature," but in that very same passage (verse 9)! So a well-meaning pastor, himself, is found guilty of throwing a verse out because it no longer applies while he sincerely believes the next verses apply always.

Why prohibit the female teacher and allow the braid? This inconsistency is, needless to say, very confusing to young believers, which is why Pauline literature (that repeatedly identifies female leaders like those listed in Romans) absolutely must, in all times and cultures, be responsibly interpreted. (And by the way, it isn't an innocent "braid" Paul is restricting, even though that is precisely what the English translations suggest. Stay tuned...)

In chapter 15 of 1 Corinthians, Paul reminds his Corinthian audience of the right and proper teaching regarding the doctrines of: 1) Christ's Resurrection (15:1–11); 2) resurrection of the dead (15:12–34); and 3) the bodily resurrection of the saints (15:35–58). The reason this was a necessary response to this congregation was because some of these believers were denying that the dead would rise again (15:12). If they were correct, Paul writes, this would make Christianity pathetic and its adherents pitiable (15:19). Step by step through this chapter, Paul takes reports about the false teachings regarding resurrection and corrects them. The first two items on this agenda are familiar to us today (that Christ rose, and we will also). The third (bodily resurrection) is where we find a seldom-taught (and therefore highly confusing) theology.

Briefly, the Corinthians were probably asking such questions as: "How can a dead body rise again? Wouldn't it be rotten and useless?" Paul counters this by explaining that a seed planted in the soil that grows into a plant was dead when it was put in the ground. Yet it, too, sprouts into a new "body" that is young, fresh, and useful for producing wheat. Just as this harvest is a miracle, our new bodies in the resurrection event will be miracles. They will be without the same sin and weakness we experience in this life. Though Paul doesn't expound on some of the questions that arise from this teaching— what the body looks like, how it will function, etc.,—he makes it very clear there is a physical and a spiritual body (15:44).

One (the physical) carries us through this life to its end; the other (spiritual) "sprouts" from the first, and is both comparable and completely different from the first. By comparing us to Adam, we see that the sin condition inherent in all humans since Creation leads to death and decay. By comparing us to "the last Adam," Jesus, we see that our transformation in the next body leads to perfection, immortality, and an imperishable form that is raised in glory. In a later Epistle, Paul explains that our current bodies will be just like the glorious body of the Risen Lord (Philippians 3:21). When Jesus rose, He was corporeal and touchable (as the account of Doubting Thomas shows). He appeared and disappeared as He chose. He also sat and ate broiled fish with His disciples...after walking through a wall. We don't have a risen saint like Him to ask what it's like, so there is much we will never know. However, as Paul here compares our future bodies with that of Christ, we can safely assume it will be physical (touching, eating) *and* spiritual (walls will not contain us)—a concept that is currently as hard for us to wrap our brains around as the reality of time. God is not limited to linear time like we are. We move in one direction only. Time travel, though fun and entertaining to think about, is not real. For God, it's a natural, given His transcendent eternality. How can we be physical and nonphysical at the same time? By the power of the One who can be in the past, present, and future all at once (2 Peter 3:8).

After this powerful teaching, Paul closes with parting greetings in chapter 16.

Recall that at the beginning of this section, we mentioned this letter we have been studying was actually the second of a known total of four. Letters one and three are lost. Before the writing of 2 Corinthians, there was a *third* letter that caused a lot of sorrow. Portions of 2 Corinthians refer to this lost third letter. As we move into Paul's next Epistle, we must remember that there was both another visit and another bit of "mail" that we cannot read, all of which transpired in less than a year between our canonical "1" and "2" Corinthian correspondences. But the context of 2 Corinthians (and references in 2:4; 7:8) shows that some seriously devastating events transpired during this time.

It's almost universally accepted that 2 Corinthians was written as a defense of Paul's apostleship authority. The cause for such defense is often believed to be related to his change of travel plans, inspiring one or more gossipers to call him a liar. This is likely, but it's not a complete picture. Whether we have one or several initial instigators in view here, before long, angry whispers led to questioning his truthfulness and reliability (2 Corinthians 1:15–17), speaking skills (10:10; 11:6), and refusal to accept their monetary support (11:7–9; 12:13). Additionally, some folks had chosen to continue in their bad habits. Paul lists some of these: "debates, envyings, wraths, strifes, backbitings, whisperings, swellings, tumults…uncleanness and fornication and lasciviousness" (12:20–21).

It appears that there has been a positive change within much of the congregation from Paul's continuing discipleship. For some, however, the Corinthians are up to their old tricks.

Because the heartbeat of this letter has much to do with Paul's self-defense as an apostle (and less to do with complicated theologies), we have little reason to spend long on this letter. However, we will say this much: If readers intend to minister in any kind of sanctioned church or ministerial organization, 2 Corinthians is a must-read! Paul says more about himself in this letter than he does in any other, and no doubt his is the best example of an apostolic missionary with a heart of gold—a description that, God willing, will apply to many who give themselves over to the call of the Lord.

Paul begins with greetings and words of God's comfort (2 Corinthians 1:1–11). In this group, Paul states: "Praise be to the God and Father of our Lord Jesus Christ, the Father of compassion and the God of all comfort, who comforts us in all our troubles, so that we can comfort those in any trouble with the comfort we ourselves receive from God" (1:3–4).

Through Christ, we see the same supernatural comfort in weariness that Jeremiah felt, and in this New Testament verse (as well as several others), we have a direct fulfillment of Lamentations!

Paul then spends several verses discussing his change of plans to visit them at a prearranged time, explaining it was done to spare them from severe rebuke (1:23). Chapter 2 launches with a continuing thought: His visit would have been painful (2:1). He goes on to explain that his last letter (missing letter 3) caused him much distress: "For out of much affliction and anguish of heart I wrote unto you with many tears" (2:4). Reading on, the context of chapter 2 illustrates that these believers had taken Paul's angry letter to heart, and they were sorry.

Verse 2:5 mentions a man who had been the cause behind all this sadness, and Paul recognizes that the Corinthians' decision to oppose him was excruciating (2:5–11). The time has come to forgive this offender lest he be overcome with despair, Paul says. (Scholars have, at times, concluded that this man was the same incestuous offender Paul instructed the Corinthians to disassociate from in 1 Corinthians 5. That is certainly a possibility, but many folks in the academic world have good reason to think these men are unrelated. We will never know for sure. The focus here is more upon the idea that Paul's top interest is in restoration, love, forgiveness, and charitable attitude.) He then mentions his trip to Macedonia and the successes he had there.

In one giant lump—from 2 Corinthians 2:14 all the way through 7:16, Paul details his apostleship. He describes what a true apostle's work looks like, how it functions, what is expected of one, and the fruits of faithful work evidenced by the successful spiritual fruits and Church growth that results from it. Verses 3:1–3 explain that the Corinthians are "living letters" that attest to this work. He also explains that these elements don't only apply to one in the office of an apostle, but to all ministers of the Gospel. The New Covenant, written in blood by the Savior, is what makes this all possible (3:4–18). A comparison of the New Contract with the Old shows the contrast between those who live in the light to those who still wallow in the darkness of the world (4:1–6). Nevertheless, even apostles and spiritual leaders still deal with frailty, like fragile, clay jars (4:7–5:10).

With this foundation laid—the glory of the New Covenant

despite the inherent weakness of its ministers—Paul now finds himself in a position to responsibly convey the importance of reconciliation of all God's "ambassadors" to God despite all our human troubles: "Now then we are ambassadors for Christ, as though God did beseech you by us: we pray you in Christ's stead, be ye reconciled to God" (5:20). Paul suffers greatly for the sake of the Gospel, as the believers in Corinth (and us) can also expect to, but in such work is great joy and virtuous reward (6:3–10). In this work, however, Christians absolutely must be willing to put away their differences and strive toward the goal of being equally yoked. Since God is among them, Corinthians should be careful not to allow unbelievers the chance to distract them or pollute their mission (6:14–18), and they must submit to being cleansed from all defilement (7:1).

The repentance of the Corinthians has brought Paul and his companions much joy! He takes this opportunity to explain that this kind of repentant sorrow is good for personal, spiritual growth, and for this reason, he cannot be sorry that the angry letter had to happen. He merely marvels at their righteous indignation and zeal for Christ (7:5–13). (From 8:1 through 9:15, Paul discusses the matter of giving in support of his ministry, using the Macedonians as an example of generosity.)

Arriving in chapter 10, we see a sharp (and fairly sudden) shift back to Paul's defense of apostleship. He explains that the Corinthians think him to be a timid man when he's in person, but bold in his letters, so he begs them to listen to what he has to say about himself so that his next in-person visit doesn't have to involve his "bold" side (10:1–2, 9–11). He compares himself and his companions against some ignorant, arrogant men who self-inflate, using themselves as the unit of measurement by which all others should be compared (10:12), making the ultimate point that it is what God thinks of man—not what man thinks of himself—that truly matters (10:18).

Though much of chapter 11 is self-explanatory, as we see Paul dealing with "false apostles," it should not be written off as unimportant merely because it's simple to understand. There are a lot of "false apostles," false teachers, and corrupt ministers in the Body today who are well beyond the need for Pauline correction and example. As Paul addresses what the NLT calls "super apostles" (11:5; "chiefest apostles" in the KJV), he shows them his logic for ministering to them for free—an act of service the super-apostles were evidently angry about. (These expressions likely refer to someone who may have been offended that Paul politely refused their monetary blessing.)

Paul speaks of the trials he's been through, including five separate accounts of lashing, multiple run-ins with death and imprisonment, his narrow escape from Damascus (being lowered in a basket down the outside wall of the city), and, on top of all this, the occasional heart-wrenching reports he hears, sometimes including brethren who have been led astray (11:16–33). Doesn't all of this prove his apostleship? Why are there still some among them who doubt? He goes on to tell of a vision he had wherein he was taken to heaven (or some heavenly place, though he is not sure if he left his body). During this episode, he heard many astounding things he knows he is never allowed to speak of, and then explains that God has given him a "thorn in his flesh" to remain modest about such things (12:1–10).

Verse 7 within this passage identifies this "thorn" as a "messenger from Satan to torment [Paul] and keep [him] from becoming proud," but it isn't clear exactly what he's describing. It's likely he didn't feel the need to include details, as his listeners had already been told in person (or in one of the lost letters) what this pain in his life or ministry was. Colin Kruse, the theologian behind *2 Corinthians: An Introduction and Commentary* by InterVarsity Press, notes:

Many suggestions have been made concerning the nature of Paul's "thorn in the flesh." They fall into one of three broad categories: (a) some form of spiritual harassment, e.g. the limitations of a nature corrupted by sin, the torments of temptation, or oppression by a demon, (b) persecution, e.g. that instigated by Jewish opposition or by Paul's Christian opponents, (c) some physical or mental ailment, e.g. eye trouble, attacks of fever, stammering speech, epilepsy, or a neurological disturbance.... Most modern interpreters prefer to see it as some sort of physical ailment, and the fact that Paul calls it a thorn *in the flesh* offers some support for this. Galatians 4:15 ["if it had been possible, ye would have plucked out your own eyes, and have given them to me"] is appealed to by those who want to identify it as an eye problem.[152]

In the end, there isn't enough information about Paul's "thorn" to know for certain what plagues him. Yet, Paul's purpose in mentioning it here is to enlighten his readers to the fact that God has allowed him a bit of a "Job-ism" to keep him from becoming proud or haughty in his line of duty. He uses this frustration to exemplify how his Corinthian fellows can adopt an attitude of praise in worship during hardships, because it ultimately means they *must* draw their strength from Christ:

> For this thing I besought the Lord thrice, that it might depart from me. And he said unto me, "My grace is sufficient for thee: for my strength is made perfect in weakness." Most gladly therefore will I rather glory in my infirmities, that the power of Christ may rest upon me. Therefore I take pleasure in infirmities, in reproaches, in necessities, in persecutions, in distresses for Christ's sake: for when I am weak, then am I strong. (12:8–10)

After having taken a moment to teach the Corinthians something about the power, strength, and glory of Christ, Paul gets back to the super-apostles, reminding them that he, in the Name of Christ, had carried out many signs and wonders, apologizing (with an obvious tone of sarcasm) for not burdening them financially as these false apostles thought he should (12:11–13). He doesn't intend to burden them on his next trip to see them, either, because, as he is their spiritual father; children don't support their parents…it is the father's duty to support his children any way he can (12:14–15). There have been reports that Paul has been accused of trying to trick them, and he addresses the rumor head-on, explaining that all he and his companions have done from the beginning has been to serve them and help them in any way. With that said, he warns that they may not like what he has to say the next time he comes, because he's aware "many" of them are still greatly involved in their sinful exploits (12:16–21). He gives them a final and dire warning:

> This is the third time I am coming to you. In the mouth of two or three witnesses shall every word be established. I told you before, and foretell you, as if I were present, [like I was] the second time [I visited]; and being absent now I write to them which heretofore have sinned, and to all other, that, if I come again, I will not spare [those sinners]. (13:1–2)

Yikes. We only wish we had just one more letter to see how the Corinthians fared!

Nevertheless, this is the end of all he has to say on that matter. His parting words of advice are for them to remain strong and faithful, examine their hearts to be sure their faith is genuine, accept the correction within his letter, stay joyful, grow in spiritual maturity, encourage others in their congregation, live in harmony, and greet each other with a holy kiss (13:3–12).

The last words Paul ever wrote to this church in Corinth—at least his last words that we have record of—are these: "All the saints [here] salute you. The grace of the Lord Jesus Christ, and the love of God, and the communion of the Holy Ghost, be with you all. Amen" (13:13–14).

Galatians

THE "THORN" IN PAUL'S FLESH he mentioned in his letter to the Corinthians is possibly the same physical ailment he refers to in Galatians 4:13, when he tells his readers he wasn't initially planning to go through the region of Galatia, but, "through infirmity of the flesh," he preached the Gospel to them for the first time. As a result of that unexpected (but enormously beneficial) happenstance, we now have this letter, in which a main theme is freedom from the Law. In 5:2, Paul writes that getting circumcised doesn't to score any "extra points" with Jesus; therefore, we can assume the audience originally included primarily Gentiles. However, Paul's first sentence in this letter acknowledges that it's not merely one congregation, but all the "churches of Galatia" (1:1). Scholars are not in agreement today whether the correspondence was initially sent to the Northern Galatian territory (where the residents would have been ethnic Galatians, named after the early Gauls, or Celtics, that allied with Rome) or the Southern territory (where the provincial cities of Antioch, Iconium, Lystra, and Derbe were).

If our book was only about Galatia, this would be an important detail, because it identifies whether the readers of Paul's letter were heavily influenced by Phrygian culture (Southern territory), which was much dedicated to the area's mother goddess, Agdistis (possibly Cybele, depending on how the ancient texts read). This "mother" is both "he" and "she" in ancient writings, as she is hermaphroditic (possessing both male and female reproductive organs), and extant effigies from the area's ruins depict a female whose draping cloth intentionally exposes her nude chest and her "manhood." Sometime after 80 BC, the goddess was the prized deity of the cult in Lesbos, a Greek island at the edge of the Aegean Sea where the famous poet Sappho, a homosexual female, wrote lyrics and music. (Sappho's self-identified sexual orientation on this island is the etymological link to our similar modern terminology: To be a "lesbian" is to associate with the homosexual Sappho of Lesbos, where the male/female Agdistis reigned supreme.) If Agdistis could be proven to be the pet deity of the Galatians prior to the region's intense and widespread conversion to Christianity, the letter's context (especially Paul's command not to use freedom to feed sexual desire in 5:13) could have a more specific meaning than the general immorality theme it's often said to have today. "The weight of evidence seems to be in favor of a south Galatian location,"[153] so this discussion can, at least, be kept in the back of our thoughts as we proceed. However, as so many scholars note, the Northern/Southern argument has been the subject of much debate, and we'll likely never know for sure until we're given the chance to speak to Paul, himself, and ask.

Paul's letter begins, as usual, with warm greetings, mentioning the "brothers" he travels with and a brief note about their common mission: Jesus who died for their sins (Galatians 1:1–5). But, unlike most of his writings—which begin with kindness and slowly set the stage for later rebuke after speaking prayers over the local church—the book of Galatians bursts with fury as early as verse 6:

> I marvel that ye are so soon removed from him [God] that called you into the grace of Christ unto another gospel: Which

is not another; but there be some that trouble you, and would pervert the gospel of Christ. But though we, or an angel from heaven, preach any other gospel unto you than that which we have preached unto you, let him be accursed. (1:6–8)

Commentaries acknowledge this as some of the strongest, most fuming language Paul ever uses, and that "every clause" he employs here "is like another whiplash."[154] The "so soon" (Greek *houtos tacheos*) language is frequently interpreted to state: "I can't believe that so soon after I left, you were given over to another false gospel." (This false gospel will be addressed in a moment.) However, the Acts narrative behind where Paul was and when he preached to the Galatians initially would have to be tweaked to match that conclusion. More likely, the reference to "soon" here doesn't refer to the time between Paul's departure and the introduction of the wrongful teaching, but to the time between the introduction of the wrongful teaching and their embrace of it. Paul is saying, "I can't believe that when this false gospel reached you, you were so soon given over to it." This interpretation isn't only more in alignment with the Acts account, it also changes the urgency of the occasion for the letter. The Galatians hadn't been worn down over time by continual preaching through the convincing and confusing teaching of false prophets who had been among them for a lengthy period. These folks gave a listening ear to pretenders, and "soon" (the Greek words insinuate "at once"[155]) they were on board with false doctrines. Paul is so mad here that he says even an angel from heaven who would teach a such vile twisting of the Gospel should be cursed! He immediately goes on to accept the fact that his message won't make him popular among men, but that if popularity was his goal, he wouldn't be a servant of Christ (1:10).

It's no mystery why the second half of his opening chapter is an explanation of where his own, *true* Gospel originates. It's not from human reasoning (1:11), nor is it from any mere human; rather, it is a direct revelation of Christ (1:12). He gives a brief history of his persecution in the early Church, noting that he was even more zealous than his ancestors in Judaism, and then explains that his conversion experience led him to a visit with Peter and James and, following this, everyone in the provinces of Syria and Cilicia were wowed by his transformation to the Gospel message (1:13–24). Fourteen years later, he travelled back to Jerusalem and met privately with apostles and leaders of the Christian Church, telling them his testimony and checking to be sure they were all on the same page with his teaching. Not only did they confirm that Paul was correct, they didn't even see the need to make his companion, Titus, get circumcised (3:1–3), though doing so would have potentially made him a more affable minister to anyone in the Jewish community (like Timothy in Acts 16:3).

Paul, after mentioning Titus in regard to circumcision, now brings up a group of spies or "false believers" who had snuck into that meeting. Scholars call this group "Judaizers," a term with more than one meaning, but in this context, it refers to men who forced the Jewish way of life upon Christian Gentiles who should have been free of it (see Galatians 2:14). Paul writes that these Judaizers "came in privily to spy out our liberty which we have in Christ Jesus, that they might bring us into bondage" (2:4). He explains that Peter is minister to the Jews, but Peter, James, and John all recognize Paul as minister to the Gentiles (2:6–10). He and Titus feel strongly that not only is circumcision (and other adherences to Jewish customs and lifestyle) unnecessary, but that the blatant refusal to give in to these "spies" was, in part, so the Galatians (and others Paul's missionary journeys reached) would have prominent leaders in the Church who set the standard of freedom from those customs: "To whom we gave place by subjection, no, not for an hour; that the truth of the gospel might continue with you" (2:5). A modern rendition of this would read: "To those spies, those fake Christians, who demanded we return to the bondage of the Jewish system, we said, 'No! Not for even a minute!' And we did this so the truth of Gospel freedom would be carried on to you and continue through you." Therein, we discover what this "false gospel" was that began the letter. That a man would have to be fully indoctrinated to the Old Contract in order to come to Christ is such an offensive idea that Paul likens the teacher of that message as one deserving to be cursed!

Oh, to have been a fly on the wall on the day Paul and Peter were face-to-face over this issue!

What Paul says next reminds these authors of Peter's earlier denials of Christ. Peter—for all his strengths and wonderful, faithful attributes as an authoritative man of Jesus for the early Church—was not a perfect man. None of the apostles were, but in Peter's case, his imperfection manifested in his giving in to pressure when he was against a wall of social expectations. Paul explains to his Galatian readers that Peter had sat and broken bread with uncircumcised Gentiles. Then, later, he chose not to break bread with them because he feared criticism from Judaizers. This decision influenced a few others in their party, including Barnabas, who snubbed these Gentiles in the same way, and the blame for such a wrong fell on Peter's head, Paul writes (2:11–13). After explaining how Peter was confronted by Paul (2:14–16), he explains that the Law of the Jews, as it exists *after* the New Contract was signed by Christ, results in condemnation, even for a man as pious as Paul used to be! If justification is to be found in Christ, alone—and it is—then insisting on the bondage of the Law for new believers leads to the question: "Is therefore Christ the minister of sin?" (2:17). In other words, if Jesus insists that He is the only way to the Father (as He stated in John 14:6), and that this path of righteousness is not through Jewish customs and Law, then He would be leading us into sin if holiness really is found in Judaism. There's no way around it: Christians must either be *free* from the Law, or Jesus is an agent of sin. This is a concept against which Paul uses some of the strongest and firmest language in the New Testament: "God forbid!" (Note for later: This is a *strong* argument for why we don't adhere to the popular dispensationalist interpretation of Revelation that teaches that the Old Covenant—including sacrifices, rituals, customs, and all of Old Testament Law—will be revived in the Millennial Kingdom. If such a teaching results in condemnation and is to be "God-forbidden" like Paul says here, it seems unlikely that God would reestablish that older form of covenantal worship at any point in the future and for any reason.)

Because of this New Contract, insisting on rebuilding the Law of Moses throughout the early Church would be sin in itself, so Paul insists it must remain torn down (2:18). The old self dies *with* Christ, and Jesus now lives in the believer. If keeping the Law made us right with God, then Jesus didn't even need to die (2:19–21).

Yet, there the Galatians were, believing the false gospel they had embraced so quickly. "Oh, foolish Galatians!" Paul writes (3:1). Did they receive the Holy Spirit through obedience to the Law? Of course not (3:2). They received it by hearing the true Gospel. "Are ye so foolish? having begun in the Spirit, are ye now made perfect by the flesh?" (3:3). Was their conversion experience all in vain then? (3:4).

Paul once again remembers Abraham, who was the father of Israel even prior to his circumcision, and teaches that all of the Old Contract looked forward to the day when Gentiles would be saved by faith. Those bound to the Law are cursed. But Jesus took this curse upon Himself when He died on the cross. We are all prisoners of sin, in its bondage through our very nature, and Christ breaks those bonds irrevocably and irreversibly (3:6–22). Before Jesus, we were under the Law, and we would remain under the Law until the time the way of faith would be revealed. Now, these Galatians can be assured of their faith in Jesus as what marks them as children and heirs of God (3:23–4:7).

Paul softens his tone, expressing his deep concern for the Galatians. He writes that he doesn't wish them to return to their days of bondage for no reason: "How turn ye again to the weak and beggarly elements, whereunto ye desire again to be in bondage?" (4:9b). He remembers back when he had first come to them. Some would have been understandably put off by his illness (or affliction) at the time, yet they took him in and cared for him as they would have a heavenly angel or Jesus,

Himself. They were so hospitable that they would have gouged out their eyes and given them to Paul to see better with if they could have! Now he fears for them and worries that he has become their enemy, just because some Judaizers disagree with his theology and knowledge of Christ! The Judaizers will do all they have to in order to win favor with the Galatians, but at the heart, they have terrible intentions, including the aim to isolate the Galatians and keep them to themselves. Paul knows his words are harsh and cold through a letter, and he so desires to be with them in person, but at this moment, he feels he has no choice but to speak the truth and hope it lands upon them the way he intends (4:10–20).

Nevertheless, since the Galatians are so eager to follow the Law, Paul asks, have they even *heard* the Law? Don't they know the story of Abraham's two sons? One, Ishmael, was born from human efforts, when Abraham and his bondwoman, Hagar, attempted to fulfill God's promise because Abraham and his wife Sarah were tired of waiting for God's own perfect timing to kick in through Sarah. The other son, Isaac, born through Sarah, was given as God promised. These two women represent the Old and New Contracts. Hagar is like Mt. Sinai. Her "son," allegorized as the Jews, were enslaved to the Law, as those in Jerusalem. Sarah is like the heavenly Jerusalem above, free from bondage (4:21–27)!

> Sarah (grace) was initially barren, but she ended up with innumerable spiritual children because of the Abrahamic Covenant. She eventually surpassed the younger Hagar. The intended comparison was between the growth of Christianity (grace) and the stagnation of Judaism (law) in the first century. Paul is challenging the Galatians to choose Christ (grace) and be a part of what God was doing in their day.[156]

These Galatians were like Isaac, children of the promise of God! But Judaizers want to place them into bondage, just as Ishmael, the child of the flesh, persecuted Isaac, the child of the Spirit. Well then, what does the Word say about that? Paul is happy to quote: "Cast out the bondwoman and her son: for the son of the bondwoman shall not be heir with the son of the freewoman" (4:28–30; see also Genesis 21:10). Therefore, the Galatians should accept their freedom, like children of the freewoman (Galatians 4:31).

And *since* they're free, they need to *stay* free, refraining from getting mixed up with Judaizers. If circumcision and Jewish customs are what the Galatians choose, then Christ is of no benefit to them at all. Plus, they will have to obey *all* of the Mosaic Law. In fact, Paul elaborates, if they choose the Law, they will be guilty of rejecting the grace and freedom of Christ, which makes them "fallen from grace" (5:1–4). The Galatians had been doing so well up to this point! Who has come after them with this false message? Surely, it wasn't God, because He has just instituted freedom. These false teachings are like yeast… If the Galatians keep giving ear to it, it will pollute all of them together, like the whole lump of dough. Whoever these false teachers are, Paul hopes the Galatians will refuse to allow themselves to be confused by them again (5:5–10).

There is a statement by Paul in 5:12 that has inspired great discussion. In the KJV, it's "I would they were even cut off which trouble you." This sounds like Paul wishes the Church would excommunicate these false teachers—kick them out of the fold, so to speak—and that is one possible interpretation adopted by the minority. However, a vast number of scholars see the Greek *apokopto* (here "cut off") as meaning something a *lot* more gruesome. *Apokopto*, without interpretational leanings, means to "cut off," but it is more than that. As it was used in ancient Greek writings from this area, regarding the practices of the native eunuch priests throughout Asia Minor, it also means to castrate, amputate, or mutilate a part of the body. In the context of a conversation about circumcision to a Galatian people rooted in a culture familiar with the castration rites of the Phrygian priests, the verdict is heavily in favor of the latter interpretation. Greek lexicons, when explaining the meaning of this word, list "Gal. 2:15" (this very verse) after this description.[157] When a verse appears in a lexicon reference, it is because lingual experts have studied not only the word's etymological roots and culture, but the grammatical structure of the verse and its context as well, and they feel assigning that meaning is most likely.

Some of Paul's writing simply requires folks to be mature in their understanding. Paul is not being crass here. If he does, as the lexicological studies say, infer that those who were bothering the Galatians would be castrated, it wasn't a cold or flippant remark, but one designed to show the foolishness of bodily mutilation for the sole sake of faith. Those who have made this connection and interpret Paul to literally be suggesting that these Judaizers deserve to be castrated for what they've done miss the heavy hyperbole (a biblical overstatement for emphasis) in his remark. Saying Paul wishes them harm in this way is like saying Jesus told His disciples to *literally* pull a giant log from their eyes before they complain about the splinter in their brother's (a lesson on being judgmental; Matthew 7:3–5). It's almost like Paul is saying here: "If those Judaizers who are bothering you are such fans of circumcision, why don't they up their piousness to the level of the Phrygian priests in the area and see whether they feel holier after castration?" (also a lesson on being judgmental).

Nevertheless, he said it, and when he did, he was no doubt infuriated by the injustice of a group of men interfering with the innocence of the Galatians' faith.

In the very next verse (5:13), Paul makes a critical statement that can and should be seen as the summarized message of the entire letter: "For, brethren, ye have been called unto liberty; only use not liberty for an occasion to the flesh, but by love serve one another." Yes, the Galatians were free, *but*, if that freedom was used to feed the sinful desires of the flesh, they failed in serving others, which is the heartbeat of ministry. Christian liberty is a means by which believers are now and forever released from the burden of the Law...*not* from the burden of the lost! Paul's following sentence strengthens this. He reiterates: "For all the law is fulfilled in one word, even in this; Thou shalt love thy neighbour as thyself" (5:14). The *entire Law* can be summarized, Paul says, in one's choice to love others as much as himself.

It kinda reminds us of something Jesus said…

Then one of them, which was a lawyer, asked him a question, tempting him, and saying, "Master, which is the great commandment in the law?"

Paul was really paying attention, wasn't he?

In the wrap-up of his letter to the Galatians, Paul expresses the necessity of living by the power of the Holy Spirit over all else, and urges them to avoid giving in to the sinful nature of humanity—"Adultery, fornication, uncleanness, lasciviousness, Idolatry, witchcraft, hatred, variance, emulations, wrath, strife, seditions, heresies, Envyings, murders, drunkenness, revellings, and such like"—because people who submit to these desires will not inherit the Kingdom of God (5:16–21). He then expresses the fruits of following the Spirit as a contrast: "love, joy, peace, longsuffering, gentleness, goodness, faith, Meekness, temperance" (5:22–23).

Some of the greatest advice for Christian living is found in chapter 6, the final chapter of this Epistle. Paul exhorts his listeners to help fellow sinners without falling into the same temptation; share burdens with others, to show obedience to the "law of Christ"; never self-inflate their own importance; take care to produce good work that doesn't need to be compared to the work of others; support ministers; live in a way that pleases the Spirit…for in this, they will "plant" seeds that grow to produce the rich, bountiful harvest of everlasting life (6:1–10). One more time, Paul reminds the Galatians that the Judaizers are simply afraid of persecution and seek the glory of being able to call the Galatians the disciples of their own movement. But the only thing that matters is that Christians have been transformed into the new creation Jesus' sacrifice triggers in the faithful. The verse, "From henceforth let no man trouble me: for I bear in my body the marks of the Lord Jesus" (6:17) could be rendered, "From now on, make sure I don't receive any more reports like these. I, myself, have marks on my body, though the only marks that matter are those that show I have suffered for His Name's sake."

He signs off: "Brethren, the grace of our Lord Jesus Christ be with your spirit. Amen" (6:18).

In this one Epistle, Paul has blasted the Church of today with several important lessons, two of which are: 1) Never let anyone tell you you're not saved if you know you are; 2) never quickly embrace the teachings of others, no matter how convincing they are, if their words don't follow the true Gospel of the Word.

Praise the Lord for Paul's insight to these souls of so long ago!

Ephesians

A LOT OF WHAT WE SAID about Corinth will sound familiar in our glimpse of this city as well. Ephesus was one of the largest cities in the ancient world, devoted not only to a level of industry, wealth, and extravagance competing with that of Corinth, but known primarily for its well-educated residents. (The people in the church at Ephesus were also the ones 1 and 2 Timothy addressed. We don't plan to cover this material again in those letters, so remember these things for those studies as well, or come back and refresh your memory if needed at that time.)

Most cities would never have bothered trying to light the streets at night back then, as this was an expensive luxury requiring oil to be burned from sunset until sunrise. But after the sun went down in Ephesus, these very lamps were lit all over the city, illuminating walkways and thereby supporting the very progressive concept of a city that never sleeps. It's also not hard to imagine that would be the case for a town with its own commercial harbor, as ships arrived whenever the weather permitted, so a night-watch needed to be standing by to receive them. When the goods were unloaded, the men would head straight for inns and taverns for food and rest.

Students with access to a wide selection of biblical dictionaries and encyclopedias can, like us, access photos of an array of advertisements still etched in the stone walls of the ruins at Ephesus. Many of the ads are for the city's brothels, which operated like inns and taverns but with "loose women"—of whom there were plenty in Ephesus—available for hire. One of these brothels shows a permanent "billboard" carved into a slab of the walkway at the end of a road called Marble Street.

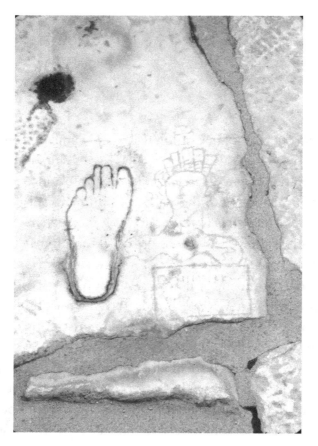

At the bottom right of the image is a woman. She looks a little bit like a male Roman soldier due to two thousand years of damage to the sidewalk carving caused by natural wear, footsteps, and weather deterioration, but you can see above her chest the frilly ruffle of the top of her dress. Her hair is the cluster of almost noodle-looking swirls above and around her head, and the towering design (that kind of looks like a New York cityscape rising from her scalp) is an ornate hairpiece. Above that is a vague "T" shape. On the left is a giant male foot carving with a lowercase "t" atop, and above that, half-cut from the photo, is a sort of polka-dot-filled heart shape. (Online searches of this same image often render the full heart. We are using this image as it is in the public domain.)

Much of the world was illiterate at this time, and even some of the wealthier inhabitants of the ancient world couldn't read, so symbols in signs like these were common. The uppercase and lowercase "T" shapes above the woman and the foot mean "at the next crossroads." The left foot instructs the viewer to turn left. The heart symbolizes love, while the woman is, for archeologists familiar with history, a clear and irrefutable reference to a prostitute. Once the symbols are understood and put together, the carving directs the men arriving on this main street near the harbor: "Looking for love? Turn left at the next crossroad for services."

How do archeologists know for sure that this is a prostitute, not just a woman offering some other service that might be comparably innocent? We have three clues. The first two are the bare shoulders and an ornamental hairpiece—two indecencies that "marked" prostitutes in those days. Women in royalty then would often dress this way and style their hair similarly in many cultures (think Cleopatra), and it wasn't an indicator of prostitution. But among the common folk in the city, it meant only one kind of service, and it was *not* "head this way if you want to meet the resident queen." The third clue is that the directions did, in fact, lead to a brothel. As for what looks like a "plaque" covering the woman's chest on the lowest right area, most experts who have weighed in on this image believe it to be an unrolled scroll (a "book" of that day, hence the lost writing on the front). Others believe it was a traveler's satchel filled with coins. If it's a book, it tells the journeyman that the library is next door to, or connected to, the brothel (and it was both). If it's money, the insinuation is that the service of the prostitutes is not free. Some go as far as to claim it made both statements: "This service will cost you, but if you can't afford it, come visit our library instead."

Do you notice that the deepest part of the carving is the foot? That was, archeologists say, a measurement tool, similar to the giant rulers standing near the entrances to rides at Disneyland or other theme parks that say, "You must be this tall to ride this ride." The carving here says: "If your foot is not as big as this one, you're too young to come see these ladies."

If journeymen or pilgrims were to go to Ephesus today and follow these very instructions from Marble Street near the harbor, going left at the next crossroads would indeed lead them down a short path to the ruins of a two-story brothel that has an underground passageway leading to the Celsus Library on the other side of the street. This supports other evidence found in Ephesus indicating that many of the women were not only wealthy, they were well-educated. The Celsus Library of Ephesus was the second largest in all of Rome in that day, with more than two hundred thousand scrolls covering nearly every imaginable topic, and the women of the brothel had constant access.

It stands to reason, then, that Ephesus' greatest features drawing travelers from the outside world was its emphasis on education, and that applied to women of the night. This is reflected not only in stone ruins and documents, but also in artistic depictions (like the ad) throughout the city. Heraclitus, one of history's most famously known pre-Socratic Greek philosophers who wrote the treatise *On Nature*, was "an enormous inspiration behind the increasing establishment of education in Ephesus. This single papyrus scroll—addressing politics, ethics, theology, and the universe—was dedicated by Heraclitus to Ephesus' prized Artemisium, one of the Seven Wonders of the Ancient World."[158] The Artemisium was the temple of Artemis (her Greek name) or Diana (her Roman name), the twin sister of Apollo and the daughter of Zeus/Jupiter. The temple was destroyed in 356 BC—and, as we stated earlier (in "Unbelievable Political Implications of the Magi"), it was believed to be the very night that Alexander the Great was born. It was rebuilt circa 250 BC, restored to its grandeur, and opened to the public by the New Testament era. The Artemisium is not the same as the brothel's advertisement we just looked at; it was down the road some distance in the opposite direction (north on an aerial map), past the stadium and gymnasium, and it was a great deal larger.

Artemis/Diana was the Great Mother goddess over all of Asia. Disciples of her cult believed that she was the deity through whom all life (humanity and the world) began. Interestingly, her "creation account" involved making Eve first, *then* Adam from Eve's rib, and the rest of humanity followed, all without the need for the seed of a man. (In this way, Artemis/Diana had a warped sort of "virginal birth" story that would have also made Christ's birth through Mary more believable to her disciples at a later point of their Christian conversion. However, before Christianity was well established in this area, the theology centering on Jesus would not *replace* that of this feminist goddess, it would be *added to* the theology surrounding her. This "Eve first, then Adam" idea is exactly opposite of the Jewish and Christian narrative of Creation, and that is important to note for the Timothy letters later on!) Salvation in this cult was found only by *gnosis* (enlightenment) of Artemis/Diana. In addition to being the creator of the world, this goddess was ruler over archery and hunting; the moon; wilderness, forests, and hills; animals (especially the deer, with whom she is frequently posed with in ancient effigies); as well as childbearing and virginity. Though she is credited to be the protector goddess of women (especially young girls), it was also believed that women could be both afflicted and healed through her power.

The three chief goddesses of mythology in this area were Artemis/Diana, Minerva, and Vesta. Because Ephesus was the "Diana capitol" of the ancient world, there was a bit of intellectual and religious snobbery amidst the Ephesians regarding her. Anyone in the Greco-Roman culture could travel to Ephesus to worship her, but residents of the city approached her temple with a chip on their shoulders that said, "You may know her, but *we* know her better. She is *our* goddess." Idol-making was an enormous trade of this city as well, and home-owners who could afford them had at least one, if not more, effigies of the goddess in their homes. Merchants and travelers abroad could visit the marketplace and return home with small, hand-held shrines of her.

Proof of the Ephesians' obsession with the Mother can be found in Acts. Paul, who stayed in Ephesus for several years until the church had taken its root there, arrives first in chapter 19 of that histori-cal record: "And it came to pass, that, while Apollos was at Corinth, Paul having passed through the upper coasts came to Ephesus" (Acts 19:1). In the Name of Jesus, Paul carried out countless miracles, signs, and wonders amongst the people—some of which occurred when the people would simply touch the handkerchiefs and aprons he had worn (19:11–12)—and the disciples there spoke in tongues through the Holy Spirit when Paul laid hands upon them (19:1–6). After a group of traveling Jews came to Ephesus, casting out devils in the name of Paul's God, they encountered a powerfully possessed man. The demon from within him snarled at them, "Jesus I know, and Paul I know; but who are ye?" (19:15). Afterward, he pounced on them, overpowering the small group, sending them naked and beaten into the streets. All the people of Ephesus heard this story, "and fear fell on them all, and the name of the Lord Jesus was magnified" (19:17). Sorcerers from all over the city attended a public bonfire, putting into the great flame all their evil possessions, scrolls, and incantation literature. This, too, added much attention to the Name of Jesus (19:19–20).

But one man, an idol-maker named Demetrius, was angered. His business of making Artemis/Diana idols was suffering because of Paul's message, so he gathered his "many" craftsmen together and started running through the streets proclaiming, "Great is Diana of the Ephesians!" (19:23–28). People from every nook and cranny in the city flooded into the amphitheater in hopes to find a voice to lead them in all the confusion, and some didn't even know why they had gone there, except that it was where people were headed for answers. Everyone was talking over one another, and Paul wasn't allowed in (both because he was unwelcome and for the sake of his safety for those who cared about him). When a Jew named Alexander took to the central stage, people started to quiet down and listen—until they found out he was a Jew; then the din roared once again: "Great is Diana of the Ephesians!" (19:29–34). The mayor finally stood at the front, calming everyone down. He stated as if it was irrefutable fact that the image of Artemis/Diana fell to them from the sky, so the citizens should not do anything irrational. (The logic here is that, because Artemis/Diana was so firmly embraced in this city, no other doctrine was a threat to her, so impulsive reactions were out of order.) Then, he suggested that, in order to avoid a riot in Roman territory, the issues Demetrius had with the travelers should be taken up in formal charges of the court, not on the streets. Everyone went their own way (19:35–41).

Needless to say, though Ephesus was influenced by more than one god, as they were as knee-deep in the Greco-Roman pantheonic religions as anyone else in the Roman Empire, Artemis/Diana was indeed their most prized deity. Ephesus hosted an annual "Artemisia Festival" that honored her in this, her "home city," drawing multitudes from the surrounding regions and promoting prostitution and orgiastic worship.

What we stated in our Corinth reflection regarding women's rights was also true here, in Ephesus, but to a greater degree. Women were still considered to be ranked lower than men on most political and social fronts, but for matters regarding educational background and religious opinion, they were a powerful voice in Ephesus. As the female body was the "conduit to the gods," females were vocal about theological concepts when Christianity was established in the area (sometime later, Emperor Theodosius closed the schools, and women quickly reverted to being second-class citizens well beyond the time of Paul).

As far as the audience of this letter, Paul makes it clear (Ephesians 2:11) that he is primarily writing to Gentiles, which stands to reason, in light of the seeming absence of Jewish religion in everything we've just discussed. With this background in mind, much of the Epistle to the Ephesians (especially chapter 5), is brought into new light.

After Paul's greetings (Ephesians 1:1–2), he writes of the spiritual blessings and inheritances that come from our adoption as children of God (1:3–14). Warmly, Paul then proceeds with a prayer over the congregation of Ephesus, asking God that they be given the spiritual wisdom necessary to discern rightful behaviors and knowledge of Him (that supplants and overcomes the messy theologies dominating the area). He prays their hearts will be receptive and growing in: 1) the understanding of the hope that has been given to God's children; 2) the full acknowledgment of God's power, which raised Christ from the dead and is available to assist believers; 3) the recognition of Christ's authority as Head of His Church; and 4) the realization that the Church is His Body (1:15–23).

With this foundation cemented in the minds of his readers, Paul proceeds by explaining that, before Christ, the Ephesians "were dead in trespasses and sins" (2:1); they had "walked according to the course of this world, according to the prince of the power of the air, the spirit that now worketh in the children of disobedience" (2:2). It is not just the Ephesians who are dead in this way, he says; all have struggled with the inherent nature of sin, provoking God to anger. But now, through the power of Christ and the living Gospel message, the Ephesians are saved and made alive in Jesus, "raised...up together, and made [to] sit together in heavenly places in Christ Jesus" (2:3–6). None should boast about this status, because salvation is not earned but given freely. This plan of God should encourage Paul's readers with the knowledge that they are examples for future generations (2:7–10).

Paul now stresses the "oneness" Christianity brings to these people. Once, they had been Gentiles, excluded from the nation of Israel and the promises of God to His people and left without any hope. Because of Jesus, they are now included in the family—and the inheritance— of this nation under God, because Christ broke down the walls of hostility that separated them, replacing the Old Contract based on Law and regulation. Finally, there is peace between the Jew and the Gentile, who are now "one" (2:11–18). With this new arrangement, concepts such as "foreigners" or "strangers" are gone forever. All believers in Christ make up the new Temple of God, the "house" built upon the foundation of the words and deeds of apostles and prophets. The Cornerstone of this building is Jesus. Therefore, together, Christians are "builded together for an habitation of God through the Spirit" (2:19–22).

This fresh and gracious plan of God has not been revealed to prior generations. As Paul is an authoritative, church-planting apostle, he writes that he is chosen to be a part of God revealing this part of the plan in this very moment, though he humbly notes that he is the least deserving of this grand position. The Jews and the Gentiles are equal inheritors of God's riches, blessings, and promises (3:1–13). Again, Paul prays for the congregation's inner strength and empowerment to understand and properly utilize the knowledge he is sharing with them; that the roots of the Ephesians will be grounded in "the breadth, and length, and depth, and height" of God's love; and that they will be made complete in the fullness of life, given through the power of God that leads to accomplishments they never thought imaginable (3:14–20).

But while there is much reason to celebrate the success of this plan of the Most High, it requires unity in the Spirit amongst the brethren. The Ephesians must show patience with others while everyone is working out their mistakes and coming into the Christian life. Each believer is given gifts by the Spirit to accomplish this task. Jesus had "ascended" to the highest place. This also shows that, while He walked the earth,

He had "descended" to the lowest place for believers. His presence is therefore illustrated to be throughout the entire universe! The Ephesians can rest in the irrefutable fact that the gifts given to them through the Spirit are not only for the health of the Body, but for the spreading of His Gospel. The new Christians are required to continue developing in the Spirit, letting go of the behaviors of children and becoming mature as adults. When this happens, they will not be thrown around in the winds of deceit, lies, and false doctrines. (Goodness, this teaching is needed today more than ever!) Instead, they will be united in truth and love, responding as a corporate Body to these threats and drawing closer to Christ, the Head of the Church (4:1–16).

Remember the Artimisium and the prostitution in Ephesus for this next portion of the letter…

Having been given the authority of an apostle for the Lord, Paul goes on to state it is imperative that the Ephesians no longer live like Gentiles, in hopeless confusion and darkness and with hearts hardened against God. The Gentiles live shamelessly, *feeding the lusts of the flesh with impurity*. Now that the Ephesian congregants have given themselves over to the ways of Christ, they must shed this old life: "put off…the old man, which is corrupt according to the deceitful lusts; And be renewed in the spirit of your mind; And that ye put on the new man, which after God is created in righteousness and true holiness" (4:17–24). If a believer is a liar, he must stop lying; if angry, he must stop allowing things to feed that anger (for anger is a "foothold" of the devil); if he's a thief, he must stop stealing; if he uses his mouth for profanity, he must replace that practice with words that are good and helpful, and that are an encouragement to others; if his behavior grieves the Spirit, he must remember that he is no longer his own, but God's child who will be saved on the day of redemption. Bitterness, rage, hatred, anger, harsh speech, and slander of the brethren are all signs of evil, and they are to be purged, replaced with kindness, tenderness of heart, and forgiveness, just as God has forgiven the Ephesians through the work of Christ (4:25–32).

All of their decisions and deeds are now expected to imitate God. Paul gives a lengthy list of examples in chapter 5. He is quick to mention the sin of "fornication" first, followed by "uncleanness," "covetousness," "filthiness," "foolish talking," and "jests" (by this, scholars believe he meant "dirty jokes"). He explains that none of these believers can be a "whoremonger," an "unclean person," a "covetous man," or an "idolater" (including those who worship Artmeis-Diana) if they wish to inherit the Kingdom of Christ (5:1–5). Folks who make excuses for these sins will incur the wrath of God. As they are now making the choice to live in the light, they are expected to act as those who live in the light. Evil and darkness are behind them now, and any evil that contradicts the nature of the Spirit is to be exposed and made accountable (5:6–14). So Christians must be careful to live in the wisdom of God, using thoughtful determination in what God hopes for us to accomplish, shedding reckless and impulsive thinking brought on by vices such as drunkenness. Being filled with the Spirit leads to singing praises, making music that delights God's ears within the heart of men and among the brethren, and giving thanks to the Lord in everything (5:15–20).

Now, Paul turns to the subject of marriages and relationships between men and women, writing of a concept that would be nearly unbelievable to the listeners of his day: *mutual* submission!

It's easy in our modern world to look at Paul's advice in this area and still see a stronghold of cultural misogyny, but when we consider the letter's background, we see that Paul is actually instilling the *opposite* idea. Chapter 5, verses 21–33, do absolutely and irrefutably identify that a woman is to submit to her husband, as the husband is the head of the household (especially 5:22–24). But this is stated just below a verse that says *both* spouses are to submit to each other (5:21). Paul also teaches that a man is to love his wife in the same way Christ loves His Church when He died for "her," making her clean and holy, without spot, wrinkle, or blemish (5:25–27). A husband is to love his wife as much as his own body. If believers are the "Body" of Christ—and nobody hates his own flesh—then husbands should see wives as part of this holy Body as well and cherish them, because they are now "one" like Christ and the Church are "one." In case it hasn't been made clear up to this point, Paul reiterates it for emphasis, closing out the chapter with: "Nevertheless let every one of you in particular so love his wife even as himself" (5:28–33).

We skim over the world-changing moment that occurred here when we read these words in contemporary culture. Remember, at this time and area of the world, women were not allowed to divorce men, and most often, they were not allowed to choose their own husbands, as they were given in marriage by parental arrangement. Men could take brides, treat them like absolute garbage all the time, and then divorce them as simply by handing them a piece of paper stating their intent to part from them (and yes, in case you're wondering, that was the literal action taken by men who wanted a divorce). This was the norm. With the exception of women in Corinth and Ephesus (as well as a few other "orgiastic worship" cities of the ancient world)—who could openly share their opinion in a public place regarding what "the gods" were "saying to the men"—women had no rights at all. They could not demand proper treatment or expect to be valued in any way above the demoralizing office of a spiritual prostitute. Reduced to a status only barely above those of the lowest slaves, women were objects that could be barked at, ordered around, and punished for disobedience to a man in ways that left them destitute, forgotten, alone, and, in a collectivist "honor and shame" society, being therefore viewed as a blight to their neighbors. A woman was lucky even to be given a husband who would provide sustenance on a dinner table that *she* had to prepare perfectly lest she make one mistake and get kicked to the curb. (We are not suggesting that every wife was treated poorly, but that it was very common, and women couldn't do a thing about it.) Nobody in Paul's day expected that a letter from an apostle who was once a Jewish leader would address the value of women to their husbands as Paul just did here. Some read his words and think,

He should have talked about women's rights and equality of the sexes! Those who respond this way miss the fact that this is precisely what Paul just did! Some preachers and/or pastors use this section of the Bible to show that women must bow to the authority of her husband starting from verse 22 forward. Even when it's unintentional, if they teach submission of a woman without also addressing the overarching theme of "mutual submission" over this portion of Scripture, then they are leaving out one of the most radical, mind-boggling verses in the whole of the Word, which is verse 22, demanding that the husband also submits to the wife!

Don't get us wrong… This letter from Paul should never be read in a way that endorses a feminist ideology that the woman is more powerful in the home than the husband at any point. Read these next words very carefully: *That approach still feeds the fleshly notion that men and women are in competition for power!* Paul is explicitly suppressing such competition…and it's noteworthy that his audience is the Ephesians. If a Roman girl's parents were wealthy enough to afford her education prior to the removal of schools in this city (which was exceptional, but it did happen), she could have grown up to be anything from a professor at the school to a philosopher and beyond. These were offices that had almost never been given to women prior, and the exceptions to that were early women's-lib-type movements that were quickly squashed before they could fully take root. Though these positions did not place a learned woman as a man's equal in society, Ephesus at the time of Paul was beginning to see a glimmer of women's liberation in the community. You can therefore imagine what kind of "competition" would be happening in the home just prior to, and during the beginning of, Christianity's hold on Ephesus. This new religion with a Man named "Jesus" obliterated the walls of what was male, female, slave, free, rich, poor, and every other status, placing everyone on an equal plane in spirit, as Paul wrote in Galatians 3:28. Though we know today that Jesus' Kingdom was "not of this world"—and therefore Galatians 3:28 should not be used to endorse a woman's liberation movement on earth—the new status of a believer was no longer identified according to gender in the operation of the Spirit's gifts and the love that is to be shared in the Body. Ephesian women, then, would have jumped at the chance to see this as an opportunity to rise up as equals, but their longsuffering and hunger for equality would have led to an aggressive nature of the flesh, leading them to dominate men. Christianity claimed believers were "free" from so many things that had enslaved them before (sin nature, the Law, and so on), and this "freedom" could have easily been interpreted by these women as if they were no longer expected to be submissive in a city where a feminist goddess reigned.

This struggle for power is what Paul is addressing, and instead of the coldness that had been written of women in this area for hundreds (if not thousands) of years, he is saying men should cherish their women, love them as much as they love themselves, and *through* that love, the Ephesian culture that assigns women strong opinions through unholy unions at the temple of Artemis will be broken! The "mutual submission" emphasis is *not*—as many preachers today teach—Paul's establishing who is in charge. The emphasis is on establishing that both husbands and wives should love each other so much as equals in the Body that the petty squabbles of power never take root in the household in the first place! The loving words of Paul about women in these passages show clearly that, unlike most men of his day, he sees the value of females in the Body, and that true love conquers the struggle for power. He isn't perpetuating the vices of misogynist culture, he's *breaking* the vices of misogyny in the Body of Christ by lifting the women up as equals. Simultaneously, he is telling the women of Ephesus: "You might be used to thinking women are the authorities in a religious setting such as the unholy Artimisium, but here, in the Body of this new system called 'Christianity,' you are not the final word. Wives, submit to your husbands."

A timeless truth that can be taken from this lesson is this: A wife should *so* love her husband that she should approach God with a daily prayer: "God, help me to really listen to what my husband needs, and help me want the same things he wants for this household." A husband should pray the same prayer regarding his wife. Then, when they come together to discuss something they don't initially agree upon, they have both prepared themselves to submit to the other so that the answer to the problem is found in mature, unselfish discussion until they come together and agree on what's ultimately best for their family. If the Pauline example in these verses is correctly applied, no spouses ever have to say *theirs* is the final word when both parties are equally interested in the precious, beautiful act of mutual submission in love. And, once that much is understood, suddenly the demand for control inherent in the competition for domination of the sexes "pops out" as the evil it truly is. (If this same kind of submission were to apply between Christian and Christian, all division within the Body would be vanquished! We have so much to learn, don't we?)

Contrary to the "who's in charge around here" teaching, Christ is in charge of *all* of us, Paul writes, as He is the Head of the Body, and we should be patient, kind, and loving toward all others within the Body while we work through our differences.

On the tail of addressing relationships in marriage, Paul instructs children to obey and honor parents (6:1–3), then he says something as equally precious for the children as he did for the women: "And, ye fathers, provoke not your children to wrath: but bring them up in the nurture and admonition of the Lord" (6:4). At this time in history, children were certainly loved by good parents, but societally, they were considered far more inconvenient than they are in Western culture today. They were, as the saying goes, to be "seen and not heard." Parenting, especially from fathers, was often stern, cold, and lacking in affection. Nurturing was "the mother's place," while the father was less present in the household. Additionally, Roman "infanticide" ("infant" and *cide*, meaning "to kill") was taking place all over the Empire.

Briefly, a mythical legend tells that the founder and first king of

Rome, Romulus, and his brother, Remus, were abandoned by their mother and left to die. A female wolf found them and nursed them in a sort of Mowgli in *Jungle-Book* fashion while Tiberinus, the god of the Tiber River, protected them. Eventually, they were discovered and adopted by a shepherd and initially raised as shepherds themselves.

The abandonment of unwanted infants is therefore sewn in to the very fabric of Roman life, and since men were the supreme decision-makers of that era, it was the father of the child who chose whether the baby lived or would become the next victim of a practice called *exposti* ("exposed"; the act of being left out in the wild without shelter). Though some babies were drowned, most of them were "exposed," meaning they were thrown into sewers, or on dung heaps or garbage dumps. Needless to say, many mothers had their precious newborns taken from their arms and disposed of like trash. At times, these infants were taken in by infertile couples, or by those who could not afford to buy a slave of their own. (It's too graphic to address at length in this family-friendly book, but sometimes babies were adopted for pedophilic purposes as well, and those stories usually ended in terrible ways.)

Jews were actually quite unique in their belief that all lives were sacred and that this early form of abortion was wrong. To the Romans, it was just a part of common life, and without contraceptives, the number of deaths was much higher than we would assume to hear in modern statistics related to abortion. Outside of the brothels, it was unusual to see that a male baby would be exposed to death, as the life of a male was more valuable to society. In areas that flourished with prostitution—such as Ephesus and Corinth—this wasn't always the case, as a female could be raised as an assistant to the older women until she was old enough to become a prostitute, herself, thus giving her value to society as well. Under and around ancient brothels, many archeological digs have found countless skeletons of male babies, while the dung heaps or garbage dumps show primarily female remains. Greek philosophers, including Aristotle, agreed that if a baby was born deformed or weak, it was to be killed for the good of both the child and the public.[159] However, a deformity was not by any means required to justify infanticide. In fact, Greek philosophy acknowledged it as a natural part of human prerogative completely unrelated to any question of immorality. Thomas Wiedemann, in his research-packed book, *Adults and Children in the Roman Empire*, states:

> Pagan philosophers had not been worried about the morality of infanticide or exposition. Democritus noted with approval that while other living creatures instinctively try to raise their offspring, it is accepted among human beings that the purpose of raising children is, consciously, to gain certain material advantages. Greek and Roman writers noted that it was a peculiarity of the Jews that infanticide and exposition were frowned upon.[160]

From the very womb, children of Rome were not frequently valued as people that God (or the gods) created and cherished. Therefore, what we read right past in Ephesians today would have landed on its original readers' ears like a gong. We can imagine the response of some of Paul's recipients: "Fathers are to respect *children*? Fathers are supposed to be careful not to provoke them to anger? Nurture them? What? Why do their feelings matter? Where did this Paul guy come from, and who does he think he is? That kid of mine is lucky I didn't leave him on a dung heap!" So again, though we skim right over it now, Paul was consistently presenting priceless defenses of yesteryear's underdogs.

It's all the more unimaginable that our Lord and Savior said, "Suffer little children, and forbid them not, to come unto me: for of such is the kingdom of heaven" (Matthew 19:14). He so loved the little ones!

Paul now turns to slaves—who were considered the least important people on the earth in those days. First, he expresses that the slave should obey his master as respectfully and sincerely as he would obey Christ. This they are to do not only when they are being watched by the master, but at all times, as their reward for good work will come in the end (Ephesians 6:5–8). Then, he addresses the masters, saying, "And, ye masters, do the same things unto them, forbearing threatening: knowing that your Master also is in heaven; neither is there respect of persons with him" (5:9). Just as it was with women and children, Paul here defends the rights of slaves to be treated well because they are humans and, therefore, are equal inheritors of the work of the cross. We simply don't "see" in Paul's writing the "gong effect" here, but it would be similar. Jews had punishments written into several parts of the Old Testament regarding their treatment of slaves, but being a slave to the Jews was considered a different thing entirely from being a slave to the Romans/Gentiles. A Jew would have already known the life of a slave matters to Yahweh (the fact that the Old Testament Law addressed punishments to those who mistreated them proves this). A slave, to the Jews, was also one who was positioned as a servant voluntarily: given room and board as well as payment like an indentured servant (think "maid" or "butler"), and the slave was always freed on the year of Jubilee. The Gentile Ephesians would not have had the same Law, and extant documents from the Roman masters in this day openly view a slave as barely a person: one who could be bought, sold, traded, and beaten at the will of the owner. Likewise, they were unable to marry or own property of any kind. Some documents in circulation at this time do recommend that a master treat his servant with care, but only because a severely beaten slave cannot serve his master well. No pause for brutality was in place to protect the human rights.

Now, suddenly, this radical apostle is saying a Gentile slave owner should view his servant as a person equal to himself, because God is not a respecter of our human title-games. As the master is over the slave in the home, the Master is over the homeowner. Paul just compared these wealthy men to slavery terms, showing that they, too, have a Master they must serve.

Goodness, Paul really was bold! And we miss so much in light readings of the Word...

As a final (yet groundbreaking) word to his readers, Paul now exhorts Christians in Ephesus to put on the whole armor of God every day (6:10–18). There are many teachings on this in modern times, so we will make this a shorter examination, but Paul here paints the picture of the enemy in military terms, as a dark warrior who strategizes against God's people. To withstand the enemy and his vices, we must put on the following pieces of spiritual armor:

1. Belt of Truth
2. Breastplate of Righteousness
3. Shoes of Peace
4. Shield of Faith
5. Helmet of Salvation
6. Sword of the Spirit (which is the Word of God)
7. Prayer in the Spirit

Paul then requests prayer for himself, that he will be successful in presenting the Gospel message to both Jew and Gentile, even while he remains shackled in his prison cell (6:19–20). He notes that Tychicus will update them further on how things are going in Paul's ministry (6:21–22), and ends this letter with: "Peace be to the brethren, and love with faith, from God the Father and the Lord Jesus Christ. Grace be with all them that love our Lord Jesus Christ in sincerity. Amen" (6:23–24).

The more of the backdrop of Paul's letters we understand more fully, the more his Epistles show that the spread of the Gospel to such a pagan world was, in itself, a miracle. Who could have ever imagined that the Roman world would be taken by such a beautiful storm?

Philippians

PHILIPPI WAS A CITY in the province of Macedonia known for its gold mining. Its location on Via Egnatia—an important military and commercial trade route that ran from Dyrrachium to the West through major cities along the Aegean Sea to Byzantium (Istanbul today) to the East—was the reason for heavy foot traffic in the city. As it was customary for our sweet apostle who so believed in planting churches in urban strongholds, it's no surprise that Philippi was, like Corinth and Ephesus, a significant draw for large crowds including travelers. Its resident deities were Liber (god of wine, male fertility, and, as the name suggests, liberty), Bendis (goddess of hunting and the moon; the earlier, Athenian "Artemis"), and the Thracian Rider (alternatively Thracian Horseman or Danubian Horseman; the demigod "hero" of ancient Thrace representing salvation). An annual festival called Liberalia was given to honor the god Liber, and it was at this celebration of a young boy's maturation that the Roman "boys" became "men" and were given the rights to vote as well as other benefits of official Roman citizenship. This was done just following the ceremony wherein the boys would remove their *bulla* and surrender it to the gods. (The *bulla* was a round, hollowed protection amulet worn by boys nine days after birth that featured a phallic [erect male organ] symbol representing fertility.) Archeological pursuits of history have shown evidence of much emperor worship in Philippi, alongside remains of the Anatolian Cybele cult (which worshipped the Egyptian gods Isis and Osiris). In addition to this, Philippi respected and venerated the pantheon of gods along with the rest of Rome.

Acts 16 shows Paul's ministry to the Philippians, including Lydia, an important tradeswoman who mastered the rare art of purple clothing dye—a fairly new skill at the time that this area was legendary for. He cast a demon out of a slave girl and got into some serious trouble with the local magistrates who had him beaten illegally and then apologized and begged him to leave the city after they realized he was a legitimate Roman citizen. (By the way, in case you're wondering, though Paul was a Roman, he had been a Jew more than anything else in his childhood, so there is no merit to the idea that he would have participated in the Liberalia festival, or that his parents would have ever placed upon him the *bulla* amulet.)

The language in this Epistle shows that Paul was in prison when he wrote to his brethren, and the evidence tends to stack in favor of his imprisonment in Rome. So here he is, writing from the shackles of a cell to the early Christians. Yet this backdrop is in sharp contrast to the central message of this letter, which is themed on the subject of joy. If *Paul* could find joy during such trying times, certainly the Christians of Philippi—a city built around the god who embodies and celebrates liberty and freedom—could as well.

The occasion of the letter is a cocktail of many issues Paul has addressed in the previous letters we've studied: persecution, false teaching, adherents to the Mosaic Law, and unification of the members in their work toward the fulfillment of the Great Commission.

He begins his letter with greetings from he and Timothy (Philippians 1:1–2), and shares prayers and thanksgiving for the church at Philippi (1:3–11). In this opening, we have a crucial reminder of

God's work in us: "I thank my God upon every remembrance of you, Always in every prayer of mine... Being confident of this very thing, that he which hath begun a good work in you will perform it until the day of Jesus Christ" (1:3–4, 6). In other words, "I thank God each time I think of you, and in every prayer I lift up on your behalf, I'm confident that God, who has began a good work of growth in you, will be faithful to complete what He started."

He moves on to mention that his presence in the prison is actually creating the opposite condition that his captors would have imagined: The whole company of guards know he is in shackles for the sake of Christ, and the local believers have become bolder in their preaching of Jesus as a result. In fact, some locals are even preaching out of jealousy, which is not a motive Paul endorses, but it does show that his ministry is inspiring a movement (that we now know in modern day to have been a world-changing and irreversible one). For others, the motive is pure, but either way, the message of Jesus is being spread and, bondage or no bondage, Paul is rejoicing in it all (1:12–19). Paul then makes the point that living at all means living for Christ. To live for Him is wonderful, but to *die* for Him is even better! Meanwhile, as long as Paul lives, he is available to help increase the strength of the churches, so though he longs to ascend to Christ's side, He is happy to go on living as well, so long as it means his existence on this earth is a constant act of worship to the Savior (1:20–26). The Philippians should understand that they are to live as citizens of heaven, showing no fear in the face of their enemies, as God, Himself, is the Author and the Finisher of their faith and good works, so their own suffering is as much an honor for them as it is for Paul (1:27–30).

If the Philippians want to receive the comfort Christ and the Spirit give during persecution and suffering, however, it requires them to be united in all things through love. This is the genuine attitude of the Christ, the Messiah, who came and condescended His own status as Deity, never worrying about maintaining divine privileges while He willingly died a cursed, criminal's death. But in this supreme act of servanthood to the Father's plan of redemption, He was exalted to the highest place; His Name is above all names; every knee will bow to Him one day; and every tongue will confess that He is Lord of Lords. This is the attitude of servanthood that the Philippians must imitate (2:1–11).

With a great emphasis on the joy of the work, Paul exhorts the Philippians to obey God in reverence and fear, choosing to live lives that are wholly pleasing to God, free of squabbling and complaint, so they will continue to be the example to a dark and perverse world. In that very work, both Paul and the Philippians can find their source of joy (2:12–18).

He makes a brief mention of the wonderful, tried-and-true companion he has found in young Pastor Timothy (2:19–24), then he commends Epaphroditus in equal praise, letting the Philippians know he will be joining them soon at Paul's instruction (2:25–30).

Whatever happens from that point out, these Christians need to rejoice in the Lord; watch for evildoers who insist circumcision is the only path to salvation; maintain confidence in their salvation through Christ; remember that all human pursuits toward goodness or righteousness (like Paul's own years in obedience to the Law) is all worthless without the Messiah whose work changed it all (3:1–11). Though perfection is unattainable, and even Paul cannot proclaim he has reached perfection, like Paul, all Christians should hold on to the progress they have already made and press on toward the goal of perfection in Christ. Paul contrasts this language with haughty folks who have become enemies of the Lord in their behaviors, and then explains that true Christians will be recognized and lifted up into their newly resurrected bodies with the almighty power of God (3:12–21).

What a joyous thought, indeed.

In chapter 4, Paul switches gears, exhorting his readers to assist Euodia and Syntyche in an apparent disagreement they are having, and to be considerate. He writes that these believers should pray to God about everything, every single little need, and to always rejoice and be thankful in what He does for them. Peace comes from this relationship, and it's a peace that exceeds all human understanding and guards their hearts and minds as they continue in the pursuit of following Christ (4:2–7). It is at this point in the letter that the beloved "think on good things" quote is shared for the first time in history with the Philippians:

> Finally, brethren, whatsoever things are true, whatsoever things are honest, whatsoever things are just, whatsoever things are pure, whatsoever things are lovely, whatsoever things are of good report; if there be any virtue, and if there be any praise, think on these things. Those things, which ye have both learned, and received, and heard, and seen in me, do: and the God of peace shall be with you. (4:8–9)

As Paul wraps up his letter, he thanks them for their generous gifts of genuine concern and financial support. Philippi was the only church that had supported Paul in this magnitude while he was travelling throughout Macedonia. Despite his gratitude, however, Paul goes out of his way to ensure his readers that he is not looking for more, because he has all he needs. He simply couldn't keep to himself the gratitude of their blessings during a time when this kind of support was important. Such a generous spirit they have, and God will supply all of their needs as well, so all glory goes to Him (4:10–20).

Paul signs off to "every saint in Christ Jesus" on behalf of himself and the saints who tend to him, and says, "The grace of our Lord Jesus Christ be with you all. Amen" (4:21–23).

Next time you're are feeling bogged down by life and wonder which Scriptures to turn to in order to receive the comfort of joy in the midst of all else, consider this letter of Paul. Whatever things are *good*, keep your mind occupied by those lovely and pure thoughts. And when you're discouraged about your spiritual growth, always remember that the One who began something wonderful within you *will* be faithful in completing what He started. *You* are a wonderful work of God—no matter what you look like; how you smell; what your parents named you; what others have said to you; whether you need to lose fifteen pounds, start exercising, or quit smoking; whether or not you're the first to sign up for the main entrée on potluck Sundays; whether you have a good credit score; whether you wrecked your new car as a teenager; what job you perform on a daily basis while you struggle to keep up with your bills, kids, and spouse; whether you've achieved your dreams; whether you don't yet know what your dreams are; whether you're young, middle-aged, or elderly; what snarky comment from earlier today you still have to apologize for; whether you still feel guilty about that secret sin you committed last week; that kid whose feelings you hurt on the playground when you were twelve; or any other man-made qualifier of human value— and you will someday reach wholeness in what God has begun in your life and in your heart. In your Father's view of you, you were perfectly formed and designed even before birth, and there is no end to the access you have to His throne while you work out your imperfections and strive toward higher goals. You *do not*, as some wrongly imply, have to have your life figured out all in a day. Allow yourself room for mistakes, and forgive yourself during this messy and confusing time in a human body.

You were defined at birth, when the Father created someone He saw as a good and worthy creation.

You were refined at conversion, when the Son made you brand new, wiping away any fault of the past and giving you a fresh start.

You are daily redefined by the Spirit, who convicts you to strive toward being the best person you can be while the Son intercedes on your behalf to the Father who has loved you from the beginning.

Defined. Refined. Redefined every day.

This is the work of the Trinity on your behalf, because each of these three Persons holds an affection for you that can never compare to any other affection you've experienced in this lifetime. There is no greater power in the universe than the Father, the Son, and the Holy Spirit who have worked together to make you great. And though you haven't arrived at perfection like you will when you're given a white robe and a seat at the Groom's table, the One who formed you in your mother's womb did so even while He was devising a plan for your life that supersedes any "whoops," "uh-oh," or "oh crud" you commit along the journey. He *will* complete that good work in you.

Meanwhile, take this good advice from history's most famous prisoner-in-chains: While you're experiencing the suffocating constraints of this rough world, occupy your mind with pleasant thoughts. Let your joy be overflowing so that, when people see what you're facing and observe your supernatural happiness, they say, "I want whatever they've got."

Colossians

IN CENTURIES PRIOR to New Testament times, Colossae was a prominent trading city located at a major crossroad along the main highway near Ephesus. According to two Greek historians, Herodotus and Xenophon, in the sixth century BC, Colossae was visited by the Persian king Xerxes, and Cyrus the Great (the founder of the Persian Empire) travelled through (or past) it en route to Greece.[161] At this time, it was large and heavily populated. However, by the time of the New Testament, the roads had been repaved to head north to Pergamum, and Colossae had dwindled to a smaller town, just southeast of the grander cities Laodicea and Hierapolis. This is likely why our church-planter—who made it a habit to convert the citizenry of larger cities and let the movement trickle out to smaller towns—never personally visited there (as far as we know; see Colossians 1:4). After an earthquake fueled its final demolition in the late twelfth century AD, the city was buried beneath the soil. Today, it remains unexcavated as a giant mound, and we therefore have much less information about this location than we do of the cities addressed by the other Epistles. As such, we cannot state with certainty whether this city had a "resident deity" over any of the rest of the Greco-Roman pantheon, or what deviant behaviors the citizens were into.

What we can responsibly say is that the Colossians were profoundly syncretized, with a population given over to a cocktail of Judaism and Gnosticism alongside the pantheon, with a bizarre angel-worship cult. Paul's audience would have been a mishmash of religiously hybridized people, as opposed to "Jews" or "Gentiles." What remaining evidence we have of this location (next to internal, biblical evidence) recognizes that Colossians saw the archangel Michael as an archetypal figure greatly resembling such pagan gods as Zeus, and they worshipped him in part for an ancient spring of healing waters they believed he brought to the city. Needless to say, they were apparently confused about who was worthy of worship and who wasn't…

This short letter begins—after Paul's hello, thanksgiving, and prayer for the church in Colossae (1:1–14)—by establishing the authority and rule of Christ, who is, was, and always will be the visible Image of the otherwise invisible God; the preexistent Ruler over all creation, through whom creation was made, including all principalities and authorities of the earth; Head of the Church, His Body; the Beginning and the First of all things; the Reconciler of all things to God; and the One who brought peace to heaven and earth through the work of the cross (1:15–20).

Paul ensures that his readers know this applies to them as well. The Colossians were once far from God, incompatible with His nature, until the Reconciler made them blameless and holy in the sight of God. Their responsibility in this work is to believe in it, wholeheartedly and unwaveringly (1:21–23). Paul then reiterates that he is happy to suffer for the sake of the Gospel, which has now spread to this sweet little town. Once, this Gospel message was hidden, but now, it applies to all, and Christ lives *within* these precious people (1:24–27). This is the motive Paul holds onto while he continues to preach and teach the Gospel with the wisdom of God and Jesus, carrying truth, encouragement, and love to those who seek Christ. Christ *is* the Mysterious

Plan God had from the beginning. Paul has personally agonized over the Colossians and their neighboring church, Laodicea. He writes to them to spare them from those who would deceive them and marvels at their strong faith and righteous living (1:28–2:5).

For the rest of chapter 2, Paul focuses on the freedom and the new life that faith in Christ brings. They must never be misled "through philosophy and vain deceit, after the tradition of men, after the rudiments of the world" (2:6–8). Christ was God, in human form, and He remains above all the authority of the world. Jesus was even powerful enough to "circumcise" them in a spiritual way, cutting them off from the sin that dominated them prior. At baptism, the Colossians were "buried" with Christ, emerging into new life for their trust in Him. The ongoing record of charges against the Colossians was nailed to the cross on the day of His death, so they need not worry about whether they are following the Law, which was merely a foreshadowing of the real salvation plan (2:9–17). Then, he addresses the issue of angel-worship:

> Let no man beguile you of your reward in a voluntary humility and worshipping of angels, intruding into those things which he hath not seen, vainly puffed up by his fleshly mind, And not holding the Head, from which all the body by joints and bands having nourishment ministered, and knit together, increaseth with the increase of God. (2:18–19)

In order to more appropriately identify what "worshipping of angels" means from a literal standpoint, scholars have deeply engaged in discussion about the ancient cult of Michael (the archangel) and what conclusion the rest of the context of Colossians supports. There are varying theories, but the chief idea is one we should be aware of in our day. It may not have been that Paul was rebuking "worship" in the way we would view it now (bowing down to, praying to, offering up sacrifices for, etc.), but as "an obsession with": "[T]he people [Paul] is opposing spend so much time in speculations about angels...that they are in effect worshipping them instead of God."[162] Paul warns his readers not to be enticed by someone's promise of a reward for "voluntary humility." This false humility should, scholars say, be read as "a synonym for the fasting which in some disciplines was believed to induce heavenly visions."[163] We can't know for sure, but the evidence stacks in favor of the idea that the Colossians were so fascinated by angels that they would spend all their focus on them over God and hope for delightful visions from heaven as a result, and God, Himself, was being neglected in this scenario. Whether anyone ever bowed before Michael, or paid him homage, or did anything else our far-removed minds can conceive, Paul still here calls that a form of "worship." That should be a warning to folks today who seek visions, dreams, or spiritual experiences above a simple and right relationship with Jesus.

Paul goes on: Dying with and through Christ has released the Colossians from the grips of the world's evil spiritual power. Paul is therefore confused as to why they religiously follow unnecessary and outward signs of piousness. Such things certainly show devotion, but they don't touch the issues of the inner man (2:20–23). In their new life, they should not be thinking about earthly things, but of using their minds to share in the glory of the Risen One (3:1–4). They must put off such things as "fornication, uncleanness, inordinate affection, evil concupiscence [sexual urges and/or lust], and covetousness, which is idolatry" (3:5). Such things incur the wrath of God, and they represent the former life without Jesus' supernatural and all-powerful freedom that has been given to these fresh Christians. The new life cannot be defined by anger, rage, malice, blasphemy, dirty words, and dishonesty (3:6–9). A man who has been given such an opportunity to begin anew must "put on" the nature of the renewed man, accepting that this gift requires one to draw ever closer to the Creator and imitate Him in his human behavior. There are no longer such walls as "Greek nor Jew, circumcision nor uncircumcision,

Barbarian, Scythian [Siberian warriors], bond nor free: but Christ is all, and in all" (3:10–11). Therefore, God's holy people should be merciful, kind, humble, gentle, patient, and quick to forgive one another's mistakes and quirks, just as God was quick to forgive them. Doing all things in love unites a body of believers more than any other attribute. Their hearts should be at peace in Christ, and they should always be thankful (3:12–17).

In a tone similar to his Epistle to the Ephesians, Paul teaches: Wives must submit to husbands, and husbands must love their wives and treat them with tenderness and respect. Children are always to obey parents, and parents are expected now to encourage their children, never allowing themselves to provoke them to anger. Slaves must obey their masters even while they're not being supervised, and they should work hard, because their true Master is Christ; what they do on earth in goodness will be seen and rewarded by the Master. Earthly masters need to remember this teaching also, showing kindness, justness, and fairness to their slaves, because they, too, have a Master in heaven (3:18–4:1).

Paul briefly addresses prayer, reminding his readers they should always pray with a thankful heart and mind. He requests prayer for his own mission, too, that he will be successful in spreading the Good News, loudly and clearly, even while he is imprisoned (4:2–4). As a final thought, he once again reminds them to live as they are among unbelievers, setting a good behavioral example and making the most of every open door to share the Gospel (4:5–6).

He closes his letter with a note about Tychicus, who will give them a more thorough report regarding Paul, his ministry, and how he's holding up in prison. Onesimus, one of their own people, will also be coming for a visit soon (4:7–9). The Jewish believers in Paul's circle also say hello, and if they travel that way, they should be welcomed (4:10–11). Epaphras, another of their brothers, says hello. Paul goes out of his way to let the Colossians know Epaphras is praying for them in their spiritual growth constantly, as well as the believers in

Laodicea and Hierapolis (4:12–13). Interestingly, Paul here mentions Luke, the physician and author of the Gospel by the same name and the book of Acts, who here sends his warm greetings alongside Demas (4:14). The Colossians should say hello to the believers in Laodicea, and while they're at it, they should swap letters with that city, so both Laodicea and Colossians can receive the words Paul wrote to the other city (4:15–16). His departing sentiment is: "Remember my bonds. Grace be with you. Amen" (4:18).

1 and 2 Thessalonians

THESSALONICA WAS NAMED after Alexander the Great's half-sister, who was married to Macedonian King Cassander, one of Alexander's military generals. At the time Paul wrote his letters to this church, it featured the central seaport of Rome's Macedonian region. It equaled in importance to Corinth and Ephesus as far as shipping and commerce. In the middle of the city was the Egnatian Way, the chief road in Rome connecting it, through Byzantium, to the Orient; this vital route linked Thessalonica to huge urban districts by both land and water.

Regarding Paul's audience: Scholars, like those who compiled *The Bible Knowledge Commentary*, are quick to point out that this city "was one of the most important centers of population in Paul's day, occupying a strategic location both governmentally and militarily."[164] This source goes on to explain that the population was around two hundred thousand, primarily made up of "native Greeks," "many Romans," "Orientals and Jews," and many proselytes as a result of the influence of the synagogue there (Acts 17:4). It also points out that this vast number of proselytes is proof that the Greco-Roman religion left a spiritual void in the people, who were therefore eager to convert to the higher moral and spiritual standards of Judaism.[165] In other words, the existence of many proselytes assumes the existence of much debased immorality that drove the people to seek God in a way they were not finding satisfactory from classic worship of the pagan pantheon.

In 1939, remains were discovered showing that the Thessalonians were open to the worship of some of the Egyptian gods that had floated into the Greco-Roman culture in earlier times, most commonly Serapis: the god of resurrection, the underworld, and agriculture. Fragments of statues dedicated to the worship of this god were found alongside those of Isis, Aphrodite (goddess of sexual love and desire, as well as beauty), and Harpocrates (Hellenistic god of secrets, confidentiality, and silence).[166] In certain locations, such as the crypt beneath the temple, well-preserved artifacts also show veneration of the Thessalonians to Dionysus/Bacchus—the god of vineyard harvest, wine, theater, and religious ecstasy whose wild and frenzied "dance" was participated in by his worshippers who sought to free themselves of self-consciousness and behavioral inhibitions. Since a fire obliterated the remains of the old city in its western area in 1917, archeologists can't be certain, but some extant ruins may be those of the "Tree of Life" synagogue of the Jews, which may be the very synagogue Paul arrived at when he first preached to Thessalonica in Acts 17:2.[167]

Syncretism was thus just as much an issue for this large area when Paul ministered as it was for the Colossians or anywhere else. (Today, the location is known as Thessaloniki or Salonica, and its population is approximately three hundred thousand. It's no secret that, due to its location, historical roots in Christianity, and the survival of the population throughout the years, Thessalonica very likely played a paramount, continual role in the spread of Christianity beyond Paul's day.)

To the new believers who carried Paul's torch after his departure, opposition, theological problems, and immoral vices remain an ongoing problem. Thankfully, however, they appear to be working out their issues in a way that shows spiritual growth.

Thessalonians 1:1 identifies that the letter is being written from Paul, though Timothy and Silas also took a part in its message. As usual, a message of thanks is given for the faithfulness of these believers, for whom Paul and his associates are in constant prayer. They are reassured of God's love, as well as the power of the Spirit who verified God's presence among them when Paul ministered prior. The Thessalonians received Paul's message, despite the extreme suffering heaped upon them, and as a result, they had imitated the behaviors of both the apostle and the Lord, becoming beautiful witnesses to all other believers throughout Macedonia and Achaia. Everywhere Paul and his companions go in the region, they hear good reports regarding how the Thessalonians have rejected idolatry, embraced the faith, and are looking forward to the return of the Son (1:2–10). Paul recalls the dismal treatment from some Philippians before he came to Thessalonica, and the contrast of that to this sincere city's welcome of him. When Paul arrived here, his motives in ministering to them were pure—it was not for flattery, money, or praise that he preached the Good News to them, and they received it. The apostle and his fellow workers worked tirelessly outside of the church so as not to become a burden to them during his stay. When he had said all there was for him to say, the believers were affronted with great opposition from the locals, and the Thessalonians' response to this showed a favorable simulation of the believers in Judea who also faced persecution from the Jews (2:1–16).

Initially, when Paul was prevented from coming back for a visit as he'd hoped, he was concerned that he might receive bad news about this congregation as a result of their trials. But after Timothy arrived with a report to Paul, it was shown that the good fruit he had planted in them is actually blossoming beautifully. Now, Paul prays that the love they are already showing for the brethren continues to be magnified in the Lord, just as the apostle and his fellows also continue to love the Thessalonians even from a distance. Paul expresses a prayer that the Lord will continue to make their hearts strong and holy before Him when He comes back (chapter 3).

Paul now urges this growing congregation to continue living their lives in a way that pleases God. Holy living requires that they refrain from all sexual sins of the flesh. Refusal to heed this advice is not just an offense against other people, but against God, Himself. The Thessalonians are already loving toward their fellow man, as is obvious by the reports Paul receives, but they are encouraged to love even more, to work hard, and maintain their grand example of the good life for nonbelievers (4:1–12).

Now we get to the crux of the letter: It appears that some of the Thessalonians are living with little hope because of some believers who have passed away. What happens to followers of Christ when they pass into the next life? Where do they go, if a Christian's mortal existence expires before Christ comes again? Jesus hasn't yet returned, and though some of the Thessalonian believers held to the idea that they and their loved ones would be alive and well for that occasion, they were starting to find out that it wouldn't happen when they thought it would. Now, Paul must help them understand that hope is *not* lost for those who have gone on before them! It is by Jesus' own design that no one will know that hour.

Paul explains: When Jesus died, He was raised again, and when He comes back, He will bring with Him the believers who have gone on to the next life. In fact, when He returns, the living will not meet up with Jesus before the dead do. Jesus will descend from heaven with a shout, with the voice of the archangel, with the trumpet blasts of God, and the dead will rise *first*! Followers alive on the earth in that day will be caught up together to meet Jesus in the clouds. All of us, from that day forward, will be with Jesus forever! And this is a message Paul received directly "by the word of the Lord," Himself, and it is one that the Thessalonians can share with each other to find comfort in these times (4:13–18). As far as *when* these events will transpire, Paul cannot offer an answer. All he can say is that it will all happen unexpectedly; the Lord will return in a way that can be compared to a thief in the night whom nobody knew to anticipate. It will be as suddenly as a woman's labor pains begin, and there will be no escaping His will and plan. Meanwhile, believers like the Thessalonians are not left in the dark about these events, and they, along with other followers, will not be surprised when it happens, though they must remain alert and on guard at all times in waiting for this moment to arrive. Sleepers sleep in the night, and drunkards get drunk in the night. Those who live in the light must continue to walk in the armor of God with a clear mind. Christ died for all of us, so whether the Thessalonians are alive or dead upon Christ's return, we will be with Him forever: "Whether we wake or sleep, we should live together with him. Wherefore comfort yourselves together, and edify one another, even as also ye do" (5:1–11).

With this enormous reassurance offered, Paul exhorts the Thessalonians to honor those who are leaders in ministry. They work hard to offer spiritual guidance. Believers should lift up the weak, warn against laziness, and encourage those who fear. No true follower of Christ would pay back evil for evil; they will show goodness to all, keeping a healthy prayer life and staying joyful no matter what happens, because this is the will of God. The Holy Spirit should never be repressed. Prophecies should never be considered a laughing matter, though they need to be tested. And while these people shun the evil from their personal homes and the church, they must hold on to what is good (5:12–22).

In his parting words, Paul prays that the God of peace will continue to make them strong in holiness, asks for prayer for himself and his associates, tells the congregation to greet each other warmly, charges them to read this letter aloud in front of the assembly, and closes: "The grace of our Lord Jesus Christ be with you. Amen" (5:23–28).

A few weeks or months later, Paul wrote to them again…

The Thessalonians were sincere in their Christianity, and that is evident, both in world history as well as internal evidence from these Epistles. However, scholars note that the material covered in the first letter didn't quite have its intended effect. A few symptoms of disbelief in the words of Paul in his first correspondence were clinging on, and he felt the need to repeat himself in a couple areas for clarity. This second letter reads with a tone that says, "Yes, you heard me correctly before. I'm writing you again to confirm what I wrote a short time ago."

The second Epistle to the Thessalonians begins with greetings nearly identical to those he sent in the first: Paul, along with Silas and Timothy, are bearing these truths to the church in Thessalonica, those believers who belong to God and Christ—may God the Father and Jesus give them grace and peace (1:1–2).

The persecution continues, and Paul is aware of that. God, however, is also aware, and He will see to those who oppose the faithful. When Jesus comes back—and He *will* come back—there will be rest for the weary. He will come with the angels, "In flaming fire taking vengeance on them that know not God, and that obey not the gospel of our Lord Jesus Christ" (1:3–8). Eternal destruction and separation from God awaits those who turn their back on the One who laid His life down for them. So Paul and the others continue to pray for the Thessalonians, asking God to provide the equipment they need to live in a way that is worthy to the call He has placed on their lives—Jesus' Name will be honored by the way they live, that is certain, because of His grace (1:9–12).

To clarify some of the confusion, Paul says, the Thessalonians should not be afraid when they hear rumors that the Day of the Lord is at hand. Prophecies, visions, and revelations from others that state this as fact—or even claims that the apostle has written such a thing to someone else—should not be believed. There is coming a lawless deceiver of the end times (Antichrist) who will cause a great rebellion against God, defiling pure worship and exalting himself above even God. In fact, he will even sit in the very Temple of God, claiming to *be* God, and people will believe in him. This deceiver will rise up *before* the Day of the Lord (2:1–4). He will not arrive earlier than the appointed time. Don't these Thessalonians recall that Paul taught them this while he was with them? Now, the lawlessness the deceiving one embodies *is* already at work on the earth, but it won't be seen for what it is as long as there is a Restraining Force at work. Then the lawless one will rise, but Jesus will strike him down with His very breath, destroying him "with the brightness of His coming" (2:5–8). This evil one will be a serious foe, coming to the earth to do the work of Satan, carrying out signs and wonders through dark power. Every kind of deception imaginable will be used to trick those who refuse the Gospel: "And for this cause God shall send them strong delusion, that they should believe a lie: That they all might be damned who believed not the truth, but had pleasure in unrighteousness" (2:9–12).

As for the Thessalonians, Paul and his friends thank God for them! They are among the first to experience the transformative power of salvation! This very salvation comes from the Spirit of truth, who assists them now in their belief and their righteous living. So, they must remain strong in Paul's teaching while Jesus continues to increase their strength and in all the goodness they produce (2:13–17).

Paul now repeats his request for prayer, that his Gospel message will continue to be rapidly spread throughout the region and received as well as it was for them. He exhorts them toward righteous living for a final time (3:1–5). But before he concludes his letter, he has one last thing to say…

Some of the Thessalonians were using Paul's teachings of the Second Coming as an excuse, claiming that "it was useless to work for a living" when Christ was about to return.[168] To those, Paul recalls the example of hard work he and his fellow ministers set while they were with them, and scolds with a strong rebuke! In the Name of Jesus, Paul writes, such folks are commanded to redirect their focus on minding their own business and working hard for their own living, because "if any [able-bodied person] would not work, neither should he eat" (3:6–12). With that said, the rest of the believers should continue carrying out what is good. They are to take note of those who don't heed this letter, and separate from them if it comes to that. They are not to be treated with disdain or hatred, but like brothers and sisters in the interest of helping them see the error of their shameful ways (3:13–15).

Paul closes again: "Now the Lord of peace himself give you peace always by all means. The Lord be with you all. The salutation of Paul with mine own hand, which is the token in every epistle: so I write. The grace of our Lord Jesus Christ be with you all. Amen" (3:16–18).

There are a few sociopolitical movements today whose adherents have attitudes that resemble the attitude of the Thessalonians in this last portion of Paul's letter. Certain spokespeople of these movements use New Testament Scriptures about sharing and caring for the destitute out of context to support their agenda. In sharp contrast, from Paul's writing to this congregation involving a very serious charge given by the apostle in the Name of Jesus, we should remember that those who *can* work must work for their living and for their food.

1 and 2 Timothy

THESE TWO EPISTLES were written from Paul to Pastor Timothy, making up two of the three books known as the "Pastoral Epistles" (the third being Titus). By now, readers have heard of Timothy several times. It's clear by what we've covered thus far that he was as devoted to Paul as anyone in the entirety of his ministry, and because of this, he was awarded the title of "apostle" (1 Thessalonians 2:7). Paul even wrote that he looked upon Timothy as a son (1 Timothy 1:2). However, though the recipient of these letters is an individual, the content is Paul's response to what is happening in the individual's church—that is, in Ephesus.

Readers who skipped ahead, or those who don't recall the discussion of the city of Ephesus at the beginning of our study on the Epistle to the Ephesians, should turn back to that now. Whereas some Epistles can be understood fairly well without devoting much time to describing the city they were written for (such as the salvation message of Romans), certain verses in these letters (especially those referring to women) are flat-out impossible to fully grasp without taking a look at what was going on in Ephesus during Paul's day. Countless Christians, albeit likely sincere and well-meaning, simply don't understand that Paul is writing to one man in these letters. His advice is about the *church*, but his immediate audience is *Timothy*.

Some things never change, and personal correspondence is somewhat the same now as it was then. We have email, texting, phone conversations, and other methods of immediate communication Paul could have never dreamed of in his day, but it doesn't mean that someone peeping into an ongoing talk between two people are going to have the full story. Such is the case with 1 and 2 Timothy more than any other section of the Word. Paul and Timothy had travelled together, planted and discipled churches together, and chatted with each other for many hours, sharing thoughts and theological conclusions that we will never know about because very little of what they discussed made it into the canon of Scripture. Christians today are "peeking into personal mail" between these two men, and as unfathomably privileged as we are to have been given this access, we are also given the responsibility of trying to fill in the gaps where that communication is not entirely clear. The conversation is also one-sided: We can read what Paul said in *response* to Timothy's problems in Ephesus, but we cannot read what Timothy wrote to Paul in the first place. Certainly, we can draw from the context and conclude answers to these issues, but that involves a process of digging. It's not a "given" that we read a "response" about problems in a city two thousand years removed from our own time and suddenly have divine insight into the details that were written first from Timothy to Paul.

Therefore, we urge you: If you are not yet informed of what the Ephesians were going through—their resident gods, the shocking practices of orgiastic worship carried out by prostitutes and courtesans, or how these women were viewed as strong religious "voices" in the community—please revisit that explanation at the beginning of our reflection on Ephesians.

Paul begins his letter to his best friend and son-figure, Timothy, with warm greetings in the Name of Christ (1 Timothy 1:1–2).

Unlike most of his letters that take time to offer up thanksgiving and prayer, Paul jumps right into the issue at hand. (Again, this could be because it is a personal letter between two men and is not addressed to a congregation.)

When Paul left for Macedonia, he asked Timothy to remain in Ephesus and bring a stop to false teaching: "As I besought thee to abide still at Ephesus, when I went into Macedonia, that thou mightest charge some that they teach no other doctrine" (1:3). The first false teaching being addressed here is, once again, the idea that the Mosaic Law must be followed in the life of a believer in order to be saved. Paul immediately dispels that the Law should even be considered "vain jangling," or meaningless blithering by those whose motive is to sound well-versed and be known as prestigious teachers (1:4–7). He explains, as he has in other Epistles, that the Law is not completely without value, as it has been the very tool God has used to help people identify what sin is. But in that application, "the law is not made for a righteous man, but for the lawless and disobedient, for the ungodly and for sinners, for unholy and profane," and those who thrive in sins of all kinds (he lists several examples; 1:8–11). Paul can relate to such things, at least in one area... He used to profane the Name of Christ and persecute Jesus' followers, but the Lord of mercy has given him another chance to make it right, and now his life stands as an example of just how limitless God's forgiveness really is (1:12–17). Paul then encourages Timothy to remain faithful and keep a clean conscious. He notes two believers who have recently been formally punished in the Church for their blasphemy (1:18–20), and then notes the importance of prayer in ministry over not just other believers, but all people, including earthly rulers, that Christians may be able to live quiet, obedient lives that please Christ (2:1–7).

From here, Paul goes on to discuss specifics regarding how the worship is being conducted in Ephesus. Men are to worship and pray in a way that leaves their anger and doubt behind (2:8). Women, Paul says, are to learn quietly and submissively, and "adorn themselves in modest apparel, with shamefacedness and sobriety; not with broided [old English for "braided"] hair, or gold, or pearls, or costly array; But (which becometh women professing godliness) with good works" (2:9–10).

As a brief reminder: In learning proper principles of biblical interpretation, the first thing a student is taught is the difference between, and proper order of, exegesis and hermeneutics. Exegesis is the process of determining the "then and there" of a passage: what the author was originally saying to the audience of his day. Hermeneutics is the process of determining the "here and now" of a passage: what the Scripture is saying to us in our day. Exegesis *must* come first. If the order is reversed and the reader simply draws from the Word what we are supposed to do today based on antiquated advice without knowing what the author intended to say, it leads to a grievous error called "eisegesis," which is the opposite of exegesis—it "places our meaning *into* the Scripture," leading to an obliteration of context and, naturally, resulting in misinterpretation. The next step in this faulty approach is to determine behavioral "absolutes": rules we absolutely must live by "because the Bible says so," even though the Bible does not, in fact, say it. For example, a preacher might read this statement from Paul about braided hair and decide that any and all braids are sinful. (We are about to explain why this is not at all what he meant.) This hairstyle then becomes a behavioral absolute, or what some scholars call a "normative standard" within places of worship: A woman can pull her hair up in a ponytail, let it lay down around her shoulders, stuff it into a turban-like wrap, perm it, curl it, dye it, or shave it off...but a *braid* is a sin. (That's simply "what the Bible says" when the author's *original intent* is not considered.)

Have you noticed that's *not* happening in regard to hairstyles today? Almost everyone who just read that last paragraph probably had the same thought: *Well, that's just silly*. We agree, and that's the initial point we want to make: Nobody worries about braids in today's Church. Likewise, most teachers of the Word today aren't bothered by a woman who wears necklaces made of gold or pearls. Why not, though?

For these ministers, such rules are a "cultural issue" that can be chalked up to, "Well, times were different then."

But Paul's very next statement regarding women is *frequently* adhered to as an "absolute" for all times:

> Let the woman learn in silence with all subjection. But I suffer not a woman to teach, nor to usurp authority over the man, but to be in silence. For Adam was first formed, then Eve. And Adam was not deceived, but the woman being deceived was in the transgression. Notwithstanding she shall be saved in child-bearing, if they continue in faith and charity and holiness with sobriety. (2:11–15)

While the vast majority of churchgoers disregard or dismiss braids or "costly array," many prohibit women teaching because of what Paul said about usurping the authority of the man. Thus, we observe inconsistent application of Scripture, which has the first statement about hair and jewelry as being a "cultural issue" and the second statement regarding women teaching is a "normative standard" to be obeyed at all times and in all cultures. Technically, if a teacher interprets the prohibition of women teachers based on 1 Timothy 2:11–15 and holds his congregation accountable to that, then he is accountable to also prohibit all braids and "bling" as well. The only other option is to dig deeper to see if Paul was not intending to establish a normative standard on *both* of these topics, which is the opinion we hold. (It is also the conclusion of many academics for two thousand years, almost all of whom, ironically, are *male* scholars—which refutes the idea that what we are about to share is "feminist theology").

First, let's address what's going on with the hair. It should be quick if you've read the intro to Ephesians.

Recall the "cityscape" hair ornaments braided into the hair of the prostitute on the brothel advertisement etched on Marble Street as seen on the image included in the Ephesus discussion? That's what Paul is referring to here. A "braid," in and of itself, was not an offense. The literal, word-for-word translation from Paul's Greek in 1 Timothy 2:9–10 was not "braided hair, *or* gold" (*plegmasin e chrysio*), it was "braided hair *and* gold" (*plegmasin kai chrysio*),[169] meaning that women were not to weave gold (or other costly decorations) *into* her hair. Why? Because that was the "mark" of a prostitute (as the ad showed). Further, as discussed in our study of 1 Corinthians (11:6), a woman's hair and head were to be covered at all times within a worship setting. Only a prostitute (or a woman wanting to look suggestive) would leave her hair uncovered. The bottom line is Paul's comparison of modesty to the popular immodesty concepts of this culture. Though Paul never endorsed Hippocratic science, there was also a teaching by Hippocrates at this time that hair was congealed body fluids that grew from the scalp as a result of intercourse between a man and woman:

> To a modern reader, the concept of hair and fertility being related in any way is foreign. However, as is heavily documented throughout this era (and especially just following it, as seen in the works of Hippocrates of Kos, the Greek "Father of Medicine"), doctors taught that hair was created by intimate body fluids. From Troy W. Martin's work, the *Journal of Biblical Literature* (2004), we read that the ancients believed "hair is hollow and grows primarily from either male or female reproductive fluid...flowing into it and congealing (Hippocrates, *Nat puer* 20). Since hollow body parts create a vacuum and attract fluid, hair attracts [the fluid shared by a male].... Hair grows most prolifically from the head because the brain is the place where the [fluid] is (78) produced or at least stored (Hippocrates, *Genit.* I)."[170] Of course this "science" seems absurd today, and it is, in light of what we know about hair now, but in the inter-

est of remaining exegetically informed, we must understand the world that Paul was immersed in. Paul did not sanction these Hippocratic teachings, but he was responding to a social and cultural issue regarding decency. The world around him believed this medical teaching, and as a result, a woman with an uncovered head was in a sense making the statement in that culture and time that it didn't matter to her if she wandered about displaying her intimacy. Whether Paul and his fellow early Christians accepted Hippocratic leanings is irrelevant [and he certainly never said that he did!]. For a woman to go into a place of worship and pray or prophesy with her head uncovered was to blatantly associate herself with the behaviors of temple prostitutes and common pagan practices.[171]

As to how this would apply to children (since they have hair before they have carried out any act of intimacy), it's a complicated explanation involving much "science" of the ancient world that dances on the edge of transforming this book into one that would not be family friendly. Suffice it to say that the children "inherit" hair through their mother and father, according to this medicinal theory. As for Paul, his interest was not to prove or disprove medicine or science, but to respond to a cultural indecency: a woman attending a Christian assembly dressed or made up as one who was...well, "for hire" in the line of work many of these women found easy and lucrative.

A longer address of the issue of Paul "suffering not the women to usurp the authority of a man" from 1 Timothy 2:11–15 can be found in Howell's *Handmaidens Conspiracy*, but we will include a quick excerpt here:

The words "I suffer not" here are from the Greek *ouk* ("not") and *epitrepo* ("do I permit"). The verb *epitrepo*, the exact grammatical variant of the word as Paul wrote it in this sentence, is first person, singular; it is being used in the *present* tense. So, a more accurate rendering into English would be, "I am not currently permitting," as opposed to the inaccurate, "I will never permit." After a serious dig into the uses of this word in the Septuagint (the Greek Old Testament; Genesis 39:6; Esther 9:14; Job 32:14; also: Wisdom of Solomon 19:2; 1 Maccabees 15:6; 4 Maccabees 4.17–18), Professor John Toews notes that the word is used to address isolated, *present-tense* circumstances (i.e., affairs occurring at the time it was written), not universal situations throughout all time.[172]

But the really tough meat to chew in this verse is the relationship between "teach" (*didaskein*) and "to usurp authority" (*authentein*). The word "teach" here has been isolated by some scholars as its own "absolute" regulation, but the majority of available research points to the conclusion that *authentein* is a copulative word to *didaskein*. Put more simply, the *kind* of teaching prohibited here is defined by whatever *authentein* means within this context, because *authentein* serves to qualify *didaskein*. Logical support for this, based purely on common sense within the overall "internal consistency" picture, is that: a) Paul commissioned women to teach; b) Jesus Christ commissioned women to teach (next two chapters [that is, the next two chapters in *Handmaidens Conspiracy*; the thread shows His approval of the female preacher, revivalist, and evangelist of Sychar while He watched her for "two days" in John 4 convert the city and even responded favorably to the harvest she sent to Him, as well as many other examples]); c) the Holy Spirit commissioned women to teach [on the Day of Pentecost], so therefore; d) if teaching is anywhere prohibited within Scripture, it *must* be qualified (limited) to a certain *kind* of teaching, and therefore it is a "relative" and not an "absolute." Thus, the qualifier here, *authentein*, is a key element to our study, as it explains what kind of teaching the prohibition addresses. But before we visit the exasperating complications raised around the translation of *authentein*, it's crucial to point out that Paul normally used a completely different word with a much more common understanding in the Hellenistic period. [Howell explains in this section that anytime Paul discussed "authority," he used a different word in Greek, *exousia*, which means "to control." We have clipped it out for space, but she then goes on to say:]

The first peculiarity is that *authentein* does not occur anywhere else in the Bible—Old or New Testament. Because we cannot rely on Paul's use of this word elsewhere for an internal comparison of how *he* would have used it in a sentence, the only places we can look are in extrabiblical documents in ancient Greek. Understand that some words—even in English—can have more than one common meaning, even when the word is spelled the same in all variables. This is called a homonym. For instance: "Row" as a verb is the action that propels a boat forward, but as a noun, it refers to a line of regularly-spaced objects. *Authentein*, as it appears in ancient Greek documents, is similar. It means different things to different writers as it is used in a sentence....

From the list provided by Henry George Liddell and Robert Scott in the *Greek-English Lexicon*, we retrieve the following instances of *authentein* in its noun form, *authentes*: "murderer" (Herodotus 1.117; Euripides, *Rhesus* 873; Thucydides 3.58; Euripides, *Hercules Furens* 1359; Apollonius Rhodius, *Argonautica* 2.754); "suicide" (Antipho 3.3.4; Dio Cassius 37.13); "one from a murderer's family" (Euripides, *Andromache* 172.2); "perpetrator," "author" (Polybius 22.14.2; Diodorus Siculus 16.61); generally "doer" (Alexander Rhetor 2S); "master" (Euripides, *The Suppliants* 442; *Leidon Magical Papyrus W* 6.46); "condemned" (Phyrnichus Arabius 96.3); "murder by one in the same family" (Aeschylus, *Eumenides* 212; *Agamemnon* 1572).[173]

Thesaurus Linguae Graeca, an online computer database, uncovered only 306 uses of *authentein* between 200 BC and AD 200 (four hundred years total, at the center of which was

Christ). Although 306 sounds like a very small number, in light
of how often it is discovered in ancient texts, this was actually a
thrilling find. Among the uses listed, these were the most common: "doer of a massacre," "author of crimes," "perpetrators of
sacrilege," "supporter of violent actions," "murderer of oneself,"
"sole power," "perpetrator of slaughter," "murderer," "slayer,"
"slayer of oneself," "authority," "perpetrator of evil," and "one
who murders by his own hand."[174]

New Testament scholar Scott Bartchy lends the following
insight: "The verb *authentein* clearly bears the nuance of using
such absolute power in a destructive manner, describing the activity of a person who acts for his or her own advantage apart from
any consideration of the needs or interests of anyone else."...[175]

[One possible intent behind *authentein* is that a woman was
not] "to represent herself as originator of man"....[176] Cultural
support for this interpretation would be: a) we know that one
meaning of the word *authentein* is "author" (i.e., "originator");
and b) native religions of Anatolia (surrounding Ephesus) taught
that Artemis/Diana was the divine source through whom all life
began. Who would teach such a thing? False teachers. What
does 1 Timothy centrally condemn? False teachers. Surrounding text support would be that the very next verses in the epistle
reestablish the creation order, essentially putting such a woman
teacher in her place.

However... 1) Ephesus, as well as the surrounding regions,
was simply *crawling* with people who practiced erotic pagan
religions that placed women equal to, and often above, men
in aggressive and sexual positions of authority; 2) historical
evidence shows instances in Ephesus and nearby regions that
women had collectively usurped the authority of men in religious settings (especially those related to the temple of Artemis/
Diana in Ephesus); 3) the words *authentein* and its noun form
authentes are repeatedly associated with some form of extremely

aggressive behavior; and perhaps most importantly, 4) there exists a substantial argument based on historical evidence that *authentein* and *authentes* were *not employed to mean* "having power or authority" until *"the second century after Christ"*!... [This is crucial! It means that the standard English KJV translation most folks draw the "women prohibition" from in 1 Timothy used a definition of Paul's word that did not even exist at the time Paul wrote this letter!]

At the time 1 Timothy was written, the common language in the Hellenistic era was Koine Greek. Insight for what the verb *authentein* might have become by this time can be credited to Dr. Cynthia Long Westfall, exegesis professor at the McMaster Divinity College: "In the Greek corpus, the verb *authenteo* refers to a range of actions that are not restricted to murder or violence. However, the people who are targets of these actions are harmed, forced against their will (compelled), or at least their self-interest is being overridden, because the actions involve an imposition of the subject's will, ranging from dishonour to lethal force."[177]

The truth is, because the Greek word the KJV translators here chose as "usurp authority over" is so rare and so homonymous (meaning many things), nobody today can be absolutely certain what Paul meant by its use. However—and this is important—it refers to something aggressive. As Howell illustrated in this excerpt (and amidst a vast array of other evidence her book covers), a far more responsible translation from a responsible, exegetic point of view allows that Paul is here silencing the kind of woman who would march in and aggressively take over the teaching of a man with her false teaching that perpetuates Artemis/Diana theology.

Suddenly, with this in mind, Paul's next note to Pastor Timothy clicks into place: "For Adam was first formed, then Eve. And Adam was not deceived, but the woman being deceived was in the transgression. Notwithstanding she shall be saved in childbearing" (1 Timothy 2:13–15a).

According to the Artemis/Diana cult, Eve was formed first, *then Adam*, and childbearing was below the expectations of the liberated woman under Artemis, who created all life without the help of a man. Paul was not against having women leaders in the Church, as he identified several and commended them (as we have shown prior). He was correcting the erroneous theology of a powerful local cult. (Howell, in *Handmaidens*, also explains why Paul here says it was the "woman [who] was deceived in the transgression" when he elsewhere attributed the Fall of mankind to Adam, not Eve [Romans 5:14; 1 Corinthians 15:21–22]. This, too, is explained in *Handmaidens*. She also shows grammatical evidence from Greek that Paul is only silencing one trouble-woman in Timothy's congregation, not "all women of all times," but we think we have covered enough of this subject for our purposes here. But just to bring this issue around to where we started: The reader is encouraged to remember that, without Timothy's correspondence, we never had access to read the report of this one woman and the incorrect theologies she was aggressively insisting on teaching. If we did, the context would be easier to grasp. Paul's response requires digging into, lest women continue to live under unnecessary prohibitions. When the Holy Spirit calls these sweet souls into action today—as He did on the Day of Pentecost when He transformed women from the Upper Room into preachers and sent them into the very streets of Jerusalem to teach the Gospel— we need to support that movement of God. We should not stand in opposition to something the Lord is doing because "today's culture" has a mainstream [but incomplete] interpretation of what they are allowed to do in His Name.)

With that out of the way, Paul goes on to discuss what the leaders of the church in Ephesus should be: above reproach; faithful to their spouses; monogamous; self-controlled; wise; of good reputation;

hospitable; good at teaching; sober; nonviolent; gentle; not argumen-
tative; not a lover of money; excellent at familial management; good
parents; not new to Christianity; and of clear conscience (3:1–13).
While Paul is not there to help in person, this is how the Church
must be conducted. It is the household of God, and therefore it is a
sacred place that must be respected as the "pillar and ground of the
truth." Godliness among members is based on a mystery: "God was
manifest in the flesh, justified in the Spirit, seen of angels, preached
unto the Gentiles, believed on in the world, [and] received up into
glory" (3:14–16).

The Holy Spirit, Paul writes, expresses with all clarity that, in the
last days, "some shall depart from the faith, giving heed to seducing
spirits, and doctrines of devils" (4:1). These false teachers speak from
hypocrisy and a dead conscience. They will make ridiculous claims,
such as the idea that it is wrong to take a wife or husband, or it is a sin
to eat particular foods, but God created these things to be enjoyed by
those who know the truth and give thanks for His blessings (4:2–5).
Timothy will be a worthy servant of Christ if he carries the truth of
these things to the congregation of Ephesus. His time on this earth is
precious, and he should never waste that time arguing over fables and
wives' tales. The Christian's hope is in the Savior, who is the Living
God over all. Timothy has the ability to teach these things, and he
mustn't doubt this ability that God gave him, even when some might
comment on his young age. He is to stay strong, and keep teaching
what is right. When the elders of the Church laid hands on Timothy
and prayed for him, he was given a very special gift in ministry, and
he cannot neglect that no matter what (4:6–16).

Paul goes on to instruct Timothy in a few specific areas: Elderly
men and women must be shown as much respect as one's own fathers
and mothers; younger men and women are to be treated as brothers
and sisters; widows who have nobody to care for them—especially
those over the age of sixty who have done well in raising good people
and dedicating their lives to matters of integrity—are to be cared for

by the Church, and if they have children or grandchildren, it is their responsibility to repay those who have invested in them first, as such an act pleases God. These instructions are to be passed on to the congregation in Ephesus, for those who cannot even care for their own families are worse than unbelievers (5:1–10)! Younger widows need not be placed on the list of those the Church sponsors, because they are of a remarrying age. Once they remarry, if all their financial needs are met by the Body, they will become idle busybodies, going from house to house with gossip and juicy tales. For this reason, younger women should remarry, have children, and guide the household. This will remove the enemy's opportunity to speak against them. (This, too, should not be taken as an absolute regulation. It was advice given from Paul to a specific congregation in the ancient world that he had personal, privileged information about. If a young woman today is single and serving the Lord, these verses should not be interpreted to mean she must hurry to the altar to start a family.) Some of the young women of Ephesus already have, Paul fears, "turned aside after Satan" (5:11–15). (With everything we now know about the ladies in this city, this otherwise seemingly harsh assertion from Paul now makes a lot more sense!) If a female believer has widow relatives, she must help take care of them also. In this manner, the Body will be freed to care all the more for the widows who are truly alone (5:16).

When elders work hard for the church, they are entitled to both respect as well as payment. If an accusation arises against an elder, two or three witnesses to his offense must be present, or else the accusation should be disregarded. But to those who have actually committed a provable offense, they should be reprimanded in a way that sets a strong warning in place for the rest of the congregants. Paul charges Timothy "before God, and the Lord Jesus Christ, and the elect angels, that [he] observe these things without preferring one [person] before another, doing nothing by partiality" and showing no favoritism for any one person over another (5:17–21). The appointment of other church leaders is not a decision that should be made in a hurry. And

Timothy should remain pure at all times, free from the sin around him, keeping himself as healthy as possible for the work he's been called to do (it is here that Paul mentions drinking wine for Timothy's chronic illness—a verse we addressed in our earlier section, "Wedding at Cana"). He should always remember that some sins are obvious and lead to observable judgment, but some sins remain undetected, though these will eventually be brought to light (5:22–25).

After addressing slaves and masters in a way similar to the way he addressed them in his previous letters (6:1–2), Paul proceeds for several verses to compare the false teachers in Ephesus with the spiritual riches that come from correct teaching. He warns that there are some who will likely come against Timothy's proper instructions, but this apostolic training is what leads to a godly life. People who show up wanting to contradict and argue with Timothy are those who love wasting time arguing semantics and words, an unhealthy habit that brings "envy, strife, railings, evil surmisings, [and] Perverse disputings of men of corrupt minds, [who are] destitute of the truth" (6:3–5). Men like this are motivated, at least in part, by easy money, but true wealth comes from spiritual godliness. We come into the world without anything, and we take nothing with us when we leave, so we should be content with merely whatever food or clothing is needed to maintain this life. The love and pursuit of money and earthly gain is the root of all sorts of evils! Unfortunately, some folks have so given into this lust for gold that they have strayed from true faith and heaped upon themselves nothing but sorrow (6:6–10).

Timothy, in contrast, is a man of God, and as such, he should flee from these things. As he has been faithful to do so far, he is to continue to run toward all righteousness, faith, love, perseverance, and gentleness. Nobody can find fault in such a man. At the right time, Christ *will* return in the clouds as King of kings and Lord of lords, so the time is now for Timothy to continue teaching those who rely on their money that this endeavor leads to unreliable ends. God gives us all we need, and people with money should be generous to share with those who have none, "Laying up in store for themselves a good foundation against the time to come, that they may lay hold on eternal life" (6:11–19).

Paul wraps up his advice and warmly concludes:

O Timothy, keep that which is committed to thy trust, avoiding profane and vain babblings, and oppositions of science falsely so called: Which some professing have erred concerning the faith. Grace be with thee. Amen. (6:20–21)

Scholars are not in unanimous agreement about exactly how much time passed between the writing of these two Epistles, but most believe the second followed the first within a few years of the first letter. Somewhat like 1 and 2 Thessalonians, much content in 2 Timothy repeats advice shared in the earlier Epistle. Nobody would question whether Timothy was a strong young man who served God faithfully, teaching the doctrines of Christ properly even in the midst of his ongoing health issues. However, even the greatest leaders in history have need to be reassured. It is apparent that what was taking place in Ephesus when Paul wrote to his son figure the first time was a rampant enough problem that Timothy desperately required Paul to remind him he was on the right track. Paul, never once being above this kind of human need, writes to his "son" once again, warmly maintaining what he had stated before, with the addition of a few details.

Paul's opening words in his second letter are much like those of 1 Timothy, identifying Timothy as his son in the faith with wishes of God's grace, mercy, and peace upon the young pastor (2 Timothy 1:1–2). Paul thanks God for Timothy once again and encourages him to be faithful while Paul prays for him night and day, always longing to see him again. Paul takes the time to confirm that Christ is worth his chains and all suffering, including those who have long since abandoned him in the work, and encourages Timothy to keep this in mind as he ministers (1:3–18).

In chapter 2, Paul states that many reliable witnesses have confirmed the teachings of Paul and Timothy, so he should stay the course and remain devoted to what he knows to be truth. He should consider his position alongside Paul as a soldier for Christ. Paul might be chained, but the Gospel never will be, and what Timothy is doing is right, so he should draw encouragement from this and keep steady, continuing to silence arguments between the brethren (2:1–14).

Timothy is here instructed to work hard, rightly dividing the Word of truth, so he will be blameless while others who have left the faith (Paul mentions Hymenaeus and Philetus) shame themselves by teaching incorrect doctrines, such as the idea that the resurrection of the dead has already occurred. The Lord always has, always does, and always will know exactly who His authentic followers are. If Timothy keeps himself pure and righteous, he will be like the special cutlery that is only removed from the cabinets of the wealthy for special occasions: a superior utensil ordained for honorable use. Again, Paul states, all petty disputes over words should be avoided. Timothy can certainly offer a gentle response for what he believes, but he is not to engage in squabbling with others. God, Himself, has the power to help them see the light, and this light will be shown brighter through Timothy if he avoids giving in to quarreling (2:15–26).

Sadly, Paul shares, the last days will only get more difficult. Wickedness will continue to thrive while people become increasingly lovers of money, boasting in themselves, acting proudly, sneering at God, and considering nothing on the earth sacred while they feed their own ingratitude. Children will grow more and more in disobedience every day, forsaking the act of forgiveness and love, slandering others, embracing their own lack of self-control and justifying it through hatred and cruelty, acting recklessly, betraying their friends and family, and doing anything that pleases them in the moment. These people will act religious while rejecting the very Power that leads to godliness. (Wow... Does this sound like our times to you readers as well?) Their faith is counterfeit, and one day, they will be exposed

(3:1–9). But Timothy, as Paul charges, cannot ever allow himself to become like these. Paul has suffered much, and so has Timothy, but that suffering will only continue; Paul cannot lie about that. All who give their lives to the purposes of Christ will face these trying times, but all Scripture (such as that Timothy grew up under) is inspired by God and is useful for training in righteousness; God uses His Word to instruct, prepare, and equip His people for good works. Someday, all men and women will stand before Christ and face judgment, so it is crucial that Timothy continues to run the race well, fight the good fight, and persevere (3:10–4:2).

A time is coming soon when people will no longer tolerate correct, wholesome teaching. They will follow their own lusts and desires, specifically seeking out teachers who will twist Scripture and proof-text the Word of God, tweaking its context to say whatever their itching ears want to hear to justify their wrongdoing. (Folks, we're there…) Rejecting truth, they will strive after myths! Timothy must prepare for this and keep his head clear while he carries the undefiled Gospel message. As for Paul, his life has already been nothing more than a constant pouring out for the Lord's purposes, and now his death is near. But he doesn't fear this end. It's merely when he will inherit all he has waited for: the crown of glory on the other side! And this reward is not only for Paul, but for all who have joined in this work and who look forward to the next appearance of Jesus (4:3–8).

Paul requests a visit from Timothy soon, noting a few who have gone on to other things, and asks Timothy to bring with him Paul's coat and papers. (Some believe this verse to be Paul's instruction for Timothy to bring him the shroud of Turin. Our book *Afterlife* explains how and why this is not a reliable interpretation based on the difference between the Greek words *phainoles* ["cloak"] and *sindon* [linen cloth, like the Shroud].) Paul says hello to a couple of believers in Timothy's midst, asks if Timothy can plan his visit for an arrival before winter, and sends greetings from the brothers and sisters he is still in contact with (4:9–21). His parting words are: "The Lord Jesus Christ be with thy spirit. Grace be with you. Amen" (4:22).

In these Epistles, we are given insight not only into the end of Paul's life, but into the end of his ministry. His writing is of one who is drawing closer to weariness. He remains ever strong, dutifully standing for what is right to his last day…but, as he wrote to Timothy, he is nearing his end. It stands to reason, then, that we would only have one more letter in the canon from this spiritual powerhouse—a father in the faith for us all.

Titus

Have you ever heard someone call someone else a "Cretan" (pronounced kret-n or kreet-n)? Even in movies or television? It occasionally shows up in scripts wherein one character is so loathsomely dishonest or has such a lack of integrity that another character struggles to find an insult powerful enough to appropriately capture the first character's corrupt nature. A contemptable cheater in Paul's day would have been called this very name, and it would have been just about as insulting as being called a "Corinthian."

Because Crete is an area of the world in Paul's day that appears to be more highly overlooked than other major cities on the mainland, we will spend a little more time on the subject of this island. Paul's letter to Titus is tiny (only three chapters), and therefore has a tendency to "get buried" under the teachings (or readings) of the longer letters. Because this Epistle isn't necessarily known as one that makes any groundbreaking statements that aren't present in Paul's other letters, Christians tend to skim through it as a believer's rite of passage, but when we really *know* who the Cretans are, Paul's words come to life on the page. His advice goes from being rudimentary and common to revolutionary and trailblazing at a time when the most hated and untrustworthy folks of the ancient world spring to life with newfound, Gospel truth being uttered from their lips. Their lives were changed almost overnight by the power of the Word...and because Paul's instructions to his young missionary associate is short, the transformation the Gospel made on this territory is far more glorious when we can "see" the people he wrote, and not just hear about them in three chapters of an antique text.

The people from the island of Crete weren't known for their honor. This concept is reflected in a circular logic problem, today called the "Epimenides Paradox" or "the liar's paradox." Epimenides was, himself, a seer from Cretan who famously stated, "Cretans are always liars, evil beasts, slow bellies [meaning "lazy gluttons"]" (a quote Paul reiterated in this very Pastoral Epistle to Titus; see verse 1:12). So the logic of the literal interpretation of Paul's quote in Titus leads to the following apparent contradiction, which is both confusing and kinda fun to ponder over:

1. If all Cretans are liars, and Epimenides is a Cretan, then Epimenides is also a liar.
2. Therefore, if anything he says is a lie, then his statement that all Cretans are liars is, in itself, false.
3. And if it is false, then it means all Cretans are honest.
4. But if all Cretans are honest, then Epimenides is honest as well.
5. So, finally, if Epimenides is honest, then his claim about the dishonest Cretans is true...they are liars.

...And we're back, full-circle, at the beginning of the problem that loops indefinitely. Throughout the years, philosophers, psychologists, and parents have sometimes used this loop to explain how dishonesty contributes to mass confusion and, before long, nothing can be certain when truth is not applied in the first place, because one lie leads to another "lie," even when that lie is the truth, and so on and so forth. Wikipedia is not—in any way, shape, or form—a reliable source for research. Anyone in the world is allowed to tweak and edit what is on that online encyclopedia, so we don't use it to support any of the claims we make in our books. However, once in a while, Wikipedia is helpful in articulating common facts the general public may otherwise find hard to grasp. Such is the case for "the liar's paradox." The Wikipedia page on this states:

> In philosophy and logic, the classical **liar paradox**…is the statement of a liar that they are lying: for instance, declaring that "I am lying." If the liar is indeed lying, then the liar is telling the truth, which means the liar just lied.… [A] classical binary truth value leads to a contradiction.[179]

Oh my gosh…what!?

Yeah… That's where dishonesty leads. You don't have to follow every moment of these complicated explanations of the liar's paradox to grasp the general idea that only one deceitful moment causes a mountain of others.

Since so much of Crete's history has to do with a labyrinth (as we will discuss shortly), it seems fitting to use a film by the same name to further illuminate this paradox.

In the 1986 Jim Henson movie *The Labyrinth*, starring David Bowie as the "Goblin King" villain "Jareth," the "liar's paradox" makes a classic (and popularly referenced) appearance. Sarah, played by actress Jennifer Connelly, must work her way through a puzzling labyrinth to save her baby brother in less than thirteen hours, or the baby will become the property of King Jareth. At one point, Sarah reaches a dead-end in the maze. She starts to turn around and head back when a mysterious wall appears behind her, entrapping her. When she starts to grumble, two doors appear on the wall that was formerly the dead-end. Over the doors are two-headed Jim Henson puppets (one head is at the top of each character, and one head is at the bottom of each, the main bodies hidden behind a large shield, resembling playing cards). This scene has become a landmark of logic in our modern day that appears all over contemporary media as one of the hardest riddles to solve: a beginner's mark of accomplishment for the pilgrim who seeks to master truth, logic, and philosophy. (We authors admit that we have watched this clip for decades and still can't follow it without slowing it way down and contemplating every word of the exchange…and even then, we still don't really get it. The reason for including it here is *not* to challenge readers to solve it, but to demonstrate the kind of backwards reasoning and judgment a person must use when confronted with the paradox.) The conversation goes:

Sarah: What am I supposed to do?

Left door, bottom head: Well, the only way out of here is to try one of these doors.

Right door, bottom head: One of them leads to the castle at the center of the labyrinth, and the other one leads to—bababa bum-mmm—certain death!

All puppet heads: Oooooo… [a moan insinuating fatality if she chooses the wrong door]

Sarah: Which one is which?… [a discussion explains that only the top heads can answer this question, but there a "liar's paradox" is embedded in this part of the maze]

Left door, top head: You can only ask *one* of us.

Right door, top head: Mm-hm. It's in the rules [points to bizarre writing on the shield]. And I should warn you that one of us always tells the truth, and one of us always lies. That's a rule, too. *He* [referring to the left top head] always lies.

Left top head: I do not! I tell the truth!

Right top head: Oh, what a lie!

Sarah, to the left top head: Alright, answer yes or no… Would *he* [pointing to the right top head] tell me that this [left] door leads to the castle?

Left door, top head: [consults the bottom heads for a moment, and then responds:] Yes.

Sarah: Then [the right door] leads to the castle, and [the left door] leads to certain death.

All puppet heads: Oooooo… [a moan insinuating they're impressed with her quick answer to the riddle]

Left top head: How do you know? *He* could be telling the truth!

Sarah: But then *you* wouldn't be. So if *you* told me that he would say 'yes,' I know the answer is 'no.'

Left top head: But *I* could be telling the truth!

Sarah: But then *he* would be lying. So if you told me that he said yes, I know the answer would still be 'no.'

Left top head, to right top head: Wait a minute! Is that right?

Right top head, to left top head: I don't know! I've never understood it! [All puppet heads laugh.]

Sarah: No, it's right! I figured it out![180]

If you're one of the few who can follow this and understand the scene, you are of a rare breed of intellect, for certain. If you can't, you're no different than many others, including these authors. This clip is widely available online, both with and without voiceovers pausing and stopping the clip to explain that Sarah's applied logic to the "liar's paradox" is actually correct. In order to find the truth in a pattern of certain lies, one must apply negative, backwards questioning. Despite the fact that Sarah solves the riddle successfully, however, viewers are quick to point out that, right after she enters the door on the right, she falls into the "hall of helping hands"—hands that form faces, reaching out and catching her midway down. She's given the choice to go back up where she was or head downward to the unknown. She chooses down, since she's headed that way anyway, and falls into an oubliette (a pit with no escape). So, even though she was right, the trap set her up to be wrong either way. (Spoiler alert: In case you're wondering, Sarah does make it out of the oubliette with help from another Jim Henson character and lives on to challenge, and then win, Jareth's labyrinth, returning her baby brother to his crib at home in the end.)

Our purpose for sharing this scene is this: The common element intrinsically embedded in the liar's paradox is proven visually through this movie… When lies are involved, even the truth can't be trusted when it is based on deception and riddles in the beginning. Thus, this scene from one of our society's most beloved '80s classics is comparable to the kind of mind games one had to play when communicating with a person from the island of Crete. Epimenides' use of language in his initial accusation and Paul's quote of this original statement are hyperbolic: Obviously neither of them was stating that every single person on the island was a liar, but that so many of them were, this statement could apply as a general rule for those who lived on the island. Communicating with a Cretan was always a puzzle, and nobody could ever be certain that what was said was true. Epimenides wasn't the only one to make this assertion, either. A common euphemism throughout Greece was the word "cretize": a verb meaning "to lie." Publius Ovidius Naso (known more simply as "Ovid") was a poet from the time of Augustus who referred to the island as *mendax Creta* ("lying Crete"). There is no doubt that the ancients expected every word a Cretan said to be a fib, and if there was a chance it wasn't, the only way to know for sure was to take a chance and hope it worked out, or to get involved in a game of "analysis paralysis" that could never be counted on anyway. To make matters far, *far* worse, by 67 BC (the year Crete transferred to Roman occupation), it had become a supreme beehive for piracy, adding thievery and violence to incoming ships on top of the problem of dishonesty.

What a morality train wreck…

As for "resident gods," Crete was highly devoted to the gods Zeus and Asklepios (god of medicine who accepted body parts at the altar as sacrifices that accompanied petitions for healing), as well as "the center of the Minoan maritime empire named after the legendary King Minos."[181] Though some of this influence had waned by the

New Testament era, Cretan culture was built upon the concepts and creeds of King Minos, the "king of Crete," son of Zeus and Europa. The goat-man Aegeus, after whom the Aegean Sea was named, was the father of Theseus, the so-called founder of Athens. Aegeus was also associated with King Minos, and their history is quite revolting and sordid.

Truncating what the Greeks believed about this area leads to an oversimplification of mythology, but to give readers the gist: King Minos prayed to the god of the sea, Poseidon, to grant him a beautiful bull for sacrifice to the sea god. Poseidon sent a beautiful, snow-white bull to King Minos for this sacrificial purpose. (In other versions, Minos bred this bull from his own livestock.) This was the Cretan Bull (or "Marathonian Bull") of the island's proud history. Minos found the bull to be so perfect that he couldn't bring himself to kill it, so he kept it and offered a substandard bull to the god instead. Poseidon, angered by the king's inferior sacrifice, caused Pasiphae—the queen of Crete, wife of King Minos, and goddess of witchcraft and sorcery—to fall in love with the Cretan Bull. Queen Pasiphae found a (rather disgusting) way of tricking the bull to mate with her. (Don't look this up around a child, please!) The offspring of this perverse union was the well-known half-man, half-bull monster identified in Greek mythology as the "Minotaur." Because this beast was neither wholly human nor wholly animal, he could not be fed in predictable ways, and eventually became the devourer of humankind. In his desperate need to contain this monster, King Minos followed the advice from the oracle at Delphi and constructed a great labyrinth with the Minotaur placed at its center. Every nine years, the Minotaur would need to be sent another shipment of "food"—fourteen children (seven boys and seven girls) to satiate his appetite and keep him contained.

Sometime later in the hard-to-pin-down chronology of events, the prince of Crete, Androgeus, competed against the goat-man Aegeus in the "Panathenaic Games" (an Athenian athletic festival) and won in every event. Aegeus, angered by his own defeat, challenged Androgeus to duel against the Cretan Bull (father of the Minotaur). Androgeus accepted the challenge against the now-adult Cretan Bull, who over-powered and killed Androgeus in the fight. King Minos was enraged over the death of his son by his once-beloved, snow-white bull and led an attack against Athens (the territory Aegeus and his son ruled). As a peace treaty, King Minos promised to pull back the attack if Athens would provide fourteen children from their own people to be fed to the Minotaur, to spare the youth of Crete. (This arrangement went on for many years, explaining why the Minotaur, King Minos, and Aegeus are all associated with child sacrifice in mythology. It also clari-fies why, circa 430 BC, the silver coin of Crete was minted to show a labyrinth on one side.) The labyrinth, archeologists (from as far back as the Bronze Age) say, may have actually been a real place, as the ruins of Knossos (located in Crete) show an extravagant architecture of weaving walls featuring antique paintings and frescoes of bulls—images that wouldn't make sense unless this was the captivity site of the Minotaur (though, obviously, nobody believes in the Minotaur as a true character in history anymore).

Later, Aegeus' son Theseus would head to the labyrinth in an attempt to kill the Minotaur and save the Athenians from sacrific-ing their children to the bull-man. Aegeus had instructed Theseus upon his departure that, if he was victorious, he should raise a white flag from his ship on his voyage home. Theseus *was* victorious, but he didn't keep up his end of this "flag plan," and when Aegeus saw his son's ships returning home without any sign of the white flag, he assumed Theseus was dead. In his grief, he drowned himself in the sea (which is why this body of water was thereafter called the Aegean Sea).

Though these tales interweave and, at times, overlap (sometimes creating a slightly different epic than the one we just described), this is the basis legend for the island of Crete.

Again…what a train wreck!

Before we proceed to Paul's Epistle to Titus, a word of caution:

Several Christian denominations are currently employing "prayer labyrinths" that symbolize a journey to wholeness (or so they say). (Another term for this practice, though not limited to labyrinths, is "contemplative prayer.") According to the designers, the prayer labyrinths are implemented as a short, spiritual pilgrimage wherein a follower of Christ can enter the labyrinth, journey to his or her own "center," and go back out into the world.

Donna Howell worked at a Methodist camp in her teens when she first saw one of these structures, which were built from sticks. Sure enough, each time a group of campers came in, the young people were instructed to enter the labyrinth, find their "center," and reemerge with an answer to prayer (or some other spiritual reward). At the time, Howell thought it looked weird, but her job was to make breakfasts and lunches happen for the campers, so she did what she was paid to do and never asked questions. Howell is not at all a "mystical" person. She doesn't normally tell stories that involve prophetic mysteries, supernatural manifestations, signs or wonders, and the like. Though she does not discredit that the supernatural world of war in the unseen realm exists, the denomination she grew up in involved many "manifestations" of "God," "angels," "demons," etc., that later proved to be born of human imagination and superstition, so if an experience can be attributed to natural causes, she prefers that explanation. Be that as it may, something quite scary did happen one day, and it remains hard for her to explain...

One day, near the end of her summer job term, the camp directors met with her to collect her keys to the facility, and, after the hugs goodbye, one director told her, "You are welcome here anytime. Even when we don't have a camp in, you are invited to come walk the labyrinth, pray, take in the trees, or whatever you want. We're only here a couple days per month in the off-season. If we see you out here wandering during those days, we will assume you're on a journey to spiritual wellness and we will not bother you, but don't be a stranger. Come say hello if we're here when you are!"

A few days following these welcoming words, Howell drove over to the nearby camp and parked her car near the labyrinth, thinking she would give it a try. *Why not?* she thought. *Maybe it will bring me closer to God.*

As she closed the car door behind her and approached the prayer labyrinth, she stood perfectly still, looking at the stick structure for a moment before proceeding. *I wonder how I'm supposed to do this?* she thought. *Just, like...start walking and praying, I guess?* She recalled that the camp directors had told her there was "no wrong way" to walk the labyrinth and the practice was personal.

In that moment, as she contemplated the structure—though she, herself, wasn't moving or breathing heavily—Howell heard a long, audible sigh and the snap of a breaking twig. The sigh sounded as if it came from inches in front of her face, and the snap sounded as if it emanated from the center of the labyrinth.

"Hello?" she asked, spinning in a circle and eying the grounds around her. The trees were far enough away that she didn't think the snap or the breath could have come from them. She checked the parking lot down the hill: not a single car. She leaned and glanced toward the windows of the distant camp facility building to see if anyone was inside, but she saw that all the lights were out. She wasn't easily spooked, so she shrugged and took a step forward, but stopped suddenly when she caught movement in her peripheral vision. Again, it seemed to have been at the center of the labyrinth. She squinted for a moment, studying what could only be described as "thin air," and saw it again. Whatever it was, it was invisible, but the outward edges of a figure slightly distorted the trees in the background of her vision, alerting her that someone—or *something*—was definitely there. As quickly as it had arrived, it disappeared. There was no further sight or sound from the area after that.

Unlike in the movies, where the central characters have almost inhuman courage and directly investigate something out of curiosity, Howell ran back to her car, glancing over her shoulder at the now-disappeared and invisible "something" that had stood in the center of the labyrinth, and said the Name of Jesus over and over. She drove out of there as quickly as possible and never again returned to that campus (even after she was offered jobs there every season following). One day, when the camp directors were out shopping in the small city of Sisters, Oregon, Howell bumped into them and told them what had happened. Their soft, reassuring smiles and nods of kindness were of those who didn't believe a word of the story, but didn't want to make her feel foolish by telling her so.

From then until now, she has never told anyone about the experience again, except for those closest to her, because the account is so unbelievable. At the time, she struggled with bad dreams. After the labyrinth incident, she had one particularly frightening dream wherein she walked the labyrinth and, once arriving at its center, was physically restrained by something she couldn't see. Though that is the extent of the nighttime terror (and therefore sounds comparatively mild), the darkness she felt from it was palpable and lingered with her for a long time.

In the years following this frightening event, after her enrollment in a certificate Bible school (in her earlier theological training prior to college), Howell took a class that studied some of the culture behind New Testament cities. When she came to the subject of Crete and read about the demonic entity the Cretans believed lived at the center of the labyrinth, a chill ran down her spine. Immediately, she took to the Internet (and later Logos Bible Software) and began searching the links between modern, Christian "prayer labyrinths of self-journeying" and this ancient Greek mythology. Though some in the Body today say there is no link between "prayer labyrinths" or "meditation prayer" and ancient paganism, there doesn't appear to be any other possible conclusion than to admit they are, in fact, interconnected. Labyrinths have been, from the earliest examples (in Crete, Egypt, Italy, and many other parts of the world), drenched in Gnosticism, mysticism, goddess worship, esotericism, spirit guides, New Ageism, and a number of other pagan ideas just as offensive to God as the

Minotaur epic (though they frequently "hide in plain sight" as a more ambiguous, harmless, and indirect form of pagan worship). Josh Peck, one of two former New Ageists who converted to Christianity and later wrote *The Second Coming of the New Age*, writes about prayer labyrinths and the "Christian" steps of "contemplative prayer":

> The [prayer] labyrinth is a single, intricate path that leads to the center of a design then back out. A prayer labyrinth is used to inspire prayer, mediation, and spiritual awareness. For centuries, prayer labyrinths have been used in Catholic cathedrals. Yet, in recent years, there has been a resurgence in popularity of prayer labyrinths in New Age, the Emergent Church, Neo-paganism, and even in the Baptist church. [Note that since this book was written, this short list has magnified exponentially to include far more Protestant denominations.]
>
> This modern resurgence of prayer labyrinths is supported and endorsed by groups such as The Labyrinth Society and Veriditas (The World-Wide Labyrinth Project). From the Veriditas website, the group's stated purpose is "to transform the Human Spirit" using "the Labyrinth Experience as a personal practice for healing and growth, a tool for community building, an agent for global peace and a metaphor for the blossoming of the Spirit in our lives." According to Veriditas, walking the prayer labyrinth includes purgation (releasing), illumination (receiving), and union (returning).
>
> Purgation happens as a person walks toward the center of the labyrinth and sheds the distractions of life while opening the heart and mind. Illumination occurs at the center of the labyrinth, in which the person is to receive whatever spiritual enlightenment is available through prayer and meditation. The last stage, union, happens as the person exits the labyrinth and invokes joining God, a higher power, or the healing forces at work in the world.

The labyrinth, in various forms, can be found through-out ancient pagan religions. Mosaics of labyrinths can even be found on the floors of Freemason lodges. Now, Christianity has joined the trend. In an article entitled "Labyrinth Transforms Prayer Life, Baptists Say," *Baptist News Global* reported on a growing trend in the Baptist church.

The article states: "The ancient practice which involves walking a maze while praying has become more popular among Baptists as Christians in general are adopting more eclectic spir-itual disciplines."…

[One Baptist church member who helped build a prayer labyrinth said:] "I've seen people reach that center point and just start sobbing…. Other times, I've seen people get to the center and just (exhale)." [Another said:] "When I would go through the labyrinth, I would say to myself, 'Stay on the path, stay on the path,' and that became not only a mantra but also a meta-phor for things that were going on in my life"…. [Note that this person just said the labyrinth involves a "mantra," which is very common in terminology associated with prayer labyrinths…]

While on the surface this might seem harmless or even beautiful, the idea of the labyrinth is not rooted in Christianity but in ancient mythologies. Greek mythology states the laby-rinth was [originally] set up with a Minotaur in the center….

With churches taking on the mystical practice of walking the labyrinth in prayer, it is evident the enemy is plunging the Church into further deception. Of course, this isn't the first time this has happened, considering the yoga, angel prayer, and everything else [that Peck's surrounding chapters addressed involving what pagan ideas the Body of Christ is implementing into our worship today]….

Contemplative prayer focuses on shifting and balancing a person's internal world rather than outward communica-tion with God. It's more about adjusting one's interior mental state with the awareness of God as opposed to reaching out to God Himself with dialog. The goal is to rise above ordinary consciousness and dissolve the false self into the presence and awareness of the Divine through contemplation, since God "is known in pure consciousness rather than by some subject-object knowledge."...

This kind of prayer is oriented more towards a self-created shift in consciousness than it is in communication with God, and it's gaining popularity in Christian mysticism as well as evangelicalism. Popularized by a group of Roman Catholic monks named William Meninger, M. Basil Pennington, and Abbot Thomas Keating, contemplative prayer is carried out in what is called a "centering prayer."...

The first step encourages us to "quiet" ourselves. Of the over thirty-one thousand verses in the Bible, not a single one tells us to...silence our mind to enter into union with God. You can't love God with all your mind if your mind is empty....

The only verse in the Bible remotely close to a command to quiet ourselves is one which has been famously hijacked by the New Age community: "Be still, and know that I am God" (Psalm 46:10). [In proper context:] The word "still" is translated from *rephah* which means "to let go, to relent, or to cease striving," and this command was given in reference to the sovereignty of Yahweh over natural disasters (v. 2–3) and war (8–9). The raging nations (v. 6) coming against His people were reminded that God is the One who breaks the bows, burns the chariots, and makes peace on the earth (v. 9). Yahweh is speaking here to the enemies of the people of Israel whom He will be victorious over, telling them that their efforts are futile and that they should be still and recognize Him as God... Since the address in v. 10, be still, and know, is plural, readers should imagine God speaking these words to the nations, among whom He will eventually be exalted....

The second step is to choose a "sacred" word....

The idea that some words are sacred is not found in the Bible, but in Hinduism under the title of "mantra." A mantra is a sacred utterance [heavily linked with "contemplative prayer" and "prayer labyrinths"] that has the ability to produce higher levels of spiritual awareness in a person through repetition. Phrases such as *Aum Namah Shivaya* are intended propel one into a transcendent state of awareness, which happens to be the apparent goal of contemplative prayer [but] through the use of English words. Using a mantra to shift one's consciousness is an overt New Age practice that has no business in a Christian's life, whose God is supposed to be Yahweh and not the alteration of his or her mind.

The third step is to let this word be gently present in our being. We are encouraged to focus on a "sacred word," not on the person of Jesus. Even at this point, notice that no vertical connection is made between man and God. Man is still in the vain, selfish business of modifying his own internal states for his own pleasure. He is not ministering unto the Lord, asking God for wisdom, worshiping God, or talking with Him. Instead, he is pursuing a personal experience in his own mind. God is a means to an end of his own psychological pleasure.

After doing even more digging into the theology and origins of prayer labyrinths, Howell found that they are only a few specific terms away from the practice of consulting a Ouija board. Ultimately, prayer labyrinths endorse the "openness" of the mind and the "center of the self" to such a degree as to make one's self empty and vulnerable to demonic activity. (The "Classical Cretan Labyrinth" design from antiquity is identical to many "Christian" prayer labyrinths in use today...so even the very lines these believers sometimes walk match those of the Minotaur epic.) And Howell isn't the only one to make that connection. *The Kingdom of the Occult*, by scholars Walter Martin, Jill Martin Rische, and Kurt Van Gorden, states:

Christians open themselves to the world of the occult when they consult astrology charts, play with Ouija boards, visit palm readers, or engage in contemplative prayer that directs them to withdraw into silence and "open" their spirits to whatever may come along. It is never possible to open the door to the soul with impunity.... [W]alking labyrinths while focused on self-awareness [is] not [biblical]. An elaborately crafted maze of chairs, prayer stations, wood or greenery (labyrinths)...will not guarantee you access to the wisdom of God, and it has never been a requirement. Jesus said, "Come to Me, all you who labor and are heavy laden, and I will give you rest" (Matt. 11:28). The Bible teaches that the path to God is simple, not complex.[183]

Paul wrote, "Beware lest any man spoil you through philosophy and vain deceit, after the tradition of men, after the rudiments of the world, and not after Christ" (Colossians 2:8). Hosea 4:6 also warns: "My people are destroyed for lack of knowledge: because thou hast rejected knowledge, I will also reject thee, that thou shalt be no priest to me: seeing thou hast forgotten the law of thy God, I will also forget thy children." If a trend such as these prayer labyrinths is sprouting up all over the West and a responsible researcher cannot find a *single* link to this idea in the Word of God—and if all known origins otherwise consistently point to ancient pagan worship—believers should avoid them at all costs. Paul may or may not have had this on his mind when he wrote to Titus in Crete; we'll never know for certain.

What we do know about the backdrop of the Epistle to Titus is that, in addition to being known for its lies and piracy, the island of Crete was built upon this grotesque history of woman-and-bull bestiality (so gross...); child sacrifices; half-man, half-beast monsters; bloodshed; and eventually suicide. It was to this bizarre world that Paul introduced the Gospel of Truth sometime around the occasion of his shipwreck recorded in Acts 27. The power of the Good News was likely the only power on the planet that could defeat the Cretans' historical dishonesty and plunge them into a spiritual awakening of the Risen Christ.

Paul ministered to this long, skinny island (170 miles from east to west and less than thirty-five miles wide) during his final missionary journey. Though, on an aerial map, this stretch of land can appear diminutive in size—like a corn flake that fell from the bowl of cereal that is mainland Greece—it is by far the largest island in the Mediterranean Sea in the body of water southeast of the mainland and southwest of modern Turkey. Paul wasn't initially intending to land in Crete when he did, but frightening weather conditions derailed his journey from Jerusalem to Rome while he was being transported as a prisoner. Acts 27, the "shipwreck chapter," as mentioned earlier, details how this severe change in weather gave Paul an opportunity to familiarize himself with the island, to which he later sent his fellow worker Titus to appoint Christian elders across the territory.

However, the Gospel message may have been brought to Crete first by the Cretans who had been present in Jerusalem on the Day of Pentecost (see Acts 2:11), making Paul and Titus' message one they had heard before. Either way, it would take a strong man of God, one filled with the Holy Spirit and fully dedicated to godly truth and wisdom, to church-plant in this territory, and a man of equal calling in the Body to maintain that church. Paul had gotten to know Titus very well, having worked with him a lot on his third missionary journey (2 Corinthians 7:6, 13, 14; 8:6, 16, 17, 23), so Titus had the best possible example of the kind of man he should be to equip him for the work on an island like Crete. Titus was no doubt a strong man of God.

Paul begins this short letter with his usual warm greetings, referring to himself as a "slave" for Christ and Titus as a second son figure (Titus 1:1–4). He proceeds to summarize the work Titus was initially sent to carry out: establishing Christian elders in each town throughout the island. He reminds Titus the elders must live as blamelessly and upright as the leaders he has described in previous letters: faithful to their spouses; with obedient children; not arrogant or quick tempered; not drunkards; not lovers of money; nonviolent; hospitable; wise; fair; devout; disciplined; and "Holding fast the faithful word as he hath been taught, that he may be able by sound doctrine both to exhort and to convince the gainsayers" (1:5–9). (In other words, they must not live in the way Cretans were known to live.) Like in many other cities of Paul's day, Crete apparently had Judaizers among its citizens, turning "whole houses" away from the Gospel by insisting on circumcision. These elders and leaders of the island needed to know this was not necessary for salvation (1:10–11). It is here that Paul quotes Epimenides: "One of themselves, even a prophet of their own, said, 'the Cretians are alway liars, evil beasts, slow bellies.' This witness is true. Wherefore rebuke them sharply, that they may be sound in the faith" (1:12–13). All Christians of Crete must stop listening to and believing in the myths of Judaism and the rumors of the unfaithful. Such people are hypocritical in their dealings with God (1:14–15).

Titus is reminded to promote correct teaching and to live according to it. Older men should exercise self-control and practice love and patience so the respect they receive will be well-earned. Older women mustn't gossip or be drunkards, but they are to teach others what is good, showing young wives how to love their husbands and children properly, in wisdom and purity, submitting to their husbands—lest God be blasphemed. Titus, himself, will be a good example for the young men. His integrity must remain consistent while he teaches what is right and how to live wisely. If he maintains this pace, no one will be able to criticize his ministry. Slaves should work hard for their masters, refusing to participate in grumbling or stealing. If they show themselves in this trustworthy way, teachings about the Savior and God will be reflected in their actions (2:1–10).

The mystery of salvation through the Savior has finally been revealed! But the Christian is called toward "denying ungodliness and worldly lusts," living "soberly, righteously, and godly, in this present world" while we await Christ's return. Jesus gave His very life for us to have this freedom from sinful lusts, so the Cretans must be cleansed and live as Christ's own people, wholly in commitment to righteousness. Paul tells Titus, "These things speak, and exhort, and rebuke with all authority. Let no man despise thee" (2:11–15).

Titus is to remind the believers that they should submit to their earthly governments, be obedient, humble, and gentle, and avoid all slandering and fighting (3:1–2). At one point in the past, even those who are saved were once foolish, disobedient people, slaves to sin, envy, evil and hatred. But now, because of the transforming work of Christ, all sin is washed away. A new life was birthed through the power of the Holy Spirit, who poured Himself out through Jesus: "That being justified by his grace, we should be made heirs according to the hope of eternal life" (3:1–7). The Cretans will be made new through this work! Titus must insist on teaching these rudimentary truths so the Cretans can reap the spiritual benefits that come with its application of good works. Quarrelling only amounts to a waste of time, so if people are causing division, Titus is to give a first, and then a second, warning. If they persist in wasting the time of this minister and the brethren, the church of Crete should move on without them, because those types of people have turned away from the truth of Christ, and their own sin condemns them (3:8–11).

In closing, Paul notes a couple people he is sending to help Titus in his endeavors, and the apostle closes with: "All that are with me salute thee. Greet them that love us in the faith. Grace be with you all. Amen" (3:12–15).

After this letter was delivered, Christianity flourished in Crete, changing the lives of many "dishonest Cretans" for life. By the late second century, Crete was one of the chief centers of Yeshua worship in Rome. This burst of Gospel momentum came from two primary Cretan cities. One was Gortyna, in the southern central area of the island (scholars say this may have been Titus' home territory). The other, believe it or not, was Knossos…the very city where the remains of the Minotaur labyrinth stood.

Talk about a Holy Spirit smack-down! Yes!

The Cretans would no longer be known in their generation as "liars, evil beasts, [and] slow bellies." They would be known as carriers of the truth, precious men and women of God, and hard-working soldiers of Christ who feed on the diet of the Word…right there on the same land where demonic forces once held the island in its grip. At least for this period in history, a "cretanizer" would no longer be synonymous with a "liar," because they were following Jesus, whose Spirit is the Spirit of Truth (John 14:17; 15:26; 16:13). During Emperor Decius' persecution of Christians in AD 249–251, ten men known as the Ten Callinica Holy Martyrs of Crete were murdered for their faith. But their deaths led to a revival and the Cretan church expanded. It wouldn't be until the ninth century that the conquest of the Arabs changed this steady growth in Jesus.

Wow. The power of God, right?

Philemon

THE INDIVIDUAL KNOWN as Philemon (a name meaning "affectionate") was from Colossae. Paul's letter to this man is the only one included in the canon that is of such a private and personal nature. As such, there is no "city history" or "resident gods" relevant to this Epistle. It is also Paul's shortest letter (only one chapter, negating the need for chapter references below). Readers may therefore assume we will have as little to say about it as most other Bible studies that summarize Philemon in a few paragraphs or a page...but our goal in seeing Jesus in the books of the Word inspires us to take a few extra minutes here. Let's see if we can't let the Savior breathe some life into this one, shall we?

The occasion of the letter is obvious from its internal content: A runaway slave named Onesimus had robbed his master, Philemon, and escaped to Rome. There, he met up with Paul while he was imprisoned (we don't know if this was a chance meeting or if the slave intentionally sought out Paul). But Paul actually knew Philemon, as he was a "fellow-worker" with Paul and his associates from before (Philemon 1), and he ran a church out of his home (2). So Paul, after

developing an intimate friendship with this runaway, leads him to the
Lord and sends him back to his former master to face him in person
and make things right…

Pause for a moment.

This backstory reminds us of the popular Broadway musical, *Les
Miserables* (based on the book by the same name by author Victor
Hugo). The plot centers around navigating the relationship between
law and grace from two angles: On the side of the law, the story makes
the statement that the law cannot be mocked or disregarded; it must
be followed and strictly upheld, or else civilization falls into chaos. On
the side of grace, the story illustrates that the law exists to increase the
value of human life, and without clemency and leniency toward the
very people it was written to assist, it becomes a dictatorial system that
only serves to oppress. Though the story ends in Paris at the time of
the June Rebellion in 1832, it begins in Digne, France in 1815, following main character Valjean, who is up for his release after almost
a lifetime of imprisonment for stealing a loaf of bread for his starving
sister way back in his youth.

Valjean is, in the beginning, a "slave" to the prison system of the
day. Despite what honorable intentions he may initially have upon his
release, he cannot find work because of his criminal record. Nobody
appears to care that his crime had been minor, or that it had been
birthed from basic human need on behalf of a loved one, so he wanders the streets, homeless and destitute. Vexed by the pitiless and brutal
circumstances he had lived under during his prison sentence and the
follow-up rejection by his fellow man once freed, he scrambles to find a
place to stay. One night, a kind bishop gives him food and a bed, and,
after everyone is asleep, Valjean sneaks into the home's dining room in
the middle of the night, steals as much silver as he can fit into his travel
bag, and flees into the night. When he is captured by constables within
hours of his escape, he is taken back to the bishop to face his crime. The
constables appear at the door, scoffing and saying the fugitive Valjean
had the nerve to say the bishop had *given* him this silver as a gift.

The bishop—in an unexpected and benevolent turn of events obviously spurned by a godly spirit of forgiveness, grace, and mercy— tells the constables that he is, in fact, giving all this silver to Valjean. He then produces even more silver and states in front of Valjean's captors that Valjean, in his eagerness to leave early, had left the best of the treasures behind, and hands the rest over to the former prisoner. Afterward, he tells the constables to release Valjean and thanks them for their service.

As soon as the confused captors are gone, the bishop privately consults Valjean and gives him a solemn charge: There is a higher plan at work here. This silver should be used to turn Valjean's life around. Valjean must serve the Lord with his life, and now, with these valu-ables, he has that chance.

Valjean spends a moment thinking about his theft, reflecting on his own internal hatred for mankind that he feels has festered long enough. One word from the bishop was all it would have taken and Valjean would have been back to prison, where he would again be beaten, cold, hungry, and viewed as worthless to society...yet this minister who could have condemned him chose instead to call Valjean a brother, giving him food, drink, a bed, silver, and his freedom, lov-ing him despite his sin and attempted robbery. In a desperate plea to God, Valjean prays he will be able to release his inner turmoil. The shame he feels on the inside is ravaging, eating at him from the inside out. A minister of God who could have been the reason he was back in shackles had carried out an act of sympathy instead, and that single gesture of mercy amplifies his feelings of guilt. In one of the most dramatic scenes in the entire musical, Valjean releases his anger and promises that the old Valjean is dead and a new life has begun.

The story then flashes forward several years to show that Valjean took the bishop's words to heart and became an honest man. He bestowed the same kind of mercy to a young woman named Fantine who works the factory he is now in charge of thanks to the fresh start on life and the resources he had received. Before Valjean knew of her,

this youthful woman had fallen prey to a smooth-talking manipulator in the past and had delivered a child out of wedlock. She was so
desperate to provide her child with a stable life and food that she
had taken her daughter to live with an innkeeper and his wife while
she now labors long, hard hours and send her meager income to the
innkeeper to pay for her daughter's lodging and food. The innkeeper
and his wife are cruel to Fantine's daughter, and the little girl is in dire
need of rescue. When a tragic misunderstanding leads to Fantine's
dismissal from her job at Valjean's factory (Valjean isn't aware of it at
the time, as his foreman handles the issue wrongfully), she takes to
selling her hair, then her teeth, and then her body so her daughter
won't starve. Valjean bumps into her while she is walking the streets
advertising her near-bald, toothless self while she is dying from a disease brought on by her desperate lifestyle. Valjean, in a state of shock,
recognizing her as a former employee of the factory and blaming himself for her plight, promises to raise her child for her. When Fantine
does pass away, Valjean makes good on his promise, giving Fantine's
daughter a promising life filled with love...the same kind of grace the
bishop had once shown him.

The story weaves around war and romance and includes many
subplots. But, when we think about Onesimus robbing Philemon
blindly and running out into the world—and then compare that to
the grace and mercy Paul requests from Philemon on behalf of the
runaway slave—we think of the initial investment of the bishop on
Valjean's behalf. Would such an unbelievable account of compassion
and the spirit of clemency apply in this case, also?

Let's look at Paul's short Epistle, and then we'll revisit that question...

When Paul finished writing his letter to the slave owner, he sent
Onesimus back to his master to deliver it in person. Paul was aware
that masters had the right throughout Roman territory to severely
punish—up to the point of death[184]—slaves who stole from them and
fled. Paul so cared for both Onesimus and Philemon that he inter-
vened with this note. He could have used his apostolic authority as a

bargaining chip to secure Onesimus' release and subsequent service to his own needs, but the fact that he didn't says a lot of Paul's integrity as a man who truly believed in his own teaching that one should show love while also "minding his own business" (1 Thessalonians 4:11–12).

After wishing Philemon grace and peace from the Father and Christ Jesus (3), Paul offers a sweet and intimate thanksgiving for his friend: "I thank my God, making mention of thee always in my prayers, Hearing of thy love and faith, which thou hast toward the Lord Jesus, and toward all saints" (4–5). Paul then prays that Philemon will exercise the generosity that comes from faith in Christ, as Philemon is already known as a loving man who brings joy and comfort to his brethren and as a kind man who brings refreshment to the hearts of God's people (6–7).

That is why, Paul explains, he is asking Philemon for a favor… He *could* demand it in the Name of Christ, and he would be justified in doing so because what he is asking is right, but because Philemon is a loving man, Paul—now an old man who is a prisoner for Christ—is choosing to frame his letter as a gentle request, instead (8–9). Paul asks Philemon to show grace to his slave, Onesimus, who became a Christian under the tutelage of the shackled Paul. In the past, Onesimus had been "unprofitable" to Philemon, but now, because of his faith, he is of great value to both Paul and Philemon. (The name "Onesimus" means "profitable," so Paul is using a play on words, showing that, by becoming a new creation through Christ, Onesimus is fulfilling the very meaning of his name.) Paul is choosing to send Onesimus back to Philemon, and along with this slave, Paul sends his very own heart (10–12).

Paul wanted to keep Onesimus with him to help him while he preached the Good News from his cell, and if that had been the case, Onesimus would have certainly been of great assistance to Paul on Philemon's behalf, but Paul wouldn't dare carry on in such a way without Philemon's consent. It would mean more to Paul if such a scenario played out with Philemon's blessing, not because he had never been given a choice in the matter. Ironically, Philemon lost his slave for a little while, but now he can have him back in a way that reflects on eternity: Onesimus is no longer defined by the title "slave"; he is now a Christian brother to Paul and Philemon, and he will mean more to Philemon upon his return to him for this reason (13–16).

So, if Philemon considers Paul his partner in the work of the Gospel, then he should welcome Onesimus—the new creation in Christ—just as he would welcome Paul. If there are any remaining damages from Onesimus' actions, they should be charged to Paul, personally, who will take care of them: "I Paul have written it with mine own hand, I will repay it." Paul doesn't need to remind Philemon that he owes his very own soul to the work of Paul, who taught him of the work of the cross (17–19).

This might sound, at the onset, to be a line of manipulation between these two friends, but through the lens of proper context, Paul is *not* crassly saying, "Need I remind you that you owe me your very soul?" as some naysayers of today's atheistic culture assume. Much to the contrary, Paul is comparing the grace Philemon has received in eternity to the grace he naturally owes his fellow man. As Knute Larson states in Holman Publisher's *I & II Thessalonians, I & II Timothy, Titus, Philemon* commentary:

> Philemon had the right, as slave master, to have Onesimus flogged, imprisoned, even executed. But Paul did not dabble in rights; he reached for divine grace. He wanted Philemon to recall the great debt that Christ paid on his behalf and the new life to which Paul had introduced him when Philemon trusted the Savior.... All that God offers, the eternal riches of the heavens, fullness of life at this moment—all these came to Philemon because Paul had faithfully preached the gospel.[185]

Paul goes on to ask that Philemon treat Onesimus kindly as a favor for the Lord's sake and for Paul's encouragement. Paul then expresses that his confidence is so high in Philemon that he believes he will do all the letter asks…and much more (21)!

Signing off, Paul asks that Philemon prepare a room for him. If God answers Philemon's prayers, Paul will be visiting him soon. He notes that Epaphras, Paul's fellow-prisoner, says hello, as well as his fellow-workers Mark, Aristarchus, Demas, and Luke. His closing statement is: "The grace of our Lord Jesus Christ be with your spirit. Amen" (22–25).

One can only envision the moment when Onesimus showed up on his master's doorstep carrying this short letter from the Apostle Paul. Would Philemon be like the bishop of *Les Miserables*, forgiving the theft of his criminal, fugitive slave? Or would he choose condemnation and harsh reprimand, as was his Roman right? Is there any historical evidence that supports either scenario?

If some historians are correct, Onesimus *was* forgiven and then freed by Philemon, and went on to become the bishop of Ephesus following Timothy. Some are quick to point out that we don't know for certain whether Bishop Onesimus of Ephesus is the same man as Philemon's slave, but there are a few factors indicating he was. Perhaps the greatest proof is in the very circulation of this letter in the early Church, which has led most scholars to come to our same conclusion that Philemon read Paul's letter and freed Onesimus, who thereafter used that freedom to become the renowned, historical bishop, leading many to Jesus and dying a martyr's death near the end of the first century. If Philemon rejected Paul's request, and Onesimus continued only to be known as his slave, then basic logic says that Philemon would have considered this good-for-nothing letter little more than kindling for the evening fire. Nobody would have known about this private exchange unless it had led to an outcome the early Church saw worthy to make an example of. That this letter was so widely talked about as to become a part of the biblical canon is almost, in and of itself, proof Onesimus was freed and went on to minister to the very churches that read, then copied, this Epistle. Why else would the Church wish to spread the word of the event? Regardless of punishment, had the plan not worked, Paul's advice would have been disregarded by Philemon and the letter would have been a blight on the rest of the early Church's Scripture by representing nothing more than a failed plea on behalf of a Christian brother. (Why would they circulate *that*?)

Furthermore, Philemon is a very different kind of letter that doesn't appear to fit in with the rest of the canon, due to its personal nature and seeming lack of addressing the topic of worship standards for a congregation (which is the purpose of the Epistles). This begs the question: Why was it ever included among the rest if it didn't support the same goal? Many learned men of God have asked this question throughout the years, and have largely come up with only two answers: 1) It sets a behavioral example for Christian living (which is true, and could surely be the reason); 2) someone very powerful in the early Church of the first century insisted that it be viewed as Scripture—by the time the canon was formed centuries later, it was well established, and Philemon was added because of this influence on the first believers. If the latter is true, it leads to a subsequent question of *who* that powerful person initially was. Onesimus, the bishop of Ephesus after Timothy, eventually became one of the more prominent names in the late first century among Church leaders, and could have easily influenced this decision. This appears to be a little bit more than mere coincidence.

Another bit of evidence is equally convincing: The letters to Philemon, the Colossians, and the Ephesians were composed at about the same time. (The dates of all three are unknown, technically speaking, but almost all academics in historical criticism have tracked the footsteps and imprisonment dates of Paul, compared those details with his travels in Acts and his notes about planned visitations and prison, and concluded that they were all three written somewhere around AD 62.) Paul's associate, Tychicus, was listed as the sole deliverer of Ephesians (6:21), while, as we stated, Onesimus delivered the note to Philemon (verse 17). However, suddenly, someone named Onesimus is said in Paul's writing to be Tychicus' companion when the correspondence to the Colossians was delivered (4:7–9). We know Philemon was a fellow worker of the church at Colossae. It then appears quite possible that Paul sent Onesimus to Philemon, Philemon freed Onesimus, and then Onesimus *joined* Tychicus in working for Paul right before they travelled together to deliver the letter to the Colossians.

After all these details are considered, it almost takes more reasoning to dismiss this connection than to accept it. If we were talking about someone with a common New-Testament name—like John, James, Paul, Simon, or Mark—then much more doubt would be cast on these theories. The chances of there being two men by the rare name of "Onesimus" who trekked this same part of the ancient world in the same handful of years and who both had connections to Paul is far less likely. Whereas we can't be absolutely certain that this slave is the same man as Bishop Onesimus of Ephesus, the facts add up to indicate he was, and this is the belief of many scholars.

But regardless of what history tells of this man, we know from Paul's letter that—*watch this!*—the slave robbed and ran from his slave master, then came into contact with Paul, who led him to believe in the very Savior-Master his own slave master served! Meanwhile, a man whose name meant "profitable" was "unprofitable" for the Kingdom Philemon served, until he got saved and became "profitable," thereby giving new meaning for a new creature in Christ! This beautiful and poetic irony will continue to speak life to us throughout all times, as this event was, against all odds, preserved in the canon.

Society told Onesimus, "You *better* run… You're toast if you get caught, and nobody will mourn your death or even remember you," but Christ says, "Return to the man you have wronged and make it right, for in Me, you are free; I have the power to soften the hearts of My people toward you and you *may* just end up a free man out there." Society said to Philemon, "Beat him! Kill him! He's just a slave—

a *nobody* to you!" but Christ says, "Call him a brother and welcome him in, for there is no longer 'slave' nor 'free' in My Family."

Come on, folks! This is not "religion." This is love, compassion, relationship, reconciliation, and *clemency*! Our Master gives pardon when "pardon" is inconceivable!

When the world's voice fails, the Master gives hope.

This new community of people called "Christians" were upholding a higher order than one the laws of the world expected…and if the majority of historians and scholars are correct, this Epistle's "Valjean" was shown mercy, and went to the grave showing the "Fantines" of the world that same grace.

Hebrews

WHO WROTE HEBREWS? Was it written by Paul—or wasn't it?: It's the question that keeps coming up among scholars, and we may never have an answer on this side of eternity. The KJV translation treats Paul's authorship as a fact (calling this book "The Epistle of Paul the Apostle to the Hebrews"), while more modern translations omit a definitive indication of the author (titling it: "Written to the Hebrews from Rome" or "Written to the Hebrews from Italy [and delivered] through Timothy"), so relying on man-made headings in the Bible that attempt clarity is of little help.

The author of the letter to the Hebrews is technically unknown. The words and phrasing styles don't appear to align with those in typical letters of Paul. One feature of ancient letter literature was its ability to be written by an amanuensis (someone who wrote down what was dictated; a scribe, secretary, clerk, or stenographer could do this, but not all amanuenses were professionals like these). Because many folks within the ancient world were illiterate, those who wished to write something down but couldn't read and write could hire a person to do the job for them. These individuals, especially in the ancient world of Greek literature, were sometimes instructed to write down exactly what was said, word for word. Other times, they were given a certain amount of liberty in the construction of sentences. Paul certainly could read and write, but toward the end of his ministry, he might have developed what scholars think may have been an eyesight problem. (This is based on interpretations of Galatians 4:15 ["if it had been possible, ye would have plucked out your own eyes, and have given them to me"] and 6:11 ["Ye see how large a letter I have written unto you with mine own hand"; the letter to Galatians wasn't lengthy, so it is sometimes assumed he was referring to the large-handed writing of a man going blind.) Outside of that possibility are a million imaginable others—all the way from Paul's growing discomfort in shackles (less likely in his late Roman imprisonment, when his "house arrest" arrangement may not have involved shackling the wrists) to possible arthritis of the hands or knuckles. (All that writing he did with the first-century, hard-reed writing utensils could do that to a person, and we have no idea how many letters he actually wrote. We have thirteen in the canon—fourteen if you count Hebrews—and we know of several that were lost [for instance, the missing Corinthian letters]. His lifestyle as described in the Epistles shows a man who was always busy writing in prison. Typing today, for a couple of straight days, requires the authors of this very book to stretch out weary fingers and wrists, and we can imagine that, in his old age, Paul was feeling much worse!) So, if the letter is Paul's, it could be that it was dictated to an amanuensis who wrote down the spirit of his teachings with some liberty in the formation of words. This is a major possibility that surprisingly gets little attention in discussions about authorship.

Because of the Pauline emphases within the book—the alignment with Paul's principles and theology and the addressing of issues known to be important to him—many scholars attribute the writing of Hebrews to Paul, claiming he either simply wrote in a different style than usual (a weak argument, forcing a dismissal of the variations rather than an explanation of them), or that the letter was scribed by someone who had a degree of freedom to form the letter in the way they saw fit. This latter idea is a real possibility that would explain away any stylistic discrepancies and make the parts of the letter that sound like Paul's "voice" bring the book back into focus as his work. However, it raises the question of why Paul wouldn't have been listed in opening and closing greetings as he was in his other Epistles, as well as in a number of other typical "Paulisms" his work is known for… regardless of who he might be telling to write for him.

Let's look deeper at a short list of clues for and against the idea of Paul as author.

Some support for Pauline authorship is found in the fact that the letter is addressed to the "Hebrews," people the former, zealously Jewish Paul knew very well how to communicate with. He had persecuted believers in the beginning, struggling with belief in the Messiah in the same way a traditional Hebrew of his day would, so he would be uniquely positioned to speak to their doubts. Further, the recipients of the letter knew its author personally and the author asked for prayer in a manner comparable to the way Paul had in prior letters (see: Hebrews 13:18–19, 22, 23b; Romans 15:30; Ephesians 6:19; Colossians 4:3; 1 Thessalonians 5:25). The author longed to see them with sentiments akin to Pauline style (Romans 15:32; Philippians 2:24; 1 Thessalonians 3:11; Philemon 1:22), and the final closing sentence of the book is Pauline in character: "Grace be with you all. Amen" (Hebrews 13:25). Whoever the author was had also worked alongside Timothy (Hebrews 13:23a), whom we all know was a close companion to Paul.

If Paul wrote this book in the Hebrew language and it was later translated by Luke—one theory famously postulated by Church father Clement of Alexandria—then it would explain why the book has a Lukan rhythm to it similar to Acts. This theory also takes care of the question of why Paul would not affix his name to the document, as we read in Eusebius of Caesarea's *Ecclesiastical History*:

He [Clement] says that the Epistle to the Hebrews is the work of Paul, and that it was written to the Hebrews in the Hebrew language; but that Luke translated it carefully and published it for the Greeks, and hence the same style of expression is found in this epistle and in the Acts.

This source immediately goes on to explain why Paul, out of respect for the Lord who dubbed him the "apostle to the Gentiles" (Galatians 1:11–15), would not want to position himself as the "apostle to the Hebrews [or Jews]." Other Church fathers and historians that take this same (or similar) stance on Pauline attribution are Origen (in a limited way, as he believed the *teaching* was Paul's but the one who *penned* it was possibly Luke or someone else), Athanasius, and John Chrysostom. But it should be noted that the central argument in favor of that conclusion is that other, wise leaders of their day (hundreds of years removed from the life of Paul) handed down this theory as tradition…ultimately proving nothing. The Pauline authorship of this book is in no way universally accepted, and it never has been at any point throughout history. Tertullian believed it was Barnabas; Gaius, bishop of Rome, refuted Paul as author outright (but without a guess as to whom it may have been); Martin Luther guessed Apollos; and some historians attribute its writing to Silas (who was partially credited as coauthor of the Thessalonian letters alongside Paul; 1 Thessalonians 1:1; 2 Thessalonians 1:1).

One major bit of evidence in favor of Pauline attribution is not reliant upon internal content, but upon the likelihood of distribution. When the early councils prayed about what books should be in the canon, they wouldn't have just allowed "pretty words" by any anonymous author to be included. The criteria of New Testament canonicity relied on the facts that the book originated from an apostle (or an apostle's apprentice), was recognized by the churches, and contained apostolic teachings. Hebrews was *almost* not chosen for inclusion because of its ambiguous authorship. The fact that it was eventually included in the Word argues for the idea that the councils largely agreed the book was written by Paul (or at least involved his direct influence, which nobody refutes because of the Pauline character in the text we've just covered).

But if that's the conclusion they reached, then why isn't Hebrews placed in order of length? (This would position it between Romans and 1 Corinthians or between 2 Corinthians and Galatians— Hebrews is shorter than Romans and 1 Corinthians but longer than 2 Corinthians, and it wouldn't have broken up the two letters to Corinth, so it would be put in one of these two places.) Or, why wasn't it placed in order of its audience? (In other words, to "a people group," like Romans, and not to a church or individual, like the rest of Paul's letters; had this idea been followed, Hebrews would be sandwiched by category between the larger Romans and the first "church" letter, 1 Corinthians.) If the councils believed Hebrews to be of Pauline origin, why is it off by itself between known Pauline Epistles and those written by James, Peter, John, and Jude? Such placement certainly does assign doubt to the early Church's belief that the work was Paul's.

Visiting the other side of the argument, a good portion of the book's content is so different than Paul's usual style that, as scholars heavily agree, it's not easy to imagine Paul behind the pen here. Not only are his typical opening greetings missing (the letter launches into theology at its onset), but nowhere internally does the book state its author is an apostle or eyewitness of Christ, which Paul did elsewhere. In fact, in a couple of verses, Hebrews gives that distinction to *others* (2:3; 13:7). Timothy is mentioned, as stated, but oddly, here, he is no longer a "son" to the author, but a "brother" to the person (13:23a; but also see 2 Corinthians 1:1; Colossians 1:1; and Philemon 1:1, where Paul identifies Timothy as a "brother" to the congregants). The personal relationship of "brother" suggests Timothy is a collaborator with the author in the Gospel work, and not as close as Paul's "son."

Most importantly, the art of historical criticism (in part, nailing down who wrote what, and when) heavily relies on comparing styles. For instance: As noted in our introduction to the Gospels, Mark is known for frequent use of "action" words (like "immediately," and so on). Had he written another biblical book with an unknown authorship, the extensive use of action words—if used in the same way he did in his Gospel—would position him at the top of the list of potential authors as a result of forensic grammar analysis, as Mark was unique in this way. Similarly, Paul has distinctive usage of grammar, and Hebrews simply doesn't "sound like" Paul. (We alluded to this idea earlier in our look at the word *authentein*. Because Paul always used *exousia* when he spoke about "authority of [one thing or person] over another [thing or person]," his sudden introduction of *authentein* provides internal evidence that "usurping authority over [the man]" had to mean something special, because "this other word is not Paul's typical style." Throughout Hebrews, the choice of words is not frequently in Paul's traditional wheelhouse.)

After the aforementioned "internal evidence" (which we will not continue to parse out here) is considered, many scholars conclude: "The likelihood is that the real author was in fact one of Paul's followers or associates."[187]

Which follower? Which associate?

Though there is no way to be completely certain, we tend not to believe Hebrews originated with Paul. Our reasons for this are more technical (with a detailed explanation that would likely bore many readers), but comparing the way this book reads against others Paul wrote ultimately leads us, along with thousands of others, to believe that it simply isn't his work. The "nail in the coffin" (so to speak) for us is Hebrews 2:3: "How shall we escape, if we neglect so great salvation; which at the first began to be spoken by the Lord, and was *confirmed unto us* by them that heard him?" (emphasis added). A modern rephrasing would say something like: "How could we ever escape if we choose to neglect such a great gift of salvation? See, salvation was first spoken about by the Lord, personally, and then later it was confirmed to the rest of *us* by the people who heard His teachings." Grouping himself in with the word "us" in this instance insinuates that this writer came to believe in Christ because of the words of witnesses, which destroys his apostolic claim and in no way can be true of his Road-to-Damascus conversion story. As addressed in previous Epistles, Paul maintained the claim that he had personally received the Gospel from Christ. It's possible that this reference to "confirmed unto us by them that heard" could be a generic allusion to "people who heard the words of Christ and told the rest of us [generically] all about it." However, if "us" is interpreted literally (and there doesn't appear to be enough reason not to), then the first time this author heard the message of the Gospel was through "them that heard" Jesus. Paul was frequently being challenged about his apostleship, and he was thus careful to maintain a clear relationship between "I" and "you" in his letters (so "us" in this application, without a Pauline identifier elsewhere, is unlikely Paul's treatment). He also knew that, with so many rising false teachers in the churches, if the letter needed to be taken seriously, his name and authority should have been included in it somewhere, as each of his other letters had done.

Scholars who do *not* attribute Hebrews to Paul have spent considerable time tracking internal evidences to a number of possible authors who were considered to be Christian leaders who were alive and in operation at the time of Paul (and who travelled with him, explaining the Pauline influence evident in the work). Though it would likely shock (and maybe even offend) some to be told the author was *female*, a good amount of evidence supports that very theory. Certainly, women were allowed to send and receive mail in those days, and since the author is unquestionably unknown, then no matter what feelings bubble up within us when we hear "woman" and "author" together in reference to the authorship of biblical books, we will never be able to say the writer was incontestably male. Despite the fact that women weren't as highly educated as men in ancient times, some absolutely were, especially when, as we stated prior, their parents were wealthy Romans.

With that in mind, the author could have been Priscilla. This theory has been tossed around the scholarly world since forever, but it didn't gain much support until Adolf von Harnack—a highly respected and influential theologian prominent during the nineteenth and twentieth centuries—built a strong case for it in the year 1900. We know Priscilla was educated well enough to correct the theology of a man with Paul's endorsement (Acts 18:18–28), and we likewise know she was a frequent church planter and companion with Paul in his work (Romans 16:3; 1 Corinthians 16:19; 2 Timothy 4:19). As she travelled alongside this apostle, she carried out duties tradition- ally given to men, including those involved in Paul's very own trade of tent-making (Acts 18:2). She is mentioned in this grand light six times throughout the New Testament, three of which list her name first—a controversial idea in this historical, Roman-Jewish society! But as covered before (in our study of Romans), when a woman's name *did* appear ahead of a man's, as Priscilla's did, it established her authority as being above, or equal to, the man in the statement.

This brings us to the infamous "male participle" argument from Hebrews 11:32(a), used by many to show the likeliness of a male author. Hebrews asks: "And what shall I more say? for the time would fail me *to tell* [or "to recount," Greek *diegoumenon*] of Gedeon, and of Barak, and of Samson, and of Jephthae; of David also, and Samuel, and of the prophets" (emphasis added). Scholars are quick to point out that the language here would typically refer to a man: "The par- ticiple 'to recount' (*diegoumenon...*) is masculine, which could imply a male author."[188] However, this source and others like it go on to state the following observation: "This is not conclusive, for a woman author might well have used the masculine generically in this very rare self-reference. To do otherwise would have called attention to her gender and distracted from the [letter]."[189] Had a woman, in a dominantly patriarchal culture, identified herself as the author of this book, it's likely that it would not have been included in the canon or even circulated in the early Church. In that sense, the silence on the matter is, at least in part, evidence that *could* be taken to support a female author who prioritized the Gospel above her "Christian freedom" above her "right to identify herself" and instruct a gender-inclusive body of Jewish believers in Rome. Scholars who disbelieve in Priscilla as author also state that "a female author (such as Priscilla...) is unlikely," while they simultaneously admit such a conclusion "rests more on silence than on anything so specific as one masculine participle in thirteen chapters!"[190] (The exclamation point at the end of that sentence infers the scholar's acknowledgment that only one word in the whole letter as proof against a woman author is incredulous...even though he just said Priscilla's authorship was "unlikely." This kind of assumption based on the argument of silence is quite popular within the scholarly world, which we find surprising. We mean no disrespect to this scholar; actually, we're encouraged by his honesty and transparency as he says it probably wasn't a woman and then admits that the only proof against a woman is hardly proof at all. We only wish that, when he says something is "unlikely," he would explain *why* that's the conclusion he comes to instead of merely going on to discredit his own deduction by showing that there remains to be a lack of supporting evidence on either side. Yet, he is not alone in this approach. Many respected teachers of the Word say, "No way!" to either Hebrews having a woman author or specifically having Priscilla as author, followed by the admission, "there's no evidence to prove otherwise." It appears that, in such cases, the main culprit of opposition rests on our culture's unfamiliarity with, and conditioned resistance to, the idea of a female author instead of hard facts.) Relevant to this is that, just as Paul referred to Phoebe as the male variant of "deacon" (*diakonos*) to establish her as an authority among men in Koine Greek (also in our study on Romans), we know the Greek language at the time of Paul allowed a woman to be referred to with a word that would normally be assigned to a male without necessarily causing a biblical, erroneous gender attribution. So, as far as the Greek *diegoumenon* disproving feminine authorship, that stance fails—and, as we just illustrated, most scholars are aware of that. But there is grammatical research that shows this word does not need to refer to a male in the first place (brackets added for clarification):

> As we know, a participle is a verbal adjective. In Greek as in English, an adjective modifies a noun or pronoun. In [Hebrews] 11:32, *telling* [or "to tell" in the KJV; "to recount" in others] modifies the pronoun *me*; *me* is in the accusative case, so *telling* is in the accusative case. This is significant because, in the accusative case, the masculine and neuter forms of the participle are identical. ["Neuter" forms are, as the term implies, gender inclusive; it could refer to a male or female.]
>
> (This source goes on to explain how it's only in the English translations that "time will fail me telling" is swapped for "I have no time to tell," thus causing an adverbial confusion of pronouns that further leads to syntactical errors not present in the Greek. The short story on this conundrum is this: When the Greek is handled responsibly and the secondary English syntax is out of the way, the whole phrase in question is in *neuter—male or female*—form. Heaps of other scholarly opinions by Koine Greek lingual experts who collectively add support to these conclusions are stacked in this source. Although the author of the quoted excerpt is a woman, and has been grouped [yet again] with the pejorative label "feminist theologians," we find no reason for her statements about Greek grammar to be discredited on account of her gender, and it is noteworthy that the scholars who had reviewed her writing and concur with her deductions are all male in the portions we've read.)

Additional support indicates that Priscilla is from Italy (Acts 18:2), as was the author of Hebrews (13:24). Romans 16 acknowledges her as a well-known authority in the early Church, and scholars who research the topic of Church history—what homes folks met in and who the leaders were within those homes—recognize her as a likely pastoral figure in Ephesus, Corinth, and most important to this theory, Rome. Because the church in Rome *was* meeting in Priscilla's house (Romans 16:5), then the audience of Hebrews becomes important in the discussion. The Jews are the intended audience (as "Hebrews" no doubt qualifies), and the letter was written to the very Jews of Priscilla's area (Rome; Hebrews 13:24). At the very least, we can narrow it down to a celebrated teacher of Paul's day who was stationed for a time in Rome and was viewed as an authority figure there, and probably to the very congregation that met in Priscilla's home—*all* of which is fulfilled in her being the author. The pronoun "we" is the most common one used in Hebrews, so it's also noteworthy to remember that Priscilla is always listed by Paul together with Aquila, her husband, possibly forming the common "we" behind the letter. But the most convincing of all evidence supporting a female author is the "clues in the personality, mode of expression, and status of the writer"; "delicacy of expression" and "elegant personality" within the letter; the scholars (plural, including men) who "detect a woman's hand"; and many other internal, psychological clues, all of which point to "ample evidence for feminine style and outlook." As one example: the phrase "I beseech you more abundantly" in Hebrews 13:19 "can be translated idiomatically as 'with all my heart I ask you' or 'with all the strength I have I plead with you.'" Scholars involved in the discussion agree that this kind of language is "less typical of a male than a female writer."[192]

We have no interest in vehemently *disproving* a male writer, or even Paul, himself, as the author of Hebrews (as is apparent from our listing several points of evidence supporting him). Rather, we believe a female writer is a real possibility, and it is therefore pertinent to our studies of New Testament books that point to Jesus: who instigated and then endorsed the first female preacher, evangelist, and revivalist in human history. In John 4, Christ had *two full days* to run after the woman at the well and tell her to stop preaching because His Father didn't approve, or to run after the men and tell them they must stop listening to a female preacher. But instead, this same Messiah—who already knew His Father had personally appointed Deborah in a position of both judicial (judge) and spiritual (prophetess) leadership over all of His Old-Testament Church, Israel—sat in Sychar for two days, watched her bring in the harvest, and responded positively to her work. Now the kind of life He wishes His followers to lead is being expressed in the Epistles after His Ascension. Might this particular letter have been the first biblically canonized Epistle written by a woman through the same Spirit that led the woman at the well to become the first biblically recognized revivalist/evangelist? It's a provocative thought, at least—and one scholars are starting to take more seriously.

As one last aside before we launch into our look at the letter itself, the content of Hebrews is rich with Old-Testament quotes and references. (Seriously, they are all over the place, as one would expect to see in a book written to the readers of the Old Testament who are now believers in Jesus, the Man who fulfilled what the former Contract promised.) In the interest of keeping things running smoothly, we'll stick to what the book of Hebrews says to its New-Testament audience, refraining from listing repetitive citations from the Old Testament, as we believe that is the job of a study Bible. (But note that we still have the book Revelation ahead of us, which will more tightly link the Testaments together.)

Now, onto the document...

Without any introduction, the letter to the Roman Hebrews springs to life in a theological address that resembles a didactic tract, what we might call a "New Believer's Pamphlet." The writer immediately dives into explaining how God, throughout Israel's history, spoke through His prophets, and, through the culmination of His salvation plan, has now spoken through the Son. The Son, who created the entire universe, was given "all things" as a magnificent inheritance. He shares in God's glory and character, and His mighty command is what sustains everything throughout the world. When this Son took away the Hebrews' sins, He ascended to heaven and sat at the right hand of the Father. Therefore, His position is far above even that of the angels, and His Name is greater than their names (Hebrews 1:1–4).

The Father never said to any of the angels that they were His Son, but He did tell the angels to worship the Son, as they are His servants (1:5–7). To the Son, God said He would rule on an eternal throne forever with a scepter of justice. Because the Son is fair, but cannot stand evil, the oil of anointing has been poured out upon Him more than anyone else, ever (1:8–9). The Father also acknowledges to the Son that He has made the heavens and the earth with His hands, and that these things will someday perish like old, worn-out clothing, but the Son will live on forever. The angels were never told to sit at the right hand of God while He humbles His enemies and makes them like a footstool under the Son's feet, but the Son *was* told this, so the angels are only to be viewed by the Hebrews as servants who assist the inheritors of Christ's salvation work (1:10–14). If the Hebrews aren't careful to listen to and preserve the truth they've heard, they may find themselves slipping away from it. Jesus, Himself, was the first to announce this Good News, followed by those who walked with Him and heard His teaching. The Father confirmed all of this with signs, miracles, and wonders, as well as the gifts of the Spirit. In the past, a disregard for the warnings and truths of God resulted in punishment. How will the Hebrews be any different now if they ignore the message of salvation given through the Son? (2:1–4).

The Scriptures alluded to the Son when it referred to the One who would be made mortal, lower than the angels for a time, but He was crowned with glory and honor and was given all things. God's plan of grace was that Jesus would take the bitterness of death upon Himself and bring the people of God into glory with Him, and Jesus was the One who made this possible. Thanks to Him, the people of God are now the *children* of God: part of His family. Even Jesus—

God in the flesh—is not ashamed to call Christians His brothers and
sisters. Because humans are made of flesh and blood, the Son became
flesh and blood. He could only perform His salvation work if He
died; He could only die if He were human; therefore, He could only
break the power of death and the devil and set people free if He consented to this plan of becoming human and dying for all of humanity!
He didn't sacrifice Himself in this way for angels, and it is as a result
of going about it in this way that He can also relate to what it's like
to face the tests and trials of a human life like the Hebrews are doing
(2:5–18).

So, the Hebrews must think about this Son, this High Priest, this
supreme Apostle of the faith, and remember Him as One similar to
Moses. Moses, too, was faithful in his calling when he served God.
(By using Moses as an example, the writer of Hebrews is intentionally
bringing in the grandest of all heroes to the Jews. Moses was, until
Christ, the ultimate model of all good things.) But Jesus deserves far
more praise than even Moses! It is kind of like comparing the praise of
a house-builder to the praise of a house, itself. The house is not worthy
of the praise, but if the house is praiseworthy, then its builder is the
one who deserves the credit for the wonderful end product. Moses'
faithfulness in the house of God is irrefutable, but everything good
that he did only pointed to the great mystery of salvation the Father
would reveal in His timing. The Son is in charge of the house of God,
and now, Christians like these Hebrews, *are* the house of God, but it
is necessary to remain confident in the hope of Him (3:1–6).

The Holy Spirit instructs the Hebrews not to harden their hearts
to Christ as their ancestors did when they rebelled against God in
the wilderness, for forty years, testing His patience despite signs and
miracles. The Hebrews *must* remember this history and make sure
they never fall away from God as unbelievers, lest they find themselves
excluded from the blessed rest of God (3:7–19).

If even some of the Hebrews fail to experience God's rest, it should
be such a frightening thought that the whole congregation should

tremble at the idea. Only those who believe can have the blessed rest of God. The source of this blessing is God, not Moses or even Joshua, but God, who Himself rested on the seventh day, and He is offering it now, today, for believers. The Word of God is sharper than even the most glittering and new double-edged blade. It has the power to cut between soul and spirit, revealing even our innermost secret thoughts and desires: Everything in creation is known by God, and there is no hiding anything from Him, to whom all people are accountable. As a result, the Hebrews should accept the message of the High Priest, holding firm to belief in Him. Jesus was human! Even though He never sinned, He went through all the same temptations the rest of humanity faces, and He understands our weaknesses and limitations. So the Hebrews must be bold in their approach to the throne of God where they will receive grace, mercy, and assistance whenever they need it (4:1–16).

As the Hebrews know, a high priest is one chosen to represent other people to God, making sacrifices for the atonement of their sins and presenting good gifts to God upon the altar for their gratitude. Because he is also a man, just like they are all regular people, he knows how to deal with them gently when they go astray. Yet, no man can simply decide he wants to hold the office of a high priest. This important position is given directly by God to the rightly appointed person who is called, as Aaron was, for this work. Christ was chosen by God to be the High Priest for humanity, in the very highest order, after the priest Melchizedek, as He was and is the Son of the Father. When Jesus became a human, He offered up prayers and pled with God near the time of His death, having to face unthinkable, mortal things, but being submissive to suffering uniquely qualified Him as the High Priest of humanity and the Source of salvation for all believers (5:1–10).

There are so many more things to be said on this matter, but the Hebrews don't appear to be listening, so it's hard to explain to them. They've been believers long enough that they *should* be teaching others by now, yet they still require being told the basics of the faith, like babies who can only drink milk and have not yet graduated to solid food... But the time is now to stop addressing the basics over and over again. Instead, the Hebrews should become mature believers, feeding on solid food and embracing a more mature understanding. They won't benefit from yet again discussing baptisms, laying hands on people when they pray, resurrection, or eternal judgment (5:11–6:3).

Those who have experienced what heaven offers—the Holy Spirit and the Word of God—then turn from Jesus and nail Him to the cross all over again are beyond help. When it rains, the ground soaks up the water and produces good harvest; this is a blessing from God. But a field covered in nothing but thorns and thistle bushes is useless. A farmer would choose to burn it down. The Hebrew recipients of this letter aren't those to whom the author refers (in this word picture). The writer of Hebrews is confident that the congregation receiving this communication will go on to experience the good things salvation brings. God will not forget their hard work for the Lord and their concern for others, but for as long as they live, the writer desires they should continue this good work of faith, loving others, so they don't become indifferent in their Gospel work (6:4–12).

God promised Abraham many descendants, and Abraham was faithful to believe in that promise until he received it. When people make oaths, they name-drop, using someone higher than themselves as collateral to show that the oath is binding. God, too, gave humanity an oath, and it is not possible for Him to lie. Therefore, believers in the promises of God can believe them with confidence. The Christian's hope in His Word is the anchor of the soul that leads believers into His presence, His inner sanctuary, and Jesus—of the high order of Melchizedek—has already entered this place on the Hebrews' behalf as their High Priest (6:13–20).

Melchizedek, whose name means "king of justice," was the king of Salem—meaning king of peace—and a priest of the Most High God. After a battle against other kings, Abraham was on his way home from a victory when he met up with Melchizedek, who blessed him. Abraham gave a tithe of ten percent of his battle winnings to Melchizedek. Melchizedek's ancestry is a mystery. He has no father or mother anyone can find, and no record of the beginning or end of his life that they know of, making him a priest forever, resembling the Son of God. And this man was great! Abraham even recognized this about him when he gave him ten percent of his winnings. The Mosaic Law required that the priests, who are Levites, get ten percent from the other tribes of Israel. But Melchizedek received his tithe from Abraham, the father of all tribes. Then, when Melchizedek blessed Abraham, who had already received God's promises, it shows believers that the person who has the power to bless is greater than the one who receives a blessing. If the order of the priesthood based on the Levites was capable of achieving the perfection God originally hoped for, then why would there be a need for a new priesthood, with a Priest in the order of Melchizedek? And *since* the priesthood is now altered, the Law must be altered to allow for that change as well. The High Priest, Jesus, came from the tribe of Judah, not Levi, and His members are not priests who serve at the altars (7:1–14).

Since Jesus appeared, the priesthood has changed. He did *not* become High Priest because of a tribe or ancestry, but through the power of defeating death. The Law never achieved perfection, but now we have hope in something that does—a system inaugurated by God's oath that is superior to anything inherited by the descendants of Abraham. God told Jesus that He was, is, and always will be the High Priest of this order forever, and that oath established Jesus as the guarantee of a new and better Covenant between His followers and God. In the old ways, priests could not stay in office forever, because they would eventually die. This Priest will never die, and therefore, His priesthood will never be replaced; it goes on forever. Nor is His office tainted with any kind of sin. His place, the highest in heaven, is far apart from sin. Likewise, the sacrifices of the past were on behalf of the priests and the people because sin affected them all, but Jesus was one Sacrifice for all, forever (7:15–28). Everything the priesthood has ever been since the system was established was a foreshadowing of this perfect Man who would replace it all. The High Priest, Jesus, reigns over the Law of the hearts and minds of people. The old system is obsolete (chapter 8).

With that said, the rules of the old system are also replaced. The children of God formerly had to follow the guidelines and policies of the Tabernacle. There were two rooms there: the Holy Place and the Most Holy Place. Priests of the Tabernacle were allowed to enter the Holy Place, but the Most Holy Place was only to be entered by the high priest one time per year, when he would offer a blood sacrifice for the sins of the people. This entire arrangement was set up to look forward to a better one. Christ became the perfect blood Sacrifice, having entered the perfect Tabernacle of heaven. If, in the old ways, the blood of animals could cleanse, how much more can Christ's blood cleanse in this new covenantal system? This is why He is the mediator between mankind and God, and believers like the Hebrews are inheritors of the eternal promise of God (9:1–15).

When a person leaves a will, nothing on that will matters while he or she is still alive. Obviously, the will only goes into effect after the person is deceased. That explains why the first Covenant was made with the blood of an animal who had died for that purpose. Without the shedding of blood, there is no such thing as forgiveness. The New Covenant was made with the shedding of blood also, but it had to be a superior kind of blood: that of Christ. And just as a person only dies once and thereafter faces judgment, Jesus only had to die once, for all time, and for all people, to conquer sin…and He is coming back again! This time, it's not to die for sin, but to consummate His salvation work (9:16–28).

Jesus communicated to the Father that He was willing to be this single Sacrifice for all. By this, the Old Covenant was cancelled and the New Covenant was put into effect. Then, Jesus sat at God's right hand in the place of honor. He waits there until His enemies become a "footstool" under His feet. His one-time sacrifice made perfect those who are holy. When sins are forgiven, sacrifices are no longer needed (10:1–18).

Therefore, now that the Hebrews have a High Priest, they should be confident moving past the curtain and entering the Most Holy Place. They must hold tight to the hope they have in Him, without wavering, trusting that God honors and keeps His promises. Their interest should become loving others and doing good, coming together in gatherings, and encouraging one another. But if they continue to sin, even after being given the knowledge of truth, then no further sacrifice will cover those sins. The only thing facing those folks is God's wrath and judgment. When someone disobeyed the Mosaic Law in the past, in front of two or three eyewitnesses, he or she was put to death. How much worse will the punishment be for those who trample the blood of the Son underfoot and consider His sacrifice common and ordinary? (10:19–31).

The Hebrews should remember their first days as believers. They remained faithful even under extreme persecution, and they did so with joy, because of the anticipation of those wonderful and eternal promises of God. They mustn't throw all of that away now! They have to think on the great reward of their work and continue to do God's will if they want to receive all that God has promised. They must not be like those who turn away from God to their own destruction, but like the faithful ones whose souls will be saved in the end (10:32–39).

It is at this point that the writer of Hebrews arrives at the chapter of the Bible Christians call the "Hall of Faith." The author first explains that faith is the things hoped for and the evidence of things we cannot see (11:1). Then, the Hebrew readers are taken, step by step, through the examples set by heroes of faith in Israel's history: Abel, Enoch, Noah, Abraham, Isaac, Jacob, Sarah... All of these people believed in the promises of God, such as His promise to lead them to the Promised Land. Even when they had every human reason to doubt that He would follow through, and even when the Promised Land was not given to them in their lifetimes, they kept believing His promise. And even more ancient characters demonstrate this same type of faith, including Joseph, Moses, the Israelites who followed Moses during the Exodus, those who marched around Jericho, Rahab, Gideon, Barak, Samson, Jephthah, David, Samuel, and all the prophets (11:1–33). These people encountered miraculous signs and wonders, like extreme victories during times of war, the closing of the lions' mouths, quenching fires, escapes from death, and many other confirmations that their faith was in the right place. Others, like the Hebrews now, suffered immensely, being tortured, killed, shackled, stoned, or wandering about the world wearing animal skins. "These were all commended for their faith, yet none of them received what had been promised, since God had planned something better for us so that only together with us would they be made perfect" (11:34–40; NIV).

Therefore, since there are so many witnesses to the new life in Christ all around the Hebrews, they must show willingness to shed whatever sin is holding them back so they can run confidently in the race they've been called to run. This is done by keeping the focus of their lives on Christ, who was so looking forward to the joy on the other side of His sacrifice that He faced the cross without shame. And now, He is seated by the Father. He is the example to follow. Unlike Christ, the Hebrews have not yet given their very lives in the struggle against sin, and they will be confronted with heavenly discipline, like a father to a child. So they must strengthen themselves for the path ahead and never give up (12:1–13).

This means they must work to live holy lives that are pleasing to God: looking after each other, being on the lookout for bitterness that might take root and lead to corruption, and upholding morality. The Israelites came to the frightening Mt. Sinai, a physical mountain of God that was sacred ground. The Hebrews of this day have come to Mt. Zion, a holy place, a heavenly city of God where thousands of angels join together, where God is the only Judge, and where the spirits of the righteous are made perfect. They have come to Jesus, the Mediator between God and mankind, whose blood poured out for forgiveness. If the Israelites could not escape when they disregarded the earthly messenger, Moses, why would they think they could now escape from the heavenly Messenger, Jesus? The ground shook at Sinai, but now God is warning that the heavens and the earth will shake, all of Creation will be removed, and all that's left are the things that cannot be shaken. The Hebrew believers are now inheriting the Kingdom of God—the only thing that cannot be shaken—so they are to worship the King of this Kingdom in reverent fear and awe (12:14–29).

In conclusion, the writer of this sweet, emotional, and endearing letter to the Hebrews tells the audience: Keep on loving! Be kind to strangers, welcome them into your own very lives, because you may just be showing that kindness to an angel of God, even though you will not know that while they are on earth. Remember those who are in prison, as if you yourselves were locked up; remember those who are hurting, as if it is your own pain. Honor the sanctity of marriage and remain faithful in it, for God will judge those who are unfaithful in their marriage. Love God and His blessings more than the pursuit of money and earthly security. Never forget those who have gone ahead and paved the way for ministry. Much goodness has come from them, and they are wonderful examples to follow. Jesus never changes; He is the same right now as He was yesterday, and He will be the same tomorrow, so the Hebrews must never be misled by strange and new doctrines about Him. God's grace is a matter of the heart, not a matter of what kinds of food or meats are put into the body. These concerns don't help anyone who obsesses about such matters. The altar Christ's followers can approach for food is not the one of the old system of priests in the Tabernacle. The priests of old sacrificed animals, and the remains of the sacrifice were carried outside the camp and burned. So, too, was Jesus sacrificed outside the city to make the righteous holy by His own blood. Therefore, believers should go to Him outside the city and bear His disgraceful burdens with Him—because this earth is not our permanent home. That perfect place is yet to come, and Christians should be offering up a sacrifice of praise to the One whose Name you have made allegiance to. Care for those in need, which is a sacrifice that pleases the Lord. Obey spiritual leaders. Their burden of watching over the souls of others is a heavy one, and they should be supported in their endeavors so they can carry out that work with joy, not sorrow (13:1–17).

The author of the letter asks for the audience's continued prayers (13:18–19), then blesses the Hebrews, saying:

> Now the God of peace, that brought again from the dead our Lord Jesus, that great shepherd of the sheep, through the blood of the everlasting covenant, Make you perfect in every good work to do his will, working in you that which is wellpleasing in his sight, through Jesus Christ; to whom be glory for ever and ever. Amen. (13:20–21)

In closing, the believers are urged to receive what is written in the letter. A quick note is made about Timothy being released from prison and the intent to bring him to see this congregation if he travels that way. The congregation and its leaders should all be greeted, and the believers in Italy also send their hellos. The document ends: "Grace be with you all. Amen" (13:22–25).

As we said, we'll probably never know whether Hebrews was written by of Paul. But because we know the writer was heavily influenced by Paul's theology and mission, it still feels like we're peeking into the *thoughts* of Paul when we read it. It may have been dictated by him, but even if it wasn't, scholars almost unanimously conclude that it was composed by someone who was taught under him directly. So, his heartbeat for ministry lives on through this Epistle.

We have been immersed in his letters for so long now that it seems strange to be leaving Paul's work and moving on to books with other known authors. With that said, a final note on Paul seems appropriate here.

Jesus said there is no greater love on earth than for one to lay down his life for a friend (John 15:13). If Eusebius is correct (and his is the most widely accepted explanation of Paul's death among Christian scholars), then Paul was beheaded at the same time as Peter was martyred by decree of Emperor Nero circa AD 64–67. (Paul was exempt from crucifixion because he was a Roman citizen, but tradition teaches that Peter was crucified upside down.) Most folks don't immediately consider Paul's martyrdom as an act of "laying down his life for a friend," but when we actually consider his life, that's precisely what he did. Paul had every opportunity to walk a path void of controversy, living the quiet life as a tentmaker of the ancient world, never travelling in harsh winds or across the seas during storms and angering the rulers of the establishment who were against Christianity. He could have even lived as a Christian in secret, choosing to believe on the sly while he watched his brothers and sisters being persecuted. If we're honest, that's what many of *us* would choose to do. Instead, he pored over the Scriptures and wielded his pen night and day and circulated his theology of the Risen Christ to the megachurches of his time, simply daring anyone to try to stop him as he pummeled the dark principalities of the spirit realm with one major Epistle-hit after another. His letters served to strengthen the early Church and root out evil from its midst, encouraging followers of Christ to stand strong against opposition—even to the point of death.

When the world said, "Paul, you're gonna get yourself killed if you don't stop talking about this Jesus," Paul said, "Then they better kill me fast, because until they do, this mouth of mine will *never* stop preaching about Him."

When the world said, "Paul, you're not listening! You really need to stop writing these letters! The Roman government is getting nervous about the work you're doing for these Christians." Paul said, "If they take my hands, I'll oversee someone who will write for me. If they gouge out my eyes, I'll dictate. If they deafen me and cut out my tongue, the power of God will find a way. I will not stop. They will *have to* kill me to silence me."

When the world said, "Paul, don't you understand? They *are* gonna kill you! You're treating this as if it's a game, but they're serious. Are you not concerned about your very own death?" Paul said, "I would consider it a privilege. Death is better than life, because I long to see my Savior."

No matter what the threat, each time the world said, "Warning! Warning!" Paul said, "Bring it on."

The question then becomes: Who was Paul doing this for? It certainly wasn't for his own benefit. Yet it doesn't require more than common sense to see exactly who Paul was willing to lay his life down for. Most immediately, considering the texts he was compiling, we see he had many friends and associates in the same line of work. It was for them he died, so they might grow as mature ministers of Christ and continue boldly in proclaiming the only message that saves. Another reason he died was for recipients of his letters—for any potential believer whose soul he cared for so tremendously that he willingly positioned himself in the line of execution to reach them. As long as he was able to help that one little, old Jewish widow over here or that young, orphaned Gentile man over there understand that Christ died for them, too, he deemed his own life as of zero importance. Paul could never consider his own mortal existence to be more important than the least of them.

But when Paul submitted himself to the cruelty of Nero that ultimately did bring an end to his time here on this planet, it was for his Friend, Jesus, whom he loved more than any other. Paul, literally, and to the fullest extent of the words, "laid his life down for a Friend," and there was "no greater love" he could have shown for his Messiah than this. It's convicting, thinking of him in a prison cell, already "dead" to society, yet living more powerfully than perhaps any other Christian in history because he so believed in his calling and would not let anything, including threats of death or torture, stand in his way of accomplishing what he knew he was supposed to do for the Savior.

Any pastor today will say that there are some challenging times on the job… Some people come into the Family of God, worship Him for a time of personal revival, then begin to slowly turn back to their old vices. They know what's right, as they've been taught the basics of the faith and morality already, but they give in to human weakness and return to their former lives, even if they keep attending church on Sundays. Pastors who know very well to follow the example of Paul then become shepherds to these people, repeating former teachings they've already said in the hopes of hitting a new heartstring or nerve and bringing them back to the message of salvation. This is a tough line of work that requires immense, supernaturally endowed patience, as these precious souls are in continual need of a shepherd who will draw them back to the flock over and over again each time they wander away. In the flesh, many of these modern leaders (if they're honest) are tempted to take these members aside and shout, "You've already been taught what is right in these situations! Why are you still doing these self-destructive things!?" And whereas that might be the right thing to do as a last resort in a very rare and intimate case (Paul wrote similar things a few times), most of the time, that human reaction would cause the accused to turn away from the flock and make them feel ostracized from the Family… So the preachers and teachers lift up ongoing prayers for patience as they try to juggle giving milk to some and meat to others in the same congregation.

It's a stressful office to hold, no doubt about it. The phrase "being pulled in multiple directions at once" barely summarizes the pressure these soldiers of Christ are under. (For those who have been there, THANK YOU for your service to the Kingdom! You *will* be remembered for the kindness you have shown to the lost!)

Though this is a position many contemporary Christians can relate to (or at least imagine, as we've heard similar stories from fellow believers in our day), it was much—*much*—more demanding for Paul. We know from the biblical account that Paul started the churches at Ephesus, Philippi, Corinth, Thyatira, Philadelphia,

Smyrna, Laodicea, Pergamum, Syria, Arabia, Sardis, and three others in Cypress and Crete (totaling fourteen). However, from the moment each of these was planted, it sprouted even more around it that Paul assisted in the early growth of. This is why the answer to the question, "How many churches did Paul establish?" is hard to answer. After following the historical and geographical trail of the first century, many scholars believe Paul was the direct authority over more than twenty churches while he lived.

If your eyes haven't bulged out of your head yet, read this again: Paul was direct "pastor" over more than twenty churches!

By itself, that is an overwhelming number that would cause the average minister today to run away screaming, but this still isn't even close to the whole picture. Christianity was in its infancy. The new Church could not, as we can today, turn to the New Testament for answers to their theological and moral problems, as it was in the process of being written, so the demands on Paul were all the more frantic, desperate, and pleading. Without his personal supervision, the believers of the first century had nobody to help them and no scriptural teaching to turn to. They were simply lost, scrambling to figure out matters of love, generosity, morality, and doctrine on their own, and he was therefore compelled (and thankfully Spirit-strengthened) to respond to the constant needs of *all of them*.

So far, in putting ourselves in Paul's place, we have the following scenario: You are a pastor of twenty-plus congregations; you have no books or scrolls on the subject to stand in for your teaching so you can take a day off; believers keep falling into the same traps of sin over and over, and you're the only one who can encourage them to correct their actions; there's a "thorn" in your flesh that makes what you do ceaselessly uncomfortable; when you're not in prison, you're travelling across tumultuous seas, enduring shipwrecks and hurricanes, or journeying across endless miles of hot sand and soil in anticipation of reaching the next town—just to arrive in hostile territory and have your life repeatedly threatened by those who hate you. Yet, somewhere in the midst of all of this, you have to find time to build those tents for commerce, because you refuse to be a financial burden on the fledgling Body.

Now add to all of this the fact that a managerial or hierarchical structure in the Church did not exist at the time. Sure, Paul had friends and associates who helped him; that much is clear. But the advantage of modern leadership gatherings did not exist—like those that fall under terms such as "General Assembly," "General Council," "Ecumenical Council," "Plenary Council," "Provincial Council," "Board of Ministers," "synods," or even smaller rallies like "regional presbytery meetings" and other such administrative groups that make up the modern denominational governing bodies of church leaders. Paul was *the* authority! If an issue arose in his time, he couldn't shoot a quick email or text to the administrators telling them: "Brothers, we have an emergency in Crete. Titus just informed me that half his congregation is secretly meeting at midnight on Tuesdays at the labyrinth of Knossos to pay spiritual homage to King Minos. We need to rally immediately and discuss what our formal, theological response and probationary actions are going to be for whichever of these believers doesn't desist immediately. Meet me at the Temple on the first Monday of next month to address this. Between now and then, I need all hands on deck to dig into everything we know of this pagan entity's history, as well as all Scripture pertinent to his legend: bestiality, demigods and idolatry, sacred labyrinths and grounds, and so on." (That was just an example, by the way, of countless problems the early Church might have had that the Bible is silent on.) Paul had no choice but to "babysit" the entire ancient world at the time, responding like an expert to *all* hiccups in the practice of worship throughout an enormous region whose believers—with all due respect—had no idea of what they were doing. He was everything to everybody, and rather than pout and moan, griping about endless responsibilities, he counted it all a great joy to serve his Master in this way!

No matter how many times we attempt to imagine what it was

like to have been Paul, we will never be able to fully understand the intense burden he bore. And his attitude never fell. He never once became discouraged and cursed God or switched theologies under the pressure of Judaizers and pagans. He never stopped loving the wanderers who continually floundered in their beliefs and ping-ponged between following his teachings and those of heretics. He wasn't given a retirement date or a going-away party wherein his fellow ministers would pat him on the back, thank him for his faithful work in the Kingdom, and then let him live out the rest of his life peacefully with a wife, kids, a white picket fence, and a cable subscription.

Before his death, on many occasions, he was beaten severely in front of large crowds who taunted him for the claims he made about the Messiah, modeling his life after the One who died for sin…and he did it all without even considering a different choice.

As we move on now to other New Testament authors and wrap up our Epistles section, we beseech readers to remember Paul as the supreme example-setter, the standard-setter of Christian behavior— just under that of Jesus, Himself.

However, that's not to say the other church leaders of the day weren't of equal zeal in their passionate ministries to the lost, or in their bold rebukes of heresy and squabbling among members. One great example of this is James.

James

WE HAVE NOW ARRIVED at the group of Epistles known as the "Catholic Letters." This term tends to infer a connection to Catholicism as a denomination, but that's not the case. The English word "catholic" is from the Latin *catholicus*, which is itself derived from an adjective in Greek, *katholikos*, meaning "about the whole," or more simply, "universal." Therefore, "Catholic Letters," as a category of literature, denotes a universal audience as opposed to a particular person, city, or church. Please note that, for our following reflection on the Epistle of James, readers may recognize some material from Howell's book, *Radicals*, which is a line-by-line study of this powerful (but short) book. In a similar way that the backdrop of Ephesians also served as the backdrop for 1 and 2 Timothy, the familial connection between Jesus and James in this section will serve as the framework for the relationship between Jesus and Jude (His other half-brother) when we reach our study of the Epistle of Jude.

In James 1:1, the writer only identifies himself as "James, a servant of God and of the Lord Jesus Christ." Although theories abound as to the authorship of this book, only three concepts deserve real focus, as they're the only ones that present any substantive connection to the timeline and development of the early Church:

1. James the Great (also "Greater"), a central apostle of Christ, brother of John, and son of the fisherman Zebedee
2. James, the son of Alphaeus
3. James, the half-brother of Christ, later a key leader of the early Church

Several valid arguments throughout the ages have strongly supported the half-brother of Christ as being the one who wrote this Epistle.

As for the first option, James the Great, he was martyred by Herod in AD 44 (Acts 12:2). The letter was dated to circa AD 60–62. Thus, James the Great was deceased by the time the letter was written, leaving only the son of Alphaeus and Jesus' half-brother as candidates.

Second, regarding James, the son of Alphaeus, we know almost nothing of this person, while the name of Jesus' half-brother James was on nearly everyone's lips around Palestine in that day. Thus, the simplicity of the introduction to this Epistle implies that a lengthier self-identification wasn't necessary. Had the son of Alphaeus been the author, an identifier would have likely been given, so the book would *not* have been attributed to the half-brother of Christ, who was such a well-known and distinguished leader at the time of the book's writing that he had been called a "pillar of the church" by Paul (Galatians 1:19; 2:9). Since a description of the author is missing from the Epistle entirely, it appears a valid assumption that no further explanation was necessary, for, of course, the half-brother of Christ and pillar of the early Church did not need a grand introduction. (The name of James, the son of Alphaeus, was not prominent in any writings of that time, including the scriptural records. Serious scholars and theologians have largely dismissed the notion that he had anything to do with writing this book.)

Third, we look at James, the half-brother of Jesus. Much internal and external documentation points to this man as being the author of this Epistle. Here are several of those indications:

1. The language style in the book matches the language style used in the speech the half-brother gave the Jerusalem council in Acts 15:13–21.

2. Descriptions of the half-brother throughout the New Testament (see Acts 12:17; 21:18; 1 Corinthians 15:7; Galatians 1:19; 2:9, 12) seamlessly agree with what is known about the writer of the Epistle.

3. The letter was written from a Jewish background, also featuring Hebrew idioms translated into Greek; it reflects a great respect for the Mosaic Law, which would have been consistent with the upbringing and education of the half-brother.

4. Jude, the *other* half-brother of Christ and largely uncontested author of the book by that name, began his writing with the same introductory identifier, referring to himself as a "servant of Jesus Christ"—much like a familial, household moniker—but then he went on to identify himself as "a brother of James [the half-brother of Christ]" (Jude 1), the aforementioned, well-known "pillar."

5. According to Donald Guthrie of *New Testament Introduction,* "There are more parallels in this Epistle than in any other New Testament book to the teaching of our Lord [Christ] in the Gospels."[193] This is significant, as theologian David Mallick says: "James is producing reminiscences of oral teaching which he previously heard for himself [from his half-brother, Christ],"[194] which is yet another familial connection.

6. Many historians and Church fathers attributed the Epistle to the half-brother, including Origen and Eusebius.

With so much evidence pointing to the fact that the "James" of the Epistle was, in fact, the half-brother of Christ, we will continue now according to that conclusion. This identification tends to raise an interesting question: "What would it have been like to be the sibling of *the* Jesus Christ?"

Though members of the Catholic faith typically believe in Mary's perpetual virginity, scriptural evidence claims otherwise. She was certainly a virgin when the Holy Spirit came upon her and Christ was conceived, but following that, she gave birth to at least six other children. In Luke 2:7, we read that Mary "gave birth to her first-born." The word "firstborn" (as opposed to "only") indicates there were other children. In Matthew 13:55 and Mark 6:3, the question is asked about Jesus, "Isn't this the carpenter's son?"; further, Christ's "brothers" (as opposed to "cousins" or other relations) are named specifically—James, Joses (Joseph), Simon, and Judas (Jude, who is of no connection to Judas the betrayer)—as well as "sisters," which is plural (meaning at least two, equaling a total of at least six siblings and possibly more). All of these would have been half-brothers and half-sisters to the immaculately conceived Jesus Christ, the aforementioned carpenter's Son—not cousins or spiritual family.

Mary, Joseph, Jesus, James, Joseph Jr., Simon, Jude, and the sisters lived together as a family unit. Christ was around the age of thirty when He began His public ministry, but prior to that, He shared a home life with them in much the same way any normal family of that time would—except for the fact that He never sinned, not even once (1 Peter 1:18–19; 2:22; 2 Corinthians 5:21; Hebrews 4:15; 1 John 3:5).

Various extrabiblical stories about Jesus' childhood have circulated throughout history. They relate accounts of how, when He was a youth, Christ purified water, made clay sparrows and breathed life into them, commanded a tree to arc its branch so He could reach its fruit, resurrected a friend, resurrected a teacher, multiplied wheat, lengthened wood in the carpentry shop, stood in an assembly of predatory animals while they worshipped Him reverently, healed a woodcutter, and healed James from a snakebite wound, as well as other less popular legends. None of these stories are biblical; we do have biblical proof that they are all the workings of uninspired human imagination. Luke 2:40 states simply that Jesus grew, became strong, gained wisdom, and was bestowed with God's grace, but there is no account of Jesus performing childhood miracles or amazing signs and wonders. As a child running around in sandals and giving warm-hearted greetings to His neighbors, Christ was like any other little boy. This is reflected in how the people of His hometown reacted to Him in His later ministry years (Mark 3:21). (Also note that in John 2:11, the miracle Christ performed when He turned the water into wine at the wedding in Cana was the "beginning" of His signs and wonders, so there would not have been any prior.)

Although Christ's childhood was comparatively normal, Hebrews 5:8 states that His obedience was "by the things which he suffered," so we know He experienced suffering and sadness. He met temptation face to face on a regular basis, as any human would, "in all points [from every angle, at each turn, in every stage of His life] tempted like as we are, yet without sin" (Hebrews 4:15). From these verses and others, we have proof that the world and the people around Christ were the same kind of world and people surrounding any normal boy being raised in a fallen state, but He was *perfect*.

The childish and prideful back talk to their parents that may have come out of the mouths of Jesus' playmates would have been enticing for Him to repeat as well. The same pretty eyes that would have caught the attention of the other young men would have caught the attention of Christ. The same theft, lies, deceit, egotism, vanity, self-gratification, covetousness, greed, laziness, enviousness, disrespectfulness, anger, frustration...*all* flew in front of His face every day of His life, or else He would not have been "tempted like as we are."

Despite this, Christ never entertained an immoral thought, had a poor attitude, challenged or defied His parents, grumbled about what was on the supper table or argued about eating all His vegetables, quarreled with his younger siblings, said a bad word, talked about people behind their backs...and He never squandered a second of His time on earth. By the time Christ was the age of twelve, if not before, He understood who He really was after it came to Mary and Joseph's attention that He was not in the family caravan leaving Jerusalem after the Passover pilgrimage. (Boy-Jesus wasn't the kind of child a parent would normally have to track down, so it wasn't until a full day's journey they realized He was missing.) They located Him in the Temple courts after three days of searching. He was visiting nonchalantly with the teachers there, who were astounded at His astute and learned interactions. When Mary asked why Jesus hadn't stayed with the family, He responded by asking her and his father why they had to search for Him in the first place. Didn't they know He would be in His Father's house, going about His Father's business (Luke 2:41–49)?

This response was not disrespectful. Instead, it was a prodigious affirmation that Jesus knew very well who He was, as He calls God "My Father" and asserts to His parents that He was aware of His charge.

He didn't get in trouble for having gone missing, either, because His parents understood there was something significant about Jesus' decision to meander through the Temple courts. Mary and Joseph knew the boy was the Son of God, thus would one day do something immense to our planet—so far be it from them to hinder His progress or punish Him during the preparative steps of His youth. The Scripture simply says that, after Jesus' response, "he went down with them [His family], and came to Nazareth, and was subject unto them [He obeyed His parents]: but his mother kept all these sayings [His response about His Father's house/business] in her heart. And Jesus increased in wisdom and stature, and in favour with God and man" (Luke 2:51–52). Even though Christ's appointment in the Temple was an ordained moment in His life, once He was discovered, He was agreeably subject to the authority of His earthly parents. And, for eighteen years following, Jesus remained with His family as a son and a brother.

As a parent, a perfect child would be the one we all would want to raise. As a sibling, however…

Imagine *that*!

Christ was fully God, but He was also fully human; therefore, He would have had boyish moments with James as they both grew. Many younger siblings follow the older ones around. They probably threw sticks together. They likely skipped rocks together. Jesus probably ruffled James' hair. The idea that they would have playfully wrestled around is not a stretch. We can see several adorable scenes unfold in our imaginations at the mere thought of boy-Jesus.

When Donna Howell was a little girl, she and her older brother, Joe Horn of SkyWatch Television, used to play "church." He would set up "pews" out of couch pillows and fill them with stuffed animals, and Howell was his "worship leader," playing an air piano (or the bricks near their fireplace), and as she sang, Joe would stand nearby strumming a real box guitar and uttering hearty hallelujahs. When the "worship service" concluded, Howell would take her seat in the front "pew" and listen to a two-minute sermon Joe would preach (usually the same one about obedience and faithfulness in a sinful world), then he would ask for a raising of hands as a response to a life-changing question, which was usually a word-for-word repetition of what he'd heard being given from the pulpit at the real church their family attended. Joe pretended there was a whole congregation, his voice rising and falling with the rhythm of the familiar words: "Every head bowed; every eye closed. How many of you men and women out there are ready to stop [doing such-and-such] and make a lifelong commitment this morning? I see that hand. I see that one, too. How many of you are willing to do what it takes to follow through with that commitment?... Hands all across the building, folks. Hallelujah. You see this, Lord? Your children are ready for Your presence this morning."

Then the young siblings would have an "altar call." Howell remembers one teddy bear she had as a girl. She had safety-pinned a handkerchief sling around its arm, and that bear must have been "healed" of its broken bones thirty times. She saw many a stuffed animal give its heart to the Lord in those days.

How did James and Jesus play? What did their youthful, brotherly love look like? Did they, too, play "synagogue"? Did Jesus practice His oratory skills before a congregation of James, Jude, Simon, Joseph Jr., a few sisters, rocks, and figs? Did they imagine that the trees' raised branches were a "response" to a call to turn over their lives to Yahweh? Were other children from the area involved, submitting themselves as "proselytes" for baptism? Certainly, we mean no disrespect by presenting such extrabiblical imaginings, but we believe too many folks want to abolish any idea of young Jesus playing like a regular Jewish boy would, as if He came out of the womb quoting from the Septuagint. Yet, the Scripture clearly indicates that, aside from having a spotless character and leading a sinless existence, Jesus' life was normal until the wedding at Cana. Doesn't it make Jesus Christ even *more* endearing and lovable as a Friend—a true Companion to humankind—to believe He enjoyed such playtime? (The notion of "playing synagogue" is not outlandish, anyway, considering how the articulate Christ during His ministry years appeared to always have an answer ready, even for the most difficult questions. Of course He was anointed, and it was from that anointing that His greatest moments sprang, but perhaps some preaching to the bushes may have been a part of His development, as well. We can't wait to ask…)

James may have challenged Jesus to races around the fields. Jesus was probably the first responder when James suffered a skinned knee. When James was sad, Jesus' arm must have been the first to land on His little brother's shoulders in comfort. When James had questions about Yahweh, no doubt that the astute and learned Jesus—the same Jesus who astounded the teachers of the Temple courts—would have been able to provide His kid brother answers.

James was *familiar* with Jesus.

Of course, this is not to say James never would have been challenged as the younger sibling of God Almighty. Many adults can remember a parent from their youth saying, "Why can't you be more like your [brother or sister]?" We wonder if, or how many times, James might have heard the equivalent of this question.

Mary and Joseph never had any reason to discipline Jesus, because He was the perfect child. All they could do as parents was show Him love and constant affection. From a human standpoint, that may be, in part, why His brothers and sisters later rejected Him as the Messiah (John 7:5). When the day came that Jesus had performed miracles and signs—and even the "unclean spirits, when they saw him, fell down before him, and cried, saying, Thou art the Son of God" (Mark 3:11)—His brothers and friends said He was crazy, that He had cracked, that He was "beside himself" (Mark 3:21). Those of His hometown were "offended at him" when He taught in the synagogue (Mark 6:3). Jesus had known that moment would happen, and His response was, "A prophet is not without honour, but in his own country, and among his own kin, and in his own house" (Mark 6:4), meaning, "A prophet is celebrated everywhere but in his own hometown, and among his own relatives, and amidst his siblings."

Familiarity with Jesus and His perfection did not inspire James to believe in His Messiahship. James didn't find it easier to believe in His brother as the Son of God just because he had witnessed His unique character and flawlessness. No—in fact, it would have likely made it much harder. Christ was perfect, yes; but to James, He was a brother, a sibling, a part of the family, and an equal to other human men. James was the oldest son of the family aside from Jesus, so he would have had the longest time of all Mary and Joseph's children to observe his brother being a regular, non-miracle-working boy during their playtime or their hours spent carpentering. Despite Christ's ability to avoid angering His parents throughout His youth, James observed the behaviors of a regular boy. A nice boy, yes. A sweet boy, certainly. But God?! Equal to Yahweh? A *part of* Yahweh? Heavens, no... So normal was Christ's childhood that when His twelve disciples gathered to follow Him in His mission, the people in his hometown were anything *but* believing. They all thought He was crazy. That's how ordinary Christ's early years were! And James was up close and personal through every moment.

Yet, though James did not believe his half-brother's claims of being God, the day Christ bled to death on the cross in front of His mother and the Roman soldiers must have been a tragic day for James, indeed. The days of ruffling hair and wrestling around were over. The sermons in the woods to siblings and figs would not be preached again. The races through the fields were but a memory. What on earth must have been going through James' mind during that event? Did he still wholly reject the idea that Christ was Lord? Did he still believe that his brother was simply a sad and tragically misled crazy person? Or, perhaps, was there just an inkling of faith rising up within James that told him his brother was the real deal?

The world will probably never know what James felt the day Christ was crucified. What we *do* know, however, is that after Christ died and rose on the third day, He appeared to James in person (1 Corinthians 15:7). What an intense meeting that must have been. We can only imagine the previously doubting James falling on his face before his now-risen half-brother and Son of God with "nail prints" in His hands and a hole in His side from the spear (John 20:24–29)—the walking proof of death defeated, the living proof that He was, is, and always will be exactly who He says He is. And James wasn't the only one of the brothers who experienced enough personal testimony to believe. After Christ ascended into heaven, Jesus' mother *and the rest of His brothers* were present among the 120 believers in the Upper Room (Acts 1:14).

That was it. The appearance of Christ changed the course of James' life, and by extension, the course of history. As a result of their coming to believe, James and his brother Jude would both go on to write letters that would one day be included in the canon of New Testament Scripture.

At this point we can see how being the half-brother of Christ would *benefit* James. How unlikely his role as a leader of the early Church seemed when Jesus was first assembling His followers. Now, though, he stood as *most* likely to understand the pure nature of Christ's mission: Well before he was confronted with talk of Jesus as

Messiah, James had walked and talked and played and wrestled and bounced around with boy-Jesus during childhood. Years before James would ever see his brother be taken to trial and made to state which kingdom He belonged to, James would have been an eyewitness to how teen-Jesus interacted with others, what truth and wisdom He lovingly bestowed upon peers who were struggling with life's hard-hitting questions, and what encouragement He offered with words and in a way unmatched by any other person. Before Christ ever visited His forerunning cousin at the famous Holy-Spirit-descending baptismal of John the Baptist, James had watched as adult-Jesus poured Himself into His relationship with His Father, produced theological conclusions with truth and insight no one else could possibly have, formed opinions about religious authority, and approached the Jewish faith with unparalleled fervor at every turn.

Every day James had observed how Jesus responded to the world around Him. He knew what made Him laugh, what made Him cry, how He reacted when questions of this earthly existence arose, what He found inspirational versus what He saw as blasphemous, whom He saw as truly righteous versus whom He saw as pretenders in robes… *James knew what made Jesus tick.* The very familiarity that made James the unlikeliest of believers came full circle to make him the most likely of crucial early Church leaders! Who else on earth—except only Mary, Joseph, Joseph Jr., Simon, Jude, and "sisters"—would have had the privilege of living in such close proximity to God, Himself, in human form? Every reaction that Christ the Son of God had as a human, by nature of the Trinity, was precisely the same reaction the Holy Spirit and Creator Yahweh would have had, and James had a front row seat to watch God-in-the-flesh react to the world around them for thirty years. James' perspective was now enlightened so that he could distinctively understand Christ's nature and purpose. He could observe something in public and think, *My Brother would have hated that…* or, *If Yeshua were still here, He would have just hugged that woman for what she just did.*

James' authority is overshadowed by Paul's much of the time today because Paul wrote a significant portion of the New Testament, but having God in human form as a sibling for three decades, refusing to believe, then coming to believe—all this would have placed James in a position to speak with massive influence and authority in his day.

And *oh* did the early Church need a leader like James…

After the day the Christian Church was inaugurated when the Holy Spirit came upon Christ's followers at Pentecost, the twelve apostles went out to the surrounding territories to spread the Gospel. Many other key figures in Christ's circle also scattered from Jerusalem after observing the stoning of Stephen. A void was left right there in the middle of Jerusalem—the heartbeat city of God's people. Without a voice to reach the Jews with the truth about Jesus as Messiah in person, the most vital historical location in all would have been lost. So James stayed there and ministered to the people, and almost overnight became the bishop of the city, the pastor of the people, the shepherd of the flock. James was also:

- Present the day Paul came to meet secretly with the leadership of the local church in Jerusalem to tell them of his conversion (Galatians 1:18–19);
- One of the first recipients Peter commissioned the believers who had prayed for him to testify to regarding the account of his miraculous escape from prison (Acts 12:17);
- A head advisor and prominent groundbreaker in the council of Jerusalem when the question of Gentile fellowship and circumcision was raised (Acts 15), and it was at this council that, under the leadership of James and Peter, the sound doctrine of purification by faith alone (not by the observance of rituals or ceremony)—through the proof of the Holy Spirit's outpouring on uncircumcised Gentiles—was established for the Church;
- Still the leader of the church in Jerusalem when Paul was tried a decade later (Acts 21).

James was unquestionably positioned dead-center as the principal leader in Jerusalem, and much of the early Christian Church's health and stability from within the Holy City rested on his shoulders. Momentous accounts were to be brought to his attention directly. Not one central, early-Church issue occurred near Jerusalem without his knowledge and/or input. He served his post faithfully, and at every turn was active in preserving the Gospel message he believed his brother, Christ, had come to bring. Out of this unadulterated passion for Jesus Christ and His crucifixion and Ascension as the Son of God, James wrote a very important letter "to the twelve tribes which are scattered abroad" (James 1:1). He wrote the letter to encourage the early Christians who were suffering, to correct erroneous theology about the nature of salvation, and to urge his readers to more appropriately understand the relationship between true righteousness and good deeds. The language used in his exhortation is bold, vigorous, fearless, and passionate. He did not set out to flatter believers or stroke egos, but to blast the early Church with an outcry for repentance and righteous living. He wrote with the authority of a man who had observed God in the flesh for thirty years, and who had lived to see Him risen. He wrote to Jewish Christians who were dispersed throughout the land in hiding from the persecution of angry mobs and Herod Agrippa with the same wisdom flavor as that used by the writer of Proverbs. His robust call for uprightness among believers earned him the name "James the Just." (According to Eusebius in *Ecclesiastical History*, James was on his knees so much for his brethren that he developed rough skin like a camel's. This is why you may have heard of James referred to as "Old Camel Knees.")

James was the most *unlikely* leader of the early Church because of the familiarity he had while watching his brother grow…

But James, upon becoming a believer as an eyewitness account of the risen Christ, became the most *likely* leader of the early Church… because of the familiarity he had while watching his brother grow.

It's amazing what God will use, isn't it?

The first verse in the book of James is a greeting from James to the twelve tribes of Israel. James wasted no time in getting straight to the point by openly acknowledging the reality of harsh spiritual living conditions as early as verse 2. Christians are then told to "count it all joy" ("rejoice") when they meet with trials of various kinds, knowing that faith and obedience to the Word will test their patience—but in this test, patience and faith will grow if they remain vigilant in trials (James 1:1–4). (In other words: "Trials are not easy, but they are necessary.") If believers ask God for wisdom, they are assured they will receive it. In fact, James writes that when believer approach the Lord with a prayer for wisdom, God "upbraideth not [He will not hold it back]; and it shall be given him [who asks for it]" (1:5). (This is strong language representing a fact. Nowhere in the Word does it say that if believers pray for money, houses, cars, careers or jobs, spouses, children, or even a meal when one is starving to death it "shall" be given. Here, in a rare biblical oath regarding the outcome of prayer, followers of Christ are *promised* that what they ask for will be given to them. Remember that the next time you're in a sticky situation. Through the very half-brother of our Savior, in a letter included in the infallible and wholly inerrant Word of God, we are told that whenever we ask for this one thing, it will be given, guaranteed.) But there is a caveat: The asker must approach God with this request as one who expects the promise to be given. Those who casually ask God for wisdom—like an unstable man floundering on the waves of the ocean who tosses his faith to and fro—should not expect the Lord to respond favorably (1:6–8).

Believers who have no money are honored by God, while the riches of the wealthy man will fade away. God will bless those who are patient during testing and trials, and they will receive a crown of reward for their good work. And it must be remembered that God, Himself, will never tempt a believer toward sin. No person can ever claim that He did. For temptation comes from fallen human nature, and when sin is fed, it brings only death. God is only good, always, and He never changes (1:9–18).

Christians should not be impulsive and quick when it comes to getting angry, but they *should* be quick when it comes to listening, making sure that they don't speak out of turn or in an inappropriate manner. Anger can't lead to the righteousness that God desires, so they must purge the filth from their lives and accept the teaching of God's Word that has been planted in their lives. Believers are required to not only receive its teaching, but to carry out the actions that teaching expects of them. There is a difference between simply being a "hearer" of the Word and being a "doer" of the Word, and Christians are to be "doers." Being a "hearer only" is like a mirror: People can see themselves their reflection, but the minute they walk away, the details about what they look like start to blur. Their self-inspection accomplishes nothing but a memory of having seen what was there. Instead, deeply taking in the life-changing teaching of God completely transforms the reflection of our spiritual mirror images; we are set free, and God blesses those who carry out His commands with action. Meanwhile, a person who claims to be religious but does not control his tongue is fooling himself, and his religion is good-for-nothing. Pure, unadulterated religion is doing things like caring for the widows and orphans in their needs (1:19–27).

How can people who call themselves "Christians" claim to have faith in Christ while they simultaneously adopt an attitude of favoritism toward some people over others? How can they give a rich man a seat of honor at a gathering while telling a poor man in wretched clothing that he must sit on the floor? Doesn't this show quite transparently that they are driven by wrongful motives in their Christianity? Yet the poor are actually richer in their faith than anyone else, and they will inherit the same Kingdom at the end of their life as any believer. In fact, it's often the rich folks who oppress others, sue people in the court system, and slander the Name of Christ! There is no favoritism in the system of belief these early Christians belong to, and they are not loving others as they love themselves the way Scripture teaches. This is an intentional breaking of the laws of God, and a person who breaks only one of these laws is as guilty as the one who breaks them all. If believers want God's mercy, they must show God's mercy to others as well (2:1–13).

It is here in his letter that James makes his famously bold statement that faith without works is dead. Before we continue, we should stop to address the "faith" versus "works" issue. Many who are new to studying the Bible see a contradiction between the "faith alone" theology (which got a serious boost at the turn of the Protestant Reformation) and the message of James' letter, which appears to state the opposite. A brief note about the person of James outside this letter will help…

Circa AD 49 (around the time of Paul's return from his first missionary trip with Barnabas), an argument arose when teachers proclaimed that Christ *was* the Savior, but that faith in Him alone was not enough to ensure one's salvation. A believer also had to be circumcised and carry out selected Judaic customs from the Law of Moses, they said. What resulted was a syncretism of salvation through faith in Christ on the one hand and ceremonial tradition—or "works"—on the other. By now, we know Paul's stance on this issue very well. According to Romans 11:5–6, salvation is now a matter of grace—and if it is a matter of grace, then it cannot be a matter of works, "otherwise grace is no more [or "no longer"] grace."

The Jerusalem council was gathered to settle the issue. Paul, Barnabas, Peter, and this same James who was Jesus' half-brother were all at that meeting—though, as the pillar of the church, James served as the chief director. After "much disputing" (Acts 15:7), Peter stood to address everyone present, delivering a very wise line of reasoning: Through the recent proof of the Holy Spirit descending upon uncircumcised Gentiles who had *not* observed Judaic customs or traditions, God now "put no difference between us and them, purifying their hearts by faith"—and that to now place upon Christ's Gospel the "yoke" (burden) of such expectations was to "tempt God" (Acts 15:9–10). In such a brilliant and evidently irrefutable approach, Peter was making the point that sinners are saved, hearts purified, and spirits reunited after death to the presence of God through faith alone, and not through works. This he said in the presence of the presiding James, who confirmed Peter's sentiment of salvation through faith alone by saying, "God…did visit the Gentiles [He met them where they were regardless of the fact that they were not stringently following Mosaic Law or ceremony and had no intention to start doing so], to take out of them a people for his name [to claim them as His people]. And to this agree the words of the prophets, as it is written." (Acts 15:14–15). James then quoted from the Septuagint, in Amos 9, saying:

> After this I will return, and will build again the tabernacle of David, which is fallen down; and I will build again the ruins thereof, and I will set it up:
> That the residue of men might seek after the Lord, and all the Gentiles, upon whom my name is called, saith the Lord, who doeth all these things.
> James was central to the early Church's acceptance of salvation by faith alone, and not by works—and he proved it with his closing remark: "Wherefore my sentence [or "judgment"] is, that we trouble not them [other translations say "don't make it difficult for them"], which from among the Gentiles are turned to God" (Acts 15:19). Therefore, with this history in mind, recall that James did not believe, or teach, that a Christian is to follow rituals in order to be approved by God.

However, in his Epistle, which James wrote around this same time, he poses the question: "What doth it profit, my brethren, though a man say he hath faith, and have not works? can faith save him?" (James 2:14). But, as just mentioned, a few verses later, he states that faith without "works" is "dead" (James 2:17). At the onset, if one is willing to isolate the verses from the Jerusalem council in Acts 15 and these two from James, and quote them alongside each other outside of their proper context, it is easy to see a clear and present contradiction. So, to which camp does James really belong?

The error is found in the personal interpretations of the word "faith" versus what that word means to followers of Christ. To some, religious faith only means believing something exists—much like a child might believe in something or someone he or she can't see, like fairies or the bogeyman—or that one "belongs to the faith," as a member of a church or religious organization, or someone who "grew up in church." To this, James states, "Thou believest that there is one God; thou doest well: the devils also believe, and tremble" (James 2:19). In contemporary language, he is essentially saying, "You claim to believe in one God. You're doing well up to this point. Good job, guys. However, even the demons of hell believe in one God, but they will not live in heaven for eternity. How could they? They're demons! They tremble at the very thought of God!"

We are also taught in Hebrews that the definition of "faith" is believing in something unseen (11:1), while here, James is adding to that definition. Yet one verse does not *contradict* the other; it further *defines* the other. If faith only means believing a thing that you can't see exists, then an evil man (much like the demons just mentioned) could go about killing, pillaging, stealing, and creating worldly havoc in the name of Satan and still be taken to heaven when he dies, merely because he believed that Christ was the Messiah. Such a man would not even need to invite God into his life, repent, try to live according to God's guidelines, pray, have a relationship with God, or even have the remotest respect for God. Merely by believing a thing exists, this man would be saved even though his life is dedicated to the workings of God's greatest spiritual enemy. Heaven forbid that salvation would work that way! This man would "believe in" both Satan and Christ, but his "works"—and, by extension, his "faith through works"—would be satanically opposed to God. Speaking about this very concept of faith being separated entirely from works, James says, "Show me thy faith *without* thy works, and I will show thee my faith *by* my works" (James 2:18; emphasis added). Today, we might reword this: "Show me this religion of yours that has nothing to do with how you live. Then I will let you see how I live, and by my lifestyle you will know my religion." Christ, Himself, said similarly, "Ye shall know them by their fruits.... Even so every good tree bringeth forth [or "produces"] good fruit; but a corrupt tree bringeth forth evil fruit" (Matthew 7:16–17). James chose a different set of words than the ones his half-brother Jesus used, but he ultimately made the same statement: Our lifestyle and decisions produce the fruit by which we will be recognized as a "good tree" or a "corrupt tree." Real faith, *true* faith, is only genuine when our decisions reflect our belief with action.

God told the Old Testament prophet Hosea to marry a prostitute as a symbol of God's relationship with His people, Israel. Israel still "believed in" Yahweh, but their "works" opposed God, because they made sacrifices to pagan idols. As Hosea knew all too personally, some aspects of God's requirements regarding faith and works can be easier to grasp when compared to marital infidelity: If a man repeatedly cheats on his wife, but still believes in her, we still call him an "unfaithful spouse." In this context, faith is seen as a devotion, a duty, and a covenantal promise kept sincerely: Being "faithful" in a marriage requires the "works" of fidelity.

James' Epistle says we will know whether our faith is real or counterfeit based on whether we back our faith claims with behavior that proves it—the behavior that produces corresponding fruit. If we have true faith in the Lord, then the Holy Spirit will be within us. And if the Holy Spirit is within us, then we must endeavor to behave as if He is. When James began to hear of Christians who were embracing debauchery and still considered themselves saved simply because they believed something existed, he brought further definition to the word "faith," alerting the green believers that faith and works are equivalent and indistinguishable.

Faith, when it comes to religion, is a *verb*. By default, it is an action. James knew this better than many of his fellows (James 2:14–20).

He goes on to say that Abraham showed his faith in action, also. When he was told to sacrifice his son on the mountain, he carried out the command and offered his son on the altar before an angel of God stopped him and it was discovered that Isaac did not have to die after all. The Old Testament therefore redefines faith in this account, not by what Abraham believed, but what he *did* with that belief—obedience to God—and God counted him as righteous because of it. Rahab was also an example. She hid God's messengers, an *action* that backed her belief. So, just as the human body dies without breath, faith dies without action or works that qualifies belief (2:21–26).

So, though "faith" requires "works," it does not require "ritual," which is often followed out of rote duty, not lifestyle.

James goes on: The tongue is a wild thing. Not all Christians should become teachers, because those who do will be judged with more strictness. Yes, people make mistakes, but if only the tongue, itself, could be perfectly controlled, even the body could be controlled perfectly as a result. A giant horse can be made to go wherever its rider instructs, just by a small bridle in its mouth. Similarly, something even as seemingly insignificant as a rudder can make a massive ship turn in any direction. The tongue is the same idea; it is a small part of the body, but it can have a tremendous effect on listeners. Just a spark can set a whole forest ablaze, and the tongue can set one's whole life on fire if the speaker is not careful. Mankind has tamed every kind of animal imaginable—birds, snakes, and beasts of all kinds—but nobody can tame the tongue, as it is an unruly evil full of deadly poison. The same tongue in a man can praise God one minute and curse other people that God has created the next, but this is terribly wrong! Does a freshwater source also produce bitter waters? Does a fig tree sprout olives, or a grapevine sprout figs? No! Believers in God must control their tongues (3:1–12).

Again, we will depart from the Epistle for only a moment to clarify something. The tongue no man can *tame*, James writes. But note that James doesn't say the tongue cannot be brought under *control.*

If a wild animal—such as a snake whose nature is to bite and inject venom into whatever it can reach or feels threatened by—is tamed, then generally speaking, that is a permanent change. Save for some special circumstances (rabies, subsequent abuse, or what have you), once an animal is tamed, it's tamed. It is no longer "wild." But the tongue will always be wilder than even the most poisonous of snakes and, James says, it is deadly.

To read James' concerns about the tongue and then misquote 3:8 as justification for why a person "couldn't control" his or her words is a serious offense to God and Scripture, as well as to the people who are hurt as a result. The tongue can be brought under control, and it should be, but it will always require a continual effort, like a serpent whose nature will always be to strike but chooses instead to retreat into his hideaway; a dog that hovers nearby baring his teeth, whose personality will always be aggressive and dangerous, but who must always be under the authority of the owner; a lion with claws extended, tempted at all times to go for the kill, but whose trainer must govern it; an animal that cannot be tamed no matter the circumstances, and whose temperament will always be to harm, but whose handler must always be in control. That is the tongue. There is no taming it, and it is always proficient for use as a deadly poison. But it is also always capable of falling under the dominion of its possessor, and it must, if any teaching (or speech) is going to be just.

The Epistle continues by noting that if these readers are truly wise and understanding of the Lord's ways, they must prove it by living humble lives, doing the kinds of work that show that wisdom. Selfishness and jealousy are actually demonic, and any time works such as these are in effect, there will be found pure evil of every kind. But God's wisdom is pure, peace-loving, merciful, produces good fruits, sincere, always gentle, and is willing to submit to, and work with, others. It shows no favoritism, and those who plant peace will harvest righteousness (3:13–18).

Specifically, James now asks: "From whence come wars and fightings among you? come they not hence, even of your lusts that war in your members?" (4:1). Where is all this fighting coming from, anyway? Don't they see that this is evil that comes from human desires? These believers want what they don't have, and they'll go to any length, including murder, to get it. They're jealous, and given over to temptations of warring amidst themselves. But these believers are silly; they don't have what they want, but they won't think to ask God for it! And when they *do* ask God for things, He doesn't give them what they want, because they are motivated by their own pleasures and lusts. This is, spiritually speaking, adultery! They are friends of the world, not friends of God. So, these followers of Christ should humble themselves before God, resisting the devil, which will make him leave them alone. If they strive to be close to God, He will come closer to them. They need purification because their loyalty is divided between their Lord and the world. For this, they should be incredibly saddened (4:2–10).

James warns his readers about judging others and criticizing. God, alone, is the Judge, so what right do they have to judge what their neighbors are doing? And some of the believers are a little too confident in what they plan for their future, to the point that it doesn't involve God's plan. What they *should* be doing, instead, is asking what God wants them to do and not boasting about their own plans or achievements. Reading Scripture, and disregarding what it tells a person to do, is nothing but sin (4:11–17).

The rich people among this Jerusalem congregation is in for a huge letdown. Their fancy clothes are no more than moth-eaten rags, and their pretty gold is filled with dross and contamination. The workers of the field who have been cheated out of their wages are crying out, and God hears them. At the Day of Judgment, all that the wealthy will have accumulated will become a testimony against them. They've spent the whole of their lives feeding their own desires, but they've really been fattening themselves for slaughter, condemning and killing the innocent (5:1–6).

While these Christians are awaiting the Day of the Lord, they must be patient, like a farmer who is patient for the rain. They simply can't waste time fighting! The Judge is standing at the door, and people who grumble against others will have to face Him. The prophets endured under great suffering, like Job, and men like him are and were given great honor. In the end, Job was shown kindness and mercy from the Lord. So these Christians must pattern their lives after him, and they can't continue swearing various oaths on things. They need to simply say "yes" or "no" about a plan and then do what they said they were going to do (5:7–12).

The practice of Christianity is simpler than they are making it:

> Is any among you afflicted? let him pray. Is any merry? let him sing psalms. Is any sick among you? let him call for the elders of the church; and let them pray over him, anointing him with oil in the name of the Lord: And the prayer of faith shall save the sick, and the Lord shall raise him up; and if he have committed sins, they shall be forgiven him. (5:13–15).

If a person sins against another, the person should confess it and pray for the brother or sister. Prayer works…its power can be seen. Elijah, for example, prayed for no rain, and none fell for three and a half years, until he prayed again for rain to return, and it did, producing good crops from the soil (5:16–18).

And finally, if a Christian wanders, the person who brings the sinner back to the faith "shall save a soul from death, and shall hide a multitude of sins" (5:19–20).

James' letter ends as abruptly as it began, without even so much as a signature (that we know of). Many things can be said of this half-brother of our Lord, but one thing is certain: He spared no offense when he spoke the truth to his readers. His heart was passionate for these new believers to shed their lives of sin, let go of their haste to fight, and stop relying on—and championing— worldly wealth and plans. As he was writing to the congregation of Jerusalem, it's very possible that there may have been some believing Pharisees in this church, perhaps even some who endorsed the death of the Savior years before…

Be that as it may, James never faltered in his leadership. In AD 62 or 63, he was martyred for his refusal to assist the scribes and Pharisees in repudiating the legitimacy of his half-brother as the Son of God. According to early Christian chronicler Saint Hegesippus (later quoted by Eusebius), James was thrown from the Temple, but he did not die from the fall. Instead, he turned his body, kneeled, and offered a prayer similar to the words of Christ as He hung on the cross: "I beseech Thee, Lord God our Father, forgive them; for they know not what they do."[195] James was there stoned and beaten to death with a staff.

But what a change his letter went on to make! It still breathes conviction today. We aren't Christians unless we truly carry out actions that prove our faith to be legitimate. No other book of the Bible makes that statement stronger than James' Epistle.

1 and 2 Peter

THESE TWO EPISTLES were written by the same Apostle Peter of the New Testament who wept after he denied Christ. Though scholars have declared a few possible reasons to doubt this, they are easily dismissible. The following is a list of the doubts and corresponding rebuttals to the *first* of these two:

1. "A Galilean Jewish fisherman would not be able to have written in Greek so fluently."—Evidently, in addition to this theoretical statement, there is a rumor going around that Peter was illiterate. Much to the contrary, as the mainstream of academia acknowledges about the historical and regional spread of Greek and the interactions of a career fisherman, Peter would easily be capable of reading and writing in the Greek of his day. Because of the influence of Hellenism, Greek was spoken all over Palestine, and a Galilean fisherman who conducted business in that language is a primary candidate for one who could read and write important documents in this language. Acts 4:13 appears to be the

culprit of the rumor, which says, "Now when they saw the bold-ness of Peter and John, and perceived that they were unlearned and ignorant men, they marvelled; and they took knowledge of them, that they had been with Jesus." Not only is this admittedly mere "perception" of these men, as further research into this verse explains, being "unlearned" in this context merely means that they were not formally trained in the rabbinical sense: "Peter and John were obviously unversed in the formal learning of the rab-binical schools," but because they spoke as if they *were* learned rabbis, the judges in Acts 4:13 concluded that it was because "they had been companions of Jesus."[196]

2. "The letter sounds too much like Pauline theology; therefore, Paul wrote it, not Peter."—This is an immediately disputable claim. The tone and style are not Pauline (similar to our dis-cussion in Hebrews), and the theology *should* be expected to be the same, since the apostles and leading disciples all agreed on teachings of the nature of the Gospel (Galatians 2:1–10; 1 Cor-inthians 15:11).

3. "The letter refers to mass persecution across the entire Roman Empire, which dates the content to a later period than Peter's life, primarily 'the time of Domitian (A.D. 81–96) or Trajan (A.D. 98–117).'"[197]—This is an old argument that has been debunked a thousand times (but still clings on in some circles). Nowhere in the letter does it describe the kind of mass persecution that would be Empire-wide. This argument was never a strong one to begin with.

Lastly, the first of these two Epistles opens with a clear identifica-tion to the apostle of this name: "Peter, an apostle of Jesus Christ."

The authorship of the second of these two Petrine Epistles is more debated, and the most popular reason is that it bears a strong resem-blance to Jude, which was written later. However, not only does 2 Peter begin with a nearly identical opener as the first, referring to its writer as *the* Apostle Peter, the author was a witness to the Transfiguration event (2 Peter 1:16–18). Denying Petrine authorship of the second letter therefore causes far more problems than it solves in attributing the text to someone else.

Therefore, we will continue under the supposition that both letters were written by the same Peter who was a witness to Christ's life, teachings, death, Resurrection, and Ascension.

The audience is vast, but identified in the first two verses of 1 Peter: "Peter, an apostle of Jesus Christ, to the strangers [foreigners] scattered throughout Pontus, Galatia, Cappadocia, Asia, and Bithynia, Elect according to the foreknowledge of God the Father, through sanctification of the Spirit, unto obedience and sprinkling of the blood of Jesus Christ." What's clear is that these are five territories of Asia Minor. What's *not* clear is why Peter is calling them "strangers" or "foreigners." Initially, due to our understanding of these words in the Old Testament, this sounds like Jews who have been uprooted from their homes and made to live among the pagans. But "strangers" is the Greek *parepidemos* (or *parepidemoi*, plural), and it requires a bit of explanation considering the context of the rest of the Epistle. Though most interpreters accept this to be "exiles" (and that's not entirely incorrect), this particular Epistle uses this word in an unusual way, and therefore words like "exile" or "sojourner" are not the complete story. As Wayne Grudem's *1 Peter: An Introduction and Commentary* explains, "strangers" sounds as if the audience didn't know their neighbors very well; "exiles" suggests they had been forcibly removed from somewhere and made to live in another location (such as the Jews during the Babylonian and Assyrian Exiles, or the diaspora after the stoning of Stephen when they fled for fear of losing their lives). Neither of these concepts is true of the new Christians of Asia Minor at this point in history. The question is not centered on where on earth they are residing and how well they are known/ accepted by neighbors, it points to the fact that they are not at home on earth at all. Grudem explains that the following verse qualifies the context by adding "elect" as another description of this particular audience. No other ancient literature—Christian or Jewish—places these words in such close proximity as a double-description.

We must first understand the word in its typical use: "The word in the New Testament (twenty-two times) always refers to persons chosen by God *from* a group of others who are not chosen, and chosen *for* inclusion among God's people, as recipients of great privilege and blessing (Matt. 20:16; 24:31; Rom. 8:33; etc.)."[198] In the Septuagint (LXX), this word means a "chosen people" (Psalm 89:3 [LXX 88:4]; 105:6 [LXX 104:6], 43; 106:5 [LXX 105:5]; Isaiah 42:1; 43:20; 45:4; 65:9, 15, 22 [LXX 23]). Peter's readers would understand this to be describing them as those in the Old Testament whom God blessed and protected: "The phrase 'chosen sojourners' thus becomes a two-word sermon to Peter's readers: they are 'sojourners,' not in an earthly sense (for many no doubt had lived in one city their whole lives), but spiritually: their true homeland is heaven (cf. Phil. 3:20) and any *earthly* residence therefore temporary."[199]

So, in this use, "elect strangers" are Christians who have been dispersed all over the earth, while "the earth" is not their true homeland—heaven is. Christians, meaning *all* believers, are "strangers" to this temporal place. We don't "fit in" here among fallen humanity; though we are absolutely fallen, we're already destined for something grander and higher than this, and those around us who don't believe will never understand us (thus the existence of persecution). Therefore, 1 Peter is not written to Messianic Jews, as the term first appears to suggest, but to Gentiles as well. As for 2 Peter, scholars note that it "was most likely written to the same readers who received 1 Peter (cp. 3:2),"[200] making the audience the same in both.

As to who these Christian recipients of the letter were: If we were to track the massive expanse of these regions of Asia Minor on a map of first-century territories, we would easily see that this letter is being copied at least five times (and it could have been many more) and delivered to major areas of Christian growth. So, unique from Pauline messages that were sent to individuals and particular churches (before they were later made into additional copies and circulated by the early Body), this letter actually began as a kind of early mass bulletin to be delivered into many hands at once, as fast as the messenger could carry it across the land.

The events requiring 1 Peter are clear from internal evidence: Christians were being persecuted and harassed by unbelievers (not necessarily involving execution in all of these areas), and they needed a lot of encouragement. Peter—not only an apostle like Paul, but one who also walked and talked with Christ before His crucifixion—was exceptionally qualified for this kind of reassurance. It's a little too easy for us to skim over this book today because the West is still quite intolerant of persecuting people because of their beliefs (thank the Lord!). We may get a mean comment from someone on Facebook or something, but it is still, at least at this moment, considered a societal injustice if someone is beaten up or killed because he or she claims to be a follower of Jesus. (We understand this is rapidly changing and the Word of God is coming to be regarded as "hate speech," but we should all continue to be grateful that we are technically still at liberty to worship the Risen Christ.) Peter's advice can, therefore, seem irrelevant or obvious to us today, but this should not be so. Each time we are made to suffer for our beliefs, no matter how great that suffering (from a Facebook insult to torture and death), Peter's words, guided by the Spirit, are capable of bringing new life to our situation. We should therefore take in his letter with the expedience of a dry sponge that's tossed in a lake, knowing that, the worse it gets for us, the more precious this apostle's approach to life matters.

As for the focus against false teachers who did not believe in the Second Coming of Christ in 2 Peter—again, not to a particular congregation or individual—remember that the Church was still forming. Peter wasn't responding to just one or two false teachers like Paul did in 1 Corinthians and other Epistles. A doubt about the return of Jesus had sprung up from many locations around the same time. This is likely because many early messianic Jews believed the apostolic teachings referring to "soon" or "last days" indicated that Jesus would come back within their lifetime. Therefore, 2 Peter is yet another kind of "early corpus bulletin" delivered all across Asia Minor at once, silencing the confusion for good from a man who had personally heard Jesus' own statements on the issue.

Peter opens his first letter in a similar manner as Paul, identifying himself and his audience, and then acknowledging them to be saved by Christ, wishing them the grace and peace of God (1 Peter 1:1–2). As encouragement to the persecuted, the apostle reminds them of the hope Christians have in the blessed and eternal afterlife in the presence of the Almighty...a greater gift by far than the relief of oppression in this life. Their forever inheritance is pure, undefiled, priceless, and certain, and is such a cause for great joy. Trials in this life are of great use, as they qualify one's faith, and though faith is more precious than gold, even gold is purified by fire. Currently, these believers are trusting in a Messiah they cannot see or touch, but they still trust in Him, and the reward for such trust is salvation of the soul. Even the prophets, who knew many things of the nature of God, sought diligently to know more about this subject, wondering about the timing and details of how the Messiah would suffer, His glory following, and how it would all be carried out in God's plan. When they prophesied of such mysteries, they knew it was not for themselves, but for these precious Christians, and the Good News of its fulfillment is now happening in real time; even the angels are watching as these exciting times play out (1:3–12).

So the believers must now prepare their minds and hearts toward action in this day, exercising self-control, placing their hope in salvation that comes in Christ. They mustn't slip back into the selfishness that defined their old lives. They didn't know any better in those days, but they do now, and they are to strive toward becoming holy in all they do. As temporary residents of earth, they should remember that God shows no favoritism in matters of the world, but He is the Judge over how people act in matters of the heart. God paid a ransom for these precious souls, not by gold or silver that corrupt over time, but by the blood of the Son, the sinless Lamb, who can be trusted because He was raised to life after death and brought into the highest level of glory. These believers were saved and forgiven of their sin when they took that faithful step to trust in Him, and they are now required to love each other as a Family of God, brothers and sisters. They are born again, into new life, but not one like this earth that withers and perishes—it is an eternal life from the living Word of God. So they must discontinue jealousy, deceitfulness, unkind words, hypocrisy, and all forms of evil behaviors (1:13–2:3).

Christ is the living Cornerstone of God's Temple, and these new believers are the stones through which that Temple is continuously being built up. The people of God are now all priests in a fresh priesthood, offering up sacrifices that are spiritual, invisible, and wholly pleasing to the Lord. To those who do *not* believe in Christ, He is the Cornerstone that has been rejected, and therefore nonbelievers trip over it, stumbling because they refuse to obey God's Word and coming to face with a different fate. But believers are not like these people. They are the royal priests who make up the holy nation, belonging to God, and called out of darkness to show others the light. Peter warns: As people who are strangers and foreigners to the world, they must live rightly amidst their neighbors. If the neighbors of this temporal place accuse the believers of any wrong, the Christians' honorable conduct will lead the neighbors to give God glory later when He judges the world (2:4–12).

For the Lord's sake, believers must submit to earthly governments. God's will is that they silence opposition by maintaining righteousness. Christianity makes one free, but that freedom is for the purpose of following God and Christ, never for evil. They are to fear God and respect kings of the land (2:13–17).

Peter tells all slaves: Respect masters, not only when they are kind, but when they are cruel, also. When a slave submits to his master, because it is the will of God, then God is pleased, regardless of the master's response. If a slave is beaten for doing something wrong, there is no glory in it. But if a slave suffers for acting rightly, it makes God happy that righteousness is the eternal motive of the slave. Christ suffered even while He was doing the right thing—never sinning, deceiving, retaliating, threatening, or any other wrong behavior—and He thus becomes the supreme example (2:18–25).

Peter tells all wives: Accept the authority of husbands. If they are rebellious to the Gospel message, the wives' pure actions can lead them to the light. They shouldn't worry about external things, like hairstyles, jewelry, or fancy clothes. Instead, they are to clothe themselves with inward beauty, as a gentle and quiet spirit is what God finds precious. The holy women of the Old Testament adorned themselves in this spiritual way, trusting in God and obeying husbands. Sarah led by this example also, and today's wives are daughters of Sarah, doing what is right at all times (3:1–6).

Peter tells all husbands: Love and give honor to wives, treating them with understanding. Even if husbands think wives are the weaker vessels, they are *equals* in the partnership of this new life, and these men must treat their women properly so their prayers will not be hindered (3:7).

Finally, Peter tells all Christians, together: Be of one mind. Sympathize with and love each other as brothers and sisters. Remain humble and gentle in attitude, refusing to repay evil with evil or insult with insult. Pay back such things with blessings, as God will bless those who follow this order. The Lord watches over the righteous and hears their prayers, but He turns from evildoers (3:8–12).

In regard to suffering and persecution, Christians are not to live in fear over the threats of others, but to live boldly believing in Christ, and as such, they must be ready at all times to explain their system of belief in case someone asks—though this should be carried out in love. Those who come against sincere believers will feel shame when they see that the believer is living a life of love. Again, it is always better to suffer for doing something good, like Christ did, than to suffer for doing something wrong. In the case of Noah, only eight people were saved from the Flood account, and this has now become a blessed image of baptism for believers of all other times, effective because of Christ's Resurrection. Now, Jesus is in heaven, and all angels, powers, and authority respect *His* power and authority (3:13–22).

As Christ is and was the supreme example, and He suffered greatly, Christians are to prepare themselves for suffering, which strengthens a person to do the will of God under all circumstances. Followers of the Messiah who suffer for His Name will no longer yearn for the ways of the world like they once did. They will be able to withstand anything and the matters of this world will appear foreign to them. Sometimes, old friends see this change and are astounded by the idea that someone they once knew is no longer interested in participating in wildly destructive things, so they resort to slandering, but they will face God, the Judge of all men—both living and dead. The end of *all things* is coming soon, so prayers of God's people should be earnest and disciplined, and love covers a multitude of sins, so the most important thing to remember in these times is that a Christian should be loving. If someone needs a place to stay, a Christian's home should be cheerfully shared. Every believer has been given a spiritual gift from the Holy Spirit, and these should be used to serve one another (4:1–11).

Persecution should not be a surprise, and in fact, it makes believers partners with Christ in His suffering, so they will share in the glory that, one day, all the world will observe. The Spirit of God rests on His people, and those who suffer for His Name will be blessed. But it is so important that God's people don't suffer for wrong things they have done, like murder, theft, making trouble for others, or meddling into others' lives. Being a Christian is not something to be ashamed of. It's a privilege to be called by His Name! Judgment starts in the household of God, so if the righteous suffer, we can't imagine the suffering that awaits those who reject God and do wrong. God will never fail His people, so while they wait in the meantime, they must keep living rightly (4:12–19).

As a final word of advice for elders and young men, Peter writes that he is also an elder, and a witness of Christ's trials. He, too, will share in the glory of the Kingdom. As an elder, he appeals to them to care for the flock that God has entrusted to them, watching over it willingly and without begrudging, and not in pursuit of reward, but out of eagerness to serve the Lord. They are not to act as lords and masters over their brethren, but as leaders of good example. There is a crown of glory and honor awaiting those who follow the Great Shepherd in this manner. Young men should follow the leaders' authority in all humility, relating to one another and leaving pride behind, so the Lord will lift them up in honor. All worries and cares should be given to God who cares for them. They are to remain alert and watchful for the devil's snares, as he wanders like a lion waiting to devour those who fall. They must remain strong against him, and always remember that members of their spiritual Family all over the world are going through the same persecution that they are. "But the God of all grace, who hath called us unto his eternal glory by Christ Jesus, after that ye have suffered a while, make you perfect, stablish, strengthen, settle you. To him be glory and dominion for ever and ever. Amen" (5:1–11).

Peter signs off with closing greetings, noting the help from Silas (or "Silvanus") in this letter, and giving the believers one last affirmation: "I have written briefly, exhorting, and testifying that this is the true grace of God wherein [which suffering] ye stand." The church at "Babylon" (by this he means Rome) says hello, along with Mark. Readers are reminded to greet each other with a holy kiss of charity. His parting words are: "Peace be with you all that are in Christ Jesus. Amen" (5:12–14).

His second letter, probably written a few years later, begins with the same manner of opening greetings as the first (2 Peter 1:1–2). He then jumps in immediately, defining the godly life: one that is void of human desires and follows the priceless commands of God toward righteous living and the eternal mindset of the believer: self-control, faith, moral excellence, patience, endurance, and brotherly affection for all. The more they practice this kind of living, the more they will grow in their knowledge of Christ, and the more useful and productive they will become in their services to Him. Those who fail at this will grow in old sin, becoming short-sighted or blind. So the faithful must keep pressing forward, working hard as those who have been chosen and called by God. If they do, they will never fall away. They will enter the eternal Kingdom as promised (1:3–11).

Peter admits this has all been taught before, but he will continue to remind them for as long as he lives. The Lord has revealed that he will soon be gone from this earthly existence; he will not fail in reminding them of what is important, so they have his words after he is gone. (We wonder if Peter had any idea that his letter would circulate not only throughout Asia Minor, but around the entire *globe*, after he was gone! Either way, we are blessed to have his advice today!) Peter goes on to say that the majesty of Christ's First Coming was witnessed by his own eyes and the eyes of his brothers while He lived, and therefore, it's not just a story they're making up when they say He is coming back! While Peter was with Christ on the holy mountain, he, himself, heard the Father identify Jesus as the Son in whom He was very pleased. This naturally increased his faith in the words of the prophets, and therefore these Christians should read what the prophets said very carefully. Above all, they should remember that the prophets did not ever speak from their own understanding. They were moved by the same Spirit of God that operates within these Christians now (1:12–21).

There were false prophets in Israel, and there will definitely be false teachers among these Christians as well. Though these men are also created by God, they will bring heresies to His people, and even deny the very Creator, Himself. In this terrible act, they are bringing destruction upon themselves. *Many* people will listen to what they say and believe them, and the truth will be slandered because of them. In their greed, they will tell whatever lies they have to in order to get money. But they are condemned, and their condemnation will not be late (2:1–3).

In fact, God didn't even spare the angels who sinned! They were cast into hell, the ultimate place of darkness, where they wait to be judged. Nor did God spare the wicked in ancient times when He sent the Flood, nor Sodom and Gomorrah. But Noah was saved for his righteousness, as well as Lot. This should be proof that God can and will rescue the righteous believers even when the wicked is punished (2:4–9).

But God's anger is increased against people who follow perversity or who despise authority. Such men are proud and arrogant. False teachers are wild animals who follow instinct, scoffing at what they don't understand, and they do so to their own destruction. Destruction is their reward for the terrible things they've caused. Disgracefully, they engage in wickedness in broad daylight, delighting in the presence of other Christians even while they break bread together. They are adulterers for their wandering eyes, and their desires for matters of the flesh is never satisfied while they draw unstable people into their deceptions. These men live under the curse of God, following in the steps of Balaam, who earned money through evil means (2:10–16).

People who give in to such ways are doomed, even while they boast foolishly. They lead others into twisted sexual perversion who have only just escaped such a lifestyle, claiming freedom and liberty while they are slaves to sin and corruption, themselves. When a man gives himself over to Christ, escaping these snares, and then he is dragged back into it by one of these false teachers, they are worse off than they were before; it would be better to have never accepted Christ in the first place than to accept Him and reject Him once again, like a dog returning to his vomit or a clean pig who runs once again to his mud (2:17–22).

Peter reminds his readers that this is his second letter to them, a document from an apostle that the Lord, Himself, appointed, and they need to keep what the prophets said in mind: The Day of the

Lord is coming! In the Last Days, scoffers will come and mock the truth, feeding the desires of the flesh. They will mock the idea that Jesus was ever really coming back (3:1–4).

Such men will forget about the Creator who brought the Flood and judgment upon the earth, and His power to destroy those who reject Him in their ungodliness (3:5–7).

But the believers *must* remember this important fact: A day is like a thousand years to the Lord, and a thousand years is like a day. His timing is not linear or limited to human understanding. He's not slow or delayed in His plan as some people claim; to the contrary, He is showing patience for the sake of humans because He doesn't want anyone to face destruction. The Day of the Lord will come, and when it does, it will come like a thief at night when nobody expects it. The heavens will pass away with a huge and frightening noise, the elements of the earth will perish in fire, and everything on the planet will be subject to His judgment. Because this is true, it's all the more important that Christians live in a godly way, looking forward to the Day of the Lord and anticipating the New Heavens and New Earth filled with nothing but God and righteousness! But believers are to remember that, while they wait for these things, living as blamelessly as possible, God's patience gives time for the lost to be saved! Even Paul wrote about these things. Some false teachers have twisted his words, and they will face destruction as well (3:8–16).

These dear friends of Peter already know these things, so they should be on guard, not carried off by the claims of wicked people. Instead, they must always grow in grace and their secure knowledge of the Risen Christ. His parting greetings are as follows: "To him be glory both now and for ever. Amen" (3:17–18).

As stated prior, Peter went on to be crucified upside-down for his faith, according to historians. While he lived, he passionately blazed a trail Christians today are obligated to uphold. He may have, in his weakness, denied Christ at His trial just before His execution, but it is clear by how he lived from that moment forward that the fruit of his life would never stop exalting and honoring his Best Friend and Messiah. These letters are an enormous part of that example. We, too, should live in harmony with the brethren as Peter did, while never fearing persecution and always standing firmly against the false teaching that denies Christ's return.

1, 2, and 3 John

READERS MAY HAVE HEARD that the first of John's Epistles is not truly a "letter." This sound argument is based on the absence of features that would follow that form, such as opening or closing greetings, identification of the sender somewhere in the document, and so on. Although this is correct, the text absolutely does fit the definition of "Epistle." Scholars have tossed out many different labels for what 1 John should instead be called, and after considering those opinions, we hold that it would most accurately be called a "tract." However, for the sake of continuity and smooth reading, we will proceed by referring to all three Johannine Epistles as "letters," noting that, technicalities aside, at the very least it serves as a general letter of doctrine to the universal Church. From there, 2 and 3 John are, in fact, true letters.

For the well-studied Christian, it's clear by the way the fourth Gospel reads that John weaves his words in a way that's vastly different than was the style of most other writers of his time. He is also nearly inimitable in his unique approach to exceedingly deep and philosophical concepts of theology. Thus, even without digging into the seemingly limitless commentaries and interpretational media that reflect on 1 John, readers can recognize the Johannine tone from the Gospel by the same author. It is therefore not a surprise that the authorship of 1 John has remained largely uncontested throughout time. Papias, Eusebius, Irenaeus, Dionysius, and the Muratorian Canon are only a few sources that have considered it an obvious and irrefutable fact that the apostle of Christ who wrote the Gospel of John is the writer of the first Epistle by his name.

Tradition holds that this is also true for 2 and 3 John, but in recent history, New Testament scholars have questioned this. The second and third Epistles under the name "John" are written by someone who merely calls himself "the Elder." Scholars note that one man named John from Ephesus in this same time period referred to himself as "the Elder," and therefore 2 and 3 John may have been written by him, and not by the Apostle John (also called "the Evangelizer"). However, "John" was an incredibly common name at the time, just as it is today. In fact, it's third on the list (just under "James" and "Robert") of the most common male names in the last one hundred years, according to the Social Security Administration.[201] Also, "elder" is too generic to insist that it originates from the man in Ephesus, or anyone else, as it, too, was a customary label for any leader of the Church. If a blog post were to go viral today and the author only called himself "Bob the Church Leader," there would be no way to know the real identity of the man behind its writing, and this is a comparable moniker. Without going into great detail, the theme of love, as well as the use of Greek language in 2 and 3 John, are so similar to the known Johannine style that we will proceed under the assumption that all three were written by the same writer as the one who wrote the Gospel by the same name.

A matter of great debate, however, is the order in which the three letters were written. We don't plan to go over this issue in great detail, as it's not pertinent to our purpose in showing how all sixty-six books of the Bible involve Jesus, but suffice it to say that some scholars believe 1 John should actually be 3 John; others say 1 John was written first, as an introductory tract that would be explained more fully in the subsequent fourth Gospel, with 2 and 3 John trailing behind; and still others believe the three letters were written all at the same time as the Gospel...and so on. For this reason, it may be helpful for readers to occasionally take in all of John's letters in a row, flipping straight from the end of his Gospel to these, to grasp the totality of what the author hoped to convey to the Church. As for the biblical order, they appear in the canon in the order of longest to shortest.

As a set of "catholic" (universal) letters, the audience *today* is obviously all believers, and the Church benefitted greatly from all of the letters regardless of their original recipients. That said, 1 John does not identify an audience, 2 John is written to "the elect lady and her children" (more on this shortly), and 3 John is written to a now-unknown person by the name of Gaius (who may have been stationed in or around Ephesus at that time as the content of the letter suggests to some). Unlike the Petrine Epistles that are viewed with more of an "all-churches bulletin" circulation in mind from the start, John appears to have been corresponding to specific people and congregations in his area of Ephesus. Since these are technically unknown, the letters have become categorized as universal. There have been many attempts to pin down exactly who John's audience was, and though we cannot know for certain, there appears to have been a specific community that hailed John as their teacher. Most often, this group is called the "Johannine Community," and its association with the population in and around Ephesus at the time suggests that these Christians were under more of a Hellenistic influence than a Jewish one.

As for the occasion requiring the response of this apostle to his Johannine Community, 1 John is clearly refuting two major heresies that had been planted by false teachers and watered by those who followed them until it sprouted an ugly weed in their midst. The first is a teaching of self-indulgence and the toleration of sin. John teaches that a lifestyle that willfully and continually gives in to sin is immutably incompatible with being a part of God's Family or Body. The second teaching twisted the nature of the Messiah in such a way that He was being denied as God in the flesh, who died for sin. In all of John's message, the issue of loving others is of the greatest emphasis. (We explained this before at the very beginning of volume 1, under the subhead labelled, "Where and How Some Went Wrong," but as a quick review: In Christology, this denial of *either* Christ's divinity or His humanity results in the renunciation of the ontological union between God and Father. The Church was *so* dedicated to fixing this in its early centuries that, gradually, the focus on Jesus became more about studying His "substance" with the Father than about how He saved humanity in God's soteriological plan by the "Economic Trinity" [the view that sees the Trinity's interaction with mankind as interested in reaching the lost]. Theologians for hundreds of years made this "ontological substance" issue such a key concentration, both in the councils and in practice, that instead of spreading the Gospel, they spread theology. The pursuit of sharpening one's understanding of theology is a wonderful endeavor, but if people lose sight of Christ's work on the cross in the Economic Trinity, the message of Jesus' Good News is traded for studying about God rather than loving or knowing Him. This first letter of John's is unique in that it tackles the ontological substance of Christ, while balancing that subject against the responsibility of believers to flee from evil and embrace love. The early Church did read John's letter, but it appears that they didn't take it as much to heart as they should have. That's a lesson we can take from his work today to ensure that this misplaced focus doesn't happen again.)

The intent of 2 and 3 John is clear from the context of the documents: Believers need to walk in truth, not deception.

Before we jump into the letters, we would like to point out that scholars have been debating for centuries (sometimes quite aggressively, calling each other names and whatnot) about interpretational difficulties found in 1 John. Such theological depth can cause the book to be the source of much division within the Body if we're not careful. However, as our book is not serving as a commentary on

John's writings, we will do as we have with the other Epistles and straightforwardly paraphrase what he wrote. We fully accept that there may be readers who do not agree with our summary, and others who believe we should have spent more time on specific interpretational problems, but for the sake of space, we will stick to the format we've used up to this point. (One exhaustive work on the study of this letter, alone, is over a thousand pages, so if we were to stop and sort out every issue that's ever been raised about this text throughout history, we would lose the sharp focus on how Christ "appears" in each book.)

John opens his first letter with a brief introduction—not of himself, but of Christ. He is eternal, and many witnesses spoke with Him, touched Him, and experienced the Father's salvation as it played out in real time in their presence. Their fellowship is now with God and Christ, and this is a fact that should stimulate joy within the Johannine Community (1 John 1:1–4).

Jesus, Himself, taught the apostles a truth about living in the light, and the Community is now being reminded of this teaching: Because God is pure Light, and there is no darkness at all within Him, people who claim to have fellowship with God while they still practice darkness are living a lie. When one truly lives in the light as God is, Jesus' blood cleanses them of sin and they are in fellowship with God. Confessing our sin is not an optional practice. We *must* confess what we have done wrong and then believe with confidence that God is just to forgive us. No person can claim he or she is without sin, and if a person does, he or she is calling God a liar and illustrating that God's Word is not within the heart (1:5–10).

John is writing this to the Community so they might not sin, but when they do, they have an Advocate, Christ, who pleads their case to the Father on their behalf, and He is truly righteous. Patterning their lives after Christ and obeying God's Word is the way these Christians can show they truly love the Lord (2:1–6).

And here John isn't writing about a new Commandment, but one that Christ, Himself, spoke—that believers should love one another as much as they love themselves. Jesus lived this way, and members of this Johannine Community now are as well, pushing away the darkness and bringing in the light. When Christians claim to be in the light but show hatred to other believers, they are actually living in darkness, fumbling around blindly. To the young, the old, those who are mature or immature in the faith, John exhorts: Sin is forgiven through Jesus who existed as the Word from the beginning; knowing the Father for real—in action and not in words—defeats the evil one (2:7–14).

When believers say they are following God while they're still following the ways of the world, the love of the Father is not in them. The ways of the world include physical pleasures, pride, and boasting about achievements. Such are not God's ways, and these things of the world will pass away (2:15–17).

Antichrist is coming in these last days, as the Community has heard, and many wannabe antichrists have already shown up in this, the last hour. These people were never truly a part of the Body, and the fact that they have now left the Church proves this. Anyone who claims Jesus was not the Christ, the Anointed Messiah, is an antichrist, and this person also can't say he is following the Father, either, since the Father and the Son are one. So the Community must remain faithful in their proclamation of the Son as they have been taught; if they do, they will be in fellowship with the Father and Son for eternity. John is writing this to warn his listeners that there are people who will lead them astray from this teaching. They have the Spirit within them, so they must believe in His teachings, which align with this (2:18–29).

The Father loves His people so much. He calls them His children, and that's truly what they are! But people of the world don't understand this, because they don't know Him personally. Christians don't yet know what they will be like when Jesus comes back, but they *do* know they will be like Him, so they will keep themselves pure. All sin is in contradiction to God's Word, without exception, so anyone who goes about sinning is breaking God's laws. The Community members cannot allow themselves to become confused or misled where the subject of sin is concerned. It's easy to tell who are and aren't children of God based on whether they choose to be righteous like Christ or to just go on sinning (3:1–10).

From the beginning, these believers have been told they should love each other. Yet, they shouldn't be surprised when the world opposes them for their goodness, as the jealous Cain killed Abel, because what Abel offered to the Lord was the right thing. To love is to truly live, and to hate is to be in death. A person who can legitimately hate another person has the spirit of murder in his heart. Real love is defined by Jesus, who gave His very life for people, and Christians should make their lives about others after His example. If a rich man says he's a Christian but doesn't care about those around him who are destitute, where is that man's love? Love is not a statement, but something people show with actions, and there is no hiding from God, who knows everything. Therefore, Christians are to hold onto the belief in Christ's Name, and be in fellowship with God. And the faithful can know for sure that God is in fellowship with them because the Spirit dwells within them (3:11–24).

However, Christians should *not* trust in the words of every person who claims to be speaking by the Spirit. There are many false prophets around who will not acknowledge the truth of Christ. The first test in examining whether a person has the Spirit of God or the antichrist spirit is to their stance on Jesus. If they deny Jesus was and is real, and came in a body to do the work of the cross, they should not be trusted. The Spirit who lives in Christians is stronger and more powerful than the spirit of the world (4:1–6). (This group of Scriptures is what Christians are referring to when they talk about "testing the spirits." Though we have treated this section as if John was addressing *people*, because it can and should be applied in that sense also, we need to remember that it applies to spirits as well. For instance, Howell had a dream once that an "angel" was going to give her a message from

God, but some of the things this "angel" said were suspect. Howell, in the dream, initially panicked because she was afraid she wouldn't know how to tell if this entity was really sent from God or not. Then she remembered the "tests of the spirits" from this section of Scripture and was able to ask this being, "Who do you say Jesus is?" A true angel of God would have praised Jesus as the Son of God, while this being smirked arrogantly, as if to suggest that the answer was so obvious he didn't need to respond. This is precisely how Howell knew when she awakened that this "angel" had not actually been sent from God.)

Let Christians continue loving each other, for love comes from God. God so loved us that He sent His Son to take away sin. Though God cannot be seen, His love is brought to full expression within believers through the proofs of the Spirit's work in them. As we continue to grow in God, our own love toward others becomes more perfect. This allows Christians to approach God in confidence, unafraid of the Day of Judgment, because they lived like Jesus did (4:7–21).

Everyone who believes Jesus came to earth as the Son of God is a child of God, and those who love the Father love His children as well. There is victory through faith. Jesus' baptism revealed Him as the Son, as well as the work of His blood on the cross, and the Spirit confirms this. Therefore, believers have three witnesses to this truth: water (baptism), blood, and Spirit, and all three attest to the same truth. If the testimony of a person can be believed, how much more can the testimony of God be? God testified about His Son, and those who follow Jesus know this to be truth also. Whoever has the Son has life; whoever doesn't have the Son does not (5:1–12).

In conclusion, John writes: He has written this to believers of the Son, so they might inherit eternal life and be confident in it. They can be confident that God hears their prayers and will answer them. The Johannine Community should also pray for those who sin. True Christians will not go on sinning, and they are therefore free from the fate the devil would want them to face. They are part of the world, which is under the control of the enemy, but the Son has come to give real understanding about God, and believers now have fellowship with Him. John ends his tract-like letter to the Community with: "Little children, keep yourselves from idols. Amen" (5:13–21).

As stated earlier, we don't know how much time elapsed between the writing of the first and second of John's letters. They may have been a few years apart, written at about the same time, or even flipped in order. With that in mind, we'll dive straight into the second. (Note that, like Philemon, 2 and 3 John are each only one chapter, so only verse references are included in the following pages.)

In his second letter, John "the Elder" writes to "the elect lady and her children." Many have weighed in on the debate as to whether this should be taken literally, as an individual woman, or figuratively, with its language referring to a church body. If the latter, it's similar to the idea that Israel would be identified by feminine pronouns (her, she, etc.), as groups of believers were called the "elect" (Matthew 24:22; Romans 8:33; 16:13; Colossians 3:12; 2 Timothy 2:10; Titus 1:1; 1 Peter 1:1; Revelation 17:14). In other words, the Johannine Community church is, poetically, personified as a "lady." From the standpoint of the former conclusion, since the third letter is addressed to one man (Gaius), then it's possible the second one is addressed to one person as well. Some early historians and Church fathers, like Clement of Alexandria, made the assumption that this document was intended for a woman named "Electa." However, that doesn't appear to be a proper name at that time. Furthermore, 2 John 13 (his closing greeting) mentions the "children of thy elect sister," which, if given the same application, would insinuate that Lady Electa had a sister with the same name (an awkward and highly unlikely possibility). But if it is not a proper name, then the recipient may have been someone referred to with a polite and affectionate term for an associate in ministry, such as "a lady among the elect of God" or, more simply, "chosen lady" (meaning a sister in the faith). Despite all of this conjecture, most scholars agree that the term is a personification of the universal Church, and "her children" are its members. This, too, causes a problem regarding the "sister" of the lady...but it is easily rectified. If the "elect lady" is the universal Church, then the "elect sister" is the Johannine Community *also* personified: John's congregation is the "sister" of all other churches, and this letter was written to the Body of all believers within that group.

After introducing himself as the Elder and addressing his recipients, John reminds the believers of his love for them all and wishes them the grace, mercy, and peace of God (2 John 1–3).

John is thrilled to see that, after meeting some of these "children," he finds them to be living in the truth as the Father has commanded. As with his first letter, he now reminds them of a paramount element of Christianity: love one another. Again, it is not a new commandment, but one that God's Family has always had from the beginning. Love includes following God's orders (4–6).

John writes this because there have been some deceivers who have claimed Jesus didn't have a real body (a heresy later dubbed "Docetism," as addressed earlier in volume 1, under the subhead, "Where and How Some Went Wrong"). People who proclaim this are antichrists at heart. Christians must watch out for this kind of deception and hold on to what they have worked so hard to build. The full reward awaits those who have been diligent in such matters. Those who dismiss Jesus' bodily nature are not of God, but those who remain steadfast in this understanding have a relationship with both Father and Son. If a man wanders into their assembly and teaches falsely about Jesus, Christians are not to invite him into their homes or encourage his heresy, because doing so is to partner with him in his evil work (7–11).

In conclusion, John says there is much more to say, but not through writing. He will visit them face-to-face soon, and their joy will be complete. "The children of thy elect sister greet thee. Amen" (12–13).

The third letter, addressed to a man named Gaius, was written to commend this man from a particular gathering or congregation who chose to live in the truth of John's teaching (and, by extension, Jesus' teaching). We have no idea who this man was, as nothing in the context ties him to other men by the same name in the New Testament (Acts 19:29; 20; Romans 16:23; 1 Corinthians 1:14), and the name was a common one in the first century.

Diotrephes, a wrongdoer who is a heavy focus of this letter, may or may not have been someone within Gaius' very own congregation (internal evidence stacks in favor of assuming he was). The context of John's text is clear that Diotrephes, out of pride, was refusing to show hospitality to travelling missionaries. Of all possibilities, it appears most likely that he felt he was "above" having to stoop to the level of serving others who were only present for a short time: He wanted to be the *receiver* of this kind of hospitality, not the *giver* of it.

As for the good man, Demetrius, scholars dismiss the notion that he is the same silversmith who is said to have built the idols to Artemis/Diana in Acts 19:24, even though he is living in the same area. Again, this was another common name in the first century. We know nothing about this person, except that, in contrast to Diotrephes, Demetrius was likely mentioned to give an example of one who *was* hospitable to missionaries.

John begins by once again identifying himself as the Elder who loves, in all truth, his associate, Gaius (3 John 1). John hopes Gaius is as well in body as he is strong in spirit. John is happy to have heard from some itinerant teachers (missionaries) that Gaius has remained faithful and is living in the light of the truth. News that John's "children" are following the way of truth is the utmost source of his joy (2–4).

Gaius has cared for the teachers of the Word who travel through his area, even though these folks are strangers to him, and this, John says, is an act of faithfulness on his recipient's part. Gaius is encouraged to continue this kind of blessed hospitality. Believers *should* be partners in support with teachers such as them (5–8).

Diotrephes is a man who loves to be a leader, but he refuses to even associate with the itinerant teachers. In fact, he has gone as far as to refuse support of any teacher in John's circle, and he tells others to ignore them as well. If the believers don't heed Diotrephes' warning to ignore the teachers, they get kicked out of the church. John already wrote to the church about this, but when he next comes in person, he will enlighten this body with some of the evil slander this man has perpetuated about his fellow ministers (9–10).

Gaius must not allow Diotrephes' bad example to influence him. Those who do good are God's children, and those who do evil prove by their actions that they don't know God, and Gaius needs to remember this. Demetrius, on the other hand, is a man everyone speaks highly of (11–12).

In conclusion, once again, John admits there's much more to say, but not with pen and ink. He is coming to speak with Gaius soon, face to face, and until then, John wishes him peace. He concludes his letter: "Our friends salute thee. Greet the friends by name" (13–14).

As stated earlier, the Western world of theology would go on to place a great amount of emphasis on the ontological substance of Christ, losing the importance of His work as a saving power and missing the balance John's letter's demanded. When Western Christianity finally circled back to the correct purpose and mission of the Good News, not directly stated as the catalyst for this restoration, we believe John's letters were a central source of that conviction. These texts have, along with the other Epistles, greatly influenced the Church since they were written, and we are strengthened immensely from his advice.

John went on to be a powerful leader in the early Church, until his influence intimidated Emperor Domitian and he was exiled to the Island of Patmos, where he shifted from his role as John the Evangelist to John the Revelator. Though we now turn to Christ's other half-brother, Jude, we're not even close to being through with John's teachings…

Jude

JAMES WAS NOT THE ONLY half-brother of Christ who had an epiphany about who Jesus was after watching Him grow up as a regular Jewish boy for thirty years and doing the work He went on to do. If you haven't yet read the sweet, endearing, and educational introduction to the book of James, we encourage you to do so now. Much of that book's background applies to the book of Jude as well, since both were written by the half-brothers of Jesus (see Jude or "Judas" listed in Mark 6:3 and Matthew 13:55). Like Philemon and 2 and 3 John, this letter is only one chapter long and will therefore not have chapters in the passage references going forward.

Jude 1:1 states that the author is the "brother of James." Authorship has not gone unchallenged, with potential contenders ranging from the brother of the apostle James (son of Alphaeus) to "Didymus Jude" of the apocryphal *Acts of Thomas* and *Gospel of Thomas*, and several others. However, once all possibilities have considered and compared with 1) what is known of Jude the half-brother of Christ and 2) the authority one's writing had to have by the end of the second century (and eventual inclusion in the canon), Jude the half-brother continually resurfaces as the most likely author. At the end of the road, as Clement of Alexandria said, it's not about familial relationships with Jesus or James or anyone else. Jude's authority is as a bondservant to Christ as an apostle.[202]

Very little is said in the Bible about Jude, except in a couple of brief passages. Acts 1:14 states that Jesus' brothers were joined with those in the Upper Room on the Day of Pentecost, and 1 Corinthians 9:5 at least applies to some of Jesus' brothers, noting that Jude may have been an itinerant missionary.

Jude's audience is technically unknown. But from internal evidence, we can put together the following: 1) This was a group of Christians who had already heard and believed in the message of the apostles; 2) as the Old Testament references in this tiny book suggest, these Christians probably had a background in Judaism; 3) this group was, like many of its day, waiting for the return of Christ, but as they had not received any new information about how to live in trying times while they waited for Jesus' Second Coming, they needed reassurance that only another of Christ's siblings could provide. Again, we see false teachers arriving to spread ideas that promised new revelations from ungodly sources, and these concepts were tempting for a congregation that had experienced personally the dramatic religious and political shifts that occurred in their day around the time of Christ, followed by a perceived silence on the matter of Christ, whose salvation doctrines were now known. As the false teachers' influence began to grow in this assembly, division amidst the body arose as they tore down the apostles' former message and traded it for a statement that assumed there was no such thing as sin when the forgiveness of the blood covers all.

Jude opens his letter, as stated, by describing himself as the brother of James. He also notes that he is a "bondservant" or "slave" of Jesus Christ, and that he is writing to "them that are sanctified by God the Father, and preserved in Jesus Christ, and called: Mercy unto you, and peace, and love, be multiplied" (Jude 1–2).

Jude notes that he had been looking forward to writing to his audience about salvation, but now he has to switch gears and address the defense of the faith of the holy people of God. Some false teachers have slithered into their assemblies, saying God's grace is so sufficient that Christians can be found living in ungodly ways, and it won't affect anything. But those who claim such wild ideas were condemned a long time ago for rejecting the Messiah's true Kingdom teachings (3–4).

So Jude now writes this letter as a reminder, aware that his recipients already know these things. He proceeds to reminisce on how Jesus first rescued Israel from Egypt, but later destroyed those who didn't believe. The angels also challenged God's authority and ended up being exiled from heaven, chained in darkness and awaiting judgment. So, too, did Sodom and Gomorrah face destruction because of their citizens' sexual immorality. These historical accounts of God's anger should serve as a warning of judgment. In the same way, these false teachers and prophets—who claim to have been given special revelations about God through dreams—live immoral lives, refusing to respect authority (5–8).

Then Jude writes something odd… In the KJV, this ninth verse reads: "Yet Michael the archangel, when contending with the devil he disputed about the body of Moses, durst not bring against him a railing accusation, but said, 'The Lord rebuke thee.'" This could be reworded in modern English to say, "Even Michael, the archangel—while he was arguing with the devil about burying the body of Moses—did not accuse the enemy of doing wrong from within his own perceived authority. He said instead, 'The *Lord* rebuke you!'"

What was that you said about the argument between the archangel and the devil about the body of Moses? Why haven't I heard that teaching before?

Even for seasoned readers of God's Word, this verse seems to come out of nowhere. Whenever the Epistle writers brought up events or people from Israel's past, they were quoting from (or referring to) the Old Testament. In this verse, the detail about Moses' burial (covered in Deuteronomy 34) is not mentioned anywhere in the Old Testament. Jude 9 reflects on an ancient Jewish teaching that the devil saw Michael getting ready to bury Moses and believed that since the earth is his dominion and Moses had been accused of murder (Exodus 2:12), it was his right, and not the angel's, to put Moses in the soil. Michael, acting on behalf of God (and whom Deuteronomy 34 states was responsible for Moses' burial), rebuked the devil in the Name of the Lord and carried out the act despite evil opposition. This tale, though its details overlap and are somewhat ambiguous, is told in the apocryphal books *Assumption of Moses*, and "the Slavonic *Wisdom of Moses* 16 gives a similar story...so does the *Targum of Jonathan* (on Dt. 34:5–6)."[203] Jude's purpose here is not to prove an account of Michael burying Moses (though this *is* the Word of God, and Jude's comment supports this as a reality), but to challenge his audience. The mainstream interpretation from Jude's standpoint is:

> If an angel was so careful in what he said, how much more should mortal men watch their words...[?] The devil was certainly bringing a slanderous and malicious accusation against Moses, but the archangel did not take it on himself to repudiate it.... Michael did not attempt to dismiss his charge as unjustified on his own authority.... What a contrast to Jude's opponents who set themselves up over against the Law, and against God who gave it.[204]

This contrast is clear in the following verse (Jude 10): "But these [false teachers/prophets] speak evil of those things which they know not: but what they know naturally, as brute beasts, in those things they corrupt themselves." The NLT renders it as this: "But these people scoff at things they do not understand. Like unthinking animals, they do whatever their instincts tell them, and so they bring about their own destruction." Jude goes on to say that only deep, vast sorrow awaits men such as this, who follow after the example set by Cain, who killed his own brother; Balaam, who deceived people for monetary gains; or Korah (known for going against Moses and Aaron in Numbers 16:1), perishing in their rebellion (Jude 11).

When such false believers fellowship and break bread with true believers as they do during such observances as communion, they are like: 1) dangerous and sharp rocks among the reefs that cause shipwrecks of the holy Body; 2) shepherds who only care about themselves and their own increase amidst Christians; 3) clouds that cover the land in darkness without bringing the rain; 4) trees that have died, bearing no fruit, and are therefore uprooted for their uselessness; 5) wild and unpredictable waves on the sea that only churn up the foam; and 6) wandering stars doomed to forever roam around in darkness (12–13).

Adam's descendant, Enoch, also prophesied of these people, saying:

> Behold, the Lord cometh with ten thousands of his saints, To execute judgment upon all, and to convince all that are ungodly among them of all their ungodly deeds which they have ungodly committed, and of all their hard speeches which ungodly sinners have spoken against him. (14–15; *Book of Enoch* 1:9)

These "teachers" and "prophets" among the believers grumble and complain, living in a way that satisfies only them, bragging and boasting about themselves and flattering others to manipulate them into getting what they want (16).

Jude returns to speaking to his audience directly, saying they are different than these fake believers, therefore, they must remember the teachings of the apostles. They already warned the Church that, in the last days, there would be scoffers whose sole purpose in life is to satisfy their own wicked lusts and desires. The people the believers were warned about have arrived, and they are the ones in their midst who are creating division within the Body. They don't have the Holy Spirit living within them, so they follow their own human instincts, like animals. But the believers must build each other up in prayer, guided by the Spirit, awaiting the mercy and return of Christ who brings eternal life through His work. This is the only way to remain safe in God's love and provision. As for those whose faith is wavering as a result of all this confusion, the rest of the Body should show them mercy, but they should offer it carefully, while hating the sin that pollutes their lives (17–23).

Jude ends his letter with a note of praise for the One who will bring them into His presence. Jesus *is* the Savior, and all glory, majesty, power, and authority have belonged to Him since before time began, in the present, and forever! Amen (24–25).

The nature of Jude's continued ministry and martyrdom is largely unknown. Some early traditions state that he was murdered at the same time as Simon the Zealot (and possibly in the same, horrific way [involving details so disturbing that we will not address them here]). However, before he died, he had a family, and it's clear in Church history that Jude, unlike the false believers he rebuked in his letter, maintained apostolic teachings for his sons and their sons after that. From Eusebius' *Ecclesiastical History*, we read:

> [W]hen this same [Emperor] Domitian had commanded that the descendants of David should be slain, an ancient tradition says that some of the heretics brought accusation against the descendants of Jude (said to have been a brother of the Saviour according to the flesh), on the ground that they were of the lineage of David and were related to Christ himself. Hegesippus relates these facts in the following words....
>
> "Of the family of the Lord there were still living the grandchildren of Jude, who is said to have been the Lord's brother according to the flesh.
>
> "Information was given that they belonged to the family of David, and they were brought to the Emperor Domitian by

the Evocatus [a Roman soldier who had been given honorable discharge from duty but who later reenlisted]. For Domitian feared the coming of Christ as Herod also had feared it. And he asked them if they were descendants of David, and they confessed that they were....

"And when they were asked concerning Christ and his kingdom, of what sort it was and where and when it was to appear, they answered that it was not a temporal nor an earthly kingdom, but a heavenly and angelic one, which would appear at the end of the world, when he should come in glory to judge the quick and the dead, and to give unto every one according to his works.

"Upon hearing this, Domitian did not pass judgment against them, but, despising them as of no account, he let them go, and by a decree put a stop to the persecution of the Church.

It appears in this material that there is great evidence showing that Jude's grandchildren became prominent leaders of the Church in the generations following their grandfather. Though Jude was likely met with one of the cruelest deaths ever sentenced upon a follower of his half-brother, his legacy outlived him...and so did his letter of rebuke against anyone who comes into the Body claiming God has given them "dreams" or "visions" that in any way contradict the sound doctrine of His Brother, the Word.

Begin Volume 3.

Notes

For complete source information on shortened references, please see the endnotes to volume one.

1. Josephus, F., & Whiston, W., *The Works of Josephus*, 532.
2. Waltke, B. K., Houston, J. M., & Moore, E., *The Psalms as Christian Worship: A Historical Commentary* (Grand Rapids, MI; Cambridge, U.K.: William B. Eerdmans Publishing Company; 2010), 34.
3. The apocryphal *Psalms of Solomon*, verses 17:25–46, as translated in: Brannan, R., Penner, K. M., Loken, I., Aubrey, M., & Hoogendyk, I. (Eds.), *The Lexham English Septuagint* (Bellingham, WA: Lexham Press; 2012), "Ps Sol 17:25–46."
4. DeSilva, David A., *Honor, Patronage, Kinship & Purity* (InterVarsity Press: Downers Grove, IL; 2000), 29.
5. Gamel, B. K., as quoted in: *The Lexham Bible Dictionary*, "Logos, Greek Background."
6. Simmons, Brian, *John: Eternal Love (The Passion Translation)* (BroadStreet Publishing Group LLC; Kindle Edition; 2014), John 1:1–4.
7. Barnes, Albert, *Barnes' Notes*, Kindle location 216298.
8. Ibid., footnote "c" regarding "Living Expression" in John 1:1.
9. Trites, A. A., William J. Larkin, Cornerstone Biblical Commentary: Volume 12: The Gospel of Luke and Acts (Carol Stream, IL: Tyndale House Publishers; 2006), 38.

10. Barnes, Albert, *Barnes' Notes*, Kindle locations 210501–210508.

11. Harris, R. Laird, Gleason L. Archer, Jr., Bruce K. Waltke, *Theological Wordbook of the Old Testament* (Chicago, IL: Moody Publishers; 2003), 672.

12. Vorster, W. S., "James, Protevangelium of," as quoted in: D. N. Freedman (Ed.), *The Anchor Yale Bible Dictionary: Volume 3* (New York: Doubleday; 1992), 632.

13. Walker, A. (Trans.), *Fathers of the Third and Fourth Centuries: The Twelve Patriarchs, Excerpts and Epistles, the Clementina, Apocrypha, Decretals, Memoirs of Edessa and Syriac Documents, Remains of the First Ages: Volume 8* (Buffalo, NY: Christian Literature Company; 1886), 362–363.

14. Ibid., 365.

15. Howell, Donna, *The Handmaidens Conspiracy: How Erroneous Bible Translations Hijacked the Women's Empowerment Movement Started by Jesus Christ and Disavowed the Rightful Place of Female Pastors, Preachers, and Prophets* (Crane, MO: Defender Publishing; 2018), 187–192.

16. But a word of caution is needed here, as some assume that Matthew "whoopsed" a few names from his list, as his genealogy omits a couple of names from the family line listed in the Chronicles. Luke's genealogy is different from Matthew's. Actually, the short explanation for this is that the common Jew's purpose was not in showing every single person ever involved, but in showing the relationships that are righteous and honorable. If someone turned away from God and his or her life was an abandonment of all God required—such as the wicked King Ahab—their line would be cut off. In 2 Kings 8:18, we see that Jorab married Ahab's daughter. Ahab's line was, in fact, cut off for four generations. Instead, Jehu's sons would serve as king (2 Kings 10:30; cf. 2 Kings 10:35; 13:1, 10; 14:23; 15:8). Thus, Matthew was being obedient to Scripture, and his culture, by choosing not to mention names that had, by the time of the New Testament, become known only as wicked. However, this does not in any way change the authenticity of Christ's lineage from King David, which is proven biblically and historically. We found at least three or four hundred explanations at the mere click of a button regarding this

"discrepancy," so we have chosen not to go into more detail on this issue in this work as we are already pressed for space.

17. Butler, T. C., *Luke: Volume 3* (Nashville, TN: Broadman & Holman Publishers; 2000), 29.

18. Morris, L., *Luke: An Introduction and Commentary: Volume 3* (Downers Grove, IL: InterVarsity Press; 1988), 100.

19. Marshall, I. H., "Luke," as quoted in: D. A. Carson, R. T. France, J. A. Motyer, & G. J. Wenham (Eds.), *New Bible commentary: 21st century edition* (4th ed., Leicester, England; Downers Grove, IL: Inter-Varsity Press; 1994), 984.

20. Biblical Studies Press, *The NET Bible First Edition Notes* (Biblical Studies Press; 2006), "Luke 2:7."

21. Jeremias, Joachim, *Jerusalem in the Time of Jesus* (Philadelphia: Fortress Press, 1969), p. 84.

22. Seal, D., & Whitehead, M. M., as quoted in: *Faithlife Study Bible* (Bellingham, WA: Lexham Press; 2012, 2016), "The Magi."

23. Krause, M., as quoted in: *The Lexham Bible Dictionary*, "Wise Men, Magi."

24. Ibid.

25. Ibid.

26. Brown, R. E., *The Birth of the Messiah: A Commentary on the Infancy Narratives in the Gospels of Matthew and Luke* (New Updated Edition., New York; London: Yale University Press; 1993), 167.

27. Ibid.

28. Ibid., 167.

29. Ibid.

30. Clement I, P., Ignatius, S., Bishop of Antioch, Polycarp, S., Bishop of Smyrna, & Lake, K., *The Apostolic Fathers: Volume 1* (K. Lake, Ed., Cambridge MA; London: Harvard University Press; 1912–1913), 193. Also note that we are not the only ones to interpret Ignatius' theory in this way. See: Brown, R. E., *The Birth of the Messiah*, 166–167.

31. Cicero, M. T., *With An English Translation.* (W. A. Falconer, Ed., Medford, MA: Harvard University Press; Cambridge, Mass., London, England; 1923), 275–277.

32. Brown, R. E., *The Birth of the Messiah*, 170–171.

33. Chancey, Mark A., Hanan Eshel, Eric M. Meyers, and Tsvika Tsuk, "How Jewish was Sepphoris in Jesus' Time?" *The Biblical Archaeology Review: Volume 26* (No. 4; July/August 2000), 18–33, 61.

34. Batey, Richard A., "Sepphoris and the Jesus Movement" *New Testament Studies: Volume 47* (No. 3; July 2001). 402–409, 408.

35. Chancey, Mark A. et al., "How Jewish was Sepphoris in Jesus' Time?", 18–33, 61.

36. Ibid.

37. Strange, James F., "Sepphoris: Sepphoris was the 'Ornament of All Galilee,'" *The Bible and Interpretation* (University of South Florida, September, 2001); last accessed March 7, 2022, https://bibleinterp. arizona.edu/articles/sepphoris.

38. Chancey, Mark A. et al., "How Jewish was Sepphoris in Jesus' Time?", 18–33, 61.

39. Ibid.

40. Ibid.

41. Ibid.

42. Strange, James F., "Sepphoris…" last accessed March 7, 2022, https:// bibleinterp.arizona.edu/articles/sepphoris.

43. Batey, Richard A., "Sepphoris…", 402–409.

44. Schuster, Angela M. H., "Archeology," Ancient Sepphoris: *Volume 50* (Archaeological Institute of America; No. 2; March/April, 1997), 64.

45. Strange, James F., "Sepphoris…" last accessed March 7, 2022, https:// bibleinterp.arizona.edu/articles/sepphoris.

46. Chancey, Mark A. et al., "How Jewish was Sepphoris in Jesus' Time?", 18–33, 61.

47. Fujishima, Issey, "The Violent Childhood of Jesus," *Reign of God*, January 24, 2018; last accessed March 7, 2022, https://www. thereignofgod.com/2018/01/24/violent-childhood-of-jesus/.

48. Kaufmann Kohler, M. Seligsohn, "Judas the Galilean," *Jewish Encyclopedia*, last accessed March 7, 2022, https://www. jewishencyclopedia.com/articles/9032-judas-the-galilean.

49. Fujishima, Issey, "The Violent Childhood of Jesus"; last accessed

March 7, 2022, https://www.thereignofgod.com/2018/01/24/
violent-childhood-of-jesus/.

50. Heard, W. J. J., & Evans, C. A., "Revolutionary Movements, Jewish,"
as quoted in: *Dictionary of New Testament Background: A Compendium
of Contemporary Biblical Scholarship* (electronic ed., Downers Grove, IL:
InterVarsity Press; 2000), 938.

51. Ibid.

52. "Mark 1:5," *Cambridge Bible for Schools and Colleges, Bible
Hub Online*, last accessed March 7, 2022, https://biblehub.com/
commentaries/cambridge/mark/1.htm.

53. France, R. T., *The Gospel of Matthew* (Grand Rapids, MI: Wm. B.
Eerdmans Publication Co; 2007), 120.

54. Charlesworth, J. H., *The Old Testament Pseudepigrapha: Volume 1*
(New York; London: Yale University Press; 1983), 794–795.

55. Ibid.

56. Kruse, C. G., *John: An Introduction and Commentary: Volume 4*
(Downers Grove, IL: InterVarsity Press; 2003), 94.

57. Gangel, K. O., *John: Volume 4* (Nashville, TN: Broadman & Holman
Publishers; 2000), 30.

58. Jamieson, Fausset, & Brown, *Commentary Critical and Explanatory on
the Whole Bible*, 416.

59. Hedlun, Randy, *The New Testament as Literature: An Independent-
Study Textbook* (Springfield, MO: Global University; 2016), 136.

60. Lewellen, E., D. Mangum, D. R. Brown, R. Klippenstein, & R.
Hurst (Eds.), *Lexham Theological Wordbook* (Bellingham, WA: Lexham
Press; 2014), "Miracles."

61. France, R. T., *The Gospel of Matthew* (Grand Rapids, MI: Wm. B.
Eerdmans Publication Co; 2007), 279.

62. Ibid.

63. Mowinckel, Sigmund, *He That Cometh: The Messiah Concept in the
Old Testament and Later Judaism* (Translated by G. W. Anderson. Reprint,
Grand Rapids: Eerdmans; 2005), 385.

64. Bruce, F. F., *The Book of the Acts* (Grand Rapids, MI: Wm. B.
Eerdmans Publishing Co; 1988), 63.

65. McClaffin, Mike, *The Life of Christ in the Synoptic Gospels* (4th ed., Springfield, MO: Global University; 2013) 218; emphasis added.

66. Ibid., 216.

67. Booker, Richard, *Celebrating Jesus in the Biblical Feasts* (expanded ed., Shippensburg, PA: Destiny Image Publishers, Inc.; 2016), 116.

68. Ibid., 115.

69. Booker, Richard, *Celebrating Jesus...* 146.

70. Horn, Thomas, *The Messenger...* 196–198.

71. Maclaren, J. J., "Jesus Christ, Arrest and Trial Of," as quoted in J. Orr, J. L. Nuelsen, E. Y. Mullins, & M. O. Evans (Eds.), *The International Standard Bible Encyclopaedia: Volume 1–5* (Chicago: The Howard-Severance Company; 1915), 1,670.

72. Ibid.

73. Ibid.

74. Ibid.

75. Ibid.

76. Ibid., 1671–1672.

77. Kloner, Amos, "Did a Rolling Stone Close Jesus' Tomb?" *Biblical Archaeology Society*, Biblical Archeology Review 25:5, September/October, 1999. Last accessed March 14, 2022, https://www.baslibrary.org/biblical-archaeology-review/25/5/1.

78. Bruce, F. F., *The Book of the Acts* (Grand Rapids, MI: Wm. B. Eerdmans Publishing Co.; 1988), 44.

79. See: Horn, Thomas, *The Messenger...* 101–129.

80. "Exodus 19:1," *Jamieson-Fausset-Brown Bible Commentary, Biblehub,* last accessed July 8, 2020, https://biblehub.com/commentaries/exodus/19-1.htm.

81. Note that the way these authors arrived at this date is complicated, and though the full explanation of it is included in our book, [BOOK OF FEASTS], pages [???], drawing research from multiple sources, we will cover the "gist" of the explanation here. (Our sources are: Brown, F., Driver, S. R., & Briggs, C. A., *Enhanced Brown-Driver-Briggs Hebrew and English Lexicon* [Oxford: Clarendon Press; 1977]; Heinrich Friedrich Wilhelm Gesenius, *Gesenius' Hebrew-Chaldee*

Lexicon, accessed online through *Blue Letter Bible Online* on March 15, 2022, https://www.blueletterbible.org/study/lexica/gesenius/index. cfm—and pay special attention to his treatment of the Hebrew words "chodesh" ["month"] and "yowm" ["the same day"] appearing in Exodus 19:1–2.) Some have suggested that these verse's refer to their departure from Rephidim, and that is all the clarification one needs, essentially arranging the facts in contemporary English like this: "The same day that the Israelites left Rephidim, they arrived at the foot of Mt. Sinai, which was sometime in the third month, Sivan." Others interpret that the day's "same as" description is grammatically joined to the word "month," ultimately rendering: "The Israelites arrived at Sinai in the third [3] month, and on the day that is numerically the same as the month, the third [3] day." (In other words, the third day of the third month.) In Gesenius' *Hebrew-Chaldee Lexicon,* the word *chodesh* was shown to refer to "the new moon" or "the day of the new moon"; i.e., "the first day of the month" (see: https://www.blueletterbible.org/lang/lexicon/lexicon.cfm?Strongs=H2320&t=KJV). Gesenius, in a lengthy explanation, shows how *yowm* stems from another root word meaning "to be hot," and therefore etymologically evolves to refer to "the heat of the day" (see: https://www.blueletterbible.org/lang/lexicon/lexicon. cfm?Strongs=H3117&t=KJV). Now, putting modern language together with what Gesenius (and countless language scholars after him) believes the true origins were behind *chodesh* and *yowm,* these two verses (Exodus 19:1–2) communicate: "On 1 Sivan, the same day that the Israelites left Rephidim on their journey away from Egypt, around noon when the sun was at its hottest, the Israelites arrived at the foot of Mt. Sinai." Amidst the ocean of Hebrew linguists that have adopted this same conclusion are a number of classic biblical literature commentators that have assisted in working out the timeline of events between Sivan 1 (their arrival) and the day the Law was given to Moses: 1) The Israelites arrived at the foot of Mt. Sinai on 1 Sivan; 2) on 2 Sivan, Moses went up the mountain to hear from the Lord and take His word to the Israelites (Exodus 19:3); 3) on 3 Sivan, Moses took the agreeable response of the Hebrew elders back up Sinai to God (19:7–8); 4) on 4, 5, and 6 Sivan, the three-day time period God gave His people in Exodus 19:11 to sanctify themselves and wash their clothes, the people prepared for the promised appearance of God, "for the third day the Lord will come down in the sight of all the people upon mount Sinai." Altogether, this is a total of fifty days exactly from the first Passover covenant with God Almighty to the day when He, Himself, descended upon Sinai. Thus, we have the event that instigated the annual Feast of Pentecost, or, the Feast of "the fiftieth day." This is why we can state that the "thunderings and lightnings" event of Mt. Sinai occurred on 6 Sivan.

82. Dr. Juergen Buehler, "Tongues of Fire: The Festival of Shavuot," *International Christian Embassy Jerusalem (ICEJ)*, last accessed March 15, 2022, https://int.icej.org/news/commentary/tongues-fire.

83. Shemot Rabbah 5:9, *Midrash, Sefaria Community Translation*, last accessed March 15, 2022, from *The Sefaria Library*, https://www.sefaria.org/Shemot_Rabbah.5.9?ven=Sefaria_Community_Translation&lang=bi&with=all&lang2=en.

84. Ibid.

85. "Topic Guide" tool, found by searching "Blasting," Logos Bible Software, accessed from personal commercial database on July 16, 2020.

86. Dioscorides, Pedanius, *de Materia Medica*, 5.17; As noted in: Liddell, H. G., Scott, R., Jones, H. S., & McKenzie, R. *A Greek-English Lexicon* (Oxford; Clarendon Press: 1996), 780.

87. As in, "When he uttereth his voice," from LXX Jeremiah 28:16 (which would be Jeremiah 51:16 in modern Bibles). As noted in: Liddell, H. G., Scott, R., Jones, H. S., & McKenzie, R. *A Greek-English Lexicon* (Oxford; Clarendon Press: 1996), 780.

88. "Bible Word Study" tool, found by searching "φέρω," Logos Bible Software, accessed from personal commercial database on July 16, 2020. Please note that this source listed countless lexicons, Bible dictionaries, and other word-study sources that confirmed this most basic meaning.

89. Swanson, J. (1997). *Dictionary of Biblical Languages with Semantic Domains: Greek (New Testament)* (Oak Harbor; Electronic Ed.: Logos Research Systems, Inc.: 1997), entry "1042 βίαιος."

90. "ὥσπερ," *Thayer's Greek Lexicon*, accessed online through *Blue Letter*

Bible Online on March 15, 2022, https://www.blueletterbible.org/lang/lexicon/lexicon.cfm?Strongs=G5618&t=KJV.

91. Marshall, Ian Howard, *Acts: An Introduction and Commentary* (Vol. 5; Downers Grove, IL: InterVarsity Press, 1980), 73.

92. Barrett, C. K., *A Critical and Exegetical Commentary on the Acts of the Apostles* (Edinburgh: T&T Clark; 2004), 113; emphasis added.

93. Ibid., 114.

94. "Acts 2 Benson Commentary," *BibleHub*, last accessed March 15, 2022, https://biblehub.com/commentaries/benson/acts/2.htm, "Acts 2:1."

95. Barrett, C. K., *A Critical and Exegetical Commentary...* 113.

96. Marshall, Ian Howard, *Acts...* 73.

97. Booker, Richard, *Celebrating Jesus...* 94–95.

98. Sam Nadler, *Messiah in the Feasts of Israel* (Word of Messiah Ministries, Kindle ed., 2011), 83–84.

99. "Exodus 19:1," *Benson Commentary, Biblehub*, last accessed March 15, 2022, https://biblehub.com/commentaries/exodus/19-1.htm.

100. Barrett, C. K., *A Critical and Exegetical Commentary on the Acts...* 118.

101. Marshall, I. H., *Acts...* 88–89.

102. Bruce, F. F., *The Book of the Acts*, 77.

103. Josephus, F., & Whiston, W., *The Works of Josephus*, 707.

104. Bruce, F. F., *The Book of the Acts*, 123.

105. Gangel, Kenneth O., *Acts: Volume 5* (Nashville, TN: Broadman & Holman Publishers; 1998), 121.

106. Marshall, I. H., *Acts...* 163–164.

107. Laney, J. C., "Peter and the Centurion Cornelius (Acts 10:1–48)," as quoted in: B. J. Beitzel, J. Parks, & D. Mangum (Eds.), *Lexham Geographic Commentary on Acts through Revelation* (Bellingham, WA: Lexham Press; 2019), 261.

108. *Acts of Paul* 3.3; cf. W. M. Ramsay, *The Church in the Roman Empire* (London, 1893), 31–32, as quoted in: Bruce, F. F., *The Book of the Acts*, 273.

109. Bruce, F. F., *The Book of the Acts*, 124–125.

110. *Acts of Paul* 3.3; cf. W. M. Ramsay, *The Church in the Roman Empire*, 31–32, as quoted in: Bruce, F. F., *The Book of the Acts*, 271.

111. Bruce, F. F., *The Book of the Acts*, 180.

112. Ibid., 183.

113. Bruce, F. F., *Romans: An Introduction and Commentary: Volume 6* (Downers Grove, IL: InterVarsity Press; 1985), 266.

114. Moo, D. J., "Romans," as quoted in: D. A. Carson, R. T. France, J. A. Motyer, & G. J. Wenham (Eds.), *New Bible Commentary: 21st Century Edition* (4th ed., Leicester, England; Downers Grove, IL: Inter-Varsity Press; 1994), 1,158.

115. Witmer, J. A., "Romans," as quoted in: J. F. Walvoord & R. B. Zuck (Eds.), *The Bible Knowledge Commentary: An Exposition of the Scriptures: Volume 2* (Wheaton, IL: Victor Books; 1985), 499.

116. Boa, K., & Kruidenier, W., *Romans: Volume 6* (Nashville, TN: Broadman & Holman Publishers; 2000), 458.

117. Dr. Deborah M. Gill and Dr. Barbara L. Cavaness Parks, *The Biblical Role of Women* (Springfield, MO: Global University, 2008), 120.

118. Eldon Jay Epp, *Junia: The First Woman Apostle* (Kindle edition, Minneapolis: Fortress Press, 2005), location 346.

119. Rena Pederson, *The Lost Apostle: Searching for the Truth About Junia* (Kindle edition, San Francisco, CA: Jossey-Bass, 2006) Kindle locations 2470–2484.

120. "Junia," *The Full Wiki*, last accessed August 3, 2017, http://www.thefullwiki.org/Junia. However, note that this quote can be found in almost every discussion on Junia anywhere. A simple Google search of the words "Junia Chrysostom" reveals hundreds of references.

121. "Strong's G653," *Blue Letter Bible*, last accessed March 20, 2022, https://www.blueletterbible.org/lang/lexicon/lexicon.cfm?Strongs=G652&t=KJV.

122. "Strong's G1722," *Blue Letter Bible*, last accessed July 17, 2017, https://www.blueletterbible.org/lang/lexicon/lexicon.cfm?Strongs=G1722&t=KJV.

123. Ibid.

124. Eldon Jay Epp, *Junia*, locations 955–956.

125. Ibid., location 958.

126. Ibid., locations 990–1006.

127. Howell, Donna, *Handmaidens Conspiracy*, 73–74.

128. "Romans 16:3," *Bible Hub*, last accessed March 20, 2022, http://biblehub.com/commentaries/romans/16-3.htm.

129. Ibid.

130. Ibid.

131. Howell, Donna, *Handmaidens Conspiracy*, 56–60.

132. Heiser, Dr. Michael, "Paul's Lost Letters," August 26, 2010, *Bible Study Magazine*, last accessed March 22, 2022, https://www.crosswalk.com/church/pastors-or-leadership/pauls-lost-letters-11637049.html.

133. Ibid.

134. Howell, Donna, *Handmaidens Conspiracy*, 87.

135. John Temple Bristow, *What Paul Really Said about Women: The Apostle's Liberating Views on Equality in Marriage, Leadership, and Love* (Kindle edition, San Francisco, CA: HarperCollins, 2011) 51.

136. D. H. Madvig, "Corinth," *The International Standard Bible Encyclopedia* (revised edition; Grand Rapids: Wm. B. Eerdmans Publishing Co.), 773.

137. William Barclay, *The Letters to the Corinthians* (revised edition; Philadelphia: Westminster Press, 1975), 4.

138. Morris, L., *1 Corinthians: An Introduction and Commentary: Volume 7* (Downers Grove, IL: InterVarsity Press; 1985), 89–90.

139. Ibid., 98–99.

140. Ibid., 130–131.

141. Blue, B. B., "Love Feast," as quoted in: G. F. Hawthorne, R. P. Martin, & D. G. Reid (Eds.), *Dictionary of Paul and his letters* (Downers Grove, IL: InterVarsity Press; 1993), 579.

142. Ibid.

143. Patzia, A. G., & Petrotta, A. J., *Pocket Dictionary of Biblical Studies* (Downers Grove, IL: InterVarsity Press; 2002), 70.

144. "The State of Theology," a survey conducted by Ligonier Ministries and LifeWay Research in March of 2020, findings released September 8, last accessed March 21, 2022, https://thestateoftheology.com/. Note

that not all of these statistics are covered on the "Key Findings" tab. One wishing to observe the list in its entirety must click on the "Data Explorer" tab at the top right of the main study page.

145. Morris, L., *1 Corinthians*, 171.

146. Ibid., 161–162.

147. "Strong's G4060," *Blue Letter Bible*, last accessed March 21, 2022, https://www.blueletterbible.org/lang/lexicon/lexicon.cfm?Strongs=G4060&t=KJV.

148. Horn, Joe, *Everyday Champions: Unleash the Gifts God Gave You, Step Into Your Purpose, and Fulfill Your Destiny* (Crane, MO: Defender Publishing; 2019), 229–232.

149. "Strong's G3551," *Blue Letter Bible*, last accessed March 21, 2022, https://www.blueletterbible.org/lang/lexicon/lexicon.cfm?Strongs=G3551&t=KJV.

150. Dr. Deborah M. Gill and Dr. Barbara L. Cavaness Parks, *The Biblical Role of Women*, 128; emphasis added.

151. Howell, Donna, *Handmaidens Conspiracy*, 104–111.

152. Kruse, C. G., *2 Corinthians: An Introduction and Commentary: Volume 8* (Downers Grove, IL: InterVarsity Press; 1987), 199.

153. G. W. Hansen., "Galatians, Letter to The," as quoted in: G. F. Hawthorne, R. P. Martin, & D. G. Reid (Eds.), *Dictionary of Paul and his letters* (Downers Grove, IL: InterVarsity Press; 1993), 326.

154. Cole, R. A., *Galatians: An Introduction and Commentary: Volume 9* (Downers Grove, IL: InterVarsity Press' 1989), 75.

155. Ibid.

156. Anders, M., *Galatians-Colossians: Volume 8* (Nashville, TN: Broadman & Holman Publishers; 1999), 53.

157. Souter, A., *A Pocket Lexicon to the Greek New Testament* (Oxford: Clarendon Press; 1917), 32; Swanson, J., *Dictionary of Biblical Languages with Semantic Domains: Greek (New Testament)* (electronic ed., Oak Harbor: Logos Research Systems, Inc; 1997), "ἀποκόπτω (apokoptō)"; Thayer, J. H., *A Greek-English Lexicon of the New Testament: Being Grimm's Wilke's Clavis Novi Testamenti* (New York: Harper & Brothers; 1889), 63, 338. And note: This is only three examples of many we could

have pointed to. However, many Logos Bible Software start-up packages
have one or more of these in their language study categories, so these
sources may be easier for many students to locate at home or in their
work office than the others we have in print here.

158. Howell, Donna, *Handmaidens Conspiracy*, 119.

159. For instance, see Aristotle's words in his *Politics*, 7.1335b.

160. Wiedemann, Thomas, *Adults and Children in the Roman Empire*
(New Haven, CT: Yale University Press; 1989) 36–37.

161. Elwell, W. A., & Beitzel, B. J., "Colossae," as quoted in: *Baker
encyclopedia of the Bible: Volume 1* (Grand Rapids, MI: Baker Book
House; 1988), 496.

162. Wright, N. T., *Colossians and Philemon: An Introduction and
Commentary: Volume 12* (Downers Grove, IL: InterVarsity Press; 1986),
126–127.

163. Ibid.

164. Constable, T. L., "1 Thessalonians," as quoted in: J. F. Walvoord &
R. B. Zuck (Eds.), *The Bible Knowledge Commentary: An Exposition of the
Scriptures: Volume 2* (Wheaton, IL: Victor Books; 1985), 687.

165. Ibid.

166. Talbert, A. R., as quoted in: *The Lexham Bible Dictionary*,
"Thessalonica."

167. Ibid.

168. Morris, L., *1 and 2 Thessalonians: An Introduction and Commentary:
Volume 13* (Downers Grove, IL: InterVarsity Press; 1984), 143.

169. 1 Timothy 2:9, Interlinear," *Bible Hub*, last accessed July 22, 2017,
http://biblehub.com/interlinear/1_timothy/2-9.htm. Notice, however,
that this very website even gets it wrong, which shows how often this
error occurs. In the interlinear comparison, the word for "and" (*kai*) is
clearly shown between "braided hair" (*plegmasin*) and "gold" (*chrysio*) in
the Greek line; later in the same Greek line, we see "or" (ē) as distinct.
But in the English translation line, it is "or" all three times.

170. Troy W. Martin, "Paul's Argument from Nature for the Veil in 1
Cor. 11:13–15: A Testicle instead of a Head Covering," *Journal of Biblical
Literature*, 123:1 (2004), 78–80.

171. Howell, Donna, *Handmaidens Conspiracy*, 97–98.

172. John Toews, *The Bible and the Church: Essays in Honor of Dr. David Ewert* (Shillington, Hillsboro, KS: Kindred Press, 1983), 84.

173. Henry George Liddell, Robert Scott, *A Greek-English Lexicon*, revised and augmented throughout by Sir Henry Stuart Jones, with the assistance of Roderick McKenzie, Oxford, Clarendon Press, 1940, last accessed July 25, 2017, http://www.perseus.tufts.edu/hopper/text?doc=Perseus%3Atext%3A1999.04.0057%3Aentry%3Dau%29qe%2Fnths.

174. List obtained from: Gail Wallace, "Diffusing the 1 Timothy 2:12 Bomb: More On Authority (Authentein)," *The Junia Project*, last accessed July 25, 2017, http://juniaproject.com/defusing-1-timothy-212-authority-authentein/.

175. Scott Bartchy, "Power, Submission, and Sexual Identity among the Early Christians," *Essays on New Testament Christianity* (Cincinnati, OH: Standard Publishing, 1978), 71–72.

176. "The Meaning of Authenteo," *Bible Discussion Forum*, last accessed July 25, 2017, http://www.thechristadelphians.org/forums/index.php?showtopic=14052.

177. As quoted in: "1 Timothy 2:12 in Context (Part 4)," *Marg Mowczko*, last accessed July 25, 2017, http://margmowczko.com/1-timothy-212-in-context-4/.

178. Howell, Donna, *Handmaidens Conspiracy*, 139–144.

179. "Liar Paradox," lasted edited February 23, 2022, *Wikipedia: The Free Encyclopedia*, last accessed April 4, 2022, https://en.wikipedia.org/wiki/Liar_paradox#:~:text=In%20philosophy%20and%20logic%2C%20the,means%20the%20liar%20just%20lied.

180. This clip can be found all over the internet with guiding voiceovers pausing and explaining how Sarah's logic is correct. To see the video playing out without the explanation, see: "Sarah Solves the Riddle | Labyrinth (1986)," uploaded by Jim Henson Company Fantasy Favorites on October 26, 2019, a YouTube video, 2:18 playing time, last accessed April 4, 2022, https://www.youtube.com/watch?v=uM3gK-OUvqE.

181. Hemer, C. J., "Crete," as quoted in: C. Brand, C. Draper, A. England, S. Bond, E. R. Clendenen, & T. C. Butler (Eds.), *Holman*

Illustrated Bible Dictionary (Nashville, TN: Holman Bible Publishers; 2003), 364.

182. Bancarz, Steven, and Josh Peck, *The Second Coming of the New Age: The Hidden Dangers of Alternative Spirituality in Contemporary America and Its Churches* (Crane, MO: Defender Publishing: 2018), 329–336.

183. Martin, W., Rische, J. M., Van Gorden, K., & Rische, K., *The Kingdom of the Occult* (Nashville: Thomas Nelson; 2008), 36.

184. Hubbard, K., "Philemon, Letter To," as quoted in: *Holman Illustrated Bible Dictionary*, 1,288.

185. Larson, K., *I & II Thessalonians, I & II Timothy, Titus, Philemon: Volume 9* (Nashville, TN: Broadman & Holman Publishers; 2000), 409.

186. Eusebius of Caesaria, "The Church History of Eusebius," *Ecclesiastical History*, 6.4.2–3, as quoted in: P. Schaff & H. Wace (Eds.), A. C. McGiffert (Trans.), *Eusebius: Church History, Life of Constantine the Great, and Oration in Praise of Constantine: Volume 1* (New York: Christian Literature Company; 1890), 261.

187. Michaels, R. J., "Commentary on Hebrews," as quoted in: *Cornerstone Biblical Commentary: 1 Timothy, 2 Timothy, Titus, and Hebrews: Volume 17* (Carol Stream, IL: Tyndale House Publishers; 2009), 310.

188. Ibid., 430.

189. Ibid.

190. Ibid.

191. Hoppin, Ruth, *Priscilla's Letter: Finding the Author of the Epistle to the Hebrews* (Fort Bragg, CA: Lost Coast Press, Kindle ed.; 2019), 196–197.

192. Ibid., 24, 29–30, 32.

193. As quoted by: David Malick, "An Introduction to the Book of James," January 17, 2014, *Bible.org*, last accessed April 7, 2022, https://bible.org/article/introduction-book-james.

194. Ibid., quote derived from note number 9.

195. Hegesippus, "Fragments from His Five Books of Commentaries on the Acts of the Church," *Early Christian Writings*, last accessed April 7, 2022, http://www.earlychristianwritings.com/text/hegesippus.html.

196. Bruce, F. F., *The Book of the Acts*, 94–95.

197. Schreiner, T. R., "Peter, First Letter From," as quoted in: *Holman Illustrated Bible Dictionary*, 1,282.

198. Grudem, W. A., *1 Peter: An Introduction and Commentary: Volume 17* (Downers Grove, IL: InterVarsity Press; 1988), 52–54.

199. Ibid.

200. Schreiner, T. R., "Peter, Second Letter From," as quoted in: *Holman Illustrated Bible Dictionary*, 1,284.

201. "Top Names Over the Last 100 Years," *Social Security Administration*, last accessed April 9, 2022, https://www.ssa.gov/oact/babynames/decades/century.html.

202. Morris, J., "Jude, Letter of," as quoted in: *The Lexham Bible Dictionary*.

203. Green, M., *2 Peter and Jude: An Introduction and Commentary: Volume 18* (Downers Grove, IL: InterVarsity Press; 1987), 196; endnote/footnote 32.

204. Ibid.

205. Eusebius of Caesaria, "The Church History of Eusebius," *Ecclesiastical History*, as quoted in: *Eusebius: Church History...* 148–149.